The Art and Science of Language Teaching

This user-friendly book is designed for language teachers of all levels and languages who seek to inform their classroom practices with current research findings on second language acquisition. Ideal for courses on second language learning and teaching, teacher reading groups, and professional development workshops, each chapter begins with a story of a real teaching scenario and a concise summary of what cutting-edge language teaching research says (and what it does not say) about the topic. Throughout the twenty-one chapters, the authors connect language learning research to the classroom, challenge misunderstandings around language pedagogy, and provide solutions. Each chapter concludes with classroom activities and instructional strategies that can be used immediately in professional development workshops or in the classroom. Additional resources are available online to supplement the activities found in the book. Applicable across all languages and levels, this book is suitable for teachers of diverse backgrounds teaching in diverse contexts.

Lara Bryfonski is an assistant professor of linguistics at Georgetown University. She has published and presented her research on a variety of topics in second language acquisition, including task-based language teaching, corrective feedback, materials development, language learning in study abroad, and methods for second language research. Her publications appear in journals such as *Annual Review of Applied Linguistics, Language Teaching Research, Modern Language Journal,* and *Studies in Second Language Acquisition* as well as a variety of edited collections. She is a former ESL/EFL teacher and an experienced teacher trainer and has worked with NGOs in Latin America, public and private schools in the United States, governmental and financial organizations, and universities to provide research-based training in language teaching.

Alison Mackey is a tenured full professor and Chair of the Department of Lingusitics at Georgetown University (with an additional professorial appointment at Lancaster University in the UK during summers), and an expert in both general second language research and language research methodology. She has published over 100 journal articles and book chapters, and 20 books in total, including the Mildenberger Prizewinning *The Routledge Handbook of Second Language Acquisition* (2012). She is editor-in-chief of *Annual Review of Applied Linguistics*, a co-founder and developer of the open-access Instruments for Second Language Research database, and, for the last two decades, co-editor of Routledge's Second Language Acquisition Research series. She has received both of Georgetown University's top honors: the President's Award for Distinguished Scholar-Teachers and the Provost's Career Research Achievement Award. She is one of the top-cited scholars internationally in applied linguistics.

"This is a volume that needs to be in every practicing teacher's library. This book is one of the few that directly connects second language acquisition research to practice in an accessible and comprehensive way for teachers."
Professor Richard Donato, University of Pittsburgh, USA, author of *Enacting the Work of Language Instruction* (ACTFL, 2016)

"Do you want an SLA book that speaks directly to language teaching? If so, then start with the real issues that teachers face and then see what SLA has to say about them."
Rod Ellis, University of Auckland, NZ, author of *Exploring Language Pedagogy through Second Language Acquisition Research* (Routledge, 2014)

"The Bryfonski/Mackey text demystifies research in second language acquisition by presenting key findings in an easy-to-read format and connecting them to the realities of classroom practice. Pre-service and in-service professionals alike will find research-based solutions that address the common classroom challenges facing today's language educators."
Eileen W. Glisan, Indiana University of Pennsylvania, USA, author of *Enacting the Work of Language Instruction* (ACTFL, 2016)

"Bryfonski and Mackey have done the impossible, demystifying second language acquisition for pedagogical contexts with concrete, ready-to-use applications. By artfully grounding the volume in both research and real-life teaching scenarios and questions, these eminent scholars bring to life the most important questions underlying language teaching for every instructional setting. An immediate must-read!"
Laura Gurzynski-Weiss, Indiana University, Bloomington, Indiana, USA

"Irony aside, language researchers and teachers have – for *decades* – lacked a shared language. Bryfonski and Mackey provide these yin–yanged audiences with a Rosetta Stone of sorts, a cipher that unlocks the door connecting the worlds of L2 research and practice. This text allows the authors' world-renowned expertise to shine while speaking with the hearts of trusted mentors."
Luke Plonsky, Northern Arizona University, USA

"Oriented around questions and answers relevant to any language teacher and language classroom, each engaging chapter is packed with vignettes, visuals, and strategies for teachers to put into practice. Ideal for pre- or in-service teachers alike, this text will answer teachers' burning questions on everything from pronunciation and feedback to lesson planning and technology."
Andrea Révész, University College London, UK

"Whether you're a new language teacher just starting out or a veteran language teacher with many years of experience, you must read this book. With charming graphics throughout, it makes solid connections between the latest research and practice, with concrete examples for the language learning classroom, and even includes links to sample lesson plans, videos, and other helpful materials."
Heather Sweetser, The University of New Mexico, USA, 2022 ACTFL National Language Teacher of the Year

The Art and Science of Language Teaching

LARA BRYFONSKI
Georgetown University, Washington DC

ALISON MACKEY
Georgetown University, Washington DC

Shaftesbury Road, Cambridge CB2 8EA, United Kingdom

One Liberty Plaza, 20th Floor, New York, NY 10006, USA

477 Williamstown Road, Port Melbourne, VIC 3207, Australia

314–321, 3rd Floor, Plot 3, Splendor Forum, Jasola District Centre, New Delhi – 110025, India

103 Penang Road, #05–06/07, Visioncrest Commercial, Singapore 238467

Cambridge University Press is part of Cambridge University Press & Assessment, a department of the University of Cambridge.

We share the University's mission to contribute to society through the pursuit of education, learning and research at the highest international levels of excellence.

www.cambridge.org
Information on this title: www.cambridge.org/highereducation/isbn/9781108837798
DOI: 10.1017/9781108943048

© Lara Bryfonski and Alison Mackey 2024

This publication is in copyright. Subject to statutory exception and to the provisions of relevant collective licensing agreements, no reproduction of any part may take place without the written permission of Cambridge University Press & Assessment.

First published 2024

Printed in the United Kingdom by CPI Group Ltd, Croydon CR0 4YY, 2024

A catalogue record for this publication is available from the British Library

Library of Congress Cataloging-in-Publication Data
Names: Bryfonski, Lara, 1989– author. | Mackey, Alison, author.
Title: The art and science of language teaching / Lara Bryfonski, Alison Mackey.
Description: Cambridge, United Kingdom ; New York, NY : Cambridge University Press, 2023. | Includes bibliographical references and index.
Identifiers: LCCN 2023025084 | ISBN 9781108837798 (hardback) | ISBN 9781108932011 (paperback) | ISBN 9781108943048 (ebook)
Subjects: LCSH: Language and languages – Study and teaching.
Classification: LCC P51 .B786 2023 | DDC 407.1–dc23/eng/20230725
LC record available at https://lccn.loc.gov/2023025084

ISBN 978-1-108-83779-8 Hardback
ISBN 978-1-108-93201-1 Paperback

Additional resources for this publication at www.cambridge.org/BryfonskiMackey.

Cambridge University Press & Assessment has no responsibility for the persistence or accuracy of URLs for external or third-party internet websites referred to in this publication and does not guarantee that any content on such websites is, or will remain, accurate or appropriate.

We dedicate this book to our mothers, whose belief in us has always been unwavering.

CONTENTS

Preface page ix
Acknowledgments xi
Note on Terminology xii
Pre-Reading Self-Assessment xv

PART I TEACHER AND STUDENT TALK

1. How do I get my learners to start and stay talking in the second language? 3
2. How do I maximize input in the second language? 22
3. Why, when, and how (much) should I correct my learners? 34
4. How do I promote peer interaction in the classroom? 48
5. What kinds of learning strategies can I teach my learners? 63

PART II DIFFERENTIATION

6. How does language learner identity influence the language learning experience? 77
7. How do I best support neurodiverse language learners? 93
8. How do learners' motivation and anxiety levels impact their language learning experience? 107
9. How can aptitude be leveraged for language learning? 123
10. It's much harder to learn (and teach) my language compared to other languages, and it takes much longer. How can I compensate for these difficulties with my learners? 136

PART III TEACHING THE SKILLS

11 How or when should I teach grammar? *153*

12 Is there a "best" way to teach pronunciation? *167*

13 How can I incorporate literacy skills in the target language? *182*

14 When or how should I teach vocabulary? *199*

15 What are some strategies for teaching learners about politeness, register, or other pragmatic skills in the second language? *217*

PART IV LESSON AND UNIT PLANNING

16 What are some of the most popular language teaching methods? *233*

17 Content, form, and activities: How do I select activities, tasks, and projects? *249*

18 Menus and maps: How can I make my classroom more authentic in terms of materials and practices? *266*

19 How could/should I best use technology in the language classroom? *283*

20 How do I assess language learning? *297*

21 How can I make the most of professional development opportunities for language teachers? *318*

Glossary 331
References and Resources 337
Index 355

PREFACE

This book was inspired by our desire to answer the many questions we receive from language teachers, administrators, teacher trainers, and parents in relation to the learning and teaching languages. Year after year, we hear the same questions, along with comments and criticisms of the differences between academic research and the experiences and practices of language teachers or learners. We wrote this book with language teachers in mind. As such, we've aimed to provide practical classroom solutions, tips, tricks, and suggestions, all grounded in empirical research into how languages are learned. We've included readable, helpful summaries of what the research says about the questions we are most often asked. We also point out places where the research is still ongoing or does not provide a clear answer, so it makes the most sense for teachers to (continue to) use their best judgment. We use vignettes and other examples from authentic language classrooms and language teachers' experiences interwoven with research findings to bring each topic and its research to life. We finish each chapter with a list of practical resources for further reading as well as discussion questions, either for self-reflection or for a teacher trainer to use as guidance during professional development sessions.

There's an increasing number of books on the market today that provide tips for language teaching or tout the latest best practices. Such books are often presented as consumable products that will produce instant, uniform results for *all* students in *all* contexts. This sort of approach, however, can mask the many nuances involved in second language research findings. So, what's unique about our book? Well, we don't attempt to sell teachers on any one particular method, product, or on "quick-fix" solutions. Instead, we've done our best to offer research-based practices that are the result of decades of studies into how languages are learned. We also don't shy away from pointing out where the research is lacking, unclear, or where there are still unknowns. Instead, we point out these areas in each chapter (in sections titled "The Science: What's Missing?") so that teachers know where there might not yet be enough research to provide a definite answer. We hope our approach will give language teachers (and those who support them) research-based tools to make informed decisions about how to best align the art of language teaching with the science of language learning.

Teachers often ask questions that are specific to the language they teach (e.g., English as a Second Language vs. Mandarin as a Foreign Language) or specific to their context (e.g., public vs. independent schools, language institutes). While some questions require the careful consideration of a particular context or situation, there is also quite a bit of research into how languages are learned that can be generally applied to all languages and contexts. The research we draw upon in this book has mostly investigated the *general processes* of language learning, not how language is learned or taught for one language or proficiency level in particular. So, this book aims to be a resource that is not language- or context-dependent. Rather, it applies to learners of various ages, proficiency levels, and backgrounds. For topics where the research findings have uncovered differences between learners' ages, proficiency levels, or languages, we point out how best practices can be adapted based on these learner differences. And, again, we also point to areas and issues where teachers themselves are best placed to make the decisions.

As part of our background work for this book, we surveyed language teachers based on our contacts around the world from a variety of backgrounds teaching a variety of different languages. We talked with teachers and administrators in Australia, Brazil, China, Honduras, Iran, Japan, Korea, Mexico, Taiwan, the United States, and the United Kingdom, from public and private schools teaching second languages such as Arabic, English, French, Greek, Mandarin, Japanese, Korean, Portuguese, and Spanish at all levels and ages. We asked them what their top questions were and what gaps they saw between language learning research and practice. What they told us formed the anonymized and de-identified vignettes we've published, which are based on the experiences of real language instructors. We limited our discussions of specific types of schools/resources because our observations suggest that regardless of how resource-scarce or -rich a given school may be, teachers tend to have the same questions about teaching.

To summarize then, we based this book on our interests and knowledge as second language acquisition researchers and as teachers and teacher-trainers, in order to bring together insights from both pedagogy (the art) and research (the science) into a book that provides helpful information about both of these areas. We hope that both novice and seasoned teachers and teacher-trainers alike will utilize it as a standalone read or a supplemental guide to a larger professional development initiative.

ACKNOWLEDGMENTS

We would like to express our appreciation to a number of people who helped make this book possible.

First, a huge thank you to our research and editorial assistants: Caitlyn Pineault, Erin Fell, Yuta Ito, Kris Cook, Lynn Nakazawa, Negar Siyari, and Alexandra Gehrke for all their help surveying teachers, and helping us with researching and editing.

Second, we are very grateful to Elizabeth Zonarich for her fabulous and fun illustrations that brought our concepts to life.

Third, this book benefited greatly from feedback from anonymous reviewers who provided valuable input at several stages of this project, as well as from the many teachers who reviewed the table of contents and key questions.

Next, and very importantly, we would also like to express our sincere gratitude to the many, many language teachers, educators, administrators, and learners whom we have worked with over the years, from whom we drew inspiration to write the book as well as to follow the style of answering key questions and providing vignettes and practical activities. Indeed, the art and science of language learning and teaching is derived from them. Finally, our publishers at Cambridge University Press have provided us with unwavering help and support with the perfect levels of patience and – when we needed it – pushes. Their belief in the book has been inspirational.

NOTE ON TERMINOLOGY

Because this book is meant to bridge the gap between second language acquisition (SLA) research and practice, we've also tried to incorporate the terms and framing that both researchers and teachers bring to conversations around language teaching. A number of factors lead our communities to develop differing shared "languages" to talk about language learning, and we present a short guide here not to advocate for one set of terms over another, but rather to show how teachers and researchers might be using terms differently. The table below shows how these terms relate to each other and serves as a primer for how they'll show up in the book. This is by no means an exhaustive list. We encourage readers to engage with us via the companion website with additional terms you'd like to discuss. The terms here are presented in alphabetical order by those frequently used by teachers.

Frequently used by teachers	Frequently used by researchers	Commentary
Comprehensible input (CI)	Input	One of the most discussed topics in teaching circles is comprehensible input (CI), with many teachers, districts, products, trainers, etc. labeling themselves as "CI." SLA research has come to a consensus in recent decades that CI is one essential type of input for language learning. However, research has also found that learners should be exposed to a variety of input, including CI, but also including input that is slightly above learners' current proficiency level, as well as input that is from authentic "real-world" sources, even if it is not 100% comprehensible. We discuss the issue of authenticity as it relates to input in Chapter 18. When we refer to input in this book, we are referring to all types of input, including, but not limited to, CI.
Heritage speaker	Heritage Language Learner (HLL)	In both teaching and research circles, someone's "heritage language" (HL) refers to a language an individual speaks due to family ties that is not the commonly used language in the surrounding environment.

Frequently used by teachers	Frequently used by researchers	Commentary
		Speakers of HLs can be more or less proficient, depending on how much the HL is used in their lifetime. Some HLLs have only minimal contact with their HL as children and decide to learn their HL as an adult. This is especially common with individuals for whom their HL is an indigenous language but can also occur in families where speaking the HL is associated with trauma (e.g., persecution, discrimination).
Language acquisition Language learning	Language acquisition Language learning	Both teachers and researchers alike talk about the difference between learning and acquisition. This might be one of the defining differences in the parlance of *language teachers* compared to teachers of other subjects: Language teachers are aware of the difference between the conscious processes involved in *learning* and the unconscious processes underpinning *acquisition*. An interesting development (and way in which usage differs between teachers and researchers) has been the way conscious learning has become unfashionable in some teaching circles. As we discuss in the book, learners need a judicious combination of both processes to be able to become proficient L2 users (more on this term below). In some cases, total abandonment of conscious, explicit learning instruction can even become an access issue, especially for L2 learners with learning difficulties, or older language learners (see especially Chapters 7 and 9).
Native language, Native [*English*] speaker	L1 L1 [*English*] speaker	Both language teachers and researchers alike use the term "native speaker" to refer to someone who grew up speaking a given language (referred to as the "native language"). SLA research is moving away from this "native" framing, however, and adopting "L1" in its place. Not only does L1 align nicely with its counterpart, L2, it also avoids essentializing or equating a person and a language, which is sometimes tied up in stereotyping or discrimination. This stereotyping is sometimes referred to as "native speaker ideology." Oftentimes, though, a person does not grow up with only *one* L1. In cases where an individual has two L1s, for example, researchers will sometimes refer to their languages as language "A" and language "Alpha" or (the Greek letter "α") or talk about a learners' "L1s." Referring to a bilingual's two L1s in this way allows SLA researchers to differentiate between their L1s, but *both are acknowledged as being first*.
Shared language	Shared language	SLA research has only recently begun to mainstream the term "shared language," thanks in large part to vocal members of the teaching and research community calling attention to the fact that not all learners in a given classroom have the same L1. Seems obvious, right? It is (or should be), but it's important to keep in mind *where* most initial SLA research was conducted: on university campuses with individuals who could afford higher education in the 1970s and 1980s and who were overwhelmingly white L1 English speakers.

Frequently used by teachers	Frequently used by researchers	Commentary
		As a result, many of the first SLA studies and publications didn't take account of multiple L1s in a classroom (unless they looked at alternative education programs or immigrant language classes).
Target language (TL)	L2 (literally "second language," but recently understood as "additional language")	Teaching circles often use the term "target language" (TL) to describe the language being taught because that is the aim, or "target," of the course. Researchers usually use the term "second language" or "L2" instead of TL to emphasize the fact that the language being studied is being learned after their native or first language ("L1"). Researchers sometimes also study individuals learning a third, fourth, fifth, etc. language. When referring to someone's third language, a researcher would call it their "L3." If a researcher wanted to lump someone's second, third, and fourth languages together, they might refer to someone's "L2s."
World language (WL)	Foreign language (FL) Second language (usually combined with the language being studied; e.g., ESL = English as a second language)	Teaching circles have moved away from referring to the languages they teach as "foreign languages" to deemphasize framing of speakers of the languages as "others." Using the term "world language" instead centers the common humanity of all language speakers. Researchers use the terms "foreign" and "second" languages to refer to how much access learners have to the language they're studying. "Foreign" language classes are those where learners don't have much access to the language when they leave the classroom, whereas "second" language classes are those where language being taught is the commonly used language outside the classroom (consider how "English as a Second Language" is a course for children learning English in the United States).

To reiterate, in presenting the terms above and relating them to each other, we do not advocate for one term of language learning over another. Instead, we hope that by presenting them together and showing the nuances in how we use the terms in both teaching and researching circles, we can help build a greater understanding and work toward more robust collaboration between teachers and researchers. We encourage readers to share any new terminology in their communities, again reiterating that one way of talking about language learning is not inherently better than another, and it's best to always try to ensure we're able to understand each other's "language" about learning and teaching.

PRE-READING SELF-ASSESSMENT

Before beginning to work through this book, we recommend taking a few minutes to assess your own ideas, beliefs, or preconceptions in relation to some of the topics you will read about. In the self-assessment below, there are several questions that correspond with each chapter. Some of the statements are aligned with the research you will read about in the chapters that follow, and some are not. You should decide how much you agree or disagree with each statement by placing a "✓" or "✗" in the corresponding column. After you read that chapter or part, we suggest that you come back to this assessment and ask yourself the following questions: *Has my response to this statement changed or stayed the same? Why did my response change (or why not)? Were there particular aspects of the chapter or part that affected my response in relation to this topic? What does this topic mean for my/my school's/my team's teaching practices?*

Further discussion of the statements in light of the content of each chapter is available on our companion website.

	Part I: Teacher and Student Talk Chapters 1–5					
		Strongly disagree (1)	Disagree (2)	Neutral (3)	Agree (4)	Strongly agree (5)
1	Learners primarily acquire new languages through imitation.					
2	The more interaction learners experience, the better their language learning.					
3	If learners' errors are not corrected immediately, learners will internalize incorrect rules about the target language.					

Pre-Reading Self-Assessment

		Strongly disagree (1)	Disagree (2)	Neutral (3)	Agree (4)	Strongly agree (5)
	Part I: Teacher and Student Talk — Chapters 1–5					
4	Using the first language always hinders progress in the second language.					
5	Learners pick up each other's mistakes.					
6	Learners are naturally equipped to succeed in a world language classroom.					
7	Training language learners to take responsibility for their own development is not effective.					
8	Language learners learn more by cooperating with each other in group activities than they do by themselves.					
9	Producing language helps the acquisition process.					
10	Language acquisition is better than language learning.					
11	It is important for learners of all levels and ages to have the opportunity to produce written and spoken language.					
12	Instructor–class interactions are more valuable than peer–peer interactions to the language learning process.					
13	Translation is not beneficial for language learning.					

Pre-Reading Self-Assessment

		Strongly disagree (1)	Disagree (2)	Neutral (3)	Agree (4)	Strongly agree (5)
	**Part II: Differentiation** *Chapters 6–10*					
1	All learners pick up languages in a similar way.					
2	Success in tasks/activities in a language classroom looks different for every learner.					
3	Learners who score well on intelligence and aptitude tests will pick up a new language more easily.					
4	Language learners will get confused if you introduce them to different varieties of the target language.					
5	Learners with diagnosed specific learning needs/difficulties will struggle more in language classes than their peers.					
6	Learning another language will confuse learners who have difficulties in their first language.					
7	Some languages are easier to learn than others.					
8	All languages should be taught the same way.					
9	Only high-achieving, high-performing learners should be allowed to add a language course to their schedules.					

	Part II: Differentiation Chapters 6–10					
		Strongly disagree (1)	Disagree (2)	Neutral (3)	Agree (4)	Strongly agree (5)
11	A good language class is structured around the needs of the learners.					
12	Learners who begin their language study at an earlier age have a greater chance of success than their peers who begin at a later age.					
13	Heritage language learners have an advantage over their peers in language classrooms.					
14	When pairing learners, it is most beneficial for language learning to pair learners who are at a similar level.					
15	Teaching strategies that are beneficial for neurodivergent learners are beneficial for all learners.					
16	Language-related anxiety is detrimental to language learning.					
17	Never correct learners who are anxious.					
18	Motivation is the greatest predictor of a learner's ability to learn a new language.					
19	Learners can become better language learners over time.					

Pre-Reading Self-Assessment

	Part III: Teaching the Skills *Chapters 11–15*					
		Strongly disagree (1)	Disagree (2)	Neutral (3)	Agree (4)	Strongly agree (5)
1	TV shows, DVDs, and apps are the best way to pick up languages outside of the classroom.					
2	Explicit grammar instruction should be limited in language classrooms.					
3	Teaching pronunciation is less important than teaching the other language skills.					
4	Grammar exercises/drills are necessary for developing communicative language ability.					
5	Explicit knowledge about grammatical forms and rules is essential in learning a second language.					
6	Repeating targeted linguistic structures over and over helps learners acquire language naturally.					
7	Reading speeds up acquisition.					
8	Learners must be able to read in their first language before they can begin to learn to read in their second language.					
9	Learners must have a large vocabulary before they can begin to read or write.					

Pre-Reading Self-Assessment

	Part IV: Lesson and Unit Planning *Chapters 16–21*					
		Strongly disagree (1)	Disagree (2)	Neutral (3)	Agree (4)	Strongly agree (5)
1	It is important for learners to master simple grammatical structures before instructors introduce more complex structures.					
2	Immersion education produces second language users with native-like abilities.					
3	Explicit grammar instruction should be the focus of a language program.					
4	Tasks/activities should be adapted to suit the learners' needs.					
5	The primary role of a language instructor is to create an environment conducive to interaction in the target language.					
6	The primary focus of a language program should be learners' accuracy in the language.					
7	Language courses should be organized around progressively more difficult tasks/activities.					
8	Language is acquired best when it is used as a vehicle for doing a task/activity rather than studied in an explicit manner.					

Pre-Reading Self-Assessment

Part IV: Lesson and Unit Planning *Chapters 16–21*						
		Strongly disagree (1)	Disagree (2)	Neutral (3)	Agree (4)	Strongly agree (5)
9	The primary role of the language instructor is teaching proper grammar and pronunciation.					
10	Language courses should be organized around progressively more difficult grammar.					
11	A good language class mainly follows the order presented in a textbook.					
12	Grammatical correctness is the most important criterion by which language performance should be judged.					
13	Comprehensible input means using vocabulary words that learners already know.					

These statements are based on Spada and Lightbown (2006), King and Mackey (2007), Ogilvie and Dunn (2010), and Bryfonski (2019).

PART I

TEACHER AND STUDENT TALK

1 How do I get my learners to start and stay talking in the second language?

KEY QUESTIONS
- The Science: Why is it important for learners to talk in the second language?
- The Art: How do I encourage learner participation in the second language?
- How do I encourage learners to talk in the second language when they work in small groups?
- How do I deal with "how do you say X?" types of translation questions?
- What should I do if learners don't participate because they are afraid to make mistakes?
- How do I incorporate opportunities for learners to use the second language in all parts of my lessons?

1.1 Voices from the Classroom

Ms. G is a high school Spanish instructor in a large U.S. public school. Her Spanish class of twenty learners meets three times a week for one hour. Ms. G knows that learners only have limited opportunities to hear and use Spanish throughout the week, so she wants to make sure she is using her class time efficiently. When her learners come to class, they take a long time to "warm up" to speaking in Spanish. An experienced Spanish teacher, Ms. G is well aware that when learners speak-among themselves, they mostly use English and only use Spanish when she directly calls on them or is standing next to them. Ms. G wants to include more small-group activities to make her classes more interactive, but she worries that learners don't feel comfortable using the language with their peers. Instead of working through activities in the L2, they often come to ask her for translations. She has told her learners they can only request help if they use Spanish, so "¿Cómo se dice X en español?" ("How do you say X in Spanish?") is now a common refrain in her class. How can Ms. G encourage more learner-to-learner interaction in Spanish? How can she encourage her learners to be creative with their Spanish and less afraid of making

mistakes? Can she encourage them to ask each other how to say something (in Spanish)? What else can she do?

1.2 The Science: What the Research Says

Participation, learner engagement, and involvement are top concerns of teachers in all disciplines. However, for language teachers, encouraging learners to participate, or generate **production** in the second language, is even more critical because production (sometimes also known as **output**, and we will use these terms interchangeably) is a key element of successful language development. In the classroom, successful language production might consist of learners speaking the second language (L2) with the teacher, with their peers, or with anyone else there who speaks the L2, like an assistant teacher or visitor. Production is not just speaking or signing, in the case of signed languages (e.g., American Sign Language, ASL) – it is also learners' informal or formal writing in the L2. Research has shown that learners need a lot of varied opportunities to produce language output through speaking or writing in the L2 in order to learn, and it's not just about getting opportunities – learners actually have to *make use of them*, too.

The importance of production for L2 learning is founded in a long history of research. Merrill Swain became a foundational researcher in this area after noticing that learners in French immersion contexts in Canada who studied French grammar, read French texts, and listened to French being spoken did not develop high levels of French proficiency, even after many years of this sort of immersion. Swain concluded this was because the French learners did not have sufficient opportunities to actually *produce* French in meaningful communicative environments. Studies that have been conducted since Swain's original work have backed this up: learners who produce the L2 on a regular basis learn faster and better. Production is one of the four key ingredients for successful language acquisition, along with access to **input** (the language learners hear, read, or see signed), opportunities for the **negotiation for meaning** (overcoming miscommunications or other language problems through interaction), and to receive and respond to **corrective feedback** (the corrections learners receive from other speakers). In this book, we explain all four of these important elements, starting here in the current chapter with production. We will cover the remaining three (input, negotiation for meaning, and corrective feedback) in more detail in Chapters 2, 3, and 4. Quite a few of the older textbooks start with input as the first "ingredient" before production. Indeed, this might seem like a logical place to start, as all language teachers come to learn very quickly that comprehension (of input) precedes production. However, our book is based on the most common questions language teachers have for us – and we find that how to get learners talking in the L2 and staying in the L2 is their number one question. So, that's where we're starting!

1.2 The Science: What the Research Says

> **BOX 1.1 Four Key Ingredients of Second Language Acquisition**
>
> - *Output/Production:* What learners produce (speak or write) in the second language
> - *Input:* What learners hear or read in the second language
> - *Interactional adjustments/Negotiation for meaning:* Opportunities to overcome comprehension or language production difficulties through interaction
> - *Corrective feedback:* Opportunities to receive, provide, and respond to feedback on language production (Note: Corrections can vary in nature, ranging from explicit mentions of grammatical patterns to implicit requests for clarification.)

While learners can produce language (i.e., by talking, signing, or writing) in a classroom when they repeat a dialogue script they have memorized, or parrot something after the teacher, this is not the type of language production we know is most helpful for language learning. The sorts of production that are most helpful include learners having frequent opportunities to (a) use language creatively, (b) discuss language, and (c) encounter and resolve language problems in authentic linguistic situations.

Closely related to the importance of language production is the opportunity for learners to modify their production after receiving corrective feedback or encountering other language problems. When learners have opportunities to adjust or self-correct their own language production, this engages some helpful cognitive processes. For example, they have the opportunity to directly compare what they produced with what they heard their teacher, or a more proficient speaker, produce. This allows them to build mental connections in the L2 that support their language development. To illustrate what we mean, Box 1.2 presents three conversations between language learners and native speakers (more often called "L1 speakers," as we noted in the Preface; we use L1 speakers from here) of English from data in the published literature and one example in Spanish.

> **BOX 1.2 Exemplar Language Learner: First Language Speaker Conversations**
>
> Example 1.1
> LEARNER: When it happen?
> TEACHER: When did it happen? ← Recast (see Chapter 3)
> LEARNER: When did it happen?
> (from McDonough & Mackey, 2006)
>
> Example 1.2
> LEARNER: And I've two-two cup.
> TEACHER: You have two cups? ← Evidence of misunderstanding
> LEARNER: Yeah. ← No modification
> (from Oliver, 2000)

> **BOX 1.2 Continued**
>
> Example 1.3
> LEARNER: What happen for the boat?
> TEACHER: What? ← Evidence of misunderstanding
> LEARNER: What's wrong with the boat? ← Modified production
> (from McDonough, 2005)
>
> Example 1.4
>
> | | **Spanish** | **English** | |
> |---|---|---|---|
> | Teacher (Regina): | ¿Cómo te llamas? | What's your name? | |
> | Learner (Alex): | Te llamas Alex. | Your name is Alex. | |
> | Teacher (Regina): | ¡Me llamo (gestures) Regina! ¿Cómo te (gestures) llamas? | My name is Regina! What's your name? | ← Evidence of misunderstanding |
> | Learner (Alex): | Me llamo Alex. | My name is Alex. | ← Modified production |

In Example 1.1 (Box 1.2), after receiving feedback on their production, the learner modified their original utterance by repeating the correct form "When did it happen?" We assume that as this happened, the learner had a chance to compare their production, "When it happen?" to the L1 speaker's production, "When did it happen?" and, as a result, they may have **noticed** the correction from the L1 speaker. Research has connected learners' noticing of corrections and modified production with development in the L2. In research studies of this, learners are sometimes asked what they were thinking about at the time they heard the correction and changed their production. In Example 1.1, the learner might have recalled, "After 'happen' again, I made a little effort to say 'did' because you made me realize you don't understand." This is a fascinating way to understand the process of language development from learners themselves.

In Example 1.2, the learner does not modify their production but instead acknowledges the corrected form "two cups." Whether the learner noticed the correction, or not, is ambiguous. Their response, "yeah," may be evidence they noticed the error or they may just simply be continuing the conversation. Again, asking learners afterward (e.g., after class, or in a reflection assignment at the end of class) what they were thinking shows researchers that sometimes they notice their teacher's corrections, and sometimes they do not.

In Example 1.3, the learner is not able to directly compare their own production, "What happen for the boat?" with the L1 speaker's version of the question, because the L1 speaker only indicates they didn't understand, by saying "What?" However, the learner seems to recognize from the L1 speaker's "What?" response that a misunderstanding has occurred. In order for the L1 speaker to understand, the learner is prompted to self-correct, also referred to as **pushed output** or **modified output**. In this case, the learner's new production is correct, and we can assume these two speakers were able to continue their conversation. Making errors in production allows learners to receive feedback, compare what they said to the interlocutor's responses, and, perhaps, help them notice gaps in their own knowledge of the new language. We cover different ways learners receive and respond to feedback in more detail in Chapter 3. For now, it's important to realize that errors are important sites for learning, and part of what makes production so helpful.

Another way producing language helps learners become more fluent in their new language is by promoting language **automaticity**, or the everyday routines of language use. Just like driving a car, which at first is made up of many simultaneous tasks that new drivers may struggle to execute fluently, language use becomes more automatic after practice. The more often drivers drive, or learners produce language, the less concentration and mental effort is needed to be accurate and fluent.

1.2.1 Connections to Practice

Supporting and increasing learners' language production is closely tied to supporting learner **engagement** in their learning. This is also talked about in the research as "investment," "active participation," and "emotional commitment to learning," among other terms. Studies have shown that learners with higher levels of engagement are more likely to produce the L2 during activities and, as a result, are more likely to create conditions for themselves that generate high-quality language learning. If learners are not actively participating and engaged in a lesson, they are less likely to produce the L2 and may be less likely to retain any new content in a class where content and language are integrated. This makes sense to teachers – learners who aren't engaged aren't learning.

Often, when learners have minimal-to-no production in the L2, this is related to learners' levels of **willingness to communicate**. In other words, the threshold where learners feel comfortable producing the L2. Willingness to communicate almost always manifests in ways unique to each learner and can change over time and activity (e.g., varying based on who the learner is talking to, their degree of interest in the conversation topic). Studies have shown relationships between learners' personality characteristics, levels and types of motivation, and their anxiety about speaking the L2. We will talk more about how these sorts of individual characteristics affect language learning in Chapters 6 through 10. In classroom settings, learners need to feel supported and comfortable in the learning environment, and need to be encouraged to make mistakes, otherwise they may be too intimidated or find it too stressful to contribute. Also, if not all learners are engaged, some can be "let off the hook," and not be held accountable for their learning. This is a hard issue for teachers to deal with, especially in differentiated classes (classes which are divided by proficiency level or some other learner characteristic; we cover this topic more in Chapter 6). Applying the old adage "You can't please all the people all the time" to the classroom, we like to think about engagement as "It's very difficult to engage an entire class all the time." However, what we *can* do is create an environment that is positive and includes many opportunities to collaborate in small groups, which usually has a positive impact on learners' willingness to communicate. We will also touch on this in Chapters 4 and 7, during the discussions on ensuring inclusivity of all learners. Content and materials that are aligned with learners' interests may also help improve engagement and encourage participation (see Chapter 8).

> **BOX 1.3 The Science! Points to Remember**
>
> - Speaking or writing in a second language is called output or language production. Producing the second language is a key element for second language development.
> - Interactions that push language learners to produce and modify their own language encourage language learning because they make it more likely that learners will notice the differences between their production and first language speakers' production.
> - Producing the second language is key to developing automatic, fluent use of that language.
> - An engaging, supportive, and positive classroom environment will increase learners' willingness to communicate and thus promote the production of output.

1.3 The Science: What's Missing?

Second language learning and teaching involve many different variables, unique contexts, and situations. This means that it is difficult to say for certain which teaching strategies will always be best for language learning outcomes in every context. No full-time researcher will ever understand a program or classroom like its teacher will. (See Chapter 21 for more information on research conducted by teachers in their own classrooms – often called "action research.") So, it is often up to teachers to use their best judgment and knowledge based on best practices. For example, while we know language production is important for language learning, the research does not stipulate the best method for encouraging production in every type of learning context. Likewise, the science doesn't tell us how many times a learner needs to use a vocabulary word or structure in order to have "learned" it and be able to produce it automatically. Similarly, the research does not tell us the precise ratio of learner-to-teacher interactions versus learner-to-learner interactions necessary for language learning. Instead, the research tells us only that learners *can* and *should* learn from each other (we talk more about peer interaction and learning in Chapter 4). Despite the ongoing research investigations into these questions, teachers need to make it work in classrooms. One way to guide decision-making is to use the science we have reviewed here to inform and follow up on issues that present in classrooms, but adjust as needed for individual learners, contexts, and teaching dilemmas.

Also, there is always variation. So, some learners might perform differently from how the research findings we talk about would suggest. For example, an individual learner who produces very little L2 might still demonstrate learning but simply need more time to develop their willingness to communicate and move their production from their head to the classroom. Or a child might have specific learning challenges or social-emotional needs that prevent them from producing language easily. In these cases, it is up to the teacher to identify how teaching strategies might be adapted to suit the needs of individual learners. We talk about language learners with specific learning difficulties in depth in Chapter 7.

The tips and tricks below provide some ideas to get teachers started, but we'd advise that teachers see them as jumping-off points. We also give a list of resources for where teachers interested in promoting L2 production in their classrooms can go for more information. Please always keep in mind what we say above – that individual instructors are always best equipped to read over these suggestions and figure out what works best for their own language learners in their teaching context.

1.4 The Art: Research-Based Strategies to Try

1.4.1 The Art of Planning for Output

How to Balance Teacher and Learner Output

In every lesson, unit, or task plan, identify first exactly what the instructor will be doing and what learners will be doing at each point in the lesson. Create a mental flowchart or organizer of the plan and what it will look like for learners throughout the lesson. Visualize the class period (or unit or task) playing out and imagine what the experience will be like for each learner in the room. Throughout the lesson plan, ask the following questions:

- When will learners have the opportunity to produce the L2?
- When will learners be silently listening to the teacher or others?
- How and how often will learners be given the opportunity to demonstrate their learning?

Make sure to strike a balance so that learners have ample opportunities to produce the L2 with the whole class and in small groups and are not spending excessive stretches of time listening to the teacher. Table 1.1 provides an example of an output-based class plan for Ms. G's high school Spanish class. The table shows a model lesson structure that plans for student output. Activities are described in terms of who is saying what, when, and to whom.

By planning this way, Ms. G, our featured teacher in this chapter, can quickly take stock of how much time learners spend listening, versus having opportunities to produce language during each class period or activity sequence.

Choose strategies that ask *all* learners to engage in the discussions and have opportunities for language production. For example, if you plan a whole-class discussion, select one of the strategies in this chapter, such as assigning roles (see below) to ensure all learners are included in opportunities for language production, even if you only solicit a public answer from a few learners.

Table 1.1 Example of student output-based class plan for Ms. G's high school Spanish class

Time	Teacher actions	Learner actions
5 minutes	Whole-class instructions: The instructor describes the next activity where learners will be debating the pros and cons of studying abroad in various Spanish-speaking countries and filling a graphic organizer. Instructions are provided in Spanish.	Learners are listening.
5 minutes	Whole-class modeling: The instructor asks one learner to come to the front of the class to model a few examples and fills in bullets on the graphic organizer.	One learner is producing the L2 during the model. All other learners are listening.
2 minutes	Questions: The instructor asks for questions.	Learners have the opportunity to produce the L2 if they have questions.
15 minutes	The instructor circulates to offer feedback.	Pair interaction: Learners work together to debate pros and cons and fill in the graphic organizer. Learners have opportunities to produce spoken language by taking turns during the activity. They will also produce written language on the graphic organizer. Learners will negotiate for meaning during the activity.

Authentic Materials

Choose content or materials that are aligned with learners' interests in the real world to increase engagement and L2 production. For example, in a high school or secondary class, learners may be more engaged if course content reflects trends and themes of pop culture as shared via blogs, social media posts, or music lyrics. For example, in a unit on "Fashion," learners may enjoy comparing the outfits of celebrities who speak the L2, as shown in the celebrity's Instagram posts, in the tabloid magazines, or clothing "try on" or "haul" videos (both common video genres) from the celebrity's YouTube channel instead of looking at generic pictures of clothing in a textbook. Pick ten to fifteen items from the celebrity outfits and ask learners to pick and discuss which items they would be most likely to wear on different occasions.

1.4.2 The Art of Encouraging Language Production

Polling Learner Interests

Survey learners throughout the year or semester to find out what topics interest them and integrate those topics into your lessons. Keep it relevant for them by using smartphone polling apps if possible. You can ask questions like "What

1.4 The Art: Research-Based Strategies to Try

upcoming school or community events are you looking forward to?" and "In which real-life situations can you imagine using the L2 in this year?" Younger or less proficient learners could draw pictures, while older learners could share or write about their preferences or fill in online surveys.

- For younger learners, before a unit on "Family Pets," learners could be asked to draw pictures of the animals they have or the animals they wished they had at home so the teacher can be sure to incorporate their interests into the unit activities. Authentic resources could include pictures, videos, or toys of the specific animals that learners identified.
- For older learners, prior to a unit on "Healthy Routines," a poll could be conducted to gauge the frequency and importance of certain routines and habits in their lives. Authentic resources could include infographics from physical education centers or extracurricular opportunities in local (or international) communities. We will discuss these types of resources in Chapter 18.
- See Figure 1.1 for more ideas on how to create tasks that connect to learners' interests.

Ask 3, Then Me

A typical understanding in the field is that when saying "Ask 3, then me," we mean, *ask three other learners, or consult three other resources, before asking the teacher for help*. Not only does "Ask 3, then me" encourage learners to produce output by forming questions in the L2 and discussing them with peers, it also promotes two important qualities: learner autonomy and learner resilience. See Figure 1.2 for an example.

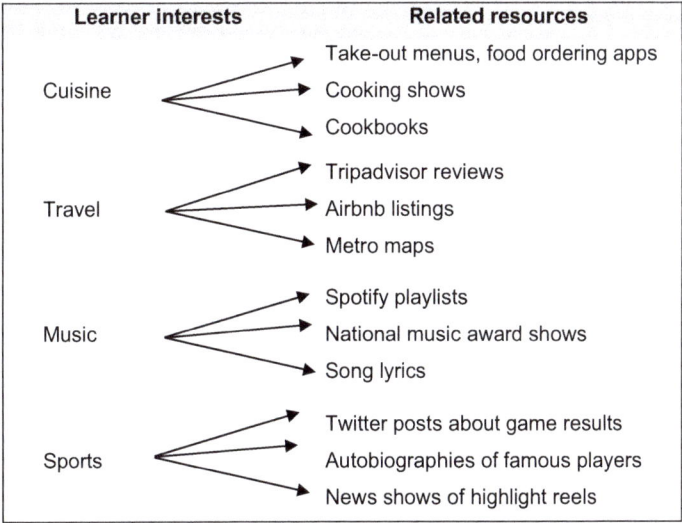

Figure 1.1 Connecting unit tasks to learner interests. This graphic shows how general learner interest can be explored through authentic resources

Figure 1.2 "Ask 3, then me" sign. The speech bubble here is intended for display in a world language classroom. It reminds students of steps they can take when they encounter an issue in the classroom. Image by: Elizabeth Zonarich

This Ask 3 strategy encourages learners to interact with each other and discuss the L2 before asking for translations or help from the teacher. If "Ask 3, then me" becomes a routine in your language class, learners will know they cannot rely on their instructor for an immediate answer before consulting other sources. This "do-it-yourself" mentality facilitates language acquisition because learners are forced to generate more utterances in the L2 by asking others for help and search through input by seeking out helpful materials in order to get the information that they need. This strategy also fosters learner motivation and investment in their own learning, which research has tied to more language development. This should also cut down on the problem of constant "how do you say X?" questions from learners.

Cold Call

This is a common teaching technique and refers to asking learners at random to answer a question posed to the whole class rather than waiting for them to raise their hands. Again, it promotes learner engagement and encourages production for all learners, even the ones less likely to volunteer. This technique allows for class time to feel more like a guided conversation than a scripted back-and-forth. It also prepares learners to answer questions, share their opinions, and pay attention throughout class. According to research on anxiety in the language classroom, while cold calling might be initially uncomfortable for some learners, once it becomes routinized and they understand how to prepare for it, it becomes much less anxiety-provoking. Special care might need to be taken for certain vulnerable individuals for whom cold calling might be a particular challenge. For example, children with audio-processing issues might best benefit from being called on when visual supports for what was just said are available so they can read to support what they hear being asked. Children with a stutter might benefit from having think-time prior to being called on; for example, just after a think, pair, share. These supports do not all need to necessarily be in place in the same way for the entire school year – nor should these learners be exempt entirely from cold calling (which other learners in the class will notice!) – but providing these supports initially, as well as discussing them with these kinds of learners, will go a long way in ensuring that learners see their L2 classroom as a supportive environment.

In this vein, teachers need to create a class culture where risk-taking is celebrated and learners are not afraid of making mistakes. Posing low-stakes questions, offering lots of scaffolding, providing visual support, and leaving plenty of wait-time can help learners transition to a learning environment where cold calling is used every day.

- *Tip:* Write your learners' names on popsicle/lolly sticks and draw them out of a jar to make sure everyone knows the selection is random. Extra tip: Have a second jar readily available and place the popsicle sticks of learners who have already taken a turn into the second jar. Continue to pull from the first jar until each learner has had a turn and then, when the second jar is full and the first jar is empty, you can reverse the jars and start the cycle again (see Figure 1.3 for an example).

- *Tip:* Sentence starters. Another helpful tip is to teach learners some phrases to say when they don't know something in the L2 (e.g., "I'm not sure, but my best guess is___" or "I don't know, but to find out I would___"). Pre-teach these phrases early

Figure 1.3 Popsicle stick jar. Using a jar of popsicle sticks is one way to call on students randomly throughout a class period. Image by: Elizabeth Zonarich

Figure 1.4 Useful phrases in the classroom. Visuals with "survival" phrases like this can be displayed throughout the classroom or distributed to students to keep on hand for quick reference. Image by: Caitlyn Pineault

in the semester/term. Post these "sentence starters" clearly in the front of the classroom so learners can reference them during whole-group discussions.
- You can even co-create a list of "survival phrases" with the class. They may have needs or concerns you don't think of! In Figure 1.4, a Spanish teacher posts "Useful Phrases [Frases útiles]" for her classroom including "Excuse me [Perdón]" and "I'm confused [Estoy confundido/a]" along with supporting graphics.

Wait-Time

Wait-time is very interesting in that research shows it varies among cultures and individual teachers. It is developmentally helpful if you can develop a habit of waiting a few seconds after you finish asking a question and before you ask a learner to begin to answer it. This strategic pause gives learners a chance to think independently and formulate their response. Here are some tips for what to do while you wait …

- Scan the rest of the class to see who else may have a comment or answer to your questions.
- Draw a hint (or write a key vocabulary word) on the board.
- Point to a key phrase or photo on the wall or to other class resources (e.g., PowerPoint, posters).

Try to develop a habit of not calling on a learner before asking your question and waiting for them to think for a minute. Doing so puts the learner suddenly on the spot, without time to think about the answer, raising their anxiety too far, which might limit their understanding of the question as they (try to!) listen and their ability to produce accurate L2. Instead, ask the question, pause, and then choose a learner to call on.

- *Tip:* If a learner looks confused, restate the question in a different way to ensure they have another chance at comprehension. You might even try simplifying your question to allow the learner the success of answering it on their own (see Chapter 2 for strategies for making your instruction more comprehensible to language learners). You can always circle back around to original questions by asking it of another learner.

1.4.3 The Art of Structuring Learner Interactions to Maximize Language Production

Talk to a Table/Buddy/Partner/"Think-Pair-Share"

In this technique, you are encouraging independent thinking followed by sharing. You ask learners to first *think* and then discuss their answer with a person sitting close to them (*pair*), before finally explaining their answer to the whole group (*share*). This way, each learner has a chance to think, to talk about their ideas with a partner in a small, non-threatening setting, and finally, be prepared for sharing in front of the whole class and the teacher. While the activity is going on, the

1.4 The Art: Research-Based Strategies to Try

teacher can circulate among the pairs, giving encouragement and feedback. This sort of preparation typically increases learners' willingness to produce the L2 in front of the whole class. Another benefit is that learners have multiple opportunities to engage with the same content. First, they formulate their own version of the answer, then they hear a peer's version, and then they hear from other classmates in the whole-class shared versions. Multiple opportunities to engage with the same vocabulary, structures, or content allow learners to develop stronger mental representations leading to more language development (see Figure 1.5 for an illustrative example).

- *Tip:* Write, discuss, share. Another version of this is to give learners the opportunity to produce the L2 first in writing before discussing. Set a timer for two–three minutes and let everyone write (or even draw!) their thinking or planning. Then solicit answers.

- *Tip:* Keep sentence starters handy for partner discussions, for example, taped to learners' desks. Sentence starters (in the L2) might say: "What's your idea?" "I was thinking the same thing," or "I agree/disagree with you because_____ ." (See Figure 1.6 for an example.)

Figure 1.5 Think-pair-share. These cat-students are engaged in a think-pair-share activity, which helps to provide each student with more opportunities to produce output. Image by: Elizabeth Zonarich

Figure 1.6 Sentence starter examples. Sentence starters like these help students get started on their own speaking or writing assignments. Image by: Elizabeth Zonarich

Choral Answers

In this fun technique, rather than asking learners to answer individually, you can mix it up by including opportunities for the class to answer in unison. This relieves the pressure on any one learner from contributing and demonstrates that everyone in class is working together for the same goal. Learners who are unsure of the accurate vocabulary or words to use will listen and follow along with the model.

Another version of the choral answer is giving out a miniature drawing board or paper to every learner or to small groups. Ask a question and let learners write the answer and hold up their board. This ensures that all learners have an answer prepared. Scan the whiteboards in the room to quickly assess learners' comprehension. Then you can follow up by calling on one learner to describe the thinking behind their answer.

You can also add physical responses to indicate comprehension and preferences to further diversify how learners engage in class. For example, classroom layout permitting, for a question where there may be several predetermined options, you can assign each option to one corner/space of the room and ask learners to stand up and move to the corner that best represents their preference (i.e., *What did you do this week? Played sports, visited with family, worked a job, watched a movie*). When they arrive at the corner, learners must turn to those next to them and ask them why they chose this spot and engage in a dialogue. This technique is especially helpful for discussing spectrums or continuums of responses (e.g., opinions ranging from "I hate X" to "I love X") where two ends of the room represent the extremes of the possible responses.

Small-Group Work

Research suggests that learning is strengthened when learners have ample opportunities to learn from each other in addition to the teacher (we discuss the science of this in more detail in Chapter 4). Make objectives for group work clear so that there is little downtime (or "what do we do now?" time) for learners. Design group activities such that interaction in or about the L2 is essential to completing the task. In order to ensure no learners can "opt out" of small-group interactions, consider assigning team roles. For example, if learners are tasked with reading a text and making personal connections to their own experiences, you might assign the following roles (or you or your learners can invent their own!):

- *The reader* reads the passage aloud to the team.
- *The summarizer* gives everyone an oral summary of the passage after the reader reads.
- *The reporter* takes notes of the team's discussions.
- *The questioner* raises three questions about what they have all read.
- *The eagle eye* reviews what the team writes for spelling or grammar mistakes.
- *The encourager* encourages everyone to contribute and supports each contribution.
- *The task manager* helps the team stay on track to finish all tasks in the time given.

1.4 The Art: Research-Based Strategies to Try

It is helpful to rotate roles during small-group work, either in that session or in future classes, so that learners have a chance to interact with a range of roles because each role offers varied language production opportunities. The reader has the opportunity to focus their comprehensibility and fluency while they read aloud to the group. The summarizer gets the opportunity to restate the key information from the selected passage, which calls on their vocabulary knowledge. The reporter has the opportunity to produce written output in the form of notes. The questioner must rephrase content into question forms as they facilitate a discussion about what was read. The encourager gets to practice memorized chunks of language, like the commands and commendations (e.g., "Great idea!") that they likely have heard their teacher use throughout the course. (See Figure 1.7 for an example.)

1.4.4 The Art: Using Language "Pledges"

Language pledges can serve as community agreements that explicitly state the expectations around language use (which language, when, and why) in a classroom, school, or program. Some teachers might find that creating a language pledge "ceremony" where learners sign, commit, or make a promise to uphold the language norms can create excitement and increase buy-in. For some learners, there might be a reward or prize if all learners follow the language pledge for a set period of time. The specifics of the language pledge vary based on learner age and proficiency level, as well as language programs themselves.

- *Tip:* Learners can create a series of statements that all start with "We agree to____."
- *Tip:* Learners can sign their names or with their thumbprints if they are young learners.

Figure 1.7 Group work roles. Each member of this group is assigned a different role to facilitate positive interactions and teamwork. Image by: Elizabeth Zonarich

1.5 Troubleshooting: How the Science Informs the Art

Ms. G knows that it's important to have her learners talk in Spanish during class. One method she uses regularly is practicing dialogues. She plays a video to her learners (who are 15 years old) of a Spanish dialogue, like ordering food in a restaurant. Then, she gives learners a written copy of the dialogue to practice with in small groups. Learners trade roles in the dialogue. Ms. G likes that the learners are speaking in Spanish and seem to enjoy the activity. However, while learners seem to memorize the exact words in the dialogue, they don't seem to be able to extend their knowledge when they are presented with a situation where they need to create their own dialogue. The learners are speaking Spanish, so why can't they use their knowledge in new contexts?

Ms. G's technique for getting learners to produce the L2 involves repeating dialogues. This allows learners opportunities to practice the sounds of a language and compare their production to a model. However, this is a *drill*. Drills do not allow for the rich production of language known to support learning. It is important to realize that communicating meaning is something that doesn't flow naturally from having done a lot of drills. Developing the ability to communicate meaning flows naturally from practice with having a need or reason to produce language in a meaningful context. While learners doing drills may produce a lot of L2, these are unlikely to be beneficial for future success in resolving communication breakdowns because learners doing drills are simply reading and repeating the words in the dialogue. Ms. G also needs to circulate in order to hear and correct pronunciation errors. A better option would be to start with a modeled interaction, like the restaurant dialogue Ms. G likes, and then asking learners to devise their *own* dialogues. Ms. G could give each learner a scenario that will push them to be creative with their Spanish. For example, one learner may be the waiter and the other learner is a customer with a specific dietary restriction. This will most likely result in communication gaps that push learners to modify their output to be better understood by their partner resulting in more language development.

The learners in Ms. G's class are producing a lot of Spanish when they use the pre-made dialogues, so why can't they use their knowledge in new contexts?

While they have practice speaking with scripts, it is likely that Ms. G's learners do not feel as comfortable speaking more spontaneously in the L2. This is because organic communication does not develop from predetermined drills, like the repetition of a model dialogue. Naturally speaking in the L2 is an ability the learners can practice during in-class activities; however, it is not an ability that will emerge if all the learners do is read scripted dialogues. If Ms. G wants her learners to use the L2 more creatively, she should design activities that support her learners in developing this skill. For example, Ms. G might start a lesson with a modeled dialogue of a restaurant interaction, but she should slowly have learners work toward composing their own. Encouraging learners to brainstorm what sorts of urgent interactions or exchanges may inspire them to think outside of the box in the L2 (e.g., What happens if your salad comes with walnuts, but you are allergic?!).

Ms. G notices that if she takes away the dialogues and allows the learners to speak completely independently, they don't talk as much as when they read from dialogues.

Even after giving her learners more support and opportunities to speak more spontaneously and creatively, Ms. G might still find that her learners get "stuck" or are reluctant to produce the L2. If this is the case, Ms. G might consider providing visual cues (i.e., posters of sentence starters, picture flashcards of key words/phrases) around the classroom that learners can look to if they are having a hard time getting started. If Ms. G does not have the ability to add posters to the room, she could add sentence starters at the beginning of the prompt page to guide learner efforts. It is possible that her learners feel more nervous about sharing their own ideas, let alone in the L2. She should be sure to be patient and encouraging and be sure that these qualities are highly valued in the classroom.

If Ms. G is including a variety of class activities, providing ample scaffolding and support, and fostering a welcoming class environment, but learners are still wary about producing the L2 independently, they might benefit from a brief discussion, in their L1(s), about the importance of output to the language acquisition process. For some learners, it is helpful to know the "why" of class routines and norms so that they can buy into the process.

1.6 The Science: Points to Remember

- Output is what learners produce in the L2 and can be oral, signed, or written.
- Producing L2 frequently, especially in meaningful interactions, is essential to successful language learning.
- The opportunity to self-correct or modify output in an interaction can help learners notice the difference between their own language and others' language.
- Producing the L2 helps learners develop automaticity, or language routines, that lead to more fluent production in the second language.
- Engagement is important for encouraging language production. If learners are not engaged, or motivated to participate, they may be less willing to communicate, which may affect their language development.
- Teachers can use a variety of strategies to promote language production and to ensure there is a balance between teacher-centered and learner-centered portions of the class.
- Learners may produce the L2 in different amounts and develop in their fluency at different paces. It is the instructor's role to identify individual needs and, where possible, tailor expectations for each learner.

1.7 Questions to Consider

1. Why do you think production is so critical to language learning? Why isn't it enough to just hear and read language input?
2. What challenges do you commonly have in getting your learners to participate in the L2?

3. What factors do you think influence your learners' willingness to communicate?
4. What are the challenges to increasing the amount of time your learners interact in small groups in the second language? What are the benefits?
5. What individual differences have you noticed in your learners? How do their engagement levels differ? With these observations in mind, how might you encourage different types of learners to produce the L2 in class?
6. How can you integrate more opportunities for learners to modify their own production in your class?

1.8 The Science of Language Learning: Research Supporting the Points Made in This Chapter

de Saint Léger, D., & Storch, N. (2009). Learners' perceptions and attitudes: Implications for willingness to communicate in an L2 classroom. *System, 37*(2), 269–285. https://doi.org/10.1016/j.system.2009.01.001.

This study investigated learners' perceptions of their speaking abilities, of their contributions to oral class activities (whole-class and small-group discussions) as well as their attitudes toward these activities, and how such perceptions and attitudes influenced the learners' willingness to communicate in the L2. Using primarily self-assessment questionnaires, thirty-two L2 French learners participated in a semester-long study. The questionnaires asked learners to "reflect on their immediate learning environment at various points in the semester and self-assess their speaking skills" (p. 269) and concluded that the learners' perceptions both of the speaking activities and of themselves as learners in the foreign language classroom both affected their willingness to communicate. In general, as learners' self-confidence increased over time, so did their willingness to use the L2 in class. However, the researchers pointed out that the learners' willingness to communicate with peers in small groups was "not uniform" and was affected by interpersonal relationships and affiliation motives.

García Mayo, M. D. P. & Alcón Soler, E. (2013). Negotiated input and output / interaction. In J. Herschensohn & M. Young-Scholten (Eds.), *The Cambridge handbook of second language acquisition* (pp. 209–229). Cambridge University Press.

This chapter from *The Cambridge handbook of second language acquisition* offers a brief overview of the research on the role of learner interaction in the language learning process. The authors explain how input and output (i.e., production) have been considered together in examinations of how interaction can be beneficial for learners. Apart from these interactions providing more opportunities for input, they also provide learners with the chance to "try out" their own understanding of the language in order to communicate larger messages. The responses of their conversation partners (whether they be peers or instructors) give them clues as to whether they were able to successfully convey their ideas or whether they need to revisit their understanding and use of linguistic features.

Swain, M. (1993). The output hypothesis: Just speaking and writing aren't enough. *Canadian Modern Language Review, 50*(1), 158–164. https://doi.org/10.3138/cmlr.50.1.158.

This article provides a concise overview of work conducted in French immersion programs in Canada and its contribution to applied linguistic research. Swain specifically highlights how French immersion research contributed to our understanding of the importance of production (i.e., output) to second language acquisition. This short article is written in an accessible way and includes examples of how learners benefit from "pushed output" and "modified output" opportunities. The article also provides implications for second language pedagogy.

VanPatten, B. (2014). Creating comprehensible input and output. *The Language Educator, 7*(4), 24–26.

This article from the American Council on the Teaching of Foreign Languages (ACTFL), the preeminent American foreign language teachers' professional association, serves as an overview for educators on the topic of "input" and "output" in language teaching. VanPatten breaks down the roles of each and offers practical implications for language educators. The article ends with the major challenges facing teachers when reading about input and output and their roles in second language development and urges teachers to reconsider the teaching methodologies, materials, and curricula of the past.

For more resources, including more sample lesson plans, videos, and other ideas, visit our companion website: www.cambridge.org/BryfonskiMackey.

2 How do I maximize input in the second language?

KEY QUESTIONS
- The Science: Why is it important to maximize input learners hear or read in the second language?
- The Art: (When) is any use of the first language okay? (and why?)
- What happens when I give instructions in the second language and then the first language?
- Is it okay for learners to use their first languages when working in groups?
- Should my instructions and classroom routines always be in the second language?
- Should the input language be the same for academic vs. nonacademic classes like art, physical education, and music?
- Should there be a "lingua franca" policy (for the school or the class)?

2.1 Voices from the Classroom

Mr. T took a course over the summer on the importance of making the language classroom a place where learners feel comfortable and confident. He read that if learners were anxious and on edge during his language class, their learning would be impacted. Because of this, Mr. T decided to let learners use their shared language (the students' first language, L1) in class when they feel it's necessary, or when it would make them more comfortable. He also decided to use the L1 when giving high-stakes instructions or sharing important administrative or school-wide information. However, since he made this change, Mr. T has noticed his learners using the L1 all the time and now they almost never speak in the second language (L2), even if the activity is low-stakes and simple. He has also found himself speaking more and more L1 in the classroom, even during instances when he recognizes, in hindsight, he could likely have communicated the same idea in the L2. When he realized he was doing this and tried to implement a stronger L2-positive culture, his learners reacted negatively and mostly ignored him. Mr. T wants his learners to feel comfortable in class, but he also wants them to use the L2 as much as possible. He is unsure what "fair" expectations are for his learners and is also unsure about how much the language of the classroom has an influence on their ultimate language development.

2.2 The Science: What the Research Says

Of the many unknowns in how L2s are best learned, there is one thing we know for certain: whether we are talking about a baby learning a first language or an adult learning a second, you will not learn a language if you are not exposed to it. Decades of research have shown that learners must have ample opportunities to receive input in the target language (TL) in order to develop language proficiency. **Input** is the language that learners hear, read, or interpret (as in signed languages) in the L2. As we discussed in Chapter 1, input is one of the four key elements for successful language acquisition along with opportunities for production, negotiation for meaning, and receiving corrective feedback. Therefore, it is critical for L2 teachers to provide access to ample target language input.

There are a number of ways to talk about the amount of input learners receive. If 100 percent of input is in the L2, this is known as "immersion." However, the degree to which teachers and programs *should* aim for 100 percent input in a target language is context-dependent. There are so many different features in the learners' environments, including the class, the program, the school, and then their home, social, and/or work lives. All of these are part of the equation when considering how much input learners need to develop in their new language.

When talking about settings, researchers often distinguish between "foreign" and "second" language, although these days, when talking about the languages themselves, the term "world language" is preferred over "foreign language." When taking about settings, the term "foreign" is still generally used. In **foreign language settings** (e.g., Arabic instruction in the United States, or English instruction in China, sometimes also called "world" languages), learners' only exposure to the target language (the one they are learning) is through the input they receive in their language classrooms. Typically, once learners leave their language classes, they are re-immersed into the setting of their shared language (normally their L1), which is usually the language outside the school, and the language they speak at home. For example, a learner enrolled in a high school French class in the United States who leaves their French language classroom and goes home to an English-speaking family, and a (mostly) English-speaking environment outside the home and school, would be said to be learning French in a foreign language context. For these reasons, it is critical for world language teachers to use the target language as much as possible in their classrooms. Owing to the restricted access to the L2 in foreign language settings, teachers should create classroom routines to acclimate learners to hearing the L2 when they first come into the classroom and then stick to their policies of using the L2 as much as possible. This is especially important for younger learners, or beginners who have limited proficiency, because they will receive repeated exposure to input in the second language. Teachers in foreign language settings are typically recommended to only speak the L1 of their learners in situations where full comprehension is paramount.

In **second language settings** (e.g., a L2 Spanish learner enrolled in summer classes in Mexico, or an English-as-a-second-language learner taking English classes in the U.K.), learners are typically exposed to the target language in a variety of contexts. For example, within the language classroom, but also in their content classes (e.g., science, art), in the cafeteria, as they travel to and from school, shop in stores, eat in restaurants, or at work. Language teachers in these contexts should still aim to speak the target language in their classrooms as much as possible. However, learners may also receive support in their L1 to access content where it is necessary, for example, to help them understand a tricky grammatical or pragmatic (relating to politeness and social norms) nuance. Many learners in second language environments have already received some instruction in their L1 and can leverage that prior knowledge to support their L2 development. Bilingual programs can increase the amount of input learners receive in the target language by offering additional courses outside the core content areas, classes often referred to as "specials" like art, music, physical education/gym, technology, or library class, in the TL, in addition to other tips we provide in the sections below. Some researchers also investigate "extramural" language learning contexts, like after-school sports teams, neighborhood play groups, collaborative video games, and other language learning contexts outside of school programs.

In mixed settings, we find situations which don't fit neatly into foreign vs. second boxes. For example, for some learners and families in mostly second language settings, it is important that the L1 or the heritage language is maintained. For example, when a family immigrates to the United States and is placed in an English-speaking school, this is a mostly second language setting for them. The learners hear and speak English in school and outside school in most contexts, but at home and perhaps in their local community, they speak their L1 (or the heritage language), or a blend, and of course, they don't want to lose their family's language. If they know the L1, teachers can support this effort by helping learners make connections between L1 and L2 structures and vocabulary. Teachers can connect learners with bilingual resources like books to further foster those connections, including in their classroom or school libraries. Regretfully, this is not always possible, such as in contexts where the instructor does not speak the L1 of the learners or when a learner's L1 does not have ample resources published in their L1 (e.g., Quechua books), or when the L1 does not have a written script, as is the case with some indigenous languages. In these cases, the onus is on schools to recognize the validity of the L1 and support their learners as much as possible. See the Preface for a table summarizing these key terms.

2.2 The Science: What the Research Says

2.2.1 Comprehension

Regardless of context, the teachers should consider the extent to which the input learners receive is comprehensible to them. This concept of **comprehensibility** originates with the researcher Steven Krashen, who suggested that learners learn best when they receive language input that is at a level slightly ahead of their current proficiency. He called this level "$i + 1$," where i is the current proficiency level of the learner. In Krashen's view, if the input learners receive is lower than their current level, for example i -1, or at their current level i, they will not hear new language forms that they can integrate into their own language system and use to develop. If the level of language the learners hear and see is too advanced ($i + 2$), and they can't understand anything, they may become frustrated and be less willing to communicate and also fail to develop.

> **BOX 2.1 The Science! Points to Remember**
>
> - **Comprehensible input (CI)** is the level of input that will be understood by a language learner and push them to develop. According to researcher Steven Krashen, the appropriate level of input should be targeted to be comprehensible but not so easy that it is at or below the current level of the learner. A level of input slightly ($i + 1$) above the learner's current level will best support their language development.
> - Note! It is likely that "$i + 1$" means something different for each learner in your class because learners progress at different speeds. What strategies can you use to differentiate instruction to make sure that all learners get input that is "$i + 1$" for them?

While this theory was groundbreaking at the time he published it, Krashen's ideas received quite a bit of criticism from researchers, mainly because it hard to test them. He doesn't define what the "i" stage is, for example. It is important to note that CI does not mean that learners will comprehend every word they hear from a teacher, read in a book, or otherwise receive in the TL input. It just means overall that they can *mostly* understand; the one or two linguistic items provided that go beyond their level of comprehension can then be noticed, paid attention to, processed, and ultimately learned. In this way, teachers can manipulate what learners pay attention to by changing the level of input. For example, if a teacher wants to target a specific grammatical structure like conditionals, they might use vocabulary that is already familiar to the learners so that the main area of focus is on the new grammatical form – the conditional. Also, teachers shouldn't habitually translate what learners don't understand into the learners' L1 to ensure they do understand the activities or tasks, or else learners will in turn grow accustomed to ignoring TL instructions and waiting for L1 input. Rather, teachers should aim to use various strategies to deliver instructions in the TL that can be understood by the learners. One thing that is very important to understand is that even if you get CI just right, that alone is not enough to promote language development (and we discuss this more in Chapters 3 and 4). Another aspect missing from "$i+1$" is that learners will approach input in different ways based on their individual abilities in language learning. This might mean certain learners can more easily notice new patterns, remember recently introduced vocabulary words, or are more likely to be creative with their language. These individual differences will affect how much of the "+1" learners can absorb, and we talk about these differences in more detail in Chapter 9.

In sum, where Krashen's theories met (and continue to meet) criticism is how we assess what that "$i+1$" means in practice and how we plan for creating an "$i+1$" task in real L2 classrooms with real learners. Subsequent researchers like Bill VanPatten, Merrill Swain, Susan Gass, Mike Long, Bill DeKeyser, Rod Ellis, and others have all grappled with this disconnect between Krashen's theoretical work and how teachers can use that theory in the classroom, each specializing in their own piece of the puzzle of what do we do after CI.

2.2.2 Connections to Practice

In order to aim for as much TL input as possible in language classrooms, language educators should utilize a variety of strategies to ensure TL input is comprehensible to learners. If learners are able to comprehend the input, there should be less pressure on the instructors to switch to the learners' L1. There has been a variety of research on strategies for effectively targeting input so it is comprehensible to language learners (e.g., Long, 1996), many of which demonstrate the power of repeated exposure to input. Language educators should be in the habit of repeating L2 instructions in several different ways (e.g., using synonyms for potentially tricky vocabulary, simplifying or expounding upon the instructions, slowing down). See Box 2.2 for an example to try.

Input that is accompanied by gestures, visuals, and role-playing can also increase comprehension. Also, learners can be asked to put instructions in their own words or explain the instructions back to the class. Learners may be called to the front of the classroom in pairs to act out the instruction or model the activity. Learners can be taught how to assess their own comprehension by frequently asking them to report the degree to which they understood the instructions. For example, a teacher might give a direction and then ask learners to show on their fingers how much they understood: three fingers mean they completely understand what to do, two fingers mean they understand some but not all of what to do, and one finger means they don't know what to do at all. If utilized repeatedly, starting with low-stakes activities (e.g., practicing playing charades to normalize using gestures), learners will develop a better sense of their own comprehension and how to report a lack of comprehension to their instructor.

Research has also demonstrated that learners can be trained to become better partners in group activities (Koh et al., 2010). This is important because if learners can successfully interact in the L2 in group work they will receive additional input from their peers. They can also be trained to support each other by providing corrective feedback (e.g., Fujii et al., 2016). Learners' ability to learn from what they hear in the input will be impacted by their ages and

> **BOX 2.2 Try It Out!**
>
> What is known as "The Paco Sentences" (Long, 2007, p. 136) have been used in empirical research to analyze how learners exposed to different kinds of input respond. Below you see the original "Paco Sentences" in four forms: the *Genuine* version, the *Simplified* version, the *Elaborated* version, and the *Modified Elaborated* version. As you read the sentences, consider what they have in common and what is different.
>
> 1. Genuine version
>   *Because he had to work at night to provide for his family, Paco often fell asleep in class.*
> 2. Simplified version
>   *Paco had to make money for his family. Paco worked at night. He often went to sleep in class.*
> 3. Elaborated version
>   *Paco had to work at night to earn money to provide for his family, so he often fell asleep in class the next day during his teacher's lesson.*
> 4. Modified elaborated version
>   *Paco had to work at night to earn money to **provide for** his family. As a result, he often fell asleep in class the next day during his teacher's lesson.*
>   "**provide for**" means   a. educate
>   b. leave
>   c. support
>
> Now you try! Pick a sentence in your target language from a book or journal article and see if you can write three additional versions of it, using the "Paco Sentences" as a model. You can also complete this exercise with a colleague and compare your versions of the same original sentence.

proficiency levels. For example, when learners are very young or low proficiency, they are more likely to use their L1 resources to communicate even when a teacher holds an entire class 100 percent in the L2. We need to recognize that learners may still fall back on their L1(s) to communicate and negotiate for meaning together. They may use their L1 to discuss a vocabulary word or correct a misunderstanding. Learners' use of their L1(s) is not always problematic, particularly if it avoids frustration. Teachers can utilize the strategies in section 2.4 to encourage more use of the L2 during group work and throughout class time.

2.3 The Science: What's Missing?

While we know that input is a critical element for second language acquisition, there are a variety of unknowns in terms of how much or how little is required for successful language acquisition. So, while we know that repeated exposure is critical, there is no specific threshold for how many times learners need to hear, read, or interpret (as in signed languages) a new word or structure in order to acquire it or use it productively and, obviously, it is likely to be different for different learners. Similarly, there is no specific threshold of L1 that we could

> **BOX 2.3 A Quick Recap**
>
> - Input is critical for second language acquisition and language instructors should aim to use the target language in as many interactions with learners as possible.
> - The percentage of target language input necessary for development varies by context: in foreign/world language contexts teachers should aim for 100 percent of the input being in the target language because learners will not have access to further input outside of school.
> - In second language environments it can be beneficial to support learners both in their first language and in the second language.
> - Input should be made comprehensible to learners so that they are able to follow instructions and access content delivered in the second language (but see Chapter 18 about the issue of authenticity).
> - Learners can be taught to assess their own comprehension of the target language input and become better language partners in small-group or partner activities.

say for certain would support but not hinder acquisition. In some second language contexts, teachers may have learners from a variety of L1s together in the same class. In this case, it is often impossible or impractical for the instructor to rely on the learners' L1 to negotiate communication breakdowns or support their development.

2.4 The Art: Research-Based Strategies to Try

2.4.1 Making Instructions Comprehensible in the TL

- After giving an instruction, call on a learner to repeat it back to the class in their own words. This way, learners can hear the instructions twice, most likely with varied vocabulary and expressions adjusted for their proficiency level.
- Model activities using gestures and the actual objects, worksheets, etc. that will be used in the activity. Provide examples of an acceptable level of completion for that activity.
- Ask learners to model the activity by coming to the front of the class or group and modeling the activity together.
- Write and/or draw the objectives for the class or task and display them in a prominent place in the classroom. Make sure the objectives are written at a level that is appropriate for learners' age or proficiency level.

2.4.2 Promoting Positivity about Second Language Learning

- Encourage L2 use while also promoting positivity about the benefits of knowing another language well by having a class discussion about bilingualism. Ask learners to discuss the following questions and record the answers on a poster or anchor chart for future reference and discussion:
    - Why is it useful to speak another language?

2.4 The Art: Research-Based Strategies to Try

- How can we help each other use [fill in TL here] in our class?
- What makes you proud about knowing two languages?

2.4.3 The Linguistic Landscape of the Classroom

The linguistic landscape of a classroom, program, or school refers to the language you see around you. For example, on entering the school is the signage in more than one language? Does the cafeteria have translations for food? Does the language classroom have print-rich displays showcasing the L2? All of these aspects can be helpful in setting the scene for language learning (see Figures 2.1 and 2.2).

Figure 2.1 Linguistic landscape wall hanging examples. These images are examples of resource that can be displayed around a classroom to support learners with the target language. Image by: Elizabeth Zonarich

Figure 2.2 Elementary word wall. This word wall is organized by sound groups with example words that students are encouraged to use in their own writing.

Figure 2.3 Bilingual classroom labels. These two classroom scenes feature items labeled in both English and Spanish. Image by: Elizabeth Zonarich

- Learners also receive input in what they read. One way to increase comprehensibility and input is to label all classroom materials in the target language. For example, label classroom supplies, furniture, and areas of the classroom.
- For younger learners, accompany the label with a picture or diagram.
- For lower-proficiency learners, provide bilingual labels. See Figure 2.3 for an example. Depending on age and ability level, involve learners in the creation and application of these labels. Turn it into a game for older learners (e.g., all learners are provided with a set of class labels and game to correctly put as many up around the room as possible within a specific time frame).

> **BOX 2.4 Example Target Language Policy for a Foreign Language Program**
>
> Mandarin Chinese teachers at our school act as language models. What does this mean?
> - They provide ample, rich, and varied types of language input for their learners to interact with each day, inside and outside of their Chinese class.
> - They support learners' acquisition of both academic and social Chinese by providing age- and proficiency level-appropriate input in Chinese and encouraging learners to speak Chinese with peers in small groups and with their teachers outside the classroom.
> - They model Chinese use in front of learners by speaking in Chinese with other Chinese teachers in the school including in the halls, cafeteria, and at recess.
> - They support learners' developing bilingualism by upholding a sense of respect toward learners' native language or languages as well as learners' multiple intersecting identities and cultures.

- Linguistic landscape is also the language that learners hear around them when they are outside their language classroom. Teachers can work together to build a community of language practice so that learners view them as language models and hear them speaking the TL together in the halls, cafeteria, and playground. An example of guidelines for Mandarin Chinese teachers at a bilingual school is shown in Box 2.4:

2.4.4 Providing Multiple Ways of Engaging with the L2

- Input can be delivered in many different forms. Make sure to vary the opportunities for learners to engage with input. For example, create stations or centers where learners engage with content in multiple forms. At one station they may read the content, at another they listen to audio versions of the content or watch videos, and at a final station they play a game.
- Learners should have the opportunity to engage with the same content on multiple occasions. Teach learners how to strategically engage in pre-, during-, and post-reading/viewing activities in order to extract as much meaning as possible from the featured content.

2.5 Troubleshooting: How the Science Informs the Art

Mr. T wants his learners to feel comfortable in class, and he wants them to follow his instructions and use the L2 as much as possible. He is unsure about what "fair" expectations would be for his learners and is also unsure of the extent to which the language that they use has an influence on their ultimate language development at all.

The fact that Mr. T's learners feel initial anxiety around using and hearing the L2, which leads them not to use it, shouldn't deter Mr. T from using some of the strategies discussed in the chapter to see if he can help his learners feel more comfortable taking risks, making mistakes, and asking questions. He can do this by providing comprehensible input in the L2 in class, and by insisting they use the L2 when possible. Mr. T might consider facilitating an open conversation with his learners around why they don't want to use it. Then he can propose some strategies (like using an agreed-upon signal to show understanding or creating a word wall) to help learners learn how to use and interpret the TL. Having a feedback box (where learners can anonymously submit written notes) about what worked well and what felt confusing in class can help ensure a strong feedback loop as Mr. T works to facilitate class more entirely in the TL. Mr. T might also find it beneficial to explain to his learners (in the L1) why input is so important to language learning and why it is okay (and actually a positive thing) if they can't understand every single word. Drawing connections to future academic or professional aspirations in international study/work abroad contexts may help motivate learners to take risks.

2.6 The Science: Points to Remember

- Input is one of the four key elements of successful language acquisition.
- The ratio of TL to L1 used in class varies based on a variety of factors including learning environment, learner age, and learner-proficiency level.
- When learners receive input that is just slightly more advanced than what they are currently capable of producing, they may be more likely to acquire it.
- Learners can be taught/helped to process input in ways that can maximize their understanding and learning potential. Designing activities that feature novel repetition is key!

2.7 Questions to Consider

1. List a few ways people communicate without language. How might you incorporate some of these nonverbal communication strategies in your classroom to increase learner comprehension?
2. A sense of routine helps learners navigate input in the TL. What routines do you have (or would you like to implement in class)? Jot down some instructions or phrases you say frequently in class. Other than translating them, how can you make sure learners understand this kind of language?
3. What different strategies could you use in class that enable learners to show you whether they understand or whether they need you to provide further scaffolding? Brainstorm several "whole-class" and "individual" polling methods that you can use in different sorts of class activities.

2.8 The Science of Language Learning: Research Supporting the Points Made in This Chapter

Ellis, R., & Shintani, N. (2014). *Exploring language pedagogy through second language acquisition*. Routledge.

In this book, chapter 7, "Teaching as 'input'," provides a concise and practical explanation of the role of input in second language acquisition for language teachers. It includes theoretical perspectives and also explains how these research findings can be applied to language pedagogy. Drawing on SLA theory and research, the authors Ellis and Shintani have addressed common language teacher concerns related to input and provide an additional list of tips for language teachers to consider implementing in their own contexts.

Gass, S. M., & Mackey, A. (2006). Input, interaction and output in SLA. In J. Williams & B. VanPatten (Eds.), *Theories in second language acquisition: An introduction* (pp. 175–199). Lawrence Erlbaum.

This chapter provides a general overview of the interaction approach in second language acquisition. Specifically, it describes in detail the four concepts – input,

2.8 Supporting Research

interaction, feedback, and output (i.e., production) – that constitute the interaction approach, and show examples of how they are interconnected and can further support second language learning. In addition, this chapter may help teachers with their understanding by listing observations related to the interactionist approach.

Gass, S. M., & Varonis, E. M. (1994). Input, interaction, and second language production. *Studies in Second Language Acquisition*, *16*(3), 283–302. https://doi.org/10.1017/S0272263100013097.

In this classic study, Gass and Varonis examine the relationship among input, interaction, and second language production and its effects on second language development. They investigated the effects of interaction and types of input (modified and nonmodified) on native and nonnative speaker pair interactions throughout a direction-giving task. Results from their study indicated that interaction and modified input improved L2 learners' comprehension and had a positive effect on L2 learners' immediate task performance.

For more resources, including more sample lesson plans, videos, and other ideas, visit our companion website: www.cambridge.org/BryfonskiMackey.

3 Why, when, and how (much) should I correct my learners?

KEY QUESTIONS
- The Science: Why is it important for learners to receive corrections on errors they make in speaking or writing?
- The Art: How can I provide effective corrections for my learners?
- Should I interrupt the learner to provide an immediate correction or wait until they finish their thought?
- Should I correct all the errors my learners make or target specific ones?
- Should I correct my learners in the same way in speaking and in writing?
- Should the type of correction I use change according to the age of the learners, the topic, or their proficiency level?
- Are certain types of corrections better for certain types of language (e.g., sounds, vocabulary, structure, etc.)?

3.1 Voices from the Classroom

Mrs. R is teaching advanced Spanish this year. As the semester progresses, she finds herself spending more and more time grading her learners' written assignments. She uses a correction key to mark errors that she thinks learners should be able to correct themselves, and she also corrects any errors that they would not be able to resolve independently. As well, she puts lengthy comments in the margins about how to strengthen the organizational structure and writing style. Though her learners are generally high-achieving, when she enters grades into the school's learning management system (LMS), she notices limited engagement with feedback. Learners spend only a few seconds accessing the documents, if they engage at all. She is frustrated that her hard work is going to waste and that her learners are not looking at their mistakes and her corrections and reflecting on their written work. In the final months of the semester, she sees quite a few learners continuing to make the same sorts of errors they made at the beginning of the year – errors she has corrected for them. This makes her doubt the effectiveness of her own instructional practices and the dedication of her learners. She wonders why she spends all this time correcting their writing assignments if they don't look at them, and it doesn't seem to make any difference anyway.

3.2 The Science: What the Research Says

Errors are a natural part of the language learning process. At some point, every learner will make mistakes in their attempts to produce their new language. While some learners may shy away from making errors, research has shown that making errors is *essential* for development. When learners make errors, they are testing out hypotheses about what is possible or not in their new language. The reactions learners encounter from teachers, native speakers, or peers when they make errors help them as they attempt to fill in the gaps between their own language and that of a more proficient speaker. Additionally, the errors learners make can help teachers to tailor instruction to meet learners' individualized needs.

Corrective feedback, typically meaning the corrections learners receive from others when they make errors in their second language (L2), is one of the four key ingredients needed for successful second language acquisition we covered in Chapter 1. Learners often receive corrective feedback when they are interacting with others in real time (e.g., in an oral conversation or in an online chat setting), but they can also receive corrective feedback on things they prepare ahead of time (e.g., a writing assignment, a presentational video). Corrective feedback might target different aspects of learners' language. For example, correction might target a grammatical error such as a verb conjugation, a mispronunciation of a sound, or a pragmatic error (e.g., an issue with politeness). Corrections also vary in how explicit they are. Some are very *explicit*, like telling a learner they have forgotten to use the correct past tense ending, or very *implicit*, like asking the learner for clarification (e.g., "Huh?"). In writing, corrections might be *direct*, like crossing out the mistake and writing the correct form for them, *indirect*, like circling the errors the learner made without pointing out why they are errors, or *metalinguistic*, like prompting a learner to check a verb conjugation without writing the correct form on the learner's paper. See Box 3.1 for examples. Learners' responses to corrective feedback can vary based on their individual characteristics, such as their current proficiency level, motivation to learn, or anxiety about being corrected. We cover these individual factors that affect language learning in more detail in Chapter 8.

3.2.1 Types of Corrective Feedback

Not all corrections of learners' spoken errors explicitly provide the corrected form. Box 3.1 defines some common strategies for providing oral feedback to learners.

The most common type of oral feedback found in language classrooms is also the most implicit, a **recast** (Long, 2016). This is most likely because recasts do not interrupt the flow of conversation but still allow learners to compare what they said to the correct way (that is, if they notice the correction; more on this later). A long history of research has shown that recasts are effective for various feedback

> **BOX 3.1 The Art! Common Types of Oral Corrective Feedback**
>
> *Example Learner Error:* **"How many cards he have?"**
> - **Recast**: reformulating or restating what the learner said with the correct form.
>   - *Example correction:* "How many cards does he have? He has three cards."
> - **Repetition**: repeating what the learner said exactly, including the error, often with a rising intonation to let the learner know there's a reason for the repetition.
>   - *Example correction:* "How many cards he have?"
> - **Clarification request**: indicating that what the learner said wasn't understandable and asking them to restate or repeat themselves to clarify.
>   - *Example correction:* "Huh? Can you try that again?"
> - **Confirmation check**: asking the learner a question about something they said to confirm understanding.
>   - *Example correction:* "Sorry. I don't understand. He have?"
> - **Metalinguistic feedback**: grammatical explanation of the learner's error
>   - *Example correction:* "Oops. You're missing 'does' in your question."
>
> (More implicit ↕ More explicit)

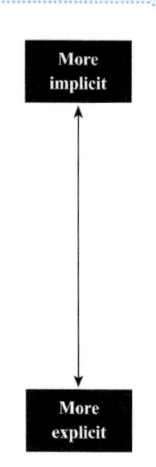

situations (different learners, languages, feedback targets). However, more explicit forms of corrective feedback are also important and shown to be effective for certain situations (Mackey et al., 2016).

The research has demonstrated that lower-proficiency learners tend to benefit more from more explicit forms of feedback (like metalinguistic feedback or direct written feedback). In contrast, higher-proficiency learners can benefit more from the implicit forms of feedback (like recasts, or in writing, indirect feedback). Why? Since lower-proficiency-level learners have not developed as much metalinguistic knowledge about their TL and do not yet have a sense of what sounds "right" or "wrong," they need more explicit feedback in order to realize their error and make the necessary adjustments. In other words, because lower-proficiency learners may be using more of their cognitive resources while they attempt to process what they are hearing or reading in their L2 than higher-proficiency learners do, they may not be able to pick up on implicit or indirect feedback. In comparison, high-proficiency learners may need to spend less time and fewer cognitive resources on trying to understand input, planning what they will say next, or puzzling through a vocabulary word. Since higher-proficiency learners have the linguistic background and communicative abilities that allow them to be more likely to notice nuance in their partner's production and attend to any error they may make, advanced learners are more likely to notice and benefit from implicit or indirect feedback.

Feedback in written modes varies by how **focused** or **unfocused** the feedback is – in other words, whether the feedback corrects *every* error a learner made in a particular piece of writing or if it is limited to a particular *kind* of error (e.g., a grammar point covered that week in class). Also, a teacher might decide whether to directly correct the learner's errors (e.g., by crossing out the error and inserting the correction for the learner) or indirectly correct errors by circling them or otherwise indicating where an error is without correcting it explicitly (see Box 3.2 and Figures 3.1 to 3.4 therein for examples).

BOX 3.2 The Art! Common Types of Written Corrective Feedback

Direct
(Teacher provides correction)

Focused: providing corrections on only one type of error (e.g., spelling of nouns, verb conjugations) in a learner's written composition and replacing them with the correct form.	*Unfocused*: providing corrections on all the errors a learner makes in a written composition and replacing them with the correct form.
Ayer, yo comió mucho ~~alado~~ *helado* y ~~hamburgesas~~ *hamburguesas* con mi amigos.	Ayer, yo ~~comió~~ *comí* mucho ~~alado~~ *helado* y ~~hamburgesas~~ *hamburguesas* con mi~~s~~ amigos.
Each day, she go~~es~~ to the store and buy~~s~~ a milk, a sugar and tea.	Each day, she go~~es~~ to the store and buy~~s~~ ~~a~~ milk, ~~a~~ sugar and tea.
Figure 3.1 Examples of focused direct written feedback	Figure 3.2 Examples of unfocused direct written feedback

Indirect
(Teacher does not provide correction)

Focused: highlighting only one type of error (e.g., spelling of nouns, verb conjugations) in a learner's written composition by circling them or underlining them but not providing the corrected version.	*Unfocused*: highlighting all the errors in a learner's written composition by circling them or underlining them but not providing the corrected version.
Ayer, yo comió mucho <u>alado</u>[sp-] y <u>hamburgesas</u>[sp-] con mi amigos.	Ayer, yo <u>comió</u>[VT] mucho <u>alado</u>[sp-] y <u>hamburgesas</u>[sp-] con mi amigos.[?]
Each day, she (go) to the store and (buy) a milk, a sugar and tea.	Each day, she (go) to the store and (buy) (a) milk, (a) sugar and tea.
Figure 3.3 Examples of focused indirect written feedback	Figure 3.4 Examples of unfocused indirect written feedback

3.2.2 Feedback for Different Scenarios

However, the topic of feedback is more complex than a simple endorsement of one kind over another. The effectiveness of feedback has been shown to vary based on *what type of language* is being corrected as well as *learner characteristics*, such as language proficiency, working memory, language awareness, and more. For example, metalinguistic feedback has been shown to be particularly effective for complex grammatical errors, whereas for pronunciation errors, implicit feedback has been shown to be particularly effective. This is because for pronunciation in particular, it is helpful for learners to hear an immediate recast and compare the correction with their own production.

In a recent study in a beginning Mandarin classroom, the researchers found not only that recasts yielded better results in learners' production of tones but also that both the instructor and the learners preferred the recasts over explicit metalinguistic feedback. This is not to say that metalinguistic feedback is never appropriate for pronunciation, but the learners studied came from L1s that did not have tones and, thus, had a steep learning curve with regards to controlling their production for tone. Because of this, getting the additional input of the recast allowed them to not only correct their errors but also keep the flow of the class going and focus their attention on the Mandarin input. See Table 3.1 for an example of how the recasts were provided.

Additionally, individual learners might differ in their preferences for certain types of feedback, and classroom tasks might lend themselves to one type of feedback over another. For example, very young children most likely will benefit the most from the more implicit forms of feedback because they can't easily understand metalinguistic comments about how grammar functions in an L2. Implicit feedback would also be appropriate in activities designed to be primarily about interaction and meaning and not grammar. More explicit feedback, on the other hand, might be necessary when targeted language structures differ significantly from the L1 or to correct repeated errors that would cause communication breakdowns. For example, if an L2 French learner repeatedly says *Je suis treize ans*

Table 3.1 Example of a recast on tone in a beginning Mandarin classroom (from Bryfonski & Ma, 2020)

(2)	Teacher:	Student:
1		*Zhe shì4 wǒ3 de ming* /nan.(This is my name card ....)
4	Nice! *Míng2 piàn4* (Name card)	
5		*Míng2 piàn4* (Name card)
6	Then, *Zhè4 shì4 wǒ3 de míng2 piàn4.* (This is my name card).	
7		Ok! *Zhè4 shì4 wǒ3 de míng2 piàn4.* (This is my name card).

(literally, "I am thirteen years"), when in French the appropriate expression is *J'ai treize ans* (literally, "I have thirteen years"), a teacher may need to explicitly correct this error by saying something like, "*Attention!* We say *j'ai treize ans* not *je suis treize ans!*" The teacher might follow up with an age-appropriate metaphor to explain the grammatical phenomenon without getting too theoretical. This French teacher might continue by saying something like the following:

> Remember, in French we think about our age like rings on a tree. Trees build new rings of bark every year and that's how they get bigger and sturdier. If you take a slice out of a tree's trunk you can see those layers of bark as rings. When you count how many rings the tree has, that tells you how many years the tree has been alive. We can think about it the same way with ourselves. We build on younger versions of ourselves and learn and grow through the years. We have these accumulated experiences – these "rings" of growing up. That's one way to think about why we say *J'ai* – why we say "I have" – when we talk about our ages in French.

This is an example of an explicit correction (i.e., the correct form is provided), with some metalinguistic explanation (though certainly "non-traditional" metalinguistics) to help learners understand how they can remember the correct form and where the idea informing the grammatical form may have come from.

Some learners can feel anxious if they are corrected too frequently or too explicitly. Others might become demotivated if they see a page of their writing covered in red ink. There is some evidence that for writing, focused feedback may be more effective than unfocused because correcting every error a learner makes can be demotivating (not to mention time-consuming for instructors). Learners who exhibit a lot of language learning anxiety might not benefit as much from too much direct or explicit feedback. On the other hand, some learners love receiving feedback and are constantly begging for more! The ways learners vary impact how they learn L2s, and we discuss these ways in more detail in Chapter 9. For these reasons, teachers should be aware of the learner and context in which they are delivering feedback and tailor their feedback to what learners need in the moment. As a result, teachers should weigh their individual learners' needs and the goals of the task against the research findings presented above when making decisions about what type(s) of feedback to use and when.

BOX 3.3 The Science! Points to Remember

What factors affect how much learners learn from feedback?

- The *type* of feedback used (recast, confirmation check, metalinguistic, etc.)
- The *target* of the feedback (pronunciation, grammar, vocabulary)
- Individual *differences* in age, proficiency level, and preferences/personalities
- The *context* (type of learning activity/task etc.)

3.2.3 How Much Learners Benefit from Feedback

Do learners have to notice the feedback that is provided to them? There is some evidence that learners who notice more feedback learn more. In other words, learners who notice they received feedback, who understand the feedback, and are given the opportunity to correct themselves might develop more language proficiency than learners who didn't notice the feedback in the first place and carried on speaking or writing without addressing the correction. Because learners often must process their feedback individually at their desks, teachers rarely have access to how deeply their learners are processing the feedback they're given. However, teachers might ask learners to think aloud while they respond to corrections in their writing or take notes about what kind of feedback they experience in the classroom. Teachers can then use this information as data about how much or little learners notice feedback and reference it during parent–teacher conferences, summarize it for whole-class reviews of common errors, review it during one-on-one learner feedback discussions, and more.

In the end, variation in the types of feedback and offering some choice or tailored options in how learners receive feedback are key to making sure that the feedback teachers give is actually understood, attended to, and acted upon by learners.

3.3 The Science: What's Missing?

While we know recasts are the most common form of corrective feedback used by language teachers in classroom settings (due to their ease of use and focus on making meaning through conversation), there is no research that definitively shows one type of corrective feedback is always better than others. What teachers should remember is that learners respond differently to corrective feedback based on their individual differences, and some might respond better to one form of feedback over another. The type of task or activity learners are completing also contributes to what kind of feedback might be most useful to learners. So, it is up to teachers to decide which type of feedback to use in any particular situation. Variation is key.

This advice is similar for writing. There is still a lot of debate among researchers about what kinds of written corrective feedback are most connected to language development.

3.4 The Art: Research-Based Strategies to Try

We find that teachers often have similar questions when it comes to providing feedback in their language classrooms. Box 3.4 provides some research-based suggestions for some common concerns with examples.

3.4 The Art: Research-Based Strategies to Try

3.4.1 Talk with Learners about Their Feedback Preferences

- Incorporate questions about the kinds of feedback they've received in the past and what kind(s) of feedback they've benefited from the most into your get-to-know-you surveys.
- Share some (brief!) information – with examples – about what kinds of feedback you will give them throughout the year and say why you use different kinds of feedback for different people, activities, content, etc. By talking about how you will teach class and give feedback, you are including the learners in the process of language learning and showing them how you will support them as they develop their

---

BOX 3.4 Common Issues about Feedback and Suggestions

Common issues and concerns about providing corrective feedback	Suggestions for teachers
• Learner is hesitant to speak or interact. • Learner's proficiency is too low for basic communication. • Learner is extremely shy.	• Learners won't participate in environments where they aren't comfortable. Make sure that their classrooms are supportive places where mistakes are acknowledged, helped, and are not a sign of being a "bad" learner. • Supply the learner with sentence frames to start conversation. These can contain symbols or pictures (Figure 3.5). I don't understand _____. What does _____ mean ? Can you help me with _____? Figure 3.5 Examples of conversational sentence frames. Sentence frames like the ones above can help students participate in a conversation in the target language • Build in opportunities for meaningful *written* interpersonal communication as well as spoken. This allows for alternative ways to build community and relationships that may help shy learners feel more willing to take risks when speaking. Examples: discussion boards, in-class chat rooms, or – for very low-proficiency learners – Post-it notes or Google Jamboard conversations/reactions (Figure 3.6).

BOX 3.4 Continued

Common issues and concerns about providing corrective feedback	Suggestions for teachers
	Figure 3.6 Post-it reactions in French class. Learners reacted with Post-its about what they hate [*déteste*], like [*aime*], love [*adore*], and don't like [*n'aime pas*]. • Incorporate games where learners interact to play but with interactions that are simple and predictable. This creates a relatively low-risk context for practicing speaking to get these hesitant learners used to using the target language. Example games include Go Fish, Battleship, UNO, etc., which are simple enough to be played in beginner classes and can be played in the first few minutes of class as a warm-up, or for longer periods of time.
• Chronic breakdowns in communication with the learner.	• Adjust speed of speech (slow down). • Use repetition. • Integrate equivalent vocabulary (alternative forms). • Wait longer (learners need time to process speech). • Incorporate gestures and visuals to support communication. • Be sure to teach your learners about nonverbal communication strategies as well!

BOX 3.4 Continued

Common issues and concerns about providing corrective feedback	Suggestions for teachers
• Learner repeats the same errors.	• Note that many errors are developmental, meaning that learners, regardless of L1 background, will make the same types of errors along their paths to higher proficiency. Not all errors are worthy of constant correction and concern. • Target errors appropriately. Consider whether the error inhibits understanding, and focus feedback on those types of errors.
• Learner does not seem to notice when the teacher corrects their errors.	• Use a more explicit form of feedback. • Vary the type of feedback provided.
• Learner is frustrated or embarrassed by error corrections.	• Make feedback more implicit, focusing on communication and meaning-making. • If possible, check in one-on-one with this learner! Make sure they understand the motivation behind your corrections and see if there is anything you can be doing differently to support their language learning in a way that is positive for them.

proficiency. Examples of learner-appropriate materials about feedback can be found on the book's companion website.

- Incorporate a post-assessment reflection opportunity where you ask learners to note the ways they prepared for the assessment (e.g., conduct mock interviews with a classmate, rewrite a story told in class from another character's perspective, review online material). This practice prompts learners to reflect on how they can take ownership of their studies. You can include questions about what kinds of feedback they think benefited them the most during the unit and what kinds of feedback they would like more/less of in subsequent units.

3.4.2 Cultivating a Positive Classroom Culture

- When learners avoid using complicated grammar or vocabulary because they are afraid of making errors, they limit their possible development. So, as instructors, we should work to build a classroom culture where learners should know that making mistakes is part of language learning and the errors are not just okay – they are encouraged!
- React positively when learners make errors. If learners are struggling to be understood, model strategies for understanding like asking clarification questions, asking a friend, or gesturing.
- Congratulate learners who attempt to use their language regardless of the number of errors.

3.4.3 Provide Keys for Writing Corrections

- Indirect feedback can be used to save time correcting writing assignments with keys or clues for the type of error the learner made. For example, S-V might mean there is an issue with subject-verb agreement. (See Figure 3.7 for some examples to try.)
- When providing corrective feedback on assessments, you can create a reference sheet of the codes or perhaps the different colored markings you use.
- If you have an online learning management system (LMS; e.g., Blackboard, Canvas, Moodle, Google Classroom), you can also make short videos explaining the most common corrections you made on a particular assessment. For example, if you found that an assessment had lots of instances of subject-verb agreement errors, you can make a short 30-second video of you explaining what the "S-V" code means. This way, if a learner is reviewing their errors and sees "S-V" on their papers, they can watch your short video and hear you explain their error to them. This is a relatively easy way to differentiate because learners will be able to watch and address only the errors they tend to make. Also, this frees up your time when you are answering questions about the assessment so that you do not have to answer the question "What does 'S-V' mean?" as each learner encounters it in their work.

3.4.4 Provide Feedback on Learners' Strengths as well as Their Errors

- Providing praise on concrete aspects of learners' proficiency goes a long way in developing and maintaining their confidence in their new language. Using a checklist format, to quickly acknowledge what a learner has already mastered and where they could improve, saves a lot of time and can fit more concrete information than a traditional rubric. Table 3.2 provides a mini example of what such a checklist might look like.

FRENCH 201 CORRECTION CODES	
ART	wrong article
FC	false cognate
INF	should use the infinitive
SP	spelling error
SV	subject verb agreement issue
WO	word order issue
VT	verb tense is incorrect
WC	word choice is incorrect
YW	use your own vocabulary!

ESOL Correction Code	
1	tense issue
2	article issue
3	wrong word
4	check collocation
5	preposition issue
6	too repetitive
7	relative clause issue
8	too informal

Italian Correction Code	
===	wrong verb form
-----	wrong word choice
*	spelling issue
^	missing word/phrase
!	not a real word/false cognate
?	unclear, rewrite

Figure 3.7 Example of written corrective feedback keys. These three correction code keys are resources that should be shared and discussed with students prior to the provision of written corrective feedback

3.5 Troubleshooting: How the Science Informs the art

Table 3.2 Excerpt from a linguistic development checklist

Throughout the unit …	Assessment strengths …	Beginning the next unit …
☑ learner maintained their "Growing [target language] Dictionary" as we added vocabulary ☑ learner interacted with peers respectfully	☑ learner accomplished the core assessment task ☑ learner used a variety of verbs ☑ learner demonstrated awareness of politeness strategies in the L2	☑ review the spelling difference between narrating past and present ☑ review the gender markers of previous units' vocabulary

- Instead of interrupting learners in the middle of a sentence or a class period to correct errors, consider sometimes summarizing the errors at the end of class.
- Some teachers allow their learners to earn back points on a test by doing test corrections. This practice involves learners reviewing an assessment, identifying their errors, correcting the errors, and providing an explanation as to why they made the error. You can expand on this idea by also encouraging learners to identify the aspects of their assessment that they did well on. For example, a learner might note that they used a variety of transition words that made their written text flow in a sophisticated way.

3.5 Troubleshooting: How the Science Informs the Art

Though her learners are generally high achieving, Mrs. R (from the start of this chapter) sees many of them throwing out their corrected writing assignments after glancing at the final grade. She is frustrated that her hard work is going to waste and that her learners are not taking more initiative to analyze and reflect on their written work. How can she encourage her learners to reflect on and internalize the feedback she provides on their writing?

Mrs. R is a thoughtful teacher who is clearly doing her best to provide her learners with feedback that can help them improve their Spanish. It seems that what her learners are struggling with is seeing the big picture of their language (i.e., being focused only on the test grade and not their overall proficiency) and how they should *use* Mrs. R's feedback. Her learners might not have many occasions to reflect on and incorporate feedback in other subjects and thus might simply not know what she is expecting them to get out of her feedback. Mrs. R should consider:

a. Scaffolding her feedback sessions so that she first models how to interpret feedback with an example text (e.g., a text written by a learner from a previous year), thinking aloud as she works through the text and showing the learners what kinds of edits the feedback is prompting.

b. Giving the learners a second example text (or the second half of the first text, if it is a long text) to correct themselves, in groups or individually. If this is her first year teaching advanced Spanish and she does not have any prior learners' texts to use, she can instead ask her learners to record themselves thinking aloud as they read through their feedback. Listening back to these recordings will offer her insight into how her learners are interpreting her feedback and help her to identify the common misunderstandings.

c. Having learners write an action plan to prepare for the final draft of the paper. In this action plan, learners can demonstrate their reflection on Mrs. R's feedback and create a plan for future improvements. In addition to having learners' set their own goals, Mrs. R can identify how the learners are interpreting her feedback and modify her instruction accordingly.

3.6 The Science: Points to Remember

- Feedback is critical for the development of both speaking and writing in an L2.
- Feedback varies by how explicit or implicit it is.
- Lower-proficiency learners may benefit from more explicit correction.
- Higher-proficiency learners may benefit from more implicit correction.
- Implicit correction is useful for pronunciation and less complex errors.
- Explicit correction is useful for more complex grammatical errors.
- Younger learners may benefit more from implicit correction than older learners.
- High-anxiety or easily demotivated learners may need more implicit correction than low-anxiety, highly motivated learners.
- Different tasks call for different feedback, e.g., tasks focused on meaning-making/communication → implicit feedback.
- Not all learners will process feedback in the same way or as deeply.
- Focus on errors that impede communication or understanding.

3.7 Questions to Consider

1. What kind(s) of feedback do you usually use? Do you make decisions about the kinds of feedback you will use for a particular error or activity prior to providing the feedback?
2. What kinds of trends have you noticed in your own classroom? Do your learners tend to prefer or react best to particular kinds of feedback? Do they dislike any kind(s) of feedback?
3. After you return an assessment and you circulate among the learners, how do the learners talk about their feedback? Do they ask each other for help/clarification? Do they reference their notes/class materials?
4. How can you involve learners in the feedback process so that they know what you want them to do with the feedback you've provided?

3.8 The Science of Language Learning: Research Supporting the Points Made in This Chapter

Li, S., & Vuono, A. (2019). Twenty-five years of research on oral and written corrective feedback in System. *System, 84*, 93–109. https://doi.org/10.1016/j.system.2019.05.006.

This article summarizes the types of oral and written corrective feedback, as well as the results of high-quality studies on these practices. Additionally, the researchers include findings on teachers' and learners' perceptions of different kinds of feedback.

Lyster, R., Saito, K., & Sato, M. (2013). Oral corrective feedback in second language classrooms. *Language Teaching, 46*(1), 1–40. https://doi.org/10.1017/S0261444812000365.

This article provides a detailed overview of research conducted on oral corrective feedback over the past four decades. Findings from a number of empirical studies are summarized and compared across a number of factors, including type and scope of feedback, the effects of feedback over time, etc. One notable point the authors make is that L2 learners report wanting more corrective feedback on their production than teachers assume they want (and more than what teachers are comfortable providing).

Park, E. S., & Kim, O. Y. (2019). Learners' engagement with indirect written corrective feedback: Depth of processing and self-correction. In R. Leow (Ed.), *The Routledge handbook of second language research in classroom learning* (pp. 212–226). Routledge.

This book chapter reports on a study conducted with beginner and intermediate L2 Korean learners as they first produced, and then corrected compositions after receiving indirect written corrective feedback via underlining. The researchers found that the learners were able to successfully self-correct approximately 36 percent of the errors noted in their compositions, but that they also quickly gave up on errors they didn't immediately know how to resolve.

For more resources, including more sample lesson plans, videos, and other ideas, visit our companion website: www.cambridge.org/BryfonskiMackey.

4 How do I promote peer interaction in the classroom?

KEY QUESTIONS
- The Science: Why is peer interaction important in language classrooms?
- The Art: How can I best leverage peer interactive learning in the classroom?
- How do I decide how to group learners to promote interaction?
- How do I encourage collaborative, cooperative learning?
- Are there any mistakes/errors my learners might pick up from each other?

4.1 Voices from the Classroom

Ms. W teaches intermediate German at the university level. She has a mix of first-year learners who were assessed as being at intermediate level based on previous German courses taken in high school, and final-year learners who began the language in their first year at university. The range of prior language learning experiences means the learners have a wide range of abilities, especially at the beginning of the semester. Ms. W always tries to use pairings and groupings to help the class feel more like a supportive community where learners feel comfortable taking risks. However, the learners' performance on their last few interpersonal speaking assessments had Ms. W feeling torn about this method of encouraging community. In reviewing the interpersonal speaking submissions over the first units, Ms. W noticed that the way in which learners communicated varied tremendously based on their assigned communication partner. For example, during one interactive task, one learner, Mica, did very well – asking questions, responding with details, and using strategies of circumlocution to navigate areas where the partners didn't initially understand each other. A few classes later, during a similar activity, Mica seemed reluctant to engage, making frequent pauses mid-sentence, appearing to have a hard time transitioning from topic to topic, and not following up on responses. The differences in performance were so significant that Ms. W followed up with Mica, asking about the difficulty level of the unit material and whether all else was well in Mica's life. Mica assured her that everything was fine. Ms. W noted that in other components of the assessment

Mica had a good understanding of the unit themes. Ms. W was even more confused. She understood that not all her learners would take an equal liking to each other, but she was surprised to see their language performance vary so much! For her upcoming class, Ms. W is considering minimizing peer–peer interaction so that she can be the students' primary conversation partner, giving all her learners a similar interaction experience. Still, she's unsure whether this is the best way to solve the problem.

4.2 The Science: What the Research Says

In most language classrooms, there are more learners than there are instructors. This means that individual learners cannot possibly spend every moment speaking in the target language (TL) exclusively with their teacher. In order to access as much input as possible, produce the TL in meaningful ways, and hear feedback (the elements of successful language learning we covered in Chapters 1, 2, and 3), learners must also spend some amount of time interacting with each other. Learners talking or writing together inside or outside a language classroom – also known as peer interaction or peer-to-peer interaction – can be an excellent way for learners to gain access to more input and feedback than a teacher could provide alone. Moreover, research findings show that learners who work on a task together tend to demonstrate more on-task behaviors and perform better than they would working independently.

4.2.1 Benefits of Peer Interaction

One advantage peer interaction provides is that when learners work together, they often discuss aspects of the language they need to be able to complete whatever task or activity they are working on. Researchers call this type of interaction a **language-related episode (LRE)** and studies have found the more often learners engage in LREs, the more they learn (see Box 4.1 for an example).

BOX 4.1 Examples of Language-Related Episodes (LREs)

The following examples from Basterrechea and García Mayo (2013) illustrate the two types of LREs. An example of a correctly solved LRE about grammar is provided in (1), in which the two learners deliberate over the verb tense of the verb *appear*. Learner 1 suggests that the tense should be past, but Learner 2 rejects the suggestion, which represents a correct resolution because the text had been in the present tense.

(1)   LEARNER 1: new bands
    LEARNER 2: that don't appear
    LEARNER 1: appeared
    LEARNER 2: huh?
    LEARNER 1: appeared
    LEARNER 2: no, that don't appear

> **BOX 4.1 Continued**
>
> A correctly resolved LRE about word choice is provided in (2). Learner 1 proposes the use of "to be in touch," but Learner 2 is not sure about its meaning, and asks about it. Learner 1 provides the correct meaning of the expression through the Spanish translation (*mantener contacto o conectar*).
>
> (2) LEARNER 1: to be in touch eh to be in touch
>   LEARNER 2: what is the meaning of it?
>   LEARNER 1: *para mantener contacto o* (to be in contact or)
>   LEARNER 2: *conectar* (to connect)
>   LEARNER 1: *sí para* (yes to) meet people to be in touch with
>   LEARNER 2: with other people
>   LEARNER 1: *vale* (alright)

As the examples in Box 4.1 demonstrate, peer interaction can be a rich site for negotiating language problems, hearing feedback, and noticing new vocabulary or grammar. These are some of the key ingredients of language development we covered in Chapters 1, 2, and 3.

Many teachers worry that learners will pick up on each other's language errors. Learners might even voice this concern themselves. Luckily, there is no evidence that this regularly occurs. Instead, research has found that learners don't make any more errors when they interact with peers of a similar proficiency level, more advanced learners, or first language (L1) speakers than they would normally make. In fact, by interacting in groups, learners more often provide each other with the correct form or help each other correct their errors. If the activities are well designed and the learners are grouped carefully, learners working in groups will participate in more conversations, discuss more language features they notice, and benefit more than they ever could in a fully teacher-centered language class.

4.2.2 Challenges of Peer Interaction

Despite the many benefits of peer interaction, there are also some challenges. Most language classrooms include a wide spectrum of personality types, levels of proficiency, and degrees of willingness to engage. Instructors must balance the needs of individual learners with the needs of the class as a whole. One of the challenges an instructor might face is grouping learners of different proficiency and ability levels. Research that has studied learners working in small groups can help guide some of these decisions. For example, studies of classrooms that include advanced second language (L2) learners show that they provide as much (if not more!) input and feedback to their L2 learner peers as L1 speakers do. So, in classrooms with large ranges in proficiency (when input and feedback are important!), grouping lower-proficiency learners with advanced learners might be beneficial. This grouping practice is called heterogenous (also called "mixed-level") grouping. If instead,

4.2 The Science: What the Research Says

learners are grouped homogeneously (in groups of the same proficiency level), research shows that the higher-proficiency group will spend more time focused on grammar and accuracy while the lower-proficiency groups will focus more on vocabulary. Overall, this research points out that grouping leaners heterogeneously (i.e., mixed-proficiency levels) might help learners of *all* levels by increasing the number of discussions around grammar and problem-solving. Higher-level learners also will be more likely to answer questions about grammar and vocabulary, which is known to support noticing of new forms for learners at all levels (see Figure 4.1).

Teachers also sometimes worry about peer dynamics when grouping learners together to interact. For example, should the confident, higher-proficiency learner be given a leadership role during small group work? Or is it more effective to assign dominant roles to the less proficient learner who might usually be less willing to share in other settings?

One study examined this issue by pairing up language learners to complete an interactive task where one learner gave the other directions on a map. This research showed that when the higher-proficiency learner was assigned the more dominant role of "direction-giver," the learners did not do much interacting and did not engage in many LREs. However, when the roles were reversed, and the less proficient learner was the direction-giver, much more negotiation and interaction occurred as they completed the task. In other words, when groups are mixed and the more hesitant or lower-level learners are given more dominant roles, there are more opportunities for learners to interact in ways we know facilitate language

If your goal is...	...then use...
"Focus on Meaning"	 Matched Groups!
"Focus on Grammar"	 Mixed Groups!
"Learning Strategy Development"	 Mixed Groups!
"Minimize Learner Anxiety"	 Matched Groups!

Figure 4.1 Pairing and grouping guide. This graphic illustrates how different pairings of students can achieve different linguistic and social-emotional goals.

development. This dynamic might seem counterintuitive, but because the higher-level learner is better able to elaborate and ask follow-up questions, they are more prepared to initiate multiple negotiations for meaning and persevere in the face of miscommunications.

In Figure 4.2, the left panel illustrates what could happen when the higher-proficiency learner is given the leadership role in a navigation task. The higher-proficiency learner provides detailed directions to the lower-proficiency learner, who, at best, is able to complete the task without saying anything themselves, or, at worst, feels very overwhelmed by the complex utterances of the higher-proficiency learner and thus disengages from the task. The right panel shows what could happen when the roles are reversed. Here the lower-proficiency learner offers a simple direction. It is not enough detail and so the partner needs to ask for more information in order to know how to move on the map. In this kind of interaction, both learners benefit. The higher-proficiency learner gains valuable practice asking questions and maintaining a conversation, while the lower-proficiency learner is encouraged to use more vocabulary and expand upon their ideas (Kim & McDonough, 2008; Choi & Iwashita, 2016).

Some learners also tend to be highly collaborative language partners, meaning they are more willing to suggest new strategies, collaborate, or provide feedback. Highly collaborative learners have also been shown to drive the number of LREs that occur when small groups interact. As a result, rather than putting all these highly collaborative individuals into a single group together, research generally recommends distributing these learners across as many groups as possible to encourage more interaction. When one learner is highly collaborative, group

Figure 4.2 Sample high-/low-proficiency pairing. These two conversations demonstrate how learners of high and low proficiency can interact in a mutually beneficial interaction. Image by: Elizabeth Zonarich

4.2 The Science: What the Research Says

members' proficiency levels will matter less, and learners will all benefit. Learners' creativity abilities have also been shown to impact how they interact in small groups. We cover creativity in more detail in Chapter 9.

But what happens when most learners in a classroom seem to be hesitant to interact with each other? Some teachers notice that after grouping learners, the room falls silent, or little TL is spoken. As we will discuss more in Chapter 8, sometimes lower-proficiency learners become anxious, especially if they are asked to partner up with a peer that they perceive is more advanced than they are. As we discussed in Chapter 2, one option instructors have is to train learners to be more effective language partners. More advanced learners can be asked to (and trained to) take a "helper" rather than a dominant role when working with lower-proficiency peers. For example, they might prompt their partner by asking questions instead of immediately supplying an answer themselves. Figure 4.3 illustrates the relationship between how much one partner controls the interaction and how much engagement will result. We see that collaboration happens when learners have more equal control of a task but are not both dominating.

Some research has found that showing learners models of peers providing each other with feedback and interacting to solve a task can help learners become

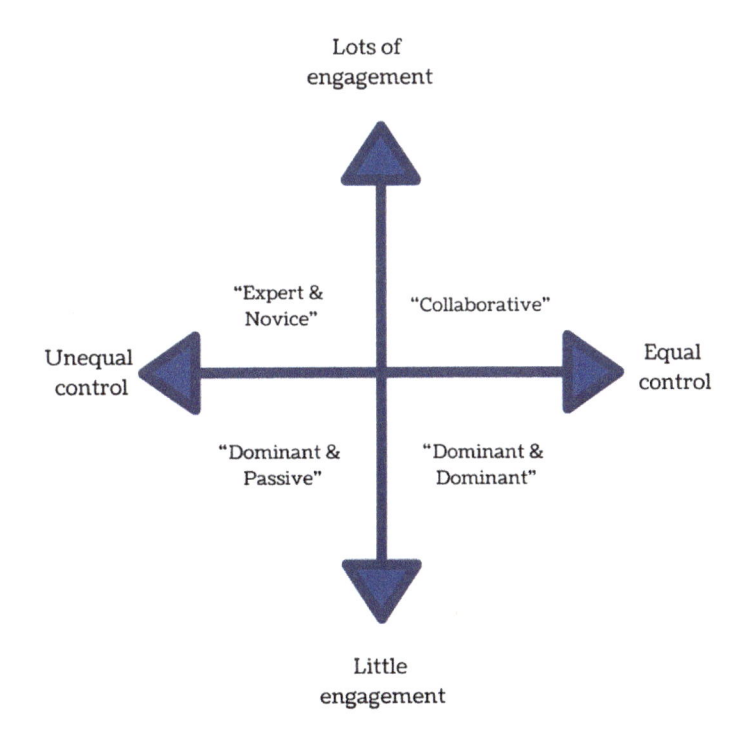

Figure 4.3 Continuums of interaction and engagement. Learner interactions can feel very different, depending on the amount of control and engagement of each individual involved. Image by Caitlyn Pineault based on Storch (2002)

better, more collaborative group members (Fujii et al., 2016). Sometimes learners will spend (some of) their group time using their shared language to interact. Research has shown that *strategic* use of the learners' L1 can help them become more confident language learners and support vocabulary learning. Lower-proficiency learners might use their L1 more with partners than advanced learners do. The research suggests this practice shouldn't be discouraged in all cases; instead, learners should know that using their L1 is one strategy they might use to solve a language problem *some* of the time. However, as we saw in Chapter 1, it is still important to encourage use of the TL to ensure learners have access to lots of rich input. Keeping this in mind, teachers and learners can brainstorm together to identify situations that merit the use of the L1 and situations where the L2 should be used entirely.

> **BOX 4.2 The Science! Points to Remember**
>
> - Learners benefit from interacting with their peers in the target language.
> - Peer interaction doesn't necessarily result in more errors.
> - Mixed-level groupings generally result in more impactful interactions than same-level groupings, especially when lower-level learners are assigned leadership roles in the group.
> - Training learners to be supportive interactants can result in better language learning.

4.3 The Science: What's Missing?

A lot of the research on peer interaction has focused on learners' proficiency levels, their willingness to collaborate, and how those differences impact the kinds of conversations they have when they work together. However, learners differ in more ways than these. For example, learners might have different levels of exposure to the L2 outside of class, they might be motivated to study the language in different ways, they might have a strong aptitude for learning languages, or they might struggle to identify language patterns. Some personalities simply clash and learners might struggle to work together for unknown reasons. Whatever the cause, interpersonal tensions can create a hostile environment for language learning. We cover some of these individual differences in Chapter 7, but when taken together, they paint a complex picture of how to group learners effectively. Only those present in the classroom with the learners themselves can fully appreciate how their learners are similar or how they differ and what that means for class dynamics. Teachers should feel empowered to try out a variety of different grouping strategies based on the unique needs of the learners (see Figure 4.4 for some considerations).

Figure 4.4 Instructor considerations. A selection of the many variables that teachers may consider when grouping their learners. Image by: Elizabeth Zonarich

4.4 The Art: Research-Based Strategies to Try

4.4.1 The Art of Planning for Interaction

Tips for Grouping Learners

- If you have a few learners who are highly collaborative (talkative, engaged, willing to collaborate and communicate), try to distribute them among as many groups as possible.
- When grouping mixed-level learners, give lower-proficiency learners more dominant roles where they must share information with the more advanced learners.
- When balanced conversation is the goal of the task (taking turns, sharing, etc.), pair learners up with peers at similar proficiency levels.
- The age of learners also plays a large role in what kinds of groupings work best. Younger learners sometimes don't work well with partners, even in their L1 classes. Working collaboratively is a social skill that younger learners are still developing, so be prepared to scaffold the transition from whole-group to small-group and partner activities carefully. The initial groundwork can be short and sweet! It might even involve turning to a neighbor, giving them a high-five, and saying "Good work!" in the L2 after successfully completing a whole-group activity.

Cultivating a Collaborative Classroom Environment

- Model and practice turn-taking, listening strategies, and using clarification strategies.
- Make sure to include opportunities for learners to get to know each other. This can happen via games, bonding activities (e.g., solving puzzles), or by having presentations where learners share their likes/dislikes. Learners who know each other are more comfortable interacting in the TL.
- Integrate brief partner chats and think-pair-shares (see Figure 4.5) into each phase of a lesson so that peer talk becomes a normal routine. This will help lessen the anxiety of learners who are more hesitant when interacting with a partner.
- Normalize a culture of risk-taking and making mistakes! You might consider using a metaphor that valorizes process-based learning like one of the following:
    - "When you work out your muscles by lifting weights or doing exercises, do you know what's happening to the muscles? You're making little microtears in the muscle as you work it. In response, your body sends nutrients to repair those little tears and the muscle is actually built up bigger and stronger than it was before. It's the same thing when we learn languages – we have to make errors so that we can figure out how the language works. It's in making and fixing errors that we learn and become better language speakers."
    - "Have any of you ever played an exploring video game? Sometimes in a video game you have a map of the world, but it's not completely filled out. You have to explore the world by playing to figure out where everything is. There isn't really a good way to figure out where all the boundaries are, sometimes, so you have to just go for it and explore until you hit a dead end. It's the same thing with learning languages. Sometimes you don't know how far a pattern extends, so we have to keep using it until we make an error. It's in getting corrected in that error that we learn a little bit more about the 'boundaries' of usage and it makes us better language speakers."
- Model and practice encouragement. Remind learners to say "Great job" to each other, and to celebrate when they successfully accomplish tasks, e.g., "We did it!"
- Change up groups frequently so that learners can benefit from interacting with everyone in the class. Create a board, poster, or display with learners' names and groups so that they can easily be shuffled.
    - For example, creating "Compass Buddies" is one way to create a rotating partner system in class (see Figure 4.6). At the beginning of the year, have learners find four partners. These four partners can work together as a compass group (i.e.,

Figure 4.5 Think-pair-share as a scaffolded student interaction technique. This graphic can be used to remind students to use think-pair-share to promote peer interaction. Image by: Elizabeth Zonarich

4.4 The Art: Research-Based Strategies to Try

one North, one East, one South, and one West partner). Additionally, you can randomly have the learners find another partner of the same direction, e.g., ask "North" learners to work with another "North" learner.

- Work together to create a set of expectations for peer-to-peer interactions. This is known as "co-constructed rubrics" (i.e., learners create the criteria used for assessment on an assignment) or "class contracts" (i.e., learners collaborate to set behavioral and environmental expectations for one another and for the teacher). Involving learners in discussions and consulting them on how to create supportive interactions is a great way to build trust and buy-in (see Figure 4.7 for an example).

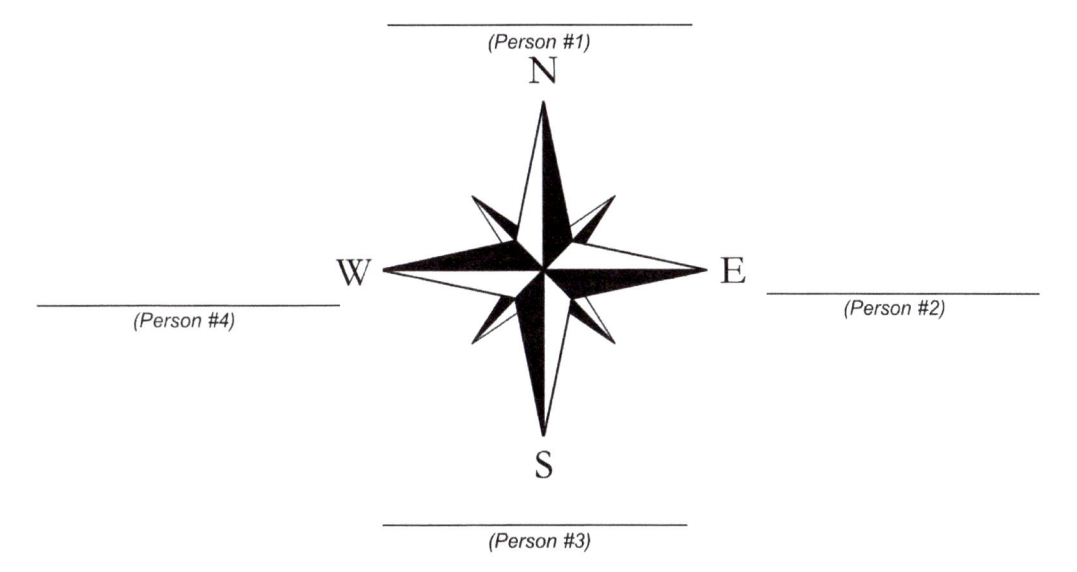

Figure 4.6 Compass Buddy template. This buddy partner system provides learners with a regular, rotating selection of classmates to work with. Image by: Caitlyn Pineault

Collaborating with a peer is...		Collaborating with a peer is not...	
• Striking balanced conversation.		• Dominating the interaction.	
• Supporting your partner through visual gestures, visuals cues and responding appropriately to their contributions.		• Shutting down your partners' contributions with your body language or language.	
• Being an active and engaged listener.		• Talking over your partner.	
• Asking follow up questions, being patient, and using clarification strategies as needed.		• Getting frustrated or giving up when you feel frustrated.	

Figure 4.7 Peer interaction expectations. This chart presents one way of explaining the goals and intentions for peer interaction to students.

Training Learners to Be Better at Peer Interaction

- Encourage more advanced learners to take on facilitative rather than dominating roles when they work with others. Model how to provide a helpful recast, ask a clarifying question, make a suggestion, etc.
- Practice giving peer feedback by doing a gallery walk. In a gallery walk, examples provided by the teacher or learners are placed spread out around a room. Learners travel in small groups or independently from example to example to discuss, leave feedback, or complete a given task. For example, do a gallery walk of writing assignments and ask learners to leave a compliment and a piece of constructive feedback on each one (see Figure 4.8 for an illustration of this concept).

Designing Collaborative Tasks

- Include activities where some learners have unique pieces of information that need to be shared with other learners. This encourages participation from everyone in the group. Some ways learners could share information include finding classmates that like to doing a particular activity, or interviewing classmates about topics they both enjoy like favorite sports, crafts, TV shows, etc. (see Figures 4.9 and 4.10 for examples). We return to the idea of tasks in Chapter 17 on task-based language teaching.
- Assign roles when making small groups. For example, one learner can be assigned as the *time checker* and make sure tasks are accomplished in the time frame given, while another learner could be the *note taker* (see Chapter 2 for more examples). Be sure to mix up roles and consider proficiency levels to make sure everyone gets a chance to talk.

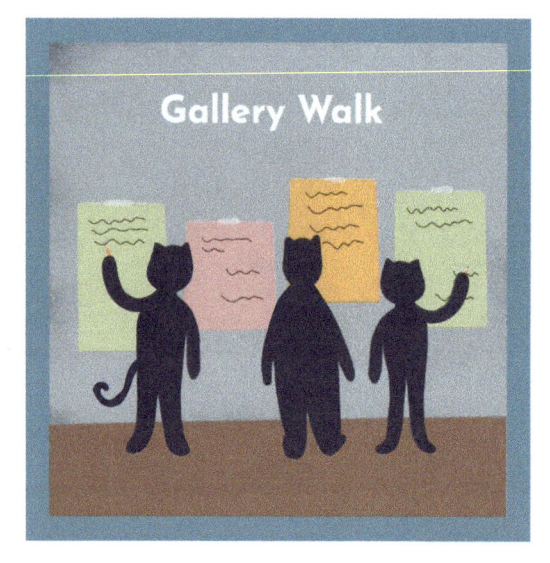

Figure 4.8 Gallery walk. For writing-based interactions, display student work around the classroom and have learners leave notes for each other. Image by: Elizabeth Zonarich

4.4 The Art: Research-Based Strategies to Try

Play outside

Have a sleepover

Visit with relatives

Watch TV

Figure 4.9 Favorite hobby exchange cards. These four themes may be topics that learners can discuss together to build community and establish foundational relationships for further interactions. Image by: Elizabeth Zonarich

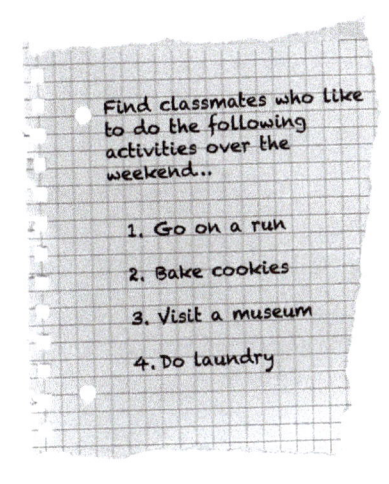

Find classmates who like to do the following activities over the weekend...

1. Go on a run
2. Bake cookies
3. Visit a museum
4. Do laundry

Figure 4.10 Classmate scavenger hunt check-in. To-do lists like this can help support students in initiating conversations with each other.

4.5 Troubleshooting: How the Science Informs the Art

Ms. W was surprised by the variation in success she saw when learners did tasks in her German class with different partners. While she realized that not all her learners were friends, she was surprised to see their language performance vary so much. For example, she wondered about her learner Mica and how their performance shifted depending on the partner they were assigned. How should Ms. W approach grouping the learners in her German class?

Ms. W's observation that learners interact differently depending on their conversation partner is an important one. Even among the best of friends, conversations can fall flat from time to time, depending on a variety of factors that may be well beyond linguistic ability. This natural variation can certainly be tricky to take into consideration in an assessment context, where standardization is often prioritized. However, the research is clear: It is beneficial for learners to interact with each other. Rather than minimize peer-to-peer interaction for the sake of a more streamlined assessment process, Ms. W might take this opportunity to reflect on the way that she assesses learner progress. For example, Ms. W could try the following:

a. She might consider incorporating more frequent, smaller check-ins rather than place a premium on several larger summative assessments. More regular check-ins can account for the ups and downs of learner participation on any given day and can capture the overall effort a learner is putting into the process of language learning.

b. Ms. W might also consider incorporating alternative measures like learner reflections or portfolios into her courses. This way, Ms. W will obtain a more holistic picture of her learners' interactive abilities. For example, she might ask them to record themselves chatting with a few different learners or completing a role play individually and add those examples to a portfolio.

c. Regardless of her assessment choices, Ms. W should continue to structure opportunities for her learners to work collaboratively. With her observation that learner experiences may vary from pairing to pairing in mind, she should be sure to mix and match learners on a regular basis so that they have the opportunity to learn from each other as they serve different collaborative roles in a variety of communicative tasks and activities.

4.6 The Science: Points to Remember

- It is important to switch up pairings and groupings on a regular basis – learners learn different linguistic and conversational skills from each other.
- There is no one "right" way to pair or group the learners in a class. The best combinations may change from day to day and activity to activity. The factors you prioritize (e.g., proficiency level, motivation, etc.) may vary too!
- Reflect actively after each class on how you pair your learners and whether your choices had the desired results. Document recent pairings along with your observations.

- While "group work" may feel uncontrolled, there is a lot you can do as a teacher before and after sending learners off to converse independently to ensure the interaction goes smoothly!

4.7 Questions to Consider

1. What kinds of qualities do you personally like in a conversation partner or small group? Make a list and then share it with your learners. What do they agree with? Is there anything they would like to add? Discussing the ways in which your conversational styles differ can be a useful opportunity for socio-emotional learning, awareness of one another's differences, and, ultimately, appreciation for those differences.
2. What makes a pairing or grouping successful? How can you tell if your pairings and groupings are going well in class?
3. What sorts of activities can you incorporate into your lesson plans to be sure you are explicitly teaching learners the kinds of conversation strategies that will maximize language learning in class?
4. Reflect with your colleagues about how it feels to divide your learners into groups and allow them to work together. If you feel confident, what actions are you taking that create that sense of security? If you feel apprehensive during these moments, what concrete steps can you take so that it feels more comfortable?
5. While learners are interacting in their pairs or groups, what do you usually find yourself doing? What would you like to do more of during these instances?

4.8 The Science of Language Learning: Research Supporting the Points Made in This Chapter

Kim, Y., & McDonough, K. (2011). Using pretask modelling to encourage collaborative learning opportunities. *Language Teaching Research*, 15(2), 183–199. https://doi.org/10.1177/1362168810388711,

The study investigates how the explicit introduction of collaborative strategies impacted group-work dynamics in a class of teenage English language learners. The researchers found that the subset of learners that learned about interpersonal modeling strategies experienced more language learning-related episodes (which have been found to be beneficial for language learning) when completing a task together than the subset of learners who did not learn about modeling strategies.

Philp, J., Adams, R., & Iwashita, N. (2013). *Peer interaction and second language learning*. Routledge.

This book explores the nuances of peer-to-peer interaction in depth across a variety of age groups, experience levels, and educational contexts. In particular, the authors address the ways in which learners use interactions with their peers to test L2 hypotheses, correct one another's L2 production, and hone their L2 skills in a less formal context than learner–teacher interactions.

Storch, N. (2002). Patterns of interaction in ESL pair work. *Language Learning, 51*(1), 119–158. https://doi.org/10.1111/1467-9922.00179.

This foundational study presents different kinds of partner collaboration dynamics observed in an adult ESL classroom and draws connections between the types of partnership and the resulting language learning opportunities. Using examples for learner conversations, the author demonstrates how the working pair relationship either supported or hindered language development.

For more resources, including more sample lesson plans, videos, and other ideas, visit our companion website: www.cambridge.org/BryfonskiMackey.

5 What kinds of learning strategies can I teach my learners?

KEY QUESTIONS
- The Science: Are certain learning strategies more effective for language learning than others?
- The Art: How can I train my learners to get the most out of my class and be more efficient, active, reflective, and autonomous learners?
- What kinds of strategies can I teach my learners?
- What strategies do self-sufficient language learners have, and how do they use them to further their learning?

5.1 Voices from the Classroom

Mr. O teaches middle school Japanese classes. All of the foreign language classes offered at the middle schools in his district are "exploratory" programs – i.e., enrichment electives taken "for fun" rather than being a core content class like math or science. As such, his classes meet relatively infrequently and are not given the same priority as the core classes like English language arts, math, and science. Though his program is restricted in scope and depth, he still wants his learners to get the most out of it and be prepared for other foreign language classes they may take in the future. Mr. O has used a student-centered approach for years now (as that's one of the criteria he is evaluated on in his yearly observations by the administration). Still, he's unsure how to support his learners in becoming more autonomous. He already uses topics that his learners are interested in, creates activities that involve learners using their language in creative ways, and ensures his learners see themselves and their identities reflected in the curriculum. These are all great student-centering techniques, but his learners are not yet able to direct their own learning in the ways the administration wants them to. How can he enable his learners to be more independent?

5.2 The Science: What the Research Says

Why is it that some learners seem to find the process of learning a language easier than others do? Why do some learners move ahead quickly and independently, while some lag behind or require a lot of scaffolding? Why don't all learners learn what teachers teach? While there are many reasons individual learners differ (more on this in Chapters 6–9), one common factor that differentiates learners is their ability to successfully employ different strategies to manage and support their own language learning. Common strategies language learners might use include setting goals, keeping notes, or reflecting on their own learning process. While using language learning strategies might come naturally to some, all learners can benefit from instruction in these techniques. Strategy instruction, also known as learner training or **strategy-based instruction**, is the explicit teaching of different practices learners can independently use to support their language learning (Oxford, 2017). Overall, research on strategy instruction has supported its use in a variety of contexts and for a variety of different strategies in second language reading, writing, speaking, and listening.

What kinds of strategies have been shown to support language learning? Researchers who investigate strategy instruction for language learning break down the many possible strategies into three subcategories: cognitive strategies for **engagement** with the target language (TL), metacognitive strategies for reflecting about the TL, and social/affective strategies interacting in the TL (see Box 5.1 for details). The strategies described below have been shown to help learners learn more effectively, although strategies that fit into the categories of engaging and reflecting have been studied the most.

BOX 5.1 Examples of Learning Strategies

Engaging

Cognitive Strategies for Enhanced Engagement
- Rehearsing or planning what to say or write
- Note-taking
- Making personal connections, linking new knowledge to prior knowledge

Reflecting

Metacognitive Strategies for Enhanced Reflection
- Organizing information
- Previewing, skimming, or summarizing a text
- Problem-solving
- Goal-setting
- Monitoring comprehension

Interacting

Social/Affective Strategies for Enhanced Interaction
- Noticing feedback from others
- Asking for clarification
- Normalizing linguistic and communicative risk taking
- Setting clear expectations for how to support peers

Why are learning strategies so important? Learning strategies can help learners become more **autonomous**, meaning they are able to be more independent directors of their own learning. Research shows that the more autonomous language learners are, the more strategies they use and the more they learn. This positive, significant correlation between strategy use, autonomy, and language learning has also been connected to learners' sense of overall satisfaction with their learning progress.

Who can benefit from learning strategies? Studies have found that intermediate and advanced language learners benefit more from strategy instruction than beginners do. However, this tendency doesn't mean that beginners can't also benefit from learning strategy instruction; rather, beginners' autonomous language strategy use is simply constrained by their limited proficiency. As a result, beginners benefit from starting with learning strategies that have fewer steps or parts, whereas advanced learners benefit the most when presented with a combination of complementary strategies, like an engaging type of strategy coupled with a reflecting strategy. Generally speaking, the more advanced a learner is, the more likely they will be easily able to adapt to new strategies and integrate them with the other learning strategies they currently use. While it may be tempting to teach more than one strategy at a time to give learners choices as they complete tasks, research has shown that being presented with multiple strategies at once can actually be overwhelming and lead to confusion or rejection of strategy use all together. Instead – no matter the proficiency of the learner – teach strategies one at a time so that learners have opportunities to practice each one in various contexts before adopting additional strategies. The practice of using each one is what will provide learners with the experience they need to figure out which strategies work best for them. After practicing using a few strategies in class, you may at that point want to consider asking learners to choose the strategies they want to use.

So, what do language learning strategies look like in practice? In Box 5.2, we list some common strategies that have proven helpful through second language research. Teachers of younger learners may recognize some of these strategies from their language arts and literacy colleagues, who often employ versions of them to support learners' linguistic skills in their first languages. Interdisciplinary collaboration could serve as helpful inspiration!

BOX 5.2 Example Learning Strategies by Communicative Mode

- *Listening strategies*
    - Selectively listening to parts of the input, such as listening for keywords or phrases.
    - Practicing "chunking" of oral input based on pragmatic or cultural norms (e.g., listening for formulaic greetings, groupings digits in a phone number).
    - Using clues from the input to guess the meaning of unknown words or phrases (e.g., using background knowledge and nonlinguistic clues like gestures and context).
    - Listening for feedback, asking for clarification.

> **BOX 5.2 Continued**
>
> - Recognizing cognates and borrowed words from the first language (L1) in the second language (L2) (e.g., teaching common L1–L2 sound correspondences and shifts in syllable stress or prosody).
> - *Speaking strategies*
>   - Rehearsal and planning (e.g., with the help of a mind map or graphic organizer).
>   - Self-monitoring and rephrasing.
>   - Talking "around" unknown or forgotten words in the target language (i.e., use circumlocution).
>   - Self-assessing speaking performance (e.g., recording oneself and reviewing).
>   - Asking and looking out for feedback from others.
>   - Modifying production after feedback.
> - *Reading strategies*
>   - Making predictions about a text (e.g., ask all students to write a prediction on a piece of paper and lock the papers away in a "time capsule" to be reopened later in the unit and the predictions evaluated).
>   - Previewing a text using a book walk: relate the topic to prior knowledge, consider questions, discuss the kind of text and topic, etc.
>   - Summarizing a text or a part of a text.
>   - Annotating a text while reading (see Figure 5.1 for different types of reading connections learners might make as they interact with a new text).
>   - Making connections from a text to the learners' own experiences, previously read texts, or other relevant themes.
>   - Using online dictionary/translator.
>   - Teaching word families and cognate patterns (e.g., connecting the French *sérpent* to the English "serpent," a synonym of "snake"; the Spanish suffix *-ción* corresponds to the English suffix "-tion").
> - *Writing strategies*
>   - Brainstorming ideas prior to writing.
>   - Team writing with learner roles (e.g., scribe, new L2 word researcher, text cohesion checker).
>   - Restructuring/editing when issues arise.
>   - Peer-based editing and feedback.
>   - Transferring skills from L1 to L2 (e.g., borrow or adapt graphic organizers and terms from L1 teachers).

How can strategies best be taught? One of the most common methods used to teach learning strategies is guided reflective practice. In this method, teachers first provide direct instruction on why the strategy is important (e.g., a teacher might explain the reading strategy of making predictions: "Before starting a new book, good readers make predictions about what the book might be about"), and then model how the strategy is used. During modeling, the teacher might "think aloud" (e.g., "When I want to make predictions about a new book, I like to look at the title and some of the pictures. In this book, I notice that the pictures all have pigs and a wolf in them. Those pictures make me think these are going to be some of the characters in the story"). In a language classroom, making predictions

5.2 The Science: What the Research Says

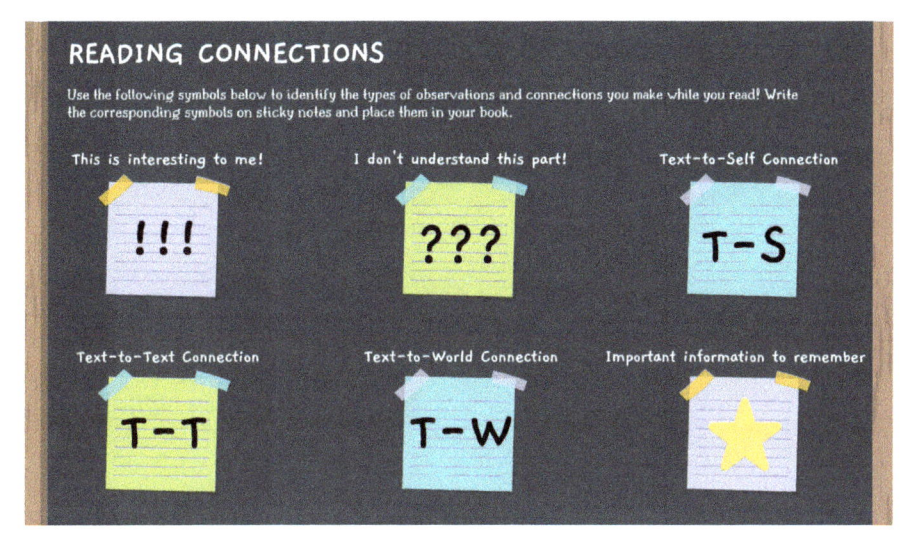

Figure 5.1 Ideas for reading connections. Image by: Caitlyn Pineault

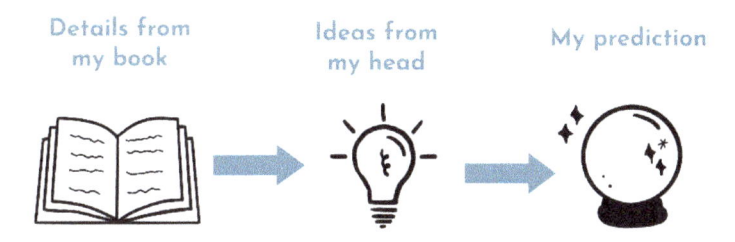

Figure 5.2 The prediction process. The process of making predictions can help learners comprehend new texts and unfamiliar language. Image by: Elizabeth Zonarich

like this can help learners anticipate vocabulary words or linguistic features they may encounter in the text so they are better prepared to make educated guesses about their meaning. Following the model, learners engage in scaffolded, structured practice in pairs or small groups (see Figure 5.2 for a visual guide that can be used to explain the prediction strategy for learners).

Learners should also be asked to reflect on how well they understand the new strategy. To what extent were they successful during scaffolded practice? Do they need more time and scaffolded engagement with the learning strategy before moving on? After several guided iterations of the strategy, learners should be expected to utilize it on their own during independent work. If space allows, it may be useful to post the language learning strategies to a highly visible space in the classroom, like a bulletin board or a door. The strategies can be presented as tools in the learners' L2 toolbox and referred to throughout the school year as new content is encountered and additional strategies are introduced. See Figure 5.3 for an example.

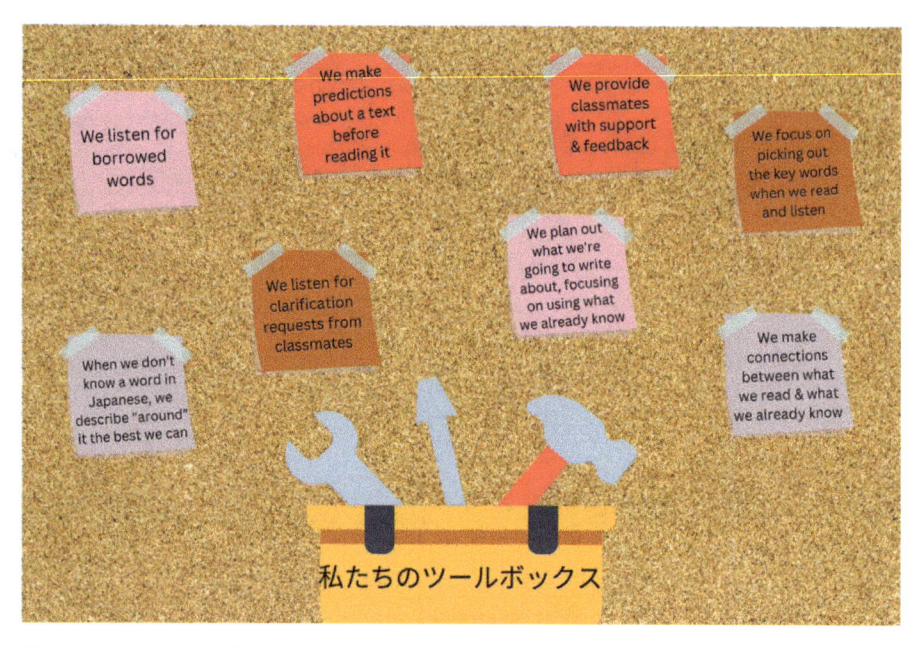

Figure 5.3 Displaying the learners' strategy "toolbox." Displaying and referring to the language learning strategies you've discussed throughout the year can be a helpful way to remind learners of what they can do to support themselves as they progress in the L2. Image by: Erin Fell

> **BOX 5.3 The Science! Points to Remember**
>
> - Research has shown that learners can use specific strategies to facilitate linguistic development and become more autonomous learners.
> - There are three kinds of language learning strategies: engaging, reflecting, and interacting.
> - Older, more advanced learners may pick up on strategies more quickly, but with intentional planning and support, learners of any age and proficiency level can be taught to use second language learning strategies.
> - Using reflective guided practice is one way to help learners adopt new language learning strategies and use them successfully on their own.

5.3 The Science: What's Missing?

While we know from prior research that teaching learning strategies can produce more autonomous, efficient language learners, there are still some aspects of strategy instruction without clear answers. For example, we don't know for sure how long learners retain the information they learn about using strategies. Will they need a refresher on the strategies they have learned before? When and how often? Here it may be important for teachers to monitor learners' use of strategies and budget lesson time for the occasional review of previously covered strategies, if necessary. This is especially important to keep in mind after learners return to class after a long holiday break.

For how long does a strategy need to be taught before learners will be able to use it independently? Is one hour of instruction effective? While there seems to be a connection between the length of time spent teaching the strategy and how well learners can use it, clearly, teachers cannot possibly spend all of class time teaching learning strategies. Therefore, teachers must conduct their own cost–benefit analyses to ascertain whether or not valuable class time can be spent on language strategies or if it is time to move on to other topics. This cost–benefit analysis should include careful consideration of which language(s) will need to be used to effectively explain, model, and practice the language strategy. Whatever is ultimately decided, remember that these questions don't have simple answers from research, so individual teachers should use their best judgment based on what learners seem to need most.

5.4 The Art: Research-Based Strategies to Try

5.4.1 The Art of Introducing Learning Strategies

- Use modeling phrases to introduce why strategies are important. For example: "When good readers read, they make connections between the text and their own lives" or "When good writers write, they use web diagrams to brainstorm their ideas first." More advanced or older learners can also be told about the research behind *why* the strategy works. Include examples in your explanation.
- Plan to introduce new strategies to capitalize on moments of increased student interest or need. For example, before watching a feature-length film, it is common for learners to be anxious about their ability to understand all the vocabulary. Acknowledge this valid concern and present several listening strategies to help learners manage the film's unsheltered input (e.g., previewing the content/context of the film, creating a prediction time capsule). Periodically check in throughout the film to ask learners if they are having success using the new strategies.
- For teachers who are trying to minimize the amount of L1 spoken in class (e.g., an immersion program) and also work with lower-level learners who may be unable to understand language learning strategies in the L2, consider dedicating some time once a week or once a month to discussing language learning strategies in the L1. This way, the TL environment can be better preserved.

5.4.2 The Art of Encouraging Autonomous Learners

- Consider asking learners to keep a journal or diary where they keep track of the strategies they notice themselves using to support their language learning. What is working for them? What isn't working? What additional tools do they want or need? See Table 5.1 for an example of how to provide time for learners to reflect on their progress and set goals for their language learning strategies in class. This can be done in the L2 or L1, depending on learners' age and L2 proficiency.

Table 5.1 Learning strategies journal prompt

이번 주에 학습에 도움이 된 공부 전략들 "Strategies that helped me learn this week"	다음 주에 새로 시도해 보고 싶은 공부 전략들 "Strategies that I want to try out next week"

- Technology can be a great tool for supporting learning strategy instruction. Learners might be able to use facilitative tools like online learner dictionaries, note-taking or brainstorming apps, and educational games. Some popular online games teachers use now are Quizlet, Kahoot, Blooket, Flippity, Gimkit, and Quizizz. These and other tools can be integrated into strategy instruction.
- Incorporating digital reflection tools like GoogleForms or Mentimeter at the end of a unit can allow for quick, anonymous check-ins about which learning strategies learners found most helpful during that unit and which learning strategies they would like more support in developing. Refer to posters in your classroom like banners (a) and (b) in Figure 5.4.
- For younger learners, picking one "learning strategy of the week/month" to focus on collectively can encourage buy-in and help learners develop autonomy in a more structured environment. At the end of each class (or on Fridays), recognize individual student efforts to use this strategy (high-fives, sticker charts, rotating "Super Strategist Award").

5.4.3 The Art of Maintaining Language Learning Strategies

- To support retention of language learning strategies, encourage learners to apply the strategies from class in the "real world" when they encounter the L2. This could be at a store, restaurant, bus station, or family event. Each week, invite learners to participate in a "show and tell" where they can bring in mementos from their encounter and report back on which strategies they used to understand and learn from the experience.
- During group work, assign one learner the role of "Strategy Advisor." This student is tasked with suggesting different learning strategies to help the group accomplish the task. When the class regroups, this student might be asked to report back on which strategy the group chose and why. For more on the benefits of assigning learners' roles in group work, review Chapters 1 and 4.
- Learners of any age and proficiency level may enjoy writing advice letters at the end of the year to the incoming class below them. Advice letters (either in the L1 or L2, depending on learner ability) present a "real-world" opportunity for learners to reflect on the language learning strategies that have been helpful to them in your

Figure 5.4 Encouragement for autonomous learners. The two banners can be created in your target language and hung in the classroom to remind learners of successful learning strategies at their disposal. Banner (a) asks learners: "What do you do when you don't know a word in Spanish? The options read: "Act! Draw! Use what you know!" Banner (b) reads: "What did you do this week?" and learners are encouraged to share strategies they used in class that week: "I wrote in my journal," "I had a positive attitude," "I made connections," and "I asked for clarification." Image by: Caitlyn Pineault

course. Older learners can write independently, and younger learners can compose group letters collaboratively with more teacher support. The incoming class may also take suggestions from their peers more seriously than they take advice from you.

5.5 Troubleshooting: How the Science Informs the Art

Mr. O's exploratory middle school Japanese course has limited time because it is only considered an elective in his district. Mr. O worries about dedicating his limited class time to learning strategies rather than language content.

Considering the limited time that Mr. O spends with his learners, it is especially important that his learners are armed with language learning strategies. Research shows that language learning is a long process that is dependent on the number of contact hours learners have in the TL. Learners in an "exploratory" program like Mr. O's may have difficulty noticing their progress and development. Introducing language learning strategies may help the learners leverage what they learn in Mr. O's program and be more prepared for opportunities to engage with the L2 in the future. Mr. O can continue to use the student-centered content he has created as he incorporates appropriate strategies. He should remember to model each strategy, explain why it is useful, and allow learners the time for controlled practice of the strategy. He can also share the list of strategies and their importance with his administration. Adding explicit instruction of language learning strategies (which may not come naturally for all learners) can help Mr. O ensure that his learners are equipped to maximize any language learning experience that comes their way!

5.6 The Science: Points to Remember

- Research shows that when learners employ language learning strategies, they demonstrate more linguistic development and overall satisfaction with their learning progress than learners who do not use such strategies.
- Identifying and using language learning strategies comes more naturally to some learners than others. Therefore, for all learners to experience the benefits, language learning strategies should be explicitly taught in class.
- When learners are aware of why certain strategies are valuable to language learning, research has shown that they are more likely to incorporate them into their daily linguistic practices. Be sure to explain the reason you are featuring learning strategies in class.
- Which language learning strategies teachers use and how they teach them varies based on classroom contexts and factors like learner age and proficiency level.
- Current research does not provide an answer for how long or how regularly to provide strategy-specific instruction to maximize student learning experiences. Check in with your learners about the strategies they remember best and find themselves frequently using in class to investigate the specific needs of your classes.

5.7 Questions to Consider

1. Think back to when you were learning a new language or first traveling abroad. What language learning strategies do you remember using to understand your surroundings? In what ways can the strategies you used then be translated into your current teaching context?
2. Partner with a colleague and ask to observe their class (see Chapter 21 if you are unsure how to broach this topic). During the observation, watch the learners who appear to be the highest performing. What do you notice them doing throughout the class period (e.g., asking clarification questions)? After the class is over, share your observations with your colleague. Were you correct? Do you think any habits of the highest-performing learners are worth sharing with the entire class?

5.8 The Science of Language Learning: Research Supporting the Points Made in this Chapter

Graham, S., Woore, R., Porter, A., Courtney, L., & Savory, C. (2020). Navigating the challenges of L2 reading: Self-efficacy, self-regulatory reading strategies and learner profiles. *Modern Language Journal, 104*(4), 693–714. https://doi.org/10.1111/modl.12670.

Set in the United Kingdom, this study examines the linguistic development of novice adolescent language learners of French. Learners were taught reading comprehension strategies to become more efficient, accurate readers. Students were introduced to strategies like using context clues and identifying synonyms, among others. Changes in their self-perceptions and linguistic development were measured with questionnaires and French tasks. Results showed that strategy instruction helped learners develop a sense of agency and control over their own development. This finding suggests that even younger, novice language learners can benefit from strategy-based instruction.

Gu, Y. (2019). Approaches to learning strategy instruction. In A. U. Chamot & V. Harris (Eds.), *Learning strategy instruction in the language classroom: Issues and implementation* (pp. 22–37). Multilingual Matters.

Strategy-based learning is not unique to language learning. This chapter begins by contextualizing strategic expertise in other fields, such as athletics and music. Next, it reviews the main approaches to strategy-based instructional strategies that have been explored in both L1 and L2 acquisition. Particular attention is paid to strategies pertaining to vocabulary retention, writing skills, and listening comprehension. The goals and effectiveness of each approach, as determined in research studies, are also discussed.

Oxford, R. L. (2017). *Teaching and researching language learning strategies: Self-regulation in context* (2nd ed.). Routledge.

This book links theories of strategy instruction with practical applications of the research. The book covers emotional, cognitive, and social perspectives to explore the dynamic nature of strategies in different contexts. Chapters include definitions and features of language learning strategies, a discussion of developing self-regulation and flexibility in learners, strategies in emotional regulation, strategies in the sub-domains of language, L2 grammar development, vocabulary, reading, writing, and listening. There is also a chapter devoted to strategy instruction and assessment. The book includes real-life scenarios, comprehensive overviews of research, and simple explanations.

For more resources, including more sample lesson plans, videos, and other ideas, visit our companion website: www.cambridge.org/BryfonskiMackey.

PART II

DIFFERENTIATION

6 How does language learner identity influence the language learning experience?

KEY QUESTIONS
- The Science: How do learners' cultural and/or linguistic backgrounds impact how they respond to instruction?
- The Art: What are some best practices to support culturally and linguistically diverse learners within the classroom?
- How are heritage language speakers' language learning experiences informed by their familial and community connections to their heritage language?
- How might learners' experiences and identities inform classroom resources and materials?
- Why is it important to consider the intersections of race, culture, and identity in second language acquisition?

6.1 Voices from the Classroom

Mrs. A teaches Spanish at a U.S. secondary school. She teaches advanced electives intended for learners in their final year who took the Advanced Placement (AP) Spanish exam during the previous year. Mrs. A often has younger learners (e.g., those in grades 9 and 10 at her school) who speak Spanish as a heritage language and who also enroll in these electives. In her district, many of these students' families come from Mexico, Guatemala, and Honduras. To be placed in an advanced elective so early on in secondary school, these learners have to take a placement exam. Like the mission and values of the district, this exam places a premium on interpersonal communication skills. Over the years, Mrs. A has observed that most heritage language learners (HLLs) do quite well on the exam and are placed in her advanced elective courses.

Because she is teaching an advanced course, Mrs. A expects all her learners to do a great deal of academic reading and writing as they analyze authentic resources like films, poems, novels, radio shows, podcasts, and newspaper articles. While many of her HLLs are interested in the course themes and are strong contributors during activities like debates or small-group conversations, she notices that some of them tend to disconnect from the activities that include authentic resources and that some have difficulty with reading and writing in more formal registers. Mrs. A regularly invites all her learners to come after school to work through exercises in a one-on-one environment, but not many learners take her up on it because of their bus schedules or after-school responsibilities. As a result, throughout the semester, she worries that her learners' linguistic abilities and engagement develop in different ways. While she tries to integrate as much cultural diversity from world Spanishes into her class, she worries about putting too much emphasis on her own culture because it's the culture she knows. How might Mrs. A adjust her curriculum next year, given the school's course offerings, and the diversity in linguistic and cultural backgrounds of her learners?

6.2 The Science: What the Research Says

In recent years, second language acquisition (SLA) researchers have begun to study aspects of *learners' identities* such as race, ethnicity, nationality, and home language backgrounds (with these factors being studied individually or in concert), to see what (if any) impact identity has on how languages are learned. Rather than viewing second language (L2) learning as a universal, uniform process, this line of research suggests that language learning is not only (or for some, not even) a cognitive process; rather it is impacted and driven by social interactions, socialized expectations, and other social factors. Some of the questions being researched in this subfield of SLA include:

- Who do we study to create our theories of how languages are learned? Do we rely too heavily on "WEIRD" populations (that is, Western, Educated, Industrialized, Rich, and Democratic – "democratic" in the sense of a governmental democracy, not in the sense of the American political party)? We provide more explanation of "WEIRD" in Section 6.3 below.
- Who do we assess using an *asset-based perspective* versus who do we assess using a *deficit-based perspective* (e.g., celebrating children from English-speaking families enrolled in immersion programs versus critiquing non-English-speaking families for not using enough English)?
- Who "gets" to be perceived as a legitimate user of the language, both as a first language (L1) speaker (e.g., how do speakers of minoritized varieties of the L2 position themselves as "legitimate" teachers of the language) and as an L2 learner (e.g., how might racialized expectations of what a Mandarin speaker "looks like" impact the experiences of a Black learner of Mandarin and an Asian learner of Mandarin?)?
- Whose variety of L2 do we decide to teach (e.g., teaching Parisian French but not Congolese French)?
- Who do we *allow* to learn languages in school (e.g., do we disallow children with learning differences or disabilities to enroll in L2 classes)?

However, there are countless other issues too numerous for a single book. The key point is this: learners' experiences in and perceptions about languages and language learning are all related to their identities, and the same is true for their teachers.

For example, when learning a language in a classroom, most learners will assume the identity of "student" and follow the social conventions associated with being a student in whatever society they were socialized into. This might look like raising a hand or an index finger when they want to speak or ask questions of the instructor. Learners might also *index* (this term is used in linguistics to mean "demonstrate," "construct," or "embody") their identity as a student through their language choices, such as using titles like "teacher" or "professor" when addressing instructors. They might further index their student identity by using informal forms of address with other students in the class, showing they perceive themselves to be on the same social level as their classmates (this is especially relevant in languages with multiple layers of formality, like those with honorific systems). On the other hand, in a study abroad context, a learner might seek to shed their "student" identity and instead immerse themselves in the host culture by seeking out peers from their new context rather than fellow study abroad learners. This might result in learners indexing their evolving relationship with the L2 in new ways, like adopting a particular dialect, accent, or vocabulary (e.g., when studying abroad in China, adopting the dialect of the city rather than speaking solely in 普通話, or Standard Mandarin Chinese). Learners will, of course, also have their own individual identities that include their familial background, their race, gender, culture, prior learning experiences, and unique personality features. It is also important to remember that identity can change over time, so how learners identify might also be different over the course of a semester, year, or academic term as they gain new experiences and interact with others. In this way, each learner will hold multiple intersecting identities, and aspects of those identities may be relatively fixed or fluid. All these factors have been shown to impact language learning opportunities and outcomes. We can see this in the research of Zoltán Dörnyei as learners' senses of their ideal L2 selves are hypothesized to impact motivation and success.

6.2.1 Identity and Language Learning

One of the key ways to strengthen learner outcomes (e.g., proficiency, sense of belonging, cultural competence) is by fostering investment and engagement within the L2 community, whether that is the classroom community or another community of language speakers in the real world. What makes one learner feel a sense of belonging may not make another learner feel the same kind of connection. Research shows that often the strongest feelings of investment come when learners are able to imagine their future selves as confident, competent, and successful multilingual individuals; SLA researchers, beginning with Zoltán Dörnyei, refer to this construct as the "ideal L2 self" or the "imagined L2 self" and often compare it to what we call the "ought-to L2 self," or what learners perceive to be expected of them in the L2 by parents, teachers, and other authority figures. In other words, if learners can imagine themselves as speakers of the L2 and feel connections to different target language (TL) communities, research indicates that their language learning experiences will be more successful. A learner's ideal L2 self varies based on the personal language goals of each person, so a Mandarin learner's ideal L2 self might involve studying abroad in China while a heritage learner of Portuguese might imagine their ideal L2 self being able to communicate easily with extended family in Brazil. This future identity is also related to learners' motivation to learner the TL. The role of motivation in language learning is discussed in more detail in Chapter 8.

When learners cannot imagine themselves or identify with the TL community, there can be consequences for their learning or participation in language learning in general. Unfortunately, research shows that not all learners see themselves represented or included in language classrooms. For example, research carried out by Uju Anya on world language curricula in the United States – where Spanish and French are by far the most commonly taught languages in K–12 (primary and secondary) education – has revealed an overreliance on Whiteness in the L2 speaking communities (i.e., Eurocentric with cultural exemplars dedicated to European art, conversational expressions, history, literature) with little to no examples of Afro-descendants of the TL communities. This lack of representation means that learners who do not identify as white are less likely to identify with the TL community or imagine themselves as part of that community when they work with these resources in comparison with their white-identifying peers. This lack of representation has measurable consequences. Language instructors who have participated in Anya's and other researchers' work have drawn connections between their learners' motivation levels and attitudes toward language class and the lack of representation in curricular materials. Black learners, for example, are underrepresented in U.S. K–12 and post-secondary L2 classrooms as well as in the SLA researcher community. Studies have found that minoritized learners – especially Black learners – often have fewer opportunities in primary and secondary school to begin learning languages, which often has a snowballing effect – meaning there are fewer minoritized language learners at the university level and fewer minoritized language instructors in all education settings.

To maximize the sense of belonging and inclusion felt by all learners, it is important that course materials give learners the opportunity to make connections between their identities and the identities of the TL community while also being mindful of ways in which Whiteness might be overtly or covertly crowding out other identities in the curriculum. This is particularly important in contexts where minoritized students might be taught (inadvertently or not) that in learning the L2 they need to adopt the language practices of white L2 speakers, not L2 speakers of color. See Figure 6.1 for an explanation from a hugely influential paper on this topic by Nelson Flores and Jonathan Rosa.

This phenomenon is especially prevalent in so-called "globalized" languages – or languages that are spoken across the world in a variety of contexts due to colonization, economic globalization, migration, and other factors – like English, Spanish, French, etc. Language teachers can reproduce racialized norms of the languages they teach by doing things like providing limited variety of geographic, dialectal, and racial diversity of L2 speakers, focusing cultural exploration on European locations and practices to the exclusion of other places where the L2 is spoken, positioning white L2 speakers as the focal characters of materials or assessments, among other practices. In writing this chapter, we want to stress nuance. We do not advocate for all references to white L2 speakers to be eliminated from curricula; rather, we, and SLA researchers as a community, advocate for reflection and mindfulness in curriculum creation and representation, acknowledging that minoritization and lack of representation have snowballing effects on learner motivation, enrollment, sense of belonging, and representation in L2 learning.

For example, French is not just spoken in France, there are other communities of French speakers with different varieties of French that learners should also have the opportunity to learn about in the classroom. Bringing in cultural artifacts from different communities that speak the TL strengthens representation of historically underrepresented or marginalized populations. Research has also explored the ways in which these artifacts (movies, TV shows, songs, etc.) can support teachers in addressing social, cultural, and political issues in their lessons. Reflective activities (like journaling) as well as experiential learning activities (like writing songs) were found to be particularly helpful in encouraging learners to reflect on the connections between cultural products, practices, and perspectives.

6.2.2 Heritage Language Learners

Learners might also enter a language class with a preexisting relationship to the language or culture because they are a **heritage language learner (HLL)**, someone who grew up hearing or speaking a language at home that was different from the language used in the external community. Research on HLLs can offer insights for how best to select curricular resources, employ inclusive pedagogical techniques, and advocate for all learners' success in world language programs.

Many classrooms around the world include both L2 learners and HLLs learning side-by-side. For example, an HLL might include a learner studying Navajo in the United States who grew up in a Navajo family (whether the language was spoken actively at home or not) or a child born to a Korean family who lives in Japan but

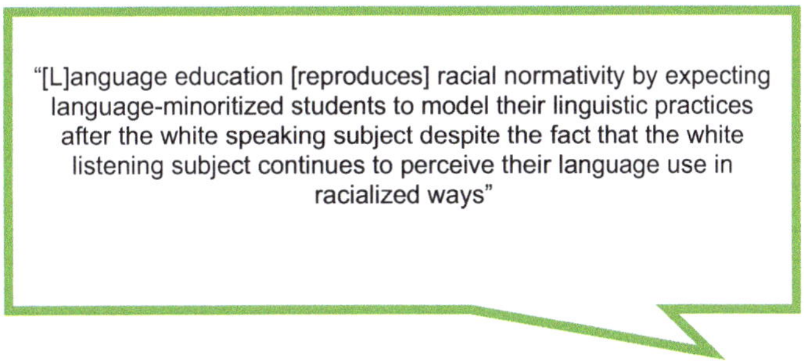

> "[L]anguage education [reproduces] racial normativity by expecting language-minoritized students to model their linguistic practices after the white speaking subject despite the fact that the white listening subject continues to perceive their language use in racialized ways"

Figure 6.1 The lack of inclusive language models in language education. Quote from Flores and Rosa's 2015 (p. 149) paper, "Undoing appropriateness: Raciolinguistic ideologies and language diversity in education."

continue to speak Korean in the home. Often, HLLs enter classrooms with better-developed speaking and listening skills that they gained from early exposure to and interaction with their heritage language at home. However, their reading and writing skills are sometimes not developed, as most of their language experiences happen informally during interpersonal conversations centered around tangible topics (e.g., cooking, recounting events of the day) or family life (e.g., telling family history, managing younger children's routines or behavior). For these reasons, HLLs often report feeling more comfortable communicating in informal, casual settings, like small talk over dinner, but not in formal or academic settings, like giving a presentation to an audience. Heritage language learners can also be beginners with low proficiency levels, but a strong cultural connection to the language or community, like a learner who wants to reconnect with a language that was spoken by older members of their family but discontinued at some point (e.g., a grandchild wanting to learn Japanese to connect with her Japanese grandfather, who only ever spoke to her in English when she was growing up). Apart from linguistic differences, there are many other social and identity-driven factors that may also play a role in how HLLs engage during class. See Figures 6.2 and 6.3.

While HLLs and L2 learners may find themselves placed in the same classes, they often have had different identities and relationships with the target language and culture, which can lead to the development of different skill sets. Studies have shown that L2 learners frequently have explicit knowledge about the language (e.g., they know and can explain grammar rules), whereas HLLs tend to have more implicit knowledge and be able to naturally tell what just "sounds right." Evidence of these differing knowledge banks has been found in standardized test scores as well as in analysis of the types of errors learners make in written

Spectrum of Language Speakers

⬅———————|———————————|———————————|———————➡

Native speaker   Heritage language learner   Second language learner

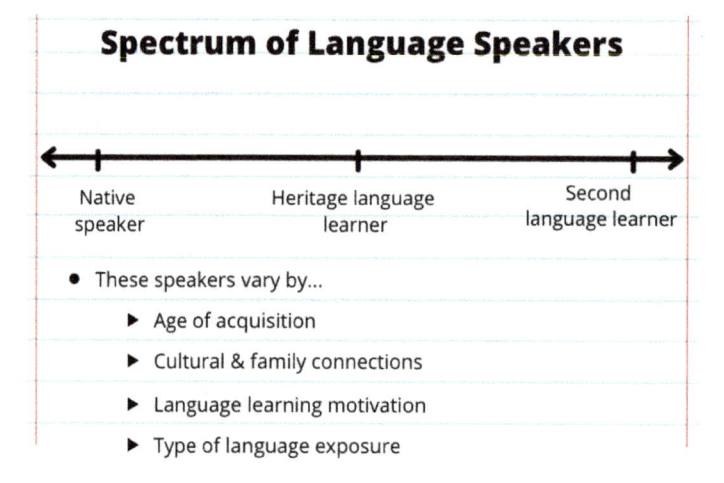

- These speakers vary by...
    ▶ Age of acquisition
    ▶ Cultural & family connections
    ▶ Language learning motivation
    ▶ Type of language exposure

Figure 6.2 Gradients of language users. Native speakers, heritage language learners, and second language learners all have different relationships with the target language. Some heritage language learners might self-describe as more than one of these identities (e.g., both a heritage language learner and a native speaker). Image by: Caitlyn Pineault

compositions. A study comparing Korean L2 learners and Korean heritage learners found that the HLLs made more spelling and punctuation errors than their counterparts, but fewer errors related to word choice, tense/conjugation choices, and particles. In general, L2 learners were also more successful at noticing and correcting their errors, whereas HLLs were more likely to be able to detect and produce nuances in phonology (sometimes due to early exposure to the heritage languages as babies, as discussed in Chapter 10). Both groups bring unique experiences and abilities to the classroom. However, in many instances, classrooms are designed with L2 learners, not HLLs, in mind. The multilingual abilities HLLs have may go unrecognized in traditional language classrooms where a "standard" (recall how this selection of a single variety can be problematic, from above) form of the TL is emphasized, and academic registers are often prioritized.

Owing to the HLLs' unique needs and skills, many programs around the world have begun offering courses specifically targeting this population. Heritage language learners may benefit from a learning environment that can be tailored to their specific needs as well as their existing linguistic and cultural knowledge. Unfortunately, being able to offer such specialized courses is a luxury that not all schools, districts, or programs enjoy. Many teachers find themselves leading mixed classes of HLLs and L2 learners without explicit training or support on how to do so. Several studies have compared how mixed groups (e.g., HL and L2 learners) and matched groups (e.g., L2 learners) have interacted, and whether those interactions produced *language-related episodes* (LREs; see Chapter 4), which have been shown to be beneficial for language learning. In the mixed groups of HLLs and L2 learners, there was a trade-off in the "expert" role depending on the

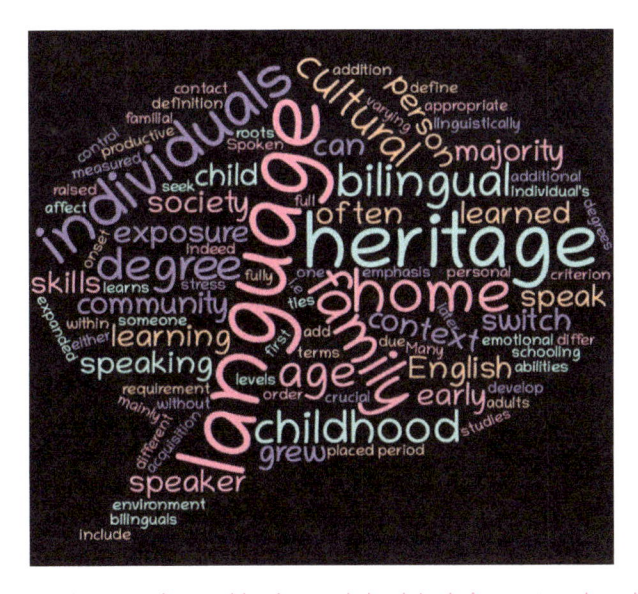

Figure 6.3 Heritage language learner identity word cloud. In their recent study on heritage language learners, García, Pineault, and Bryfonski analyzed fifteen of the most commonly used definitions for HLLs in SLA research, summarized in this word cloud. Image by: García et al., 2022

issues that arose during the task at hand. Heritage language learners assumed an "expert" role in questions that arose related to vocabulary and meaning-making, whereas L2 learners took over the "expert" role for questions related to spelling and using a more formal language register. When all group members contributed actively to their shared tasks, there were more LREs. However, in studies examining partnership dynamics between HLLs and L2 learners, some of the partners did not recognize the ways in which interpersonal collaboration could be advantageous. To maximize language learning opportunities, it may be necessary for the teacher to review language learning strategies and expectations for the group work. One study that explored interaction patterns between high school-age HLLs and L2 learners also considered the teacher role and discovered that teacher intervention did help mixed partnerships become more collaborative.

> **BOX 6.1 The Science! Points to Remember**
>
> - Learners' intersecting identities (e.g., race, heritage background) impact their perceptions of and experiences in language classrooms.
> - Curriculum has not historically represented all learner identities – especially in terms of race – which marginalizes some learners and makes it more difficult for them to see themselves as successful second language users.
> - Heritage and second language learners exhibit different linguistic skills and have different relationships with the target language and target culture(s) that may impact how they respond to in-class instruction and peer interaction.
> - All learners will benefit from a language class that draws on inclusive pedagogies and supports those pedagogies with rich, authentic resources that accurately reflect the diversity of the language, culture, and multilingual populations around the world.

6.3 The Science: What's Missing?

While we know from prior research that learners' identities impact their experiences learning second languages, there is limited intersectional identity research, or *layered* research into how learners' multiple identities impact their motivation and engagement in the language classroom. For example, little is known about how gender AND race impact one another and a learner's experiences in the L2 classroom. A study examining this intersection would need to ask questions about how learners from multiple genders and races experience their L2 class and make comparisons across both gender *and* race. Second language acquisition as a field and L2 teachers as a community are in dire need of these data, but robust comparisons like these are difficult to achieve in a singular study because they require significant coordination, data collection, participant numbers, etc. At the moment, like most applied linguistics research, what we know is limited by the overreliance of studies of white-identifying university students who are usually studying a commonly taught language such as English, Spanish, or French. As noted above, this population of learners is often referred to with the acronym WEIRD. This WEIRD population is so commonly studied because they *live* in places where applied linguistics research is commonly produced (e.g., in the U.S., the U.K., Canada), and they are easily recruited by the people conducting the research – university-affiliated researchers like professors and laboratory directors. Linguistics professors – including the authors – will give university students extra credit in linguistics courses, or other academic incentives, to participate in research, making it likely that most of the participants in a study are enrolled in the university. Additionally, there are relatively few concerns raised by ethics boards (sometimes called "IRBs" or "Institutional Review Boards") when researchers work with university students because they are not considered a traditionally *vulnerable population* (a term used commonly by ethics boards) like minors, individuals with profound intellectual disabilities, refugees, unhoused persons, or the incarcerated. In all, WEIRD participants are often seen as the "path of least resistance" to carrying out a study. While applied linguists are increasingly acknowledging that general conclusions cannot be drawn from research that only focuses on WEIRD language learners or only examines one facet of diverse learners' identities, much more research is needed.

Another crucial area less discussed in current research is how to best support teachers, both pre-service and in-service, to incorporate pedagogies into their teaching contexts that are representative of intersectional learner identities. What resources are teachers most likely to incorporate? How do teachers find and implement recourses provided to them? What kinds of training about learners' identities are most effective for teachers? Increased teacher–researcher collaboration could help to find the answers to these pressing questions.

In terms of classes with HLLs, it is important to remember that such learners are not a homogeneous group (see Figure 6.3). Depending on an individual's age of acquisition (e.g., from birth, from infanthood), proficiency level, the amount of heritage language used at home, the strength of cultural/familial ties to the heritage language/culture, and overall interest in learning the heritage language, learners may present very differently in the classroom. Therefore, the traits and learning strategies that some HLLs display during peer work cannot be generalized to all HLLs. Moreover, much research to date has focused on how older, more advanced HL and L2 learners interact when paired together. Whether younger or lower-proficiency language learners recognize each other's linguistic areas of expertise and adopt the same interaction dynamics during group work remains unexplored.

6.4 The Art: Research-Based Strategies to Try

6.4.1 The Art of Selecting or Designing Inclusive Material

- Increase representation of the variety of communities of your target language speakers and cultures. When selecting resources for your class, be sure to consider the context of the resource (its social and historical settings), the content of the resource

itself, and the content's commentary on social and political themes. Consider if historically underrepresented communities are systematically missing from your curricular materials.
- Include classroom material, topics, and curricula that reflect student experiences and cultures. If you teach Spanish, be sure you are not exclusively discussing large Spanish-speaking countries like Spain and Mexico. Equatorial Guinea is also a Spanish-speaking country that is rarely the topic of discussion in Spanish courses, and countries like the Philippines and Morocco have significant relationships with Spanish, despite not having it as an official language.
- To make sure all learners feel included, take a critical look at the resources you use and how the visuals present speakers of the TL. Look at the authors, singers, painters, musicians, celebrities, and athletes featured in your curriculum. Who is featured? Do they reflect the larger global communities of TL users or do they represent a smaller section of it?
  - Make a list of every country where their language is a recognized language, and then compare that list to the list of countries represented in their textbooks.
- Make sure vocabulary lists include vocabulary that relates to all student experiences.
  - If the unit is on describing yourself or people in your family, there should be words in the TL that describe diverse physical features, not just white learners. A 2017 analysis of Novice-level curricular material for a Spanish course found that the commercial textbook and corresponding digital learning suite did not have vocabulary that Black learners would need to describe themselves and people in their family. This was described as "color-evasiveness," which runs contrary to creating and advancing equity and inclusiveness in curricular resources and instead erases Black identity.
    - If you are unsure what words or phrases your learners may need to describe their experiences, contact experts or community members who can speak to the experiences of learners in your teaching context. You can also ask your students directly to help co-construct vocabulary lists. Ask your entire class to do this anonymously, through exit tickets that learners turn in at the end of class or through online surveys.
  - Invite HLLs to add the words or phrases their own language varieties use in your vocabulary lists. Being aware of language variation is important for all learners as they may interact with language users from many different countries. Give learners the opportunity to play and experiment with language variation in their assignments.
    - If you teach lower-level HLLs who may not be aware of language variation, do your own research on what words and phrases are used in different TL communities. The graphic in Figure 6.4 shows how you could set up a variety-friendly vocabulary list to co-create as a class.
    - At the end of the year, challenge learners to demonstrate their language variation expertise with a friendly individual or group competition. Depending on age and proficiency level, learners could race to match flashcards to the

6.4 The Art: Research-Based Strategies to Try

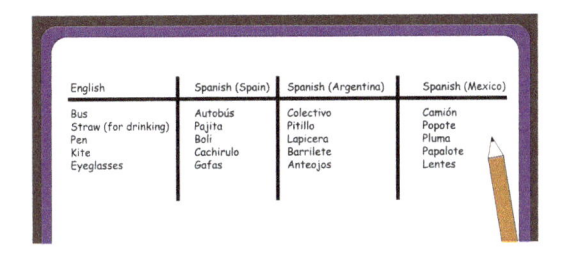

English	Spanish (Spain)	Spanish (Argentina)	Spanish (Mexico)
Bus	Autobús	Colectivo	Camión
Straw (for drinking)	Pajita	Pitillo	Popote
Pen	Boli	Lapicera	Pluma
Kite	Cachirulo	Barrilete	Papalote
Eyeglasses	Gafas	Anteojos	Lentes

Figure 6.4 Multi-dialectal vocabulary lists. Multi-dialectal vocabulary lists highlight linguistic diversity and honor the various varieties of the target language spoken around the world. Image by: Elizabeth Zonarich

  appropriate country on a map, brainstorm as many country-specific words within a given time frame, listen to short audio clips from TV shows or interviews, and then correctly identify what countries the speakers are from.
- Elevate student voices and experiences and de-center your own during class discussions, especially when discussing topics that your learners may know more about.
  - For older learners with a higher language proficiency: Try out rotating small-group discussions with poster paper and one full class debrief; one facilitator is assigned to a permanent table and does not rotate – this person summarizes and shares out the ideas from their table at the debrief.
  - Take care not to essentialize learners' identities by calling out specific learners to share about their culture; calling on someone – especially a younger learner or one who hasn't expressly agreed to it – to be a "representative" of their country or community can highlight how they are different from their peers in ways that can prove to be isolating and alienating. This is particularly relevant in classrooms that are mostly homogeneous, with only one or two learners having a background that is different from the majority of the class. Instead, provide choice and options so that learners who *want* to share about some aspect of their identity or culture have the space to do so but do not feel obliged. For example, if you want learners to present on common celebrations in countries where the TL is spoken, provide a sign-up and let learners choose from options or propose their own.

6.4.2 The Art of Building Connections

- Write language learning autobiographies at the beginning of the semester. Composing language learning autobiographies is a way to encourage any individual to reflect on their experiences, perceptions, and motivations toward a target language or community. Autobiographies can be written in any language. They can include pictures, drawings, or multimedia components. They can be shared or private.
  - Particularly for teachers with HLLs, inviting a class to author language learning autobiographies can help teachers understand the wide range of learner expertise, goals, and worries about being in a language classroom. Teachers can use this information to inform instructional decisions throughout the semester.

- Beginning and ending a language class with language learning autobiographies can celebrate learner growth and motivate continued study and/or engagement with the target language or community.
- Survey the families and learners in your school district about their experiences in the world language program, what they would like to see more of, attitudes and enrollment. The survey results may inform your teaching but may also reveal important enrollment trends that can be shared with administrators to help make sure that the opportunity to learn a language is not just an opportunity for learners of certain backgrounds.

6.4.3 The Art of Prioritizing Self-Education Experiences

- Seek out opportunities to learn more about how the African Diaspora and other diaspora communities connects to your target language. This can be accomplished through independent research, attending virtual or in-person conferences/workshops, or through engagement and discussion with your learners' community or the target language community. If you are a world language teacher, start with the list of resources of the American Council on the Teaching of Foreign Languages (ACTFL) that address issues of race, diversity, and social justice (available on their website: www.actfl.org) and the associated issue in the journal *Foreign Language Annals* that is written for language educators. Another excellent resource is the MI-BRIDGE project, which provides faculty training workshops and educator toolkits for Hispanic-Serving, Historically Black Colleges and Universities (HBCUs) and other minority-serving institutions (https://laccmibridge.fiu.edu/).
- Investigate the most common heritage languages in your community. If there are any heritage languages that are also taught at your world language program, connect with community centers, and find ways to increase in-class representation of local language use.

6.5 Troubleshooting: How the Science Informs the Art

Mrs. A teaches upper-level Spanish electives at her secondary school that enrolls both advanced L2 learners of Spanish and heritage language learners. Because of the large discrepancy in proficiency levels in her elective courses, Mrs. A struggles with selecting course material and designing activities that are accessible for her learners.

The differences between her learners' proficiency levels does not have to be a negative quality of Mrs. A's classes. However, it does require Mrs. A to consider some factors she may not have thought about before. Mrs. A can certainly capitalize on shared interests among her students as she selects resources for class. She can use different pairing and grouping strategies to make the resources meaningful for all learners, including heritage learners. For example, Mrs. A might consider using stations that each feature a resource of a different modality (a text, a video, an image, an infographic, etc.) and encouraging learners to select the resource that they are most interested in using. All the resources should relate to an overarching

6.5 Troubleshooting: How the Science Informs the Art

theme so learners can discuss a shared topic together, but the variety in modalities allows learners to pick the type of language they feel comfortable practicing.

Mrs. A also has heritage language learners of Spanish enroll in these electives. Because they are upper-level courses, Mrs. A expects all her learners, regardless of language background, to do a great deal of academic reading and writing as they interpret and analyze authentic resources. While the HLLs are often quite interested in the course themes and participate frequently during activities like debates or small-group conversations, she notices that they disconnect from the activities that include authentic resources and also often have difficulty with reading and writing in the more formal registers.

Owing to enrollment numbers and course offerings, this is not an unusual problem, but that does not make it any easier to address! The variation in student population requires a great deal of individualized instruction, which may or may not be possible, depending on Mrs. A's additional class preparations. Again, it is encouraging that the HLLs in Mrs. A's class are engaged in the themes of the course. As she plans for class, Mrs. A should be sure to consider the purpose of each of her activities and use that information to shape how she matches her learners. For example, for an in-class writing workshop where there is a greater focus on grammatical features, Mrs. A might consider using mixed groups so that learners can help to bring each other's attention to discrepancies between the work of group members and so that they can problem-solve together. To ensure that the mixed-group dynamic remains collaborative, Mrs. A could specify writing workshop roles so that each student has something concrete to contribute, regardless of their linguistic and cultural connections to Spanish.

She regularly invites all her learners after class to work through exercises in a one-on-one environment, but not many take her up on it. As a result, throughout the semester, learner abilities and engagement levels become more disparate. While she attempts to integrate as much cultural diversity from world Spanishes into her class, she worries about putting too much emphasis on her own culture. How might Mrs. A adjust her curriculum next year, given the diversity in linguistic and cultural backgrounds of her learners?

Given that the learners on her course have such different backgrounds, Mrs. A should not expect that all her learners should leave her course at the same level. Rather than having a common "end goal" based around a proficiency level, she should encourage her learners to set individuals goals for how they want to grow and develop. One way some teachers do this is by setting level-change goals rather than end-of-course goals. This could mean that Mrs. A aims for each of her students to grow by one ACTFL Proficiency sub-level (e.g., progress from Intermediate-Low to an Intermediate-Mid or from an Intermediate-Mid to an Intermediate-High) rather than setting a singular Proficiency sub-level as her goal (e.g., all learners will be Intermediate-Mid by the end of the academic year). Mrs. A can use these goals to help learners develop a sense of accountability for their own growth. Her learners' goals may also help Mrs. A select topics and design activities that her learners will be excited to complete. Throughout the year, Mrs. A can have regular "check-ins" with each learner about their goals in a one-on-one environment. Having more structure for what to accomplish during these independent meetings may help learners feel more comfortable participating in them, and may even encourage them to schedule additional sessions as they work toward their own goals. Additionally, Mrs. A should take care to ensure that her curriculum, the vocabulary she chooses to present, and the cultural issues she highlights are reflective of the diversity of Spanishes spoken globally, as well as by the families of her students. She should ensure that Afro-Latino culture is not absent from her curriculum and that images of global Spanish speakers and learners are representative in her materials and in the way she presents and discusses Spanish use in class.

6.6 The Science: Points to Remember

- Regardless of linguistic and cultural differences between partners, any peer–peer interaction has the potential to be a positive experience for language learning so long as there is a collaborative dynamic.
- It is important to consider how real and/or perceived power/social dynamics between learners may influence the prospective of collaboration and take pro-active steps to select and scaffold activities so that each student has something to contribute to the shared effort.
- Learners who seem disengaged or uninterested in language class may feel that way because they feel alienated from the curriculum linguistically, culturally, or socially.
- Incorporate your learners' experiences and expertise into the course curriculum and defer to them on areas that are unfamiliar to you. This helps ensure that all learners feel represented in the curriculum and helps to build trust and strong relationships.

6.7 Questions to Consider

1. What sorts of learning strategies (see Chapter 5) might be important to teach learners in a linguistically and culturally diverse world language classroom? Why?
2. Do all learners of color have equal opportunity to enroll in language classes at your school? Why or why not? Are there institutional policies that may be disproportionately discouraging some learners from enrolling in language courses?
3. What sort of deficit mindsets toward learners of linguistically and culturally diverse backgrounds have you encountered in your professional career? How might you challenge some of those mindsets using information you learned in this chapter?
4. What sort of subliminal messages does your textbook or curricular resources send about who legitimate speakers of your target language are?
5. Look at the curricular materials used in your program and consider whether they facilitate Black learners' participation and success in the languages you offer.

6.8 The Science of Language Learning: Research Supporting the Main Points in This Chapter

Anya, U. (2021). Critical race pedagogy for more effective and inclusive world language teaching. *Applied Linguistics*, *42*(6), 1055–1069. https://doi.org/10.1093/applin/amab068.

This article reviews two studies of Spanish language curriculum from a critical perspective. Excerpts from student and instructor interviews, as well as descriptions of curricular resources show how language programs regularly centralize white experiences and minimize multilingual Afro-descendant populations through the curricular resources they provide including textbook illustrations, vocabulary lists, supplementary articles, and more. The ramifications of this are discussed in terms of student motivation, retention, and attitudes toward language learning. Anya explains the analysis process and provides concrete steps to help educators and researchers who wish to conduct explorations of their own curricular material.

Carreira, M. (2020, September 22). *Instructed Heritage Language Acquisition* [Audio podcast]. https://international.ucla.edu/nhlrc/article/238479.

In this podcast, Dr. Maria Carreira, a researcher from the National Heritage Language Resource Center, and Dr. Melissa Bowles, a professor in Spanish and Portuguese at the University of Illinois at Urbana-Champaign, discuss research-based teaching practices for HLLs. Tools for supporting HLLs' development in their reading, writing, speaking, and listening skills are shared and connected back to empirical findings. The social and emotional dimensions to HLLs' linguistic development and classroom experiences are also explored.

Frieson, B. L. (2022). "It's like they don't see us at all": A Critical Race Theory critique of dual language bilingual education for black children. *Annual Review of Applied Linguistics*, 1–8. https://doi.org/10.1017/S0267190522000022.

This article demonstrates how the language policies and academic structures of dual-language bilingual programs can minimize the lived experiences of HLLs and Black students. Through sharing student perspectives on their school, Frieson shows the complexities of advancing bilingual agendas and underscores the importance of recognizing all students' identities and backgrounds in the classroom. The article concludes with suggestions for teachers and administrators within bilingual programs to improve equity and representation.

For more resources, including more sample lesson plans, videos, and other ideas, visit our companion website: www.cambridge.org/BryfonskiMackey.

7 How do I best support neurodiverse language learners?

KEY QUESTIONS
- **The Science: How might learning differences (e.g., dyslexia, dyspraxia, autism spectrum disorder, attention-deficit/hyperactivity disorder, among others) impact language learning? What advantages or challenges might there be for neurodiverse learners in relation to language learning?**
- **The Art: How do I best support my learners with specific learning needs and differences?**
- **How can I organize my language classes to benefit all learners, including neurodiverse ones?**

7.1 Voices from the Classroom

Ms. V teaches Russian in a middle school that offers foreign language classes to learners with gifts and talents (those who demonstrate exceptional intelligence and/or aptitude for learning), but not to the general population. One of her gifted learners was just screened for learning disabilities and was diagnosed with dyslexia. This child's parents are worried that, though the child is exceptional in many ways, his dyslexia may make learning Russian more difficult for him and the extra work may lower his grades overall, putting his continued enrollment in gifted programs in jeopardy. Ms. V is also worried because she doesn't have any experience working with dyslexic children (that she's aware of, although many dyslexic children go undiagnosed). She worries that the Russian script may exacerbate her student's difficulties. However, since the beginning of the school year she's come to understand her student as a hard worker with lots of potential, and she doesn't want to unenroll him from the class just because of his new diagnosis. She wonders what steps she can take to evaluate where his strengths and struggles lie or what strategies she can employ in one-on-one instruction time and in whole-class instruction so that he is supported in developing the literacy skills he needs to be a successful Russian language learner. She wonders how to go about reassuring his parents that all children can be (and already are!) language learners, regardless of learning challenges.

7.2 The Science: What the Research Says

All language learners bring their own individual needs and differences to the table of language learning. Put differently, like any other human characteristic, there is diversity – in this case, **neurodiversity** – of strengths, needs, and experiences in all language learners. When second language acquisition (SLA) researchers investigate neurodiversity, they often focus on one aspect of neurodiversity, or **individual difference**, at a time – for example, a researcher might look at how a learner's **working memory** (their ability to store, manipulate, and analyze information in real time) impacts how they interact with their peers. See Table 7.1 for a list of some commonly studied individual differences.

Table 7.1 Common individual differences associated with neurodiversity

Individual difference	What is it?	What role does it have in L2 learning?
working memory (WM)	A learner's capacity for storing, manipulating, and analyzing information in real time.	When learning a second language (L2), WM helps with holding onto information in real time so that learners can detect patterns across input, interpreting feedback, etc. When a learner has low WM capacity, they struggle with noticing patterns on their own. L2 teachers can help by providing extra supports like (1) allowing learners to access notes while conducting focus-on-form noticing activities or (2) *enhancing input* to make certain aspects of the L2 easier to notice.
phonological awareness (PA)	Phonological awareness (PA) is a learner's ability to recognize new sounds, rhyme words, and divide words up into syllables. Low levels of PA are associated with dyslexia.	Learners who struggle with these three skills have a difficult time detecting the boundaries between words when listening in the L2, decoding new words, and manipulating known words. Explicit instruction of these skills is important to help enable learners to be successful and independent users of the L2. L2 teachers can support learners who struggle with PA and related skills by incorporating rhyming games, spot the difference tasks, and even instructional strategies used by reading coaches (i.e., those who provide reading support to children with dyslexia and related PA disorders).
phonemic awareness	A learner's ability to distinguish between segments of sounds of a word and put them together to form words.	
phonological decoding	A learner's ability to apply spelling cues to identify words and retrieve their meanings.	

7.2 The Science: What the Research Says

Table 7.1 (Continued)

Individual difference	What is it?	What role does it have in L2 learning?
grammatical sensitivity	A learner's analytical ability regarding grammar. This skill is closely related to *noticing* because it relies on pattern recognition and inductive reasoning.	Learners who exhibit high levels of grammatical sensitivity "pick up" on grammatical features like verb conjugations, gender agreement, and word order with relatively little effort. Learners who struggle with this skill need additional support (and explicit instruction, oftentimes) to (1) notice patterns in the L2's grammar and (2) become more adept at noticing subsequent patterns in the future. L2 teachers can use tactile representations of grammar, gestures, and noticing strategies to help L2 learners with low levels of grammatical sensitivity.

Those learners with specific learning diagnoses (e.g., autism spectrum disorder, attention-deficit/hyperactivity disorder, dyslexia, among others) – or *neurodivergent* learners – vary in terms of their general learning, social, mood, or attention skills and abilities. There is a common misperception that neurodivergent learners cannot or should not speak multiple languages at home or be enrolled in language classes out of fear that they will either be unable to learn the second language (L2) or that learning the new language will somehow impede their current language abilities. As a result, many parents of neurodivergent learners are counseled into monolingual learning settings, with children of minoritized communities (e.g., racial/ethnic minorities, those from homes where the dominant language is not spoken) being more likely to be recommended for monolingual schooling.

Importantly, though, there is no data or research supporting the idea that neurodivergent learners should avoid additional language learning. In fact, the opposite has sometimes been shown to be true. For example, studies comparing monolingual and bilingual children with autism spectrum disorder (ASD) have not found any differences in general language abilities. One study of children with autism spectrum disorders from Guangzhou, China, found that exposure to other languages and dialects (e.g., Mandarin, Yue [of which Cantonese is a major dialect], Hakka, Xiang, and Southern Min) was not associated with additional language challenges. In other words, bilingual or bidialectal children with ASD do not experience any additional delays in language development compared to monolingual children with ASD. Instead, neurodiverse people reap the same benefits as neurotypical people when learning a second language.

Studies show language learning can improve learners' **executive functioning**, meaning language learners show gains in attention, self-control, and mental flexibility skills. Bilingualism has also been shown to improve people's ability to understand, produce, and think *about* language as well as their ability to recall information and switch between tasks. Since these are also the areas in which, for example, people with ASD sometimes have difficulty, neurodivergent learners may actually stand to benefit *more* from bilingualism than neurotypical learners. Research also shows that bilingualism can be beneficial in improving peoples' ability to understand others' beliefs and take others' perspectives. One study with children with ASD found that bilingual children with ASD had an advantage in understanding others' beliefs over their monolingual ASD peers. This kind of research shows how learning a second language is far from a disadvantage and can actually be advantageous for some neurodivergent learners in particular.

BOX 7.1 Important to Note!

Children who speak multiple languages are overrepresented in disability support programs or designated as "special needs" after being anecdotally diagnosed as neurodivergent. However, the assessments used to place learners often test vocabulary in the language dominant at school, thus incompletely representing learners' linguistic ability. In fact, bilingual children usually have larger vocabularies than monolingual children when both languages are taken into account! Because monolingual assessments typically under-assess bilingual children's language skills, not only are bilingual children *over*-represented in special education, but they are also *under*-represented in gifted education programs.

While this chapter focuses on children who have been formally diagnosed as neurodivergent and are learning second languages, parents and teachers of any multilingual child should advocate for assessments that include *all* the languages their child speaks. This way, the child's full linguistic repertoire is accurately assessed, and parents can avoid incorrectly placing them in a program that is designed for neurodivergent learners.

7.2.1 Advantages Some Neurodivergent Learners May Have in Language Learning

Neurodivergent learners may also have advantages in the language learning process. Some neurodivergent learners, like learners with attention-deficit/hyperactivity disorder (ADHD), can have hyper-focused attention and sometimes fixate on a narrow range of ideas. When learners' interests are leveraged, this can become an advantage for learning, given that research shows learners need to notice or attend to features of the language input in order to acquire it. Learners with ASD often have extraordinary skills in pattern recognition. As we discuss in Chapter 9, language learning aptitude is related to pattern recognition and pattern-seeking in language forms. As a result, some language learners with ASD may demonstrate advantages in detecting grammatical patterns. Memory has also been shown to influence language learning. Certain types of neurodivergent learners have excellent memory capabilities and may leverage those during the language learning process to recognize and integrate input or corrective feedback (we explain why these are important in language learning in Chapters 2 and 3). Cognitive creativity has also been tied to language learning, specifically learners' ability to produce out-of-the-box ideas and more complex language while interacting during tasks. Some people with dyslexia have been shown to score higher on creativity tests than a normed sample and perform better on tasks where they are asked to carry out unusual combinations of ideas or find nontraditional uses for objects (e.g., "A chair can be used for ... (a) sitting, (b) reaching for something on a high shelf, (c) as a bookcase, (d) shelter during an earthquake."). All of these unique skill sets of neurodivergent learners can be leveraged during the language learning process.

7.2.2 Struggles Some Neurodivergent Learners May Have with Language Learning

While some neurodivergent learners may experience advantages during language learning, they may also struggle in specific ways related to their learning needs. Understanding the frequently cited needs of these learners can help educators design their classrooms to be supportive. For example, learners with dyslexia struggle with **phonological awareness** – specifically, the skills of manipulating sounds, segmenting words into sounds, blending sounds together, and associating sounds with symbols – and may require targeted lessons to build their phonemic awareness skills. This association – dyslexia and phonological awareness – might surprise some, as there is a common misconception of dyslexia as being a visual, rather than an auditory processing issue. Early researchers of dyslexia even referred to it as "word blindness" – something we now know to be a misunderstanding of the disorder. Instead, learners with dyslexia have trouble recognizing discrete sounds and patterns in sounds. This can manifest in trouble detecting and creating rhyming words, word retrieval (e.g., "It's on the tip of my tongue!"), and memorizing words.

Learners with attention difficulties (e.g., ADHD) often have trouble with executive functioning – a set of skills that help to regulate thinking and behavior – and the ways in which these skills are impacted can vary from learner to learner. Executive functioning skills include working memory, emotional control, response inhibition (e.g., how we react when things don't go our way), sustained attention, planning and organizing, time management, goal-directed persistence, flexibility, metacognition, and others. As a result, learners with ADHD and other disorders related to executive functioning can have a hard time with instruction that relies on inference, implicit learning, or noticing a gap. This difficulty stems from the tendency for learners' shorter attention spans to make sticking with a hard task more difficult or prompt the learner to involuntarily divert attention to another task and away from working to comprehend input.

The possible space for supporting neurodivergent learners is vast and it is beyond the scope of this – or any – book to provide suggestions for every possible specific learner need. However, we do know that it is critical to work with all others involved in the education of neurodiverse learners to understand the specific learning needs of each learner as much as possible, and to not jump immediately to the conclusion that enrollment in a second language course will be detrimental for learners who are neurodivergent.

> **BOX 7.2 The Science! Points to Remember**
>
> - All language learners are differently abled, meaning everyone experiences language learning differently based on their individual needs and differences. We cover other ways learners might be neurodiverse in Chapter 9 including in terms of their personalities, working memory, aptitude, and creativity.
> - Neurodivergent learners are learners who vary from their neurotypical peers in terms of their general learning, social, mood, or attention skills and abilities, and they bring both specific strengths and specific needs with them to their language classrooms.
> - There is no evidence that learning a second language has negative consequences for neurodivergent learners; in fact, it seems that the opposite is true. Language learning has benefits that both neurotypical and neurodivergent learners can enjoy.
> - Neurodivergent learners have some advantages in the language learning process in addition to specific areas where they may require extra support.

7.3 The Science: What's Missing?

Unfortunately, there is relatively little research so far that has included and investigated neurodiverse L2 learners specifically. Often, L2 researchers find themselves relying on research conducted in other fields, like psychology, general education, early childhood education, etc. due to a lack of resources within the field of L2 teaching and learning. The L2 research that does exist often compares neurodivergent learners with neurotypical control group learners, instead of neurodivergent peers with the same or other diagnoses. In other words, the research does not compare learners with similar backgrounds, educational experiences, access to instructional resources, and learning need diagnoses. As a result, we do not currently have a clear understanding of what progress looks like for neurodiverse learners learning languages or benchmarks normed specifically for neurodivergent populations. The research also often collapses many specific learning needs together, rather than exploring the needs of neurodivergent learners separately based on diagnoses (e.g., learners with ASD compared to learners with dyslexia, compared to learners with ADHD). As a result, we don't have many specific recommendations for specific profiles of neurodivergent language learners. But we hope this will be changing as society increasingly begins to recognize and value neurodivergence.

7.4 The Art: Research-Based Strategies to Try

Research has suggested that instructional modifications that benefit neurodivergent learners will also benefit neurotypical learners. Remember that all classrooms are neurodiverse and that learning differences are not always readily apparent (and sometimes are not disclosed by learners' families due to stigma).

7.4 The Art: Research-Based Strategies to Try

7.4.1 The Art of Differentiating Instruction

- For learners with hyper-focused attention:
  - Focus on learner interests and integrate interests into the language learning process. This may lead to more learning while avoiding frustration and increased anxiety during the learning process. For example, find a speaker of the TL who has created something related to the learner's interest – like a YouTuber who makes videos on robotics or an author who's written a comic book about samurai.
- For learners with specific sensory needs:
  - Integrate movement and embodied interaction into the language classroom. For example, have learners act out scenes as plays, manipulate objects, or complete tasks that require body motions.
  - When focusing on form, incorporate tactile activities to explain grammatical features like conjugation, affixes, direct object placement, etc. For example, to demonstrate what conjugation is, use multicolored blocks to build the root of a verb, and then switch out the conjugation endings to show how just one section of a word can change. In Figure 7.1, the rainbow-colored blocks represent the conjugation endings for French regular -er verbs. Each subject pronoun has one color (e.g., "I" or *je* being red, "you" or *tu* is orange) and the students must remove and add blocks to make the conjugation's ending match the subject pronoun.
  - Headphones can be used to prevent auditory overstimulation. Have headphones available in reading corners or at any times learners need to quietly be working independently. When completing assessment tasks involving listening, consider having learners with auditory processing disorders listen to the input tasks (e.g., a video or audio recording) using headphones. This will help filter out echoes in the classroom testing environment and allow them to focus on what they understand in the L2, rather than regulate their listening.
  - Store quiet fidget toys in a drawer and show your learners with specific sensory needs how to access them, use them, and store them at the end of class. You can also consider using a chair band (i.e., a large rubber band that stretches between the front two legs of a standard chair) so that learners who need to fidget their

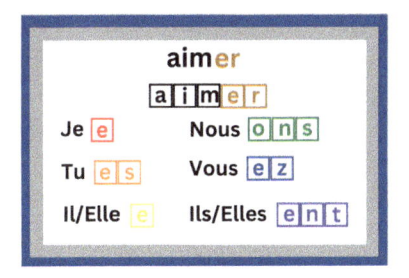

Figure 7.1 Exemplar tactile activity. Tactile activities can support learners in noticing linguistic patterns needed to successfully make meaning they otherwise might not have noticed. Based on an activity designed by Erin Fell.

legs can bounce their legs using the band. Additionally, if your school allows it, you can incorporate nontraditional seating in your classroom. Making a variety of seat kinds available to all learners – not just those with specific sensory needs – helps to normalize neurodiversity in the classroom.
- For learners with attention-regulation difficulties:
  - Attention is necessary for noticing a gap, so engaging in activities that involve games, problem-solving, or competition can be helpful for maintaining attention. Additionally, breaking larger tasks into a series of smaller tasks can help learners who struggle with attention to persist through the task and still get the "win" of understanding the input, solving the problem, etc.
  - Learning from spoken or written output and implicit feedback may be more difficult, so explicit, specific feedback can be helpful. In addition, you can pose frequent comprehension-checking questions to see whether learners were able to understand all aspects of the feedback.
  - "Carrying" information from one task to another can be difficult for learners with attention difficulties, so building in resources that learners can use from task to task can help learners keep track of what they're learning throughout the lesson (or even the unit). For example, during an input task, learners can record their observations in a graphic organizer that they then use to help them complete a production task. Learner-made supports like these are better for L2 learning than teacher-made ones (e.g., giving learners a teacher-made vocabulary list for the production task) because it is more actively engaging learners in all steps of the lesson.
  - Explicit teaching can be more helpful and yield better results than inductive reasoning activities or implicit feedback, where attention may wander or meaning may not be fully comprehended.
  - Harness creativity by allowing for multiple ways for learners to demonstrate learning (e.g., through graphic design, making a website, a group project, a short story, a news video, a podcast).
- For learners with dyslexia:
  - Provide multiple modes for engaging with content. If text is provided, include an audio version or visuals such as graphic organizers.
  - Play rhyming games like singing nursery rhymes or schoolyard hand games (e.g., jump rope, clapping games) to practice phonological awareness.
  - For alphabetic languages, incorporate instruction on prefixes, suffixes, and common letter combinations and *how they sound*. When implementing instruction on spelling and phonics, be sure to integrate it into multiple points in the curriculum, as students with dyslexia will need repetition for the instruction to be most effective.
    - You can incorporate word games and riddles that involve splitting and combining sounds to create new words. These are sometimes found in elementary education where small pictures replace words. See Figure 7.2 for an example of this.

7.4 The Art: Research-Based Strategies to Try

Figure 7.2 Word visualization strategies. Word visualization strategies may be particularly helpful in drawing learners' attention to cognates in compound words.

- You can even practice having learners create nonsense words in the L2 by combining common sounds in the L2. You can frame this practice as a game, for example, by having the learners create imaginary animals based on their nonsense words, and according to the age and interests of the learners.
  ○ Try not to penalize spelling. One way around this could be to allow the learner to use a word processor. In fact, all learners benefit from using a word processor because it allows learners to edit and reformulate (and spellcheck!) before turning in their work.
- For learners with other reading-related difficulties:
  ○ Online resources with voice-to-text, text-to-voice, and parsing functions can help those with reading-related difficulties to read and write more efficiently. Many programs and machines now provide voice-to-text as a standard function (often accessible as a microphone icon near a keyboard), but text-to-voice is also becoming more common. When selecting resources to provide learners, check to see that the L2 you are teaching is one of the languages provided by the service.
  ○ Parsing programs transform heavier reading into broken-down, digestible chunks without changing the content of the text. Parsing programs use syntax-based algorithms to arrange the words and phrases of a text into shorter stanza-like lines (where the cuts are based on English syntax) for greater comprehensibility. See Figure 7.3 for an example.

> Parsing programs
>   break up
>   blocks of text
>   to make them
>   easier to comprehend
>
> This technique
>   maximizes processing capacities
>   for learners
>   who might struggle
>   with long stretches
>   of text

Figure 7.3 Parsing example. This screen capture shows an example of parsing that may increase comprehensibility, especially for weaker readers.

7.4.2 The Art of Centering Learners' Needs

- For ALL learners:
  - Increase wait time. As discussed in Chapter 2, this benefits all learners to have time to process input. However, this is even more important for neurodivergent learners.
  - Increase use of nonverbal communication.
    - Gestures, facial expressions, and the use of objects can help all learners better understand input, but it is even more critical for neurodivergent learners who may struggle to attend to speech.
    - Note that hand gestures may hold different meanings for different cultures. It's important to be mindful of the cultures in one's classroom and use gestures appropriately. For example, in some cultures, it is considered especially rude to draw attention to something with pointed fingers or items (e.g., pen, marker, eating utensils) in general. Pointing with an open, upward-facing hand may be considered more polite or respectful in some contexts.
  - Don't expect all learners to progress at the same pace. All learners will learn at different rates, neurotypical and neurodivergent alike. Work with individual learners (or their families, if they are young children) to set benchmarks that are reasonable and achievable. Don't compare the language learning rates of learners with different abilities to one another.
  - Create routines.
    - All language learners benefit from routines so that they can form expectations about what's coming next, learn language in manageable chunks, and associate language forms with certain activities/contexts. However, many neurodivergent learners thrive off routine even more, and classroom routines will aid in comprehension and lessening anxiety.
  - Provide scaffolded supports.
    - Graphic organizers, visuals, and realia (real objects) support comprehension in all learners and are critical for learners who may struggle with different forms of input (e.g., reading/writing).
    - When using stations (e.g., a series of short activities where learners move from activity to activity at their own pace or when prompted by a timer), consider posting answer keys on the wall or whiteboard. You can cover the answer keys with a piece of paper so that those who don't want to use the key don't need to look at it, but those who do want to check their answers have an easy way to do so.
  - Consider roles in group activities that play to learner's strengths.
    - We know interaction is a critical component of language learning (see Chapter 4), but not all neurodivergent learners are able to interact with their peers in the same ways. Consider supporting your neurodivergent learners by designing roles in small group work that play to their strengths. For example, instead of assigning a learner with dyslexia to be the group note-taker, consider putting them in a role like "problem-solver" that builds on creative solutions. A learner with ASD may be asked to take the role of the group

encourager, making sure the group stays positive and doesn't become frustrated. Of course, learners should never get stuck in the same role every day such that they never have the opportunity to build other skill sets; rather, always seek ways they can offer their unique abilities to the group activity.
- Use nontraditional forms of assessment.
    - Include a variety of teaching and assessment activities to serve diverse learner learning and developmental profiles. For example, teachers may ask the learners in their class to develop a portfolio of their assignments or projects throughout the semester.
    - Exit tickets for the entire class could be distributed in order to see how your learners are doing in class.
- Plan your units around what learners *can* do rather than what they *cannot*. For example, at the start and end of the unit, have learners check off a list of can-do statements per unit so they can self-monitor their own learning.
- Model valuing neurodiversity in your classroom:
    - Point out frequently and consistently how each of your learners has unique strengths and skills for language learning and that those strengths are valued.
    - Model different methods of achieving the same goal of communicating meaning (e.g., writing the answer vs. drawing the answer vs. telling a friend vs. recording the answer via audio or video).
    - Include activities that allow all types of learners in your classroom to use their strengths. Include activities that involve art, music, bodily motion, creativity as well as the traditional skill sets of reading, writing, listening, and speaking.
    - Implement a grading system that makes it possible for all learners to track and reflect on their unique growth patterns over the duration of your course.
    - Consider using an "un-grading" system that replaces traditional letter or number grades with portfolios. This might not be feasible everywhere but disentangling L2 progress from grades can be a boon to L2 learners who enjoy the process of language learning but might struggle in aspects that might negatively impact graded performances (e.g., spelling errors). Additionally, focusing the portfolio assessment on proficiency-based statements like the ACTFL *Can-Do* statements (rather than strict adherence to accuracy-only assessment) can enable learners with difficulties to have their successes and progress celebrated.

7.5 Troubleshooting: How the Science Informs the Art

Ms. V wondered what steps she can take to evaluate her learner with dyslexia's strengths and struggles and what strategies she can employ in one-on-one instruction time and in whole-class instruction so that the child is supported in developing the literacy skills he needs to be a successful Russian language learner.

Ms. V is demonstrating the reflection and care for her students that is essential to L2 teaching, especially when considering how her instructional practices can support her learner's needs. With dyslexia, her learner may find it beneficial to have multiple ways to engage with texts. Online services that provide read-aloud assistance could be a good option for not only this learner but also his peers! Other options include splitting up the text into manageable chunks, supporting written texts with aural and visual input (e.g., read-alouds, graphics, videos), partner reading, and multimodal textual annotation. Incorporating explicit instruction around phonological awareness might also help this learner develop decoding and word recognition skills. When it comes to listening, the learner may benefit from extra time or repeated listening sessions (especially when it comes to assessments). Setting the learner up in a quiet area with access to the listening text (e.g., in a computer lab with headphones) can allow the learner time to fully process the information and perform at his best. With any adjustments, it is important that Ms. V communicate with her learner's family and the school's administrative team to be sure that everyone is on board with a new learning plan and expectations for language development.

Ms. V also wondered how to go about reassuring the child's parents that all children can be (and already are) language learners, regardless of learning challenges.

It is certainly a big challenge to change the preexisting beliefs people may carry about what neurodivergent learners are capable of achieving in a language classroom. Ms. V should keep in close communication with the learner's family to keep track of progress and demonstrate ongoing success learning Russian as a second language. She might consider including activities that highlight how Russian learning supports the learner's learning in other areas, such as history or art, and even in reading/writing.

7.6 The Science: Points to Remember

- *All classrooms are neurodiverse*, as every language learner brings unique strengths, needs, and experiences with them to their language class.
- To support the diverse needs of their learners, teachers can incorporate a variety of learning and teaching supports that learners can use as they progress through their language learning. Many of these supports benefit all learners, not just those who are neurodivergent.
- There is no research-based data that show that learning additional languages is detrimental for neurodivergent learners. In fact, research suggests otherwise, that learning additional languages brings cognitive benefits for all learners.

7.7 Questions to Consider

1. Based on your reading of this chapter, what sort of information do you think it would be important to share with the administrative staff and/or learning support team at your school?

2. A parent asks you about their child, who has been diagnosed with a specific learning disability, about their ability to succeed in learning a second language. How will you apply what you've learned in this chapter to respond to their enquiry?
3. Even if learners do not progress at the same rate, it does not mean that they are not learning. Knowing this, how might you adjust your rubrics or grading instruments accordingly to recognize all learners' abilities and development over the course of a year/semester?
4. What are actionable steps that you can immediately take as a language instructor to ensure equitable and inclusive education within your classroom context(s)?

7.8 The Science of Language Learning: Research Supporting the Points Made in This Chapter

Cheatham, G. A., & Hart Barnett, J. E. (2017). Overcoming common misunderstandings about students with disabilities who are English language learners. *Intervention in School and Clinic*, *53*(1), 58–63. https://doi.org/10.1177/1053451216644819.

English language learners are making up an increasingly significant portion of students enrolled in special education programs in the United States. This column addresses the need for special education teachers, administrators, and others to better understand the role of facilitative bilingualism in improving outcomes for English language learners with special needs. The authors highlight five key misunderstandings about bilingualism in special education and how these misunderstandings might be addressed in productive and culturally responsive ways.

Kormos, J., & Smith, A. M. (2023) *Teaching languages to students with specific learning differences* (2nd ed.). Multilingual Matters

This book is a must-read for L2 teachers looking to align instruction in their programs to the needs of L2 learners with learning differences. Kormos and Smith propose adopting a *multisensory structured learning approach* that uses all of the senses when interacting with new L2 lexis and L2 structures to help encode these into learners' L2 schema. While the entire book is practical in nature, the appendices of the book are particularly useful to classroom teachers, as they provide concrete suggestions for screening questions, and sample lesson plans to help L2 teachers enact what they learn in the book.

O'Connor, R. E., Beach, K. D., Sanchez, V. M., Kim, J. J., Knight-Teague, K., Orozco, G., & Jones, B. T. (2019). Teaching academic vocabulary to sixth-grade students with disabilities. *Learning Disability Quarterly*, *42*(4), 231–243. https://doi.org/10.1177/073194871882109.

This empirical study examined middle school adolescents with disabilities who were experiencing difficulty with academic content and language in middle school. The authors taught teachers of sixth-grade learners with learning disabilities, including English language learners (ELLs), to implement about 15 minutes of daily interactive vocabulary instruction in their intact special education English/language arts classes. Three schools were assigned randomly to treatment or control conditions. The researchers uncovered that the interactive vocabulary instruction which introduced four new words per week led to greater gains in vocabulary knowledge for the treatment condition. The intervention was found to benefit both learners with disabilities who were ELLs and native English speakers.

Rogers, M., & Meek, F. (2015). Relationships matter: Motivating students with ADHD through the teacher-student relationship. *Perspectives on Language and Literacy, 41*(1), 21–22.

This short, teacher-friendly article describes how to motivate students with attention-deficit/hyperactivity disorder (ADHD), one of the most prevalent childhood learning differences. The authors note that despite the high prevalence rate of ADHD, with most teachers having taught learners with ADHD, teachers report limited access to professional development opportunities to increase their knowledge of ADHD, address the needs of learners with ADHD, and decrease their stress about working with learners with ADHD. The article ends with five strategies for improving the teacher–student relationships in order to better motivate students with ADHD.

Shaywitz, S. E., & Shaywitz, J. (2020).*Overcoming dyslexia* (2nd ed.). Hachette UK.

This book is the second edition of S. E. Shaywtiz's (2003) book of the same name (with the subtitle *A new and complete science-based program for reading problems at any level*). This second edition is a nuanced, helpful primer on what dyslexia is, how it manifests in the learner, and how it can best be treated. Over the course of the past forty years, S. E. Shaywitz and J. Shawitz have worked together on the Connecticut Longitudinal Study (sponsored by the Yale Center on Dyslexia and Creativity), which is the most robust and nuanced research available on dyslexia across the life span. Though not a resource specifically dedicated to L2 learners with dyslexia, this book is a valuable resource on dyslexia in general and can help orient readers interested in supporting learners with dyslexia and other reading-related disorders to the larger field of study.

For more resources, including more sample lesson plans, videos, and other ideas, visit our companion website: www.cambridge.org/BryfonskiMackey.

8 How do learners' motivation and anxiety levels impact their language learning experience?

KEY QUESTIONS
- The Science: How do learners' motivation and anxiety levels impact their language learning experience?
- How can I increase motivation, or is motivation fixed?
- How does anxiety matter? Is anxiety good or bad for language learning?
- The Art: What can I do in the classroom to best motivate learners?
- What can I do to support my anxious language learners?

8.1 Voices from the Classroom

Mr. C teaches a Level 1 high school French class in a district where two years of a foreign language are mandatory for graduation and university admission. As a result, many of his learners are only enrolled in Mr. C's class because it is a requirement. Mr. C tries to motivate his learners by integrating games, skits, music, and other activities that he thinks would motivate this age group. However, sometimes learners seem to hesitate to participate even when they know the vocabulary and material well. He finds he has to cold call learners to get volunteers. A few learners routinely fall asleep. Because learners must receive a passing grade in order to complete their language requirement, they have a lot of anxiety around submitting assessments; however, this anxiety does not translate into productive learning habits or practices. How can Mr. C better structure his course to motivate his learners without triggering heightened language learning anxiety? How can he use what he knows about his learners' personalities to motivate them to engage with their classmates in productive ways?

8.2 The Science: What the Research Says

Most teachers agree that it is most enjoyable to teach when learners are motivated, engaged, and excited about their own learning. Unfortunately, learners can be unmotivated, anxious, or too uncomfortable to speak in the target language (TL) in class. Understanding what motivates learners and what causes them anxiety about language learning can empower teachers to make their classrooms more conducive to learning. Motivation and anxiety are two learner emotions that can have big impacts on second language (L2) development. Luckily, learners' motivation to improve their language skills and balance their anxiety so that it does not negatively impact learning are areas where teachers can have a direct impact. There is evidence that when teachers can tailor their instruction to their learners' interests and understand their motivations for language learning, learners achieve more.

8.2.1 What Researchers Know about Language Motivation

Definitions of motivation have evolved as researchers learn more about how motivation differs between learners and across a range of educational contexts. Once viewed as a primarily static learner characteristic resulting from learners' attitudes, motivation was most simply described as **intrinsic** or **extrinsic**. Intrinsically motivated learners aren't motivated by teachers, peers, or anyone else but instead through their learning opportunities. Extrinsically motivated learners, on the other hand, are motivated by outside influences. They might be motivated by gaining rewards, like good grades, praise from a teacher, or a reward from their parents or caregivers. Extrinsically motivated learners may also be motivated by their own fears of letting others down, avoiding embarrassment, or making mistakes.

Another earlier view of motivation was centered around the idea of **integrativeness**, which described an individual's desire to learn the language of a valued community in order to communicate with and/or join that group of people. If learners are motivated by integrative purposes, they might have positive associations or attitudes about the language or the community that speaks the language. They might aspire to be integrated into the community and their way of life. Other learners' language learning process may be more driven by instrumental motives. Learners with **instrumental motivation** have more practical reasons for studying their new language. They might not necessarily imagine being integrated into a community but instead want to use their language to achieve a goal, like getting a job where they use the language.

Research in the 1990s and early 2000s discovered that motivation can also be dynamic and situation-specific, which unsettled the previous understanding that motivation was a stable trait grounded in learners' integrative aspirations, or lack thereof. Based on this finding, studies on motivation began to explore the processes of initiating and sustaining motivation in language learners. From this body of research, the present-day conception of motivation emerged. Now most researchers believe motivation to be a fluid variable that changes because of both external and internal experiences that individuals encounter during their learning. For example, research on motivation among children found that younger learners observe and assess the motivational levels of their peers and assimilate to the average level of motivation in the room during any given activity.

8.2 The Science: What the Research Says

Motivation is also often closely tied to learners' identities. When learners identify with a language community (maybe because they are a heritage language learner [HLL]; see Chapter 6) or strive to be accepted in a new language community, their identity becomes a powerful motivator. Research shows that people tend to want to close the gap between who they imagine themselves being and who they are right now. As we discussed earlier, they want to be their **ideal self**, whatever that might look like. Their ideal self might come in a variety of forms; maybe they envisage themselves making jokes in their new language or making friends with other speakers of the language. A learner's ideal self contrasts with their **ought-to self**, which is who the learner thinks others expect them to be (their teacher, peers, parents, families, etc.). Exploring who learners imagine themselves to be and encouraging them to write or say the hopes or dreams they have as a second language user can be fun ways to help learners understand their own motivations for language learning (see Figure 8.1).

What do all these different types of motivation mean for language learning? Motivation has been shown to be a powerful indicator of ultimate language learning success, surpassing even other well-known factors like starting age. Some research in this area has pointed out that learners who have strong integrative motivations or clear ideal selves tend to have better outcomes than learners who are motivated by instrumental purposes or by their ought-to selves. For example, a great deal of research has looked at learners' attitudes around writing in the TL, particularly in ESL contexts, and found that positive orientations toward writing are related to improved writing achievement. Given this, teachers might consider how to increase learners' integrative motivations by tailoring classwork to their interests, integrating cultural learning, and creating opportunities for learners to engage with the TL community through field trips, study abroad, or online collaborations.

Figure 8.1 Visualizing learner identities. This cat-learner imagines an ideal self and an ought-to self. Image by: Elizabeth Zonarich

8.2.2 What Researchers Know about Language Anxiety

Independent of their motivations for language learning, many individuals will also experience some type of language learning anxiety. Everyone experiences anxiety in some form, whether during a musical performance, after being asked to complete a math problem in front of the class, or even public speaking in a native language. Some individuals might consider themselves to be generally anxious people (with or without a clinical diagnosis), with their language learning experiences as no exception. Others may not identify as anxious individuals and may feel surprised to feel nervous when using their new language in specific contexts, like making a phone call to an advanced speaker in another language. In fact, speaking anxiety is the most common form of language learning anxiety among L2 learners. The more anxiety learners face, the worse their speaking performance will be. However, it is listening skills that are actually the most negatively impacted by anxiety. Researchers hypothesize that this is because of the natural time constraints of listening-oriented tasks. In contrast, learners' performance in reading-oriented tasks do not appear to be strongly impacted by anxiety, likely because of the greater freedom and flexibility of reading tasks.

In addition to type of language skills, other situational and contextual factors have also emerged as important determinants of language-related anxiety. They include insufficient preparation time, fear of evaluation, and pressure for perfection. Adjusting these factors may reduce the amount of anxiety learners feel and enhance their performance. For example, in a listening activity, a teacher may mitigate the amount of anxiety learners feel by giving them several opportunities to listen to a news interview so they have time to more efficiently direct their attentional resources toward comprehending the main ideas rather than panic.

Learner-specific factors, like age, have also been explored in relation to learner attitudes toward language development. Research shows that primary school learners are more likely to experience negative effects from language learning anxiety than their older counterparts. Older leaners are often more familiar with how to mediate their anxiety so that it does not compromise learning. However, older learners in higher-stakes learning contexts may still experience spikes in their reported anxiety levels. This finding highlights the complex and dynamic nature of language learning anxiety. Researchers have also explored the relationship between anxiety and motivation. For some, too much anxiety may impact their motivation to engage in positive language learning behaviors, like seeking feedback and negotiating for meaning (discussed in Chapter 1 and Chapter 2).

8.2.3 Language Motivation and Anxiety over Time

Because both motivation and anxiety levels are susceptible to change due to a combination of psychological and social factors, researchers tend to view both qualities as dynamic states rather than fixed traits in the language learning process. These dynamic states are influenced by a variety of factors. One of the

8.2 The Science: What the Research Says

factors that researchers have examined is the classroom environment itself. There is overwhelming evidence that positive and inclusive classrooms help facilitate a positive mindset and encourage behaviors that are beneficial for linguistic development. This includes using the TL, taking risks, seeking feedback, and connecting with peers. Based on these findings, researchers recommend that teachers be granted certain instructional freedom so that they can tailor their teaching pedagogy to the needs and interests of their learners, creating environments that minimize anxiety and maximize positive emotions like motivation and enjoyment.

Of course, with each new experience, whether it be moving from German I to German II or writing a five-paragraph essay after only ever having written one-paragraph responses, learners may feel different amounts of motivation and anxiety even in supportive classroom environments with trusted educators. Even within the same communicative modality (i.e., writing) adjustments to composition tasks have been shown to impact learners' anxiety. For example, some research has shown that reducing task complexity (using a simpler narrative task rather than an argumentative writing task) also led to reductions in learners' self-reported anxiety.

Experiences learners have with the TL outside of the classroom will also affect learners' feelings toward the language learning process in the classroom. Imagine a high school learner who mainly studied Arabic to strengthen her college applications was able to study abroad for a summer in Egypt. Her experience studying in Egypt, making friends, and getting to know a new community might impact her original instrumental motivations to learn Arabic. Now she might have more integrative motivations – to keep in touch with her new friends. She might also return to her Arabic class with less anxiety about speaking with her peers after having many positive experiences speaking to others in Egypt. Teachers can impact their learners' motivations and anxiety levels by providing rich language learning experiences that push them out of their comfort zones and toward new ways of seeing the utility of their new language skills. In the past ten years, technological innovations, specifically in the fields of **Computer-Assisted Language Learning (CALL)** and Mobile-Assisted Language Learning (MALL), have proven to be useful tools in motivating learners. Software with photo-shop, artificial intelligence (AI), or avatar-building capacities hold potential for helping learners develop their ideal L2 selves. One recent study had learners develop short animated videos in the TL where they created a virtual main character based on themselves. In the design process, learners were encouraged to build a protagonist that looked, moved, and behaved like themselves to help them see themselves as valid language users. Gaming platforms with virtual environments like Second Life and OpenSim have also been shown to boost learners' motivation levels and encourage them to engage in behaviors that are beneficial to language learning. The relationship between technology and language learning is discussed in greater detail in Chapter 19.

> **BOX 8.1 The Science! Points to Remember**
>
> - Motivation comes in a variety of forms and will vary in terms of how intrinsic vs. extrinsic and how instrumental vs. integrative it is.
> - All people learning a new language will experience anxiety at some point, but some learners have persistent language anxiety related to particular contexts.
> - Motivation and anxiety are not necessarily fixed over time – they can change based on experience.
> - Anxiety may present as trait, state, or situation-specific feelings.
> - Motivation and anxiety are not unidimensional; they fluctuate over a life, a semester, or even a class period.

8.3 The Science: What's Missing?

As you can see from reading about the different types of motivation and anxiety, there is no singular way to classify learners. So far, the majority of the research on motivation and anxiety in language learning contexts is descriptive, meaning that it primarily explores learner attitudes in different situations and the relationship between these attitudes and performance outcomes. It has yet to explore how certain instructional techniques may change attitudes, or how instructors can develop educational contexts that maximize motivation and minimize anxiety in pursuit of improved linguistic development. Some teachers might be interested in measuring their learners' fluctuating motivation or anxiety within their language classrooms. It can be difficult for researchers and teachers alike to pin down exactly what type of motivation a learner might have and how it might be impacting their language development. Likewise, there is no one way to examine learners' motivations or anxiety levels either. In practice, researchers have used many different tools to explore how different learners respond to different learning environments, learning tasks, and activities, and we have provided some examples that teachers could try below. Teachers should use the methods that work best for their learning population to find out what motivates or causes anxiety in their own learners. Other areas that have limited research so far include the following:

- Why some learners have domain-specific anxiety, for example anxiety for specific types of language use like writing, and the implications of that for language learning.
- Whether there is a relationship between anxiety and achievement, depending on the TL. Most studies that do exist are focused on English language learners, and so we don't know whether similar trends are also true in different language learning contexts and among more diverse language learner populations (i.e., HLLs discussed in Chapter 6).
- The characteristics of L2 tasks or activities as they contribute to learners' motivation/anxiety.
- Motivation and anxiety within learners who are not neurotypical (see Chapter 7).

- Motivational group dynamics – how learner–learner interaction impacts learner motivation (see Chapter 4).
- Long-term studies on how learners' motivation or anxiety levels evolve based on specific assessment practices (oral proficiency interviews, Advanced Placement exams; see Chapter 20) or pedagogical approaches (task-based language teaching vs. naturalistic approach vs. grammar–translation, see Chapter 16).

Motivation and anxiety are only two ways in which individual language learners can differ from one another. As you'll see in Chapter 9, many other factors interact with motivation and anxiety, like learners' prior learning experiences, personality traits, age, and aptitude for language learning. All these factors might work together to motivate or demotivate a language learner or increase or lower their anxiety levels. We cannot think about motivation or anxiety without thinking about learners' many characteristics. Teachers should consider the *whole* learner when they think about how individual differences impact how quickly or slowly they are learning a language compared with their peers.

8.4 The Art: Research-Based Strategies to Try

8.4.1 The Art of Measuring Learners' Internal States

Like researchers, teachers can use surveys to better understand their learners' motivation and anxiety levels. Understanding learners is the first step toward creating a learning environment that meets their needs and helps them achieve their linguistic goals. Several typical uses of surveys are presented below. The exemplar formats can be modified to best fit learner age and proficiency level, or the larger educational context.

- Explore learners' motivation for language learning. Collecting information on why learners are enrolled in language classes can help teachers pick topics and design activities that align with learners' needs and wants.
- Measure learners' orientation toward the target culture or community. This may help teachers select resources to bring into class that connect with learners' intrinsic motivation. This type of survey may also spark learners' curiosity, which may in turn increase their motivation. Teachers could include questions like these at the end of quizzes, journal entries, or as exit tickets at the end of class (see Table 8.1).

Table 8.1 Motivation questionnaire excerpt

Cultural interests
1. Do you like Korean music (e.g., pop music)?
2. Do you like watching Korean movies?
3. Do you like watching Korean TV shows?
4. Do you like Korean magazines, newspapers, or books?

Table 8.1 Continued

Attitudes to L2 community
5. Do you like meeting people from Korean-speaking countries?
6. Would you like to travel to Korea? Where would you like to visit in Korea?
7. Would you like to know more about people from Korean-speaking countries?
8. Do you like Korean foods? What kinds of foods do you like? What would you like to try next?

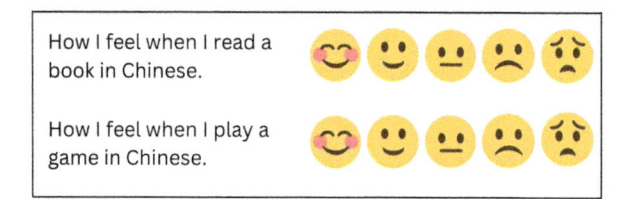

Figure 8.2 Learner motivation-anxiety exit ticket. This example of an exit ticket with a picture-based scale is more appropriate for younger or lower-level learners to share how they felt throughout class.

- For learners with more knowledge about the target culture, teachers may also add more specific questions like "Which K-pop band is your favorite?" or "What Korean TV shows have you watched before?" and tailor their instruction based on learners' responses.
  - Learners with developing literacy skills may write out their answers to these questions on paper exit tickets or virtual discussion boards. However, learners who do not yet read or write can point to visual aids, like smiley faces, to share their motivations (see Figure 8.2 for an example).
  - Grounding tasks in areas that learners already have background knowledge or experience in can boost motivation and lower anxiety.
- Ask learners to report on their anxiety levels during new activities or instructional choices. Knowing what types of corrective feedback styles or interactional features heighten or minimize their learners' anxiety can inform how teachers tailor their instruction in future classes. One of the most reliable and trusted L2 anxiety-related questionnaires asks learners to indicate their agreement to statements like "It embarrasses me to volunteer answers in my language class" or "Even if I am well-prepared for language class, I feel anxious about it." Teachers might use similar types of prompts to get to know their learners at the beginning of the school year, or to check in mid-semester.
- Collect learner responses to class with anxometers (anxiety "thermometers") to capture changes in their anxiety levels over the course of a lesson. The worksheet in Figure 8.3 illustrates how these anxometers can be designed and presented to learners. Each learner would receive a copy of the worksheet. Throughout the class

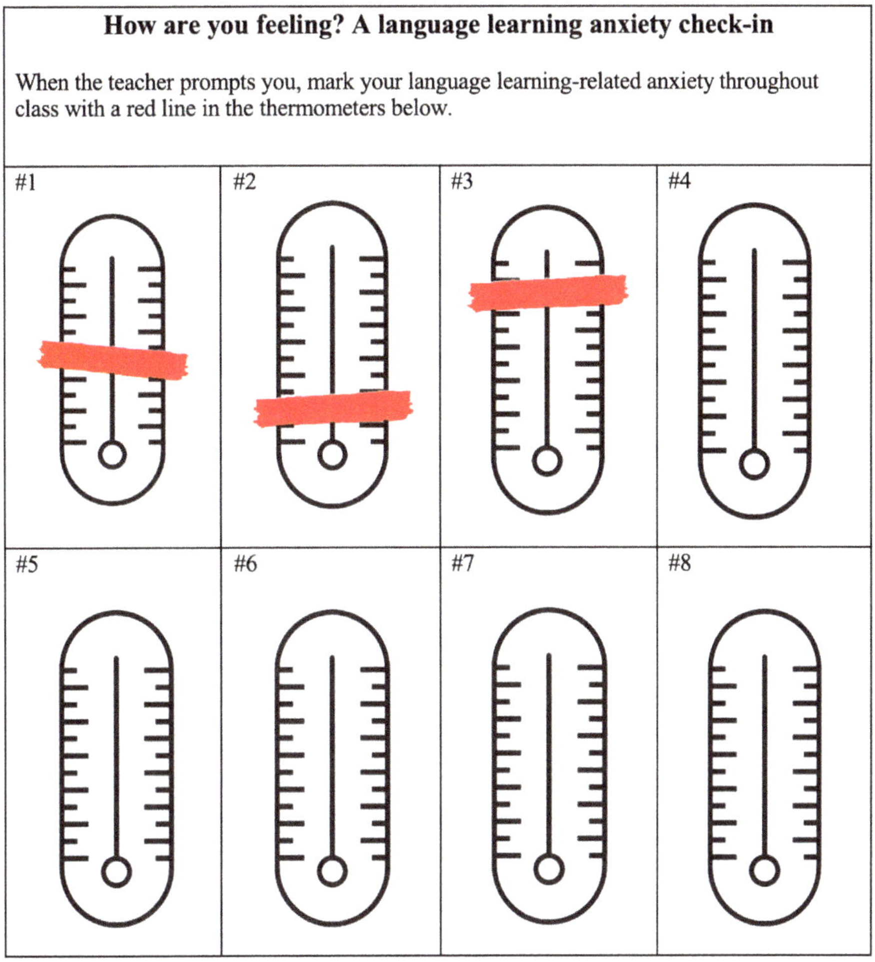

8.4 The Art: Research-Based Strategies to Try

How are you feeling? A language learning anxiety check-in

When the teacher prompts you, mark your language learning-related anxiety throughout class with a red line in the thermometers below.

| #1 | #2 | #3 | #4 |
| #5 | #6 | #7 | #8 |

Figure 8.3 Anxometer worksheet. A series of anxometers allows learners to share changes in their feelings over a period of time. In this example, the higher temperature on the anxometer relates to higher anxiety.

period, teachers would prompt learners to do a brief check-in where they mark their anxiety level on one of the anxometers, ranging from 0 (indicating the lowest anxiety) to 100 (the highest).

Learners can use this information as a self-reflection, too ("Why did that activity make me more anxious? Why do I feel more relaxed at the beginning of class, and more anxious at the end?"). (See Figure 8.4 for an example.)

Depending on the technology available in the classroom, teachers may also choose a more environmentally friendly and digital option, such as using interactive online presentation software such as Mentimeter (www.mentimeter.com/).

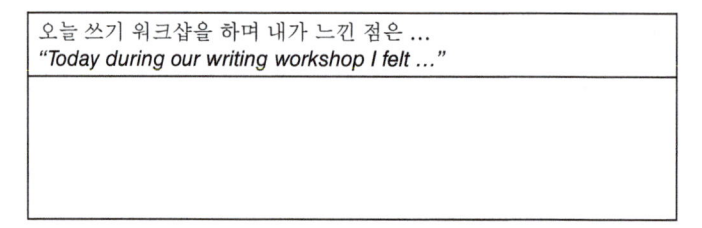

> 오늘 쓰기 워크샵을 하며 내가 느낀 점은 …
> *"Today during our writing workshop I felt …"*

Figure 8.4 Reflection journal prompt. A sample reflection journal prompt in Korean and in English encourages older learners to share more about their in-class experiences.

Introspective activities like the examples described can help teachers understand how to adapt the class to make sure learners are not experiencing too much anxiety (although some anxiety will be inevitable, so zero anxiety should *not* be the goal. Some language situations will be anxiety-inducing (e.g., presenting a task in front of the class as discussed in Section 8.2), and that is okay. When learners are aware of their fluctuating anxiety levels, they can better prepare themselves for success in class activities.

8.4.2 The Art of Creating a Responsive Classroom

With a better understanding of learners' motivation and anxiety, teachers can adapt their classroom culture to align with and increase learners' motivation while remaining sensitive to any language-related anxiety that may also be present.

- Consider your classroom environment.
    - A calm and relaxed classroom environment can limit learners' anxiety and help support learners' visions of themselves learning and being successful. This can be accomplished in many ways, including establishing a regular classroom routine. This may help more anxious language learners know what to expect throughout a lesson. Routines may also help learners sustain their motivation if they know they have certain activities or games to look forward to at predictable points in the lesson.
- Clearly state objectives.
    - Make sure to explicitly tell learners how much time and effort will be needed for an activity.
    - Tell learners why and the purpose of learning activities. Learners who see an activity as meaningful and worth their time and effort are more likely to be successful.
    - Clear goals allow learners to track their own achievement, promoting autonomy and limiting anxiety.
- Offer choices and options.
    - People tend to value activities or actions that they selected themselves and take more ownership over outcomes. Give learners the choice of activities or even assessments to help increase their motivation.
    - For example, younger learners might engage in "centers" or "stations" where they move from activity to activity around the classroom. For example, one

station might be "record yourself reading a story in the target language," a second station might be "do a crossword," and a third might be "play a word game with a partner." You can place a number of clothespins or other type of clip at each station depending on how many learners can be at each station at the same time. Then learners can go around the room and choose the station they want to explore. If there is a free clip, they can take it and complete the activity at that station. When they are done, they can remove the clip from that station and find a new station with a free clip. This allows learners ownership of their own activity choices, which has been shown to be associated with increased motivation to perform the activity. You might ask that learners make a choice, and then stay at their chosen station for a specific amount of time before switching.
- With older learners, targeted linguistic functions and communicative tasks (i.e., delivering a persuasive speech) can also be successfully achieved on a variety of topics. Encouraging older learners to pick their own topics based on their academic, professional, or extracurricular interests may help increase their motivation to engage. Coincidentally, it also helps create situations with informational gaps and nonlinguistic outcomes that are facilitative for language learning. Learn more about ideal task qualities in Chapter 17. While adult learners may be able to independently select and research topics, older adolescents may require some more scaffolding. In these settings, providing three to five topic options as well as a resource bank for each topic may be more manageable. Table 8.2 presents several tasks and topic combinations. The target communicative task is broken down into different topics and learners should be invited to choose the topic that is of most interest to them.
- Challenge your learners.
  - Tasks that are too easy or difficult may contribute to learners' motivation or anxiety levels.
    - To increase motivation: Focus on devising tasks or activities that are just slightly above your learners' current level so they are challenged without becoming demotivated. This is similar to thinking about anxiety; a little anxiety is okay since learners will become more aware of their own speech and

Table 8.2 Thematic topic choices

Communicative task	Thematic topics
To give step-by-step instructions on …	How to make a recipe
	How to play a favorite sport
	How to be a successful student
To deliver a persuasive speech on …	Why pets should be allowed in school
	Why homework should be optional
	Why every student needs recess
To identify main ideas in a story about …	Celebrity house sizes and prices
	School lunch menus
	Popular social media applications

pay close attention to the conversation. Too much anxiety, however, will negatively impact their ability to listen and speak.
- If there is a specific task that learners are reporting causes spikes in their anxiety, make small alterations that simplify it. This may include allowing learners more time to complete the task or giving them access to their notes or other resources or providing rehearsal/practice time.
  ○ Promote learners' autonomy, teach self-regulation strategies, focus on taking responsibility for their own learning (see Chapter 5 for more on developing learning strategies).
- Integrate more small-group work (see Chapter 4).
  ○ Some research shows that small-group work invokes less anxiety than whole-class or individual activities.
  ○ For example, building in additional peer-to-peer writing workshops before learners are required to submit a final draft of their writing may minimize anxiety surrounding writing skills.
  ○ Another way to get learners writing together is through introducing dialogic journal writing, where pairs write and respond to each other in their journals. Research has shown that this type of task not only can reduce feelings of anxiety but can also increase learners' ease and comfort when writing in the TL.

8.4.3 The Art of Connecting Learner, Language, and Culture

- Make TL cultural knowledge and experiences central to language learning to help learners develop a stronger sense of their future "ideal" selves.
  ○ Field trips, like going to a community restaurant representing the TL culture (bonus if learners can order in the language), study abroad opportunities (even short-term experiences), or online collaborations (pen pals from the TL community, telecollaboration where learners are partnered to do activities with peers who are learning their first language, L1) are all ways to increase integrative motivation by demonstrating the value of membership in a TL community.
- Cultivate strong relationships with your learners.
  ○ Research shows that strong learner–teacher relationships limit anxiety. Find out what your learners are interested in and how you can demonstrate your support. For example, attending a soccer game or an art show. When learners feel supported, they are more likely to envisage success for themselves.
- Be positive, encourage learners to try their best.
  ○ The research shows that when learners believe they can do something, they are more likely to meet their own expectations.
  ○ Demonstrate progress visually – have learners keep records of what progress they are making toward their self-identified goals. This could be fun, like steps on a ladder or a path on a map. (See Figure 8.5 for an example.)
  ○ Cultivate an environment where learners are comfortable taking risks and making mistakes.
- Provide consistent feedback.
  ○ Feedback on learners' language or performance can help keep them motivated.

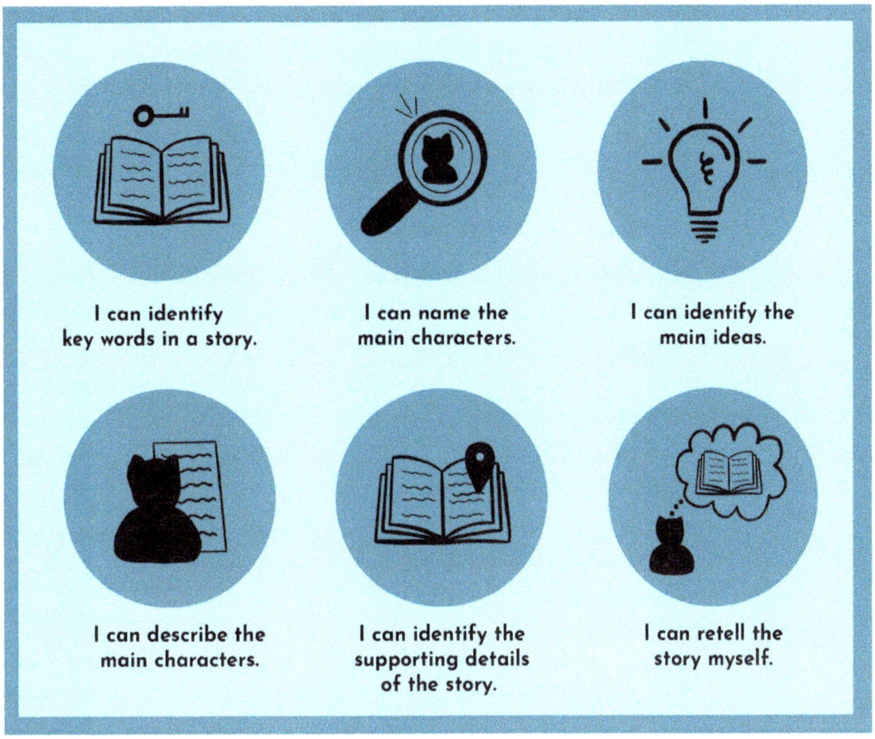
I can identify key words in a story.
I can name the main characters.
I can identify the main ideas.
I can describe the main characters.
I can identify the supporting details of the story.
I can retell the story myself.

Figure 8.5 Learning progress checklist. Clearly articulate learning goals to students. Image by: Elizabeth Zonarich

- See Chapter 3 for more about feedback on language learning.
- Incorporate more opportunities for peer-to-peer feedback, computer-mediated feedback, asynchronous feedback, or a combination of all three. Using these feedback methods, as opposed to only teacher feedback, has been shown in some populations to reduce learner anxiety and increase self-confidence.

8.5 Troubleshooting: How the Science Informs the Art

Mr. C teaches a Level 1 high school French class in a district where two years of a foreign language are mandatory for graduation and university admission. As a result, many of his learners are only enrolled in the class because it is a required course. Mr. C tries to motivate his learners by integrating games, skits, music, and other activities that he thinks would motivate this age group. However, sometimes learners seem to hesitate to participate even when they know the vocabulary and material well.

Because Mr. C's learners do not bring high levels of motivation to their coursework, he may consider incorporating some reflective activities that call on learners to explore their future "ideal" selves, thereby making connections between how learning the French language can help them arrive at their aspirational selves. Mr. C might also consider inviting his learners to take a more active role in choosing course topics and daily activities by asking them to complete surveys on what they would like to get out of the class. With this information, Mr. C can make sure that the course syllabus aligns with learners' needs and wants.

Because learners must receive a passing grade in order to complete their language requirement, learners have a lot of anxiety around submitting assessments; however, this anxiety does not translate into productive learning habits or practices.

To address his learners' anxiety, Mr. C may consider polling his learners to find out if there is any particular type of assessment (speaking vs. writing, interpersonal vs. presentational, etc.) that they find to be particularly anxiety-provoking. If possible, Mr. C could add intermediary stages where learners are able to submit drafts for additional feedback. These intermediary stages may involve peer-to-peer workshops or peer-to-teacher workshops. The chance to review their work may not only minimize anxiety but also boost motivation as learners receive concrete steps on how to take their work to the next level. Mr. C may also consider dedicating some class time toward discussing some of the strategies of effective language learners discussed in Chapter 5.

8.6 The Science: Points to Remember

- There are many factors that impact learners' motivation and anxiety levels. Some of these may be language learning specific and others may have nothing to do with the classroom. Providing learners with strategies (see Chapter 5) to manage their own internal landscape during class may help them sustain the emotions that are positively associated with language learning (i.e., motivation) and reduce others (i.e., anxiety) that are negatively associated with language learning.
- Learners with clear visions about their future L2 selves are more motivated and often experience more language learning success than their counterparts who do not have a strong sense of how language skills may relate to their future selves.
- Anxiety impacts learners' performance differently depending on the task they are expected to complete (i.e., watching a video vs. reading an article).
- New language learning demands may heighten language learning anxiety, even for learners' who previously had not been feeling anxious.

8.7 Questions to Consider

1. What factors impact your learners' anxiety and motivation levels?
2. If you teach a range of grades, what changes in learners' anxiety and motivation have you noticed as they progress through the course levels?
3. Think of a teaching moment when all your learners seemed highly motivated. What type of classroom environment and learning experiences led up to this moment? How could you apply this information to recreate a similar moment in your next class?
4. Have you ever had an explicit conversation with your learners about their language learning motivation or anxiety levels? Why or why not? What information from this chapter do you think it could be beneficial to share with your learners?

8.8 The Science of Language Learning: Research Supporting the Points Made in This Chapter

Dewaele, J. M., Witney, J., Satio, K., & Dewaele, L. (2018). Foreign language enjoyment and anxiety: The effect of teacher and learner variables. *Language Teaching Research*, 22(6), 676–697. https://doi.org/10.1177/1362168817692161.

Within the larger theme of learner emotion on SLA, these researchers pay special attention to the studies that have examined the relationship between classroom environments and younger learners' anxiety levels. In this study, they look at how 189 adolescent world language learners of French, Spanish, German, and 12 other L2s experience anxiety and enjoyment. The learners completed a survey on their proficiency levels, attitudes, use of the TL in class, and class environment. The results indicated that more advanced learners reported less anxiety and more enjoyment, that more positive learners had less anxiety and more enjoyment, and that learners could feel both high enjoyment and high anxiety levels simultaneously. In addition, there was a positive relationship between learners' enjoyment and whether they felt positively toward their teachers. However, there was no relationship between learners' anxiety and their attitudes toward their teachers. Other factors were more influential in triggering anxiety, including peer relationships, attitudes toward the language itself, and proficiency level. Based on these results, Dewaele and his co-authors recommend that teachers focus on sparking learners' curiosity and maximizing their enjoyment of class rather than fixate on minimizing anxiety, which, according to these findings, is attributed to factors outside teacher control.

Mahmoodi, M. H., & Yousefi, M. (2021). Second language motivation research 2010–2019: A synthetic exploration. *The Language Learning Journal*, 1–24. https://doi.org/10.1080/09571736.2020.1869809.

This article reviewed 100 studies on motivation in second language learning that have been published since 2010. In this synthesis, Mahmoodi and Yousefi describe all the ways in which language learning motivation has been characterized over the past decade. They also present the different theoretical and analytical frameworks that researchers have used to explore learners' motivation. Findings emphasize the complexity of both defining, measuring, and influencing learners' motivation levels. It is this very complexity that has captured the attention of both researchers and teachers alike. Finally, the authors conclude their synthesis with a list of topic areas that are yet to be thoroughly explored, including the causes, demotivation strategies for remotivation, and teachers' motivational practices. Citations for studies included in the synthesis are included so that readers may investigate the sources that are of interest to them.

Rassaei, E. (2015). Oral corrective feedback, foreign language anxiety and L2 development. *System*, 49, 98–109. https://doi.org/10.1016/j.system.2015.01.002.

It is already known that both recasts and metalinguistic feedback can be effective for promoting the development of L2 knowledge. This researcher examined whether these two types of feedback, recasts and metalinguistic, had different effects on L2 development based on their self-reported L2 anxiety levels. Rassaei found that learners with high anxiety benefited most from recasts, which is a type of implicit corrective feedback, which learners probably considered a gentler form or receiving corrections for oral L2 production. Meanwhile, learners with low anxiety unsurprisingly benefited from both types of feedback but benefitted most from metalinguistic corrective feedback. Ultimately, there is no single most effective corrective feedback to promote L2 development for all learners, even in a single instructional context. We must always consider L2 anxiety levels and keep other such individual differences in mind.

For more resources, including more sample lesson plans, videos, and other ideas, visit our companion website: www.cambridge.org/BryfonskiMackey.

9 How can aptitude be leveraged for language learning?

KEY QUESTIONS
- **The Science: How do learners vary in terms of their aptitude for language learning?**
- **The Art: Aptitude, memory, and attention. What do they mean for teaching?**
- **(When) Should I assess aptitude, memory, and attention? How?**
- **Can I increase learners' aptitude to help them learn faster?**
- **How does creativity relate to language learning?**

9.1 Voices from the Classroom

9.1.1 Scenario 1: An Intensive Polish Class

Mr. K teaches an intensive Polish class at a language institution that hosts future missionary workers, armed service members, humanitarian workers, and other travelers who need a high level of language proficiency on an accelerated timeline. Possibly because of the urgency and immediateness of their language needs, most of his learners are diligent and hard-working in their Polish studies. However, he notices that some of his learners have an easier time remembering new words and paying attention to the accuracy of their production. Those learners generally perform the best in their classes and attain the highest level of proficiency offered at the institute. He wonders whether this ease is something that comes to them naturally, if they have studied languages in the past, which makes their task easier, or if they've simply developed extremely effective memorization techniques. While he does administer his own surveys at the end of his courses, asking questions about what they enjoyed most/least about the course, how they studied the material outside of class, how they plan to use their Polish, etc., none of those data seem to tell him anything about why some of his learners achieve outsized success. He knows that things like memory and attention can vary from person to person but wonders whether they could be used in a way that improves outcomes for those learners who seem less adept at learning languages. How can Mr. K match his instructional approach to his learners' aptitude levels? Is there anything he can do to better support his learners without a strong aptitude for language learning?

9.1.2 Scenario 2: A French World Language Class

Ms. F teaches a beginning French-as-a-world-language class in a secondary school. There is one learner who, despite demonstrating strong reading and writing skills in French, consistently seems to not pay attention to directions when they're given to the class in the target language (TL). Each time Ms. F has finished explaining an activity or task to the entire class and starts to walk around the room to monitor learners' progress, this learner consistently approaches her and asks, in English, "Ms. F ... what are we doing?" After months of repeatedly providing additional one-on-one instructions to this learner, in both French and English, Ms. F becomes frustrated. It seems that the learner is deliberately choosing not to listen to the instructions with the rest of the class as an attempt to gain special attention from the teacher. One day, Ms. F teaches a new vocabulary word to the entire class and has them repeat the word after her. This word contains a nasal vowel, which is unfamiliar to L1 speakers of English. This learner tries to repeat the word, but Ms. F can immediately tell that something is off – at that moment, Ms. F realizes that the issue with the learner's ability to follow directions is not due to attention or behavior, but rather because this learner is experiencing a phonological processing issue; she cannot identify French sounds quickly enough to parse through the meaning of Ms. F's words as she addresses the class. While Ms. F technically knows that phonological processing is one of the many skills under the umbrella of language learning "aptitude," she still wonders, "What does this mean for my learner, my class – and how can I help?"

9.2 The Science: What the Research Says

All people learn at different rates, whether they are learning to ride a bike, pass an algebra exam, or learn a new language. This is because every person brings a wealth of unique characteristics, or **individual differences**, to each learning situation. People vary based on their prior experiences, personality, age, motivation to learn (as we covered in Chapter 8), learning difference (as in Chapter 7), and other factors. One individual difference that research has found to be important for language learning is language learning **aptitude** – the range of abilities that predict how quickly or easily someone will learn a language compared to others. Unlike motivation or anxiety, which can vary based on the situation, lesson, activities, interlocutor, or even by day, research on language learning aptitude seems to suggest aptitude may be more of a fixed characteristic, especially for adult learners. This is often known as a learner "trait" as opposed to a learner "state," such as satisfaction with one's language learning progress. Simply put, states can change but traits are less changeable.

9.2 The Science: What the Research Says

Language learning aptitude is related to learners' abilities to recognize and discriminate between new sounds, detect and analyze grammatical patterns, remember new second language (L2) words, and related skills (see Box 9.1). All learners will have slightly different aptitudes for language learning that will enhance or hinder their learning in the myriad of instructional situations we create in the classroom. It can be useful for teachers to understand the ways in which their learners vary in terms of their aptitude so that they can tailor language and strategy instruction to better meet learners' individual needs. One way to do this is to administer a language aptitude test; the most commonly used aptitude test in second language acquisition (SLA) research is the LLAMA, a collection of free, online aptitude tests targeting each of the components of language aptitude (https://www.lognostics.co.uk/tools/LLAMA_3/). It's important to remember, however, that these tests should not be used in high-stakes enrollment decisions (e.g., inclusion or exclusion from a language program) but rather can be used by teachers to better understand their students' language learning strengths and areas of potential difficulty.

BOX 9.1 Language Aptitude Self-Assessment

- *Phonetic abilities*
    - How well can I distinguish between different sounds?
    - How well can I detect the boundaries between (un)familiar words?
    - How well can I make connections between sounds and the symbols representing them?
    - How well can I remember new sounds?
- *Grammatical and reasoning abilities*
    - How well can I identify the grammatical functions of words in sentences (e.g., verbs, nouns, adjectives)?
    - How easily can I work out the rules and patterns in a new language?
    - How accurate are my predictions and inferences about novel rules and patterns in a new language?
- *Memory abilities*
    - How quickly can I memorize the meanings of new words?
    - How long can I remember the meanings of new words?
    - How long can I "hold onto" new words in conversation (e.g., hear and use novel words or sounds)?

Why and how does language aptitude support language learning? For learning to happen, learners must be exposed to some input (Chapter 2) and pay **attention** to it, so they notice it. Key to this process of attention and noticing is a type of memory called working memory. One way to understand working memory is to think of it as the ability to "juggle" tasks or attend to multiple tasks at once; by contrast, we can think of long-term memory as our ability to store information and take it with us into new tasks. Those with higher levels of working memory

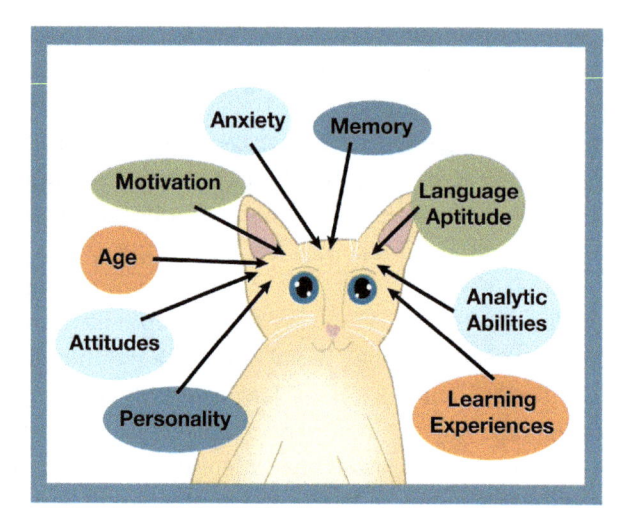

Figure 9.1 Anatomy of a language learner. There are many factors that impact how an individual learns a new language. Image by: Elizabeth Zonarich

can "juggle" more, and those with higher levels of long-term memory have a bigger "backpack" to store language information.

Researchers believe the different kinds of memory play an important role in helping learners notice relevant language input (working memory) and internalize it for subsequent production (long-term memory). This is because if learners have larger memory capacities, they have a greater chance at processing and understanding input, making it more likely to integrate into their language skills. All this happens without learners necessarily trying hard to remember! A related aptitude skill is language-analytic ability – recognizing grammatical patterns and deducing the underlying structures. Learners with strong language-analytic abilities will also be better at integrating new language with their current knowledge. High-aptitude learners will be able to do all of this faster and more automatically than learners with lower aptitude scores (see Figure 9.1).

9.2.1 What Does Language Aptitude Mean for Language Teachers?

While many of us have encountered friends, family, learners, and school stakeholders who think some people are "just not good at learning languages," researchers tend to challenge this fatalistic notion of language aptitude – everyone can learn languages! Instead, researchers suggest viewing aptitude as a tool to inform where learners allocate their time and energy while learning languages. Teachers might consider playing memory games or designing activities that test learners' ability to interpret and retain new language input to get a sense of which learners have higher or lower memory capacities. If time allows at the beginning of the school year, teachers can also administer freely available aptitude tests like the LLAMA and provide learners with their results to facilitate a meta-conversation about how to leverage their highest-scoring aptitude components to their advantage. Many schools also administer career aptitude testing for learners who are nearing the end of secondary schooling to help them discern which career(s) they might be interested in pursuing; tests like the LLAMA could be integrated into those test administration days, with language aptitude scores being added to the learners' profile of results. There is also some research that has linked aptitude with creativity, or the ability to create new products or ideas that are novel or useful in specific contexts. Creativity isn't just about the number of new ideas someone has. It is also about how original, flexible, and elaborate their ideas are. Some very new research links highly creative individuals with higher language aptitude as well. In interactive situations, creative learners tend to use more out-of-the-box strategies and ideas to solve problems using more complex language.

Importantly, assessing learners' language aptitude can help teachers differentiate instruction and increase student success in the classroom. For example, learners with lower working-memory capacity may benefit from more explicit instruction about the new language, as they will be less able to pick up on patterns in the input naturally. By contrast, learners with higher working-memory capacity are more likely to notice and integrate new patterns into their developing language schema because of their increased ability to "juggle" meaning and language forms in the input. When providing feedback on written assignments, teachers might consider providing more explicit feedback for their learners with lower working-memory capacity and more implicit feedback for their learners with higher working memory.

BOX 9.2 The Science! Points to Remember

- Language learning aptitude comprises phonetic abilities, grammatical and reasoning abilities, and memory abilities.
- Language aptitude is not the only determiner of success – the strategies learners develop over the course of language study will impact the ease with which they continue to learn.
- Learners with higher language learning aptitude may learn faster and with more ease than their peers with lower language learning aptitude.
- Research has also linked an individual's creativity levels with their language learning aptitude.
- Teachers can use what they know about their learners' language learning aptitude to inform how they provide feedback and which learning strategies they bring into class.

9.3 The Science: What's Missing?

Can learners improve or increase their own aptitude through studying or practice? As we said above, many researchers think of aptitude as a fixed characteristic that can't be improved through teaching or training; however, it is important to note that not all researchers agree with this. Some believe that certain aspects of aptitude might be improved through targeted training. Since there is disagreement about this point, it is unclear how much time or energy teachers should spend on trying to increase learners' aptitude and we cannot endorse spending a large amount of class time on activities designed to increase learners' working-memory capacities, language-analytic ability, or other aptitude-related skills.

We also don't have unequivocal information from the science in terms of how (or if) tailoring teaching to adjust for lower-or higher-aptitude learners can help them learn better or more efficiently. This is a relatively new area of research, and while there are some signs that this approach can be effective, it is far from certain. Teachers should plan to investigate individual needs in each class and adjust when new techniques seem to be working or not working. Collecting "data," in the form of notes, grades, or scores in games/activities that are repeated, can help teachers keep track of what kinds of teaching strategies seem to benefit learners who are suspected of having lower or higher aptitude. For learners who have undergone testing for specific learning difficulties, parents may already have information on their child's working memory, phonemic discrimination abilities, etc., and they may be willing to share this information to develop personalized plan for their child's success in the language classroom.

9.4 The Art: Research-Based Strategies to Try

There are many engaging games a teacher can play in class to assess and leverage learners' language learning aptitude. These games can be altered as needed for different ages and proficiency levels.

9.4.1 Play a Memory Game to Assess Learners' Memory Abilities

- There are a variety of games that can be played that test learners' memory using language. For example, the classic card game "concentration" with pairs of key vocabulary words or words with matching pictures shuffled face down in a pile. Learners take turns flipping over cards and flipping them back over. When they remember seeing a pair, they have to say the word and uncover the pair. Whoever gains the highest number of pairs wins. This type of game tests both visual–spatial memory (where are the cards) and the memory of the words (see Figure 9.2).

Find the definition!

Wallet	2	3	4
5	6	A place where you keep your money and credit cards.	8

Figure 9.2 Vocabulary memory game. Incorporate memory games using the target language needed for the real-word tasks learners are working on accomplishing.

- This kind of game could be enhanced by using categories of words or phrases that demonstrate certain patterns in the language you are teaching (e.g., adjectives vs. nouns or preterit versus imperfect verbs). This would enable learners to seek out patterns in the pairs of cards they see.
    - Note: While playing this kind of game may strengthen learners' metalinguistic awareness (i.e., noticing verb endings), that improved awareness does not directly translate into learners' communicative competence (i.e., narrating a story in multiple time frames).

9.4.2 Use an Imitation Task to Test Learners' Memory for New Sounds

- Ask learners to repeat back increasingly long and complex sentences in the TL. When used with unfamiliar language, this type of task has been shown to be a reliable measurement of the memory component of aptitude because learners cannot rely on meaning to help assist with recalling what they heard. When researchers develop nonsense words for this kind of task, it is called a "nonword repetition task," but completely unfamiliar TL words could also be used with very novice language learners, as they do not have any sense of what the words mean yet.
- "Telephone" is another fun linguistic memory game that also involves elements of imitation. Standing in a circle, the first student comes up with a sentence in the TL and whispers it to the student on their right. That student then repeats what they heard to the student on *their* right, and so on until everyone has heard the sentence. The last person says the sentence they heard aloud. Learners can try to improve their ability to hear and remember sentences (and even race to complete the task more quickly), which tests their memory for hearing and repeating sounds in the TL.
- Running dictation is another activity that calls on learners' phonetic and memory abilities. Split the class into partners and instruct one half of each pair to stand on one side of the classroom (or a hallway, gymnasium, courtyard, etc., depending on the teaching context). Give that group of learners a text appropriate for their age and proficiency level (e.g., a short joke, a poem, a chorus of a song, or a passage from a story). Then, instruct the other half of each pair to take a pencil and stand along the opposite wall, where there is a blank piece of paper taped on the wall for each pair. The far learners must then run/walk between their partner (with the complete text) and the opposite wall with the blank paper. This student must listen as the text is read aloud, remember each sentence, and write on the blank page based on what they remember. The pair who completes the transcription most quickly and most accurately wins! Running dictation tests student memory for hearing sounds, remembering them, and then transcribing them accurately.

Keep in mind that research has shown that learners are more likely to remember and reproduce language accurately when they have a more developed understanding of that language. In other words, these activities described above are likely to tell you more about a learner's *aptitude* when used with beginner learners and more about a learner's *proficiency level* when used with more advanced learners. As a result, using a running dictation with an advanced-level class may be less helpful for determining learners' phonetic and memory abilities, but would indicate which words, phrases, or structures learners have yet to master.

9.4.3 Play a Puzzle Inference Game to Assess Learners' Language-Analytic Abilities

- One of the aspects of aptitude that teachers sometimes overlook is learners' ability to infer or deduce rules about the language from input. Even when input is comprehensible (e.g., referring to visuals or glosses of new TL words to discuss an unfamiliar topic), learners differ in their ability to both attend to meaning *and* notice grammatical aspects of the language. Thus, some learners may exhibit high levels of comprehension but have much lower command of aspects of production that makes it difficult for them to interact in meaningful ways with others in the classroom. Rather than simply waiting for the learners to get enough input for them to eventually notice crucial aspects of language, purposefully crafting activities that facilitate noticing can speed up this process without getting caught in traditional grammatical activities.

9.4.4 Play Imaginative Games to Assess Learners' Cognitive Creativity

- How creative are you or your learners? Try this fun and easy creativity test called the paperclip test (Figure 9.3).
- *The Paperclip Test:* Ask learners to think of a paper clip and, in three minutes, write as many new uses as possible for a paper clip as they can think of. (If learners are younger and the paperclip prompt is too abstract, give them ten empty shapes, like triangles or diamonds, and ask them to draw whatever they want in as many as possible in three minutes. You can use the same scoring system below and reference the example in Box 9.3). Count their score in the following dimensions of creativity:
  - **Fluency:** *the number of different alternate uses.* Count the number of ideas or things drawn for a fluency score.

Figure 9.3 The Paperclip Test. The test offers insight into learners' cognitive creativity, which research suggests is relevant to language learning! Image by: Elizabeth Zonarich

9.4 The Art: Research-Based Strategies to Try

- **Originality**: *how unusual or unique the ideas were.* Look at the ideas/drawings across the entire class. Give a point to each idea that nobody else had.
- **Flexibility**: *the number of different types or categories.* Count the number of categories the ideas fell into. For example, five different "tool" uses for the paper clip count as one category "tools." Five drawn faces count as one category "faces." Give a point for each category they used.
- **Elaboration**: *the number of additional details provided for each idea.* Count how many details were included in each idea. Was it more than the absolute minimum? For example, were details such as earrings, hair, or other details included in a drawing of a face? Was the paperclip used for something simple or something complex? Give a point for each extra detail included.

BOX 9.3 Sample Responses to the Paperclip Test

Learner 1	Learner 2	Learner 3
• earrings • necklace (use several linked together) • bracelet • hang up a picture • eject a SIM card from a smartphone • hold papers together • replace the metal tab on a zipper • hold thin cables together	• put papers together • mark a page in a book • help you flip between sections in a book • poke a hole in paper	• chain • bracelet
Fluency: 8 ideas (high degree of fluency) **Originality**: 5 out of 8 (most ideas are original, i.e., not mentioned by other learners) **Flexibility**: 5 categories (jewelry, hanging, ejecting, holding together, zipper) **Elaboration**: some elaboration (e.g., direction to use several paperclips linked together for a necklace, specified what the SIM card would be ejected from)	**Fluency**: 4 ideas (mid-level degree of fluency) **Originality**: 3 out of 4 (most ideas are original, i.e., not mentioned by other learners) **Flexibility**: 1 category (all ideas stayed within the realm of books and paper) **Elaboration**: little elaboration (e.g., hole is poked in a particular substance – paper)	**Fluency**: 2 ideas (low degree of fluency) **Originality**: 1 out of 2 (but the two ideas are almost the same – you use a chain to make a bracelet) **Flexibility**: 1 category (all ideas stayed within the realm of jewelry) **Elaboration**: no elaboration
Fluency = 8 Originality = 5 Flexibility = 5 Elaboration = 2 Total = **20**	Fluency = 4 Originality = 3 Flexibility = 1 Elaboration = 1 Total = **9**	Fluency = 2 Originality = 1 Flexibility = 1 Elaboration = 0 Total = **4**

Unlike in other chapters, the descriptions of games listed in Section 9.4 are not intended to maximize language acquisition. For the most part, they do not provide much comprehensible input, they do not offer many opportunities to negotiate meaning, and there may be very little interactional feedback involved, depending on whether learners play in the TL. Language learning takes place during communicative interactions where learners are engaged with using the language to accomplish larger, nonlinguistic goals. As a result, these activity ideas (note the use of the term "activity" and not communicative "task"!) should be used sparingly as *supports* to help teachers and learners understand language learning aptitude, rather than as the focal point of a lesson or unit of study.

9.5 Troubleshooting: How the Science Informs the Art

9.5.1 Scenario 1: An Intensive Polish Class

What Mr. K has noticed is the differing levels of language learning aptitude among his learners. Mr. K can consider incorporating some exercises in Section 9.4 (Research-Based Strategies to Try) to get a sense of his learners' strengths and struggles related to language learning. He can use what he learns about his learners to inform what sorts of exercises and activities he includes in his class.

If Mr. K notices that many of his learners have high reasoning abilities but low memory abilities, he can add more opportunities for his learners to leverage their reasoning abilities to create memory aids like mnemonic devices, word associations, word families, and other ways to compensate for their weaker memory skills. Since his learners are older, Mr. K might also consider sharing what he has learned about memory and attention with his learners so that they are better able to reflect on their own learning and become more autonomous learners. For example, if a student realizes they have lower phonetic abilities, they might choose to dedicate more time working on noticing the differences between different sounds as they study. However, Mr. K and his learners should keep in mind that there is no conclusive research on whether different instructional strategies or exercises can significantly impact aptitude. For that reason, Mr. K should continue to experiment with his classes and maintain open lines of communication with his learners so that they can share which in-class activities are beneficial and which are not.

9.5.2 Scenario 2: A French World Language Class

Ms. F suspects she has a learner with a phonological processing issue, which might be the reason why the learner is "checked out" when Ms. F gives directions to the whole class in French.

The first step would be for Ms. F to make sure that this learner's difficulty relates to language aptitude, not only pronunciation. At the moment, Ms. F is assuming that the learner cannot identify the nasal vowel simply because the learner cannot reproduce the teacher's pronunciation in speaking. Remember in Box 9.1, there are other guiding questions that teachers could consider in order to assess their learners' phonetic abilities. For example, another indicator of phonetic ability is to make connections between sounds and the symbols representing them. In this case, Ms. F could further implement a listening activity. Ms. F could read out a word to the class and ask the learners to write the word with the correct spelling. Then, if the learner is still having trouble distinguishing the nasal vowel sound in listening in addition to pronunciation, Ms. F has more evidence to prove that language aptitude (for phonetic abilities) is having an influence on the learner. Ms. F can now differentiate instruction for this learner. For example, Ms. F can provide more explicit feedback for this learner and try to find opportunities throughout the semester to practice the learner's areas of difficulty (in this case, nasal vowels). Finally, Ms. F should remember that language aptitude is not the sole determiner of success in language learning. Ms. F can identify and harness the learner's individual strengths in order to help them continue their language learning journey.

9.6 The Science: Points to Remember

- The research is inconclusive on whether certain instructional practices or study habits can significantly improve language learning aptitude. Even among researchers who believe that this kind of aptitude can be improved, research still doesn't offer any indication of how much effort is required to make a positive change.
- If teachers or learners are curious about their own language learning aptitude, there are lots of different games and exercises they can complete to reveal their strengths and challenges as language learners.
  - A "low" language aptitude does NOT mean that a student is incapable of learning a language. It just indicates that it may take more time and explicit effort.
- Engaging in the process of learning another language has been shown to strengthen learners' future language learning readiness should they choose to learn another language later in life.
- Different student aptitude profiles (i.e., high phonetic ability and low grammatical aptitude vs. high grammatical aptitude and low phonetic ability) may benefit from different instructional strategies. Experiment with your classes, ask learners to reflect on their experiences, and take notes on what you observe to inform later instructional choices you make.

9.7 Questions to Consider

1. Given your current curriculum and final assessments, what kind of language learning aptitude is valued most in your classes?
2. What support and resources do you have available for learners who may (by no fault of their own) be learning the L2 at a slower pace and with more difficulty?

3. To what extent does your grading/assessment system account for learners of different language learning aptitudes? After reading this chapter, are there any changes you might make?
4. What would you say to a student who comes to you frustrated because they feel they have to work harder than their peers and still feel "behind" in class? What would you say to the student who finds class easy and advances more than their peers?

9.8 The Science of Language Learning: Research Supporting the Points Made in This Chapter

Sok, S., Shin, H. W., & Do, J. (2021). Exploring which test-taker characteristics predict young L2 learners' performance on listening and reading comprehension tests. *Language Testing, 38*(8), 378–400. https://doi.org/10.1177/0265532221991134.

Language learning aptitude has the potential to inform many subfields within applied linguistics. This study explores how aptitude may relate to second language acquisition and language testing for young language learners. A group of Korean adolescents who were learning English completed a series of listening and reading tests. Their scores were then analyzed to see whether their language learning aptitude, as well as other factors like their motivation, gender, and socioeconomic status, could predict their performance on these tests. Both aptitude and working memory were found to be strong predictors of how the learners performed on their language assessments.

Wen, Z., & Skehan, P. (2021). Stages of acquisition and the P/E Model of Working Memory: Complementary or contrasting approaches to foreign language aptitude? *Annual Review of Applied Linguistics, 41*, 6–24. https://doi.org/10.1017/S0267190521000015.

This source considers how working memory, input processing, and language-analytic ability contribute to learners' language aptitude. Through exploring early and current conceptualizations of aptitude, the authors aim to strengthen readers' understandings of aptitude and how it can be measured. First, they describe the original understanding of aptitude, the Stages Approach, developed by John Carroll in 1990. Then, a more recent model for aptitude, the Phonological/Executive Model developed by Zhisheng Wen in 2012, is introduced. A comparison of both models highlights how they can complement each other and support future research about how aptitude influences language learning efforts.

Yeldham, M., & Gao, Y. (2021). Examining whether learning outcomes are enhanced when L2 learners' cognitive styles match listening instruction methods. *System, 97*, 102435. https://doi.org/10.1016/j.system.2020.102435.

This article explores a theory that applies language learning aptitude to instructional practices in the language classroom. The Aptitude-Treatment-Interaction (ATI) theory states that learners have unique strengths and that when they are taught in a way that aligns with these strengths, learning outcomes are improved. In this study, university-level English language learners learned better when they experienced an instructional approach that matched with their cognitive learning style. These findings call for more research on how individualized learning experiences, such as online learning modules, can support linguistic development.

For more resources, including more sample lesson plans, videos, and other ideas, visit our companion website: www.cambridge.org/BryfonskiMackey.

10 It's much harder to learn (and teach) my language compared to other languages, and it takes much longer. How can I compensate for these difficulties with my learners?

KEY QUESTIONS
- **The Science:** Is it actually much harder to learn (and teach) some languages compared to others?
- **The Art:** How can I compensate for first vs. target language differences in my teaching?
- The language I teach has a different script than my learners are used to in their first language. How should I account for those differences?

10.1 Voices from the Classroom

Mrs. J is an Arabic teacher in a high school that also offers French and Spanish. Her colleagues are very friendly and the department meets regularly to check in on one another, plan curriculum, and share department administrative tasks. Despite this, Mrs. J has been the only Arabic teacher since the addition of the language to the school's World Language Department several years ago and often feels like she's on her own. Most of the professional development that is offered by her district is geared toward languages that use the Latin alphabet – especially the Romance languages. Because of this, she feels her department and administration do not provide her with appropriate instructional support and feedback. For example, the target ACTFL proficiency level for French and Spanish level I courses is Novice High (the equivalent of CEFR A2.1) in all modes of communication (interpretive listening/reading, interpersonal communication, presentational writing/speaking). Mrs. J is usually able to get her learners to Novice High in interpretive listening and interpersonal speaking tasks, but her learners usually only reach the Novice Mid-level (A1.2) in presentational, interpretive, or interpersonal tasks involving reading and writing. As a result, her learners' performance scores indicate she is underperforming compared to her colleagues in the department. However, a simple comparison of end-of-year proficiency scores doesn't consider the amount of time and effort invested by Mrs. J's learners to learn a new script and manner of writing/reading (right to left instead of left to right) before even beginning to work on higher-order literacy skills. Mrs. J wonders if there is a way to compensate for learners' difficulties learning the new script and manner of writing to expedite the task of acquiring novice literacy skills in Arabic. How can Mrs. J facilitate learners' acquisition of the new script? Should she initiate a conversation with her department regarding expected proficiency targets as it relates to reading and writing? How can she present her situation to her administration without them perceiving her to be "lowering the bar" relative to her other language teacher colleagues?

10.2 The Science: What the Research Says

Are some languages harder to learn than others? The answer is more compilated than a simple "yes" or "no." All languages are complex in their own ways, and those complexities are relative. Some linguists have hypothesized that languages that seem to be "easy" in one regard compensate for that simplicity with added complexity embedded elsewhere in the linguistic system. Some languages might be easier for learners depending on other languages they know. The term "complex" has been used among linguists studying second language acquisition (SLA) to refer to many different aspects of language learning (e.g., we talk about complexity with regards to assessment in Chapter 20). Importantly, when attempting to determine which language(s) are "harder" or more "complex," researchers and teachers must acknowledge that complexity is relative and depends on whose perspective is being taken. For example, a language might be relatively easier for some learners due to some of their individual characteristics like their first language (L1) background, aptitude for language learning, or motivation. Learning French might be relatively easier for an L1 Spanish speaker due to the similarities between the two languages in terms of lexis (i.e., French–Spanish cognates), word order (e.g., formulating possession as [OJBECT] of [POSSESSOR]), usage of certain tenses or moods (e.g., using the subjunctive mood to express doubt). These similarities do not mean that French is not a complex language or will be equally easy for all learners.

Language complexity can also be considered from an absolute perspective, by examining the quality of specific linguistic structures and how functionally or structurally complex they are. Absolute complexity can be looked at from many different angles. For example, a feature of a language could be considered complex when form and meaning are not in one-to-one correspondence. For example, in English, -s is added to the end of nouns to make plurals ("the cats"), but it is also

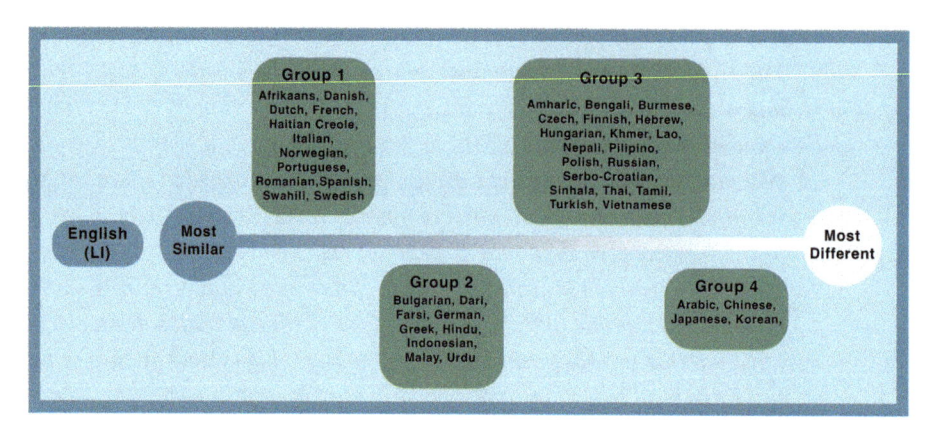

Figure 10.1 Language similarity spectrum. The perceived difficulty of learning particular L2s from the perspective of a monolingual L1 English speaker. Image by: Elizabeth Zonarich

added to the end of verbs to conjugate for third person ("she walks to work"). A form might be complex when it contains multiple components. For example, the simple past in English has one past form ("the sun rose"), whereas the present perfect has multiple components ("the sun has risen"). Complexity has different implications for grammar, vocabulary, pronunciation, and writing across languages. Researchers who examine language learning difficulty investigate the extent to which the presence or absence of certain linguistic features influence the cognitive efforts required of all second language (L2) learners. In the United States, for example, the Foreign Service has grouped languages into four categories based on their linguistic features (see Figure 10.1). The relative difficulty for an L1 English speaker to learn the languages in each category is represented by the number of hours of training needed to achieve target levels of proficiency (to take one example language from each category: 600 hours for Spanish, 750 hours for German, 900 hours for Amharic, 1,100 hours for Russian, 2,200 hours for Korean). However, it is important to consider who these learners would likely be (adult, highly educated, highly motivated working professionals) when drawing conclusions about how many hours your learners may take to progress through the proficiency levels.

Language teachers are often concerned with relative language learning difficulty by considering the differences between the language(s) their learners already know and the language the learners are learning. **Crosslinguistic influence** is the impact of a learner's L1(s) on the language they are learning. Crosslinguistic influence is when information from one language system transfers to the new system. This transfer can have positive and negative impacts on the learner's interpretive or productive abilities. **Positive transfer** is cases where one language facilitates the acquisition of the other. In the example in Figure 10.2, the learner's L1, Italian, facilitates the acquisition of Spanish because both the syntax (the order of sentence) and the vocabulary are similar in the sentence "I am from

10.2 The Science: What the Research Says

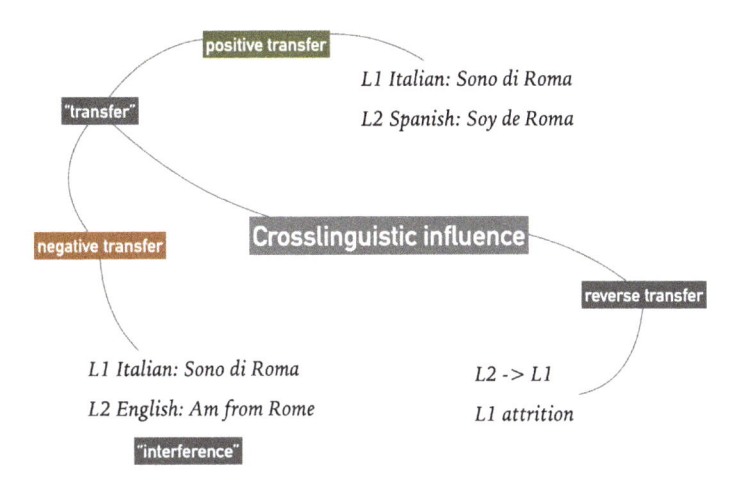

Figure 10.2 Crosslinguistic **Influences**. The languages you already know can have a positive or negative influence on your efforts to learn another language.

Rome"). By contrast, because Italian allows speakers to drop the subject (i.e., "I"), Italian L1 learners of English might struggle to consistently include their subjects in English utterances; this is negative transfer because it causes interference in the learner's L2 English. **Reverse transfer** is also possible! Especially when an L2 learner is immersed in the L2 environment for a long time, the L2 can have an impact on the L1. **Attrition**, or a decrease in language skills in a particular language, can also occur. Often, attrition occurs in L2s when learners have little opportunity for practice and interaction. However, there are also cases where the L2 becomes stronger than the L1.

How can we tell which languages will result in transfer? Language differences can be broken down in many ways. Two possible ways to look at differences are geographic proximity and language genealogical proximity. Geographic proximity describes the physical distance (on the globe) between two communities where the L1 and target language (TL) are primarily spoken. Genealogical proximity describes language families where languages within the same family are more structurally similar than languages from different families. Oftentimes, languages that originate from nearby locations are genealogically similar, but this is not always the case. For example, Hungarian is genealogically close to Finnish and Estonian and dissimilar from the languages that are in close geographic proximity (e.g., Czech, Slovak).

Language genealogy is particularly relevant to transfer because languages within the same families are more likely to have cognates or borrowed words than languages from different families. They might also have a similar word order. For example, most world languages have the order Subject-Object-Verb (e.g., Japanese, Korean, Pashto, Afrikaans) or Subject-Verb-Object (e.g., English, Russian, Mandarina, Spanish, Czech). But quite a few languages have the order

Verb-Subject-Object (e.g., Arabic, Hebrew, Irish, Māori, Tagalog). There are even languages with no dominant word order at all (e.g., Berber, Syrian Arabic, Cherokee)! Learning to use a word order that differs from the L1 means added cognitive effort for language learners.

10.2.1 Proximity, Genealogy, Transfer: Caveats and Caution

All of the above being said, it's important to note that proximity, genealogy, and transfer will not account for all learner errors in the L2. A variety of studies have pointed out that learners pass through stages of development that are similar no matter what their L1 is. For example, all language learners acquiring English pass through the same developmental stages when they learn how to use negation. All learners will be heard making mistakes like "I not like that" even if their L1 has the same negation pattern as English (e.g., German or Swedish). Instead, the difference will be that speakers from a language background with a similar pattern will have an advantage in that they will still make this error at some point in their development but will pass through this stage faster than those who speak languages with a different pattern. A study investigated this phenomenon by comparing learners from a variety of L1 backgrounds learning a variety of L2s. The researchers found that regardless of the L1–L2 pair, all learners exhibited similar patterns when they first started learning their new language; they tended to use simple structures and word order patterns, avoided inflections if the language had an inflection system, and started sentences with the main topic and avoided pronouns, articles, and conjugations. Again, learners were found to make these adjustments even if their L1 had the same pattern as the language they were learning.

There are also researchers who argue that differences between the L1 and the TL are not an issue. In fact, researchers who study the acquisition of pronunciation often say the opposite; in many pronunciation studies, researchers have found that the bigger the differences between the sounds of two languages, the easier the new sounds will be to acquire. This research indicates that learners have the most difficulty when a sound in their new language is very close to a sound in their L1, and they have less difficulty when sounds in the new language are very different from sounds in their L1. For example, in English, /r/ and /l/ are considered distinct sounds. The distinction between these sounds is important because they are used in words "red" and "led" that have different meanings. In Japanese, however, /r/ and /l/ are not distinct sounds; as a result, differentiating these sounds can cause challenges for monolingual Japanese learners studying English.

As this section has suggested, just because an L2 has many differences from a learner's L1 does not mean that the L2 will be impossible to acquire. Again, not all differences result in issues during acquisition and not all learners will acquire the language in the same way (for more on how individual differences contribute to language learning, see Chapters 7, 8, and 9). This is important when considering young children enrolled in bilingual or dual immersion programs. Research examining children enrolled in such programs does not suggest that these learners will be confused as they navigate different languages, even when those different languages are quite different from each other, as is the case with English and Arabic or English and Chinese. In fact, the early exposure facilitates their acquisition! These encouraging findings about the language learning capacities of primary school-aged children support the case for early education bilingual programs.

For older learners who are introduced to the TL in a more traditional language classroom setting (i.e., not an immersion or dual language setting), the difficulty of the language may impact the instructional approach that is most effective. For example, using a "natural approach" (see Chapter 16 for more on teaching methodologies) for English L1 learners of Chinese would be particularly challenging because L1 Chinese speakers develop their orthographic knowledge by drawing connections to words they already have in their oral–aural repertoire when they are learning to read. In comparison, L2 Chinese learners are frequently trying to develop all four linguistic skills (reading, writing, speaking, listening) at the same time and across the three modes of communication (interpersonal, interpretive, presentational). They would not have the background knowledge or exposure to the TL that L1 Chinese speakers do. Given the sheer number of characters and character combinations, research suggests that it is important for L2 learners to have explicit metalinguistic knowledge so that they can problem-solve effectively when they inevitably come across an unfamiliar character or section of a text.

10.2.2 Difficulty and Writing Systems

Typographical similarity, or how similar the writing systems are in different languages, has also been shown to be a factor in determining how challenging learners will find learning the new writing system. Writing systems can be broken down in several ways. Writing systems can be organized by *script type*; for example, languages that use a Latin script (e.g., English, Spanish, Polish, Turkish) versus those that use a non-Latin script (e.g., Chinese, Japanese, Korean, Hindi, Tamil, Cherokee). Writing can also be categorized by *system type*; for example, some languages use an alphabetic system (e.g., Croatian, Greek, Indonesian, Korean, Portuguese, Vietnamese, Ukrainian), while others use a logographic system (e.g., Chinese, Japanese) where characters are used to represent syllables, words, etc. Some languages use an *abjad script* where only consonants are written and not vowels (e.g., Arabic, Hebrew, Persian, Urdu), while others use an *abugida system* where vowels have a secondary status to consonants (e.g., Bengali, Lao, Tamil).

Some research in this area has pointed out that the more different a script is from the learners' L1, the more difficult it will be for them to learn. This could be because writing systems seem to be processed in different areas of the brain, so learning a new writing system could mean activating a new brain region. Languages that have different levels of **grapheme–phoneme correspondence**,

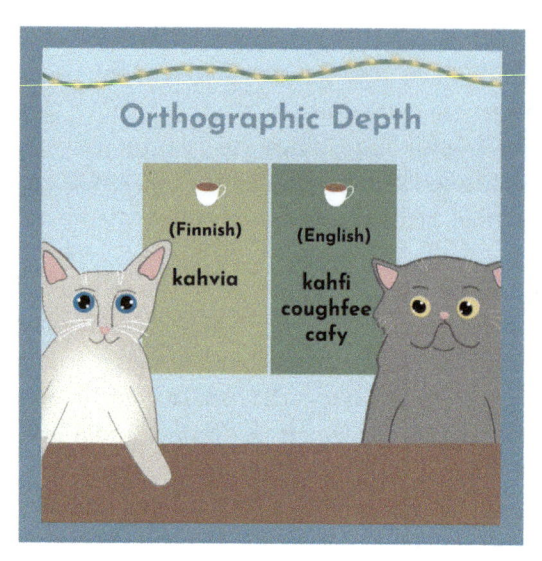

Figure 10.3 Orthography depth. The depth of a language's orthography can impact how difficult it is perceived to be by those learning it. Image by: Elizabeth Zonarich and Erin Fell

or the degree to which there is a one-to-one correspondence between sounds and symbols, can also pose challenges. Some languages, like Finnish, have a one-to-one correspondence between sounds and symbols (in this case Latin alphabetic letters). These languages are said to have **shallow orthography**. By contrast, languages like English have a **deep orthography** where sounds can correspond to multiple letters. As referenced above, some languages, like Hebrew, are said not to represent certain sounds with symbols at all. While learners of "deep" languages struggle at first even when learning to write as a first language, research shows they eventually catch up to speakers of "shallow" languages (Figure 10.3).

How do learners navigate these differences when learning to write in a new language? Research suggests that L2 learners tend to rely on the same skill sets they used in the L1 when faced with literacy-based challenges in their L2. This strategy will help learners when they are learning a language that is typologically similar to ones they already know, but it will be problematic in cases where the strategies from their L1 don't apply to the L2. For example, Spanish speakers will try to use the same phonological processing techniques (e.g., sounding out letters) they used as primary school learners; however, with a language like Chinese, these phonological processing strategies will not be as helpful. However, this reliance and preference for L1 literacy strategies diminishes as learners become more proficient in the L2.

The development and use of strategies has been shown to be an effective way to overcome typological differences when learning a new language (see Chapter 5 for a longer discussion of strategy use). Some strategies that have been investigated include improving attention to form, memorization strategies for retrieval of letters/characters, and comprehension strategies for using context clues and background information. In studies of learning logographic systems (e.g., Chinese), the most popular and effective cognitive strategies involved making connections between previous knowledge and visual, aural, and oral characteristics of the new character via repeated exposure. Studies on student preferences, study habits, and performance have revealed that beginning learners generally find it helpful to learn about the individual radicals that make up characters as they begin to develop their literacy skills because they can then leverage explicit knowledge of those radicals to figure out the meaning of new characters.

Research has also examined the effects of different instructional strategies on the success of learning new writing systems across proficiency levels. For lower-proficiency learners, learning characters of a logographic language via writing activities was found to be more effective than reading activities. Using a computer animation (e.g., animated movies of character strokes being drawn) to learn new characters also helped to enhance student performance. Even though today most writing occurs via keyboards or touch screens, research suggests that the act of writing characters not only supports the development of the physical skill but also aids in memory, retention, and understanding of new scripts, especially for those learners whose L1 is not logographic. Computer-assisted language learning technology may also support form–meaning connections in ways that more traditional reading- and writing-based activities do not (see Chapter 19 for an in-depth look at technology in the classroom). This finding encourages teachers and learners to get creative and incorporate different technological resources into their teaching and learning strategies. Interestingly, for higher-proficiency learners who were already familiar with a bank of common characters, reading-based activities were more effective in improving student performance than writing-based activities. As a result, teachers of lower-proficiency learners may want to consider more hands-on, productive practice and teachers of higher-proficiency learners may want to focus on more comparative, receptive practice.

BOX 10.1 The Science! Points to Remember

- Language complexity is relative and the ease of learning a new language depends on individual factors such as similarity to the learner's first language(s).
- Crosslinguistic transfer occurs when learners carry over aspects of their first language(s) to the languages they are learning. Crosslinguistic transfer can be positive (facilitating language acquisition) or negative (causing interference).
- Not all errors will come from negative transfer from the learners' first language.
- Learners go through universal stages of development, regardless of their first language background.
- Research suggests that the more different a writing script is from the learners' first language, the more difficult it is for them to learn.

10.3 The Science: What's Missing?

Much of the research centered around language learning difficulty has been conducted by the Foreign Services Institute of the U.S. Department of State. As a result, the studies and their findings are primarily U.S.-centric and target L1 English speakers learning world languages. Within this realm, language difficulty is studied to establish reasonable proficiency targets for the various Foreign Service officers enrolled in language classes and other trainings. Proficiency targets are tailored to the specific professional duties of diplomats and foreign service workers and are presented alongside the number of in-course hours estimated to be needed to accomplish those linguistic goals. Clearly, this represents a unique population of language learners that is not necessarily applicable to people learning languages around the world. Foreign Service Officers (FSOs) are government agents whose career goals are aligned with language learning, travel, and cultural immersion. Many of these FSOs learn multiple languages to a high-proficiency level over their years of service. Estimates provided by government agencies often do not necessarily take into consideration the impact of learners' individual differences, like motivation and aptitude (see Chapters 8 and 9), which we know play a substantial role in the acquisition process. Overall, there is substantially less research that examined relative difficulties from non-English starting points or from learners with preexisting relationships with the TL (e.g., heritage language learners).

In terms of research on acquiring a new writing system, most prior studies have also focused on English learners, typically those learning Chinese. Most of this research examines low-proficiency Chinese learners working on recognizing characters. There is much less research on other non-alphabetic languages. So far, research does not provide much guidance on the most effective ways to structure cyclical review of previously learned letters/characters to help learners retain them. Many variables could influence how to design reviews. These include learner age, proficiency level, and the amount of in-class time learners spend working with a teacher each week. Though research does not offer "best practices" in this area yet, teachers should consider these factors as they experiment with different review activities and consider some of the tools and tips below.

10.4 The Art: Research-Based Strategies to Try

10.4.1 The Art of Teaching a New Writing System

For L2s that differ greatly from the learners' L1(s), additional language learning strategies can help students navigate these new challenges. As with all language learning strategies (see Chapter 5), some learners are more apt to identify and independently make use of them, while others require more guidance and support. As a result, it is important to spend time modeling and reflecting on language learning strategies in class. As learners become more advanced in their L2, the strategies they use change. More advanced L2 learners (or those with experience learning other L2s) will tend to use strategies that rely on previously established knowledge. As learners continue to advance, they will be able to use more metacognitive strategies and become more autonomous learners. Instructors can facilitate this transition to self-reliance by designing activities that allow learners to review their own work and reflect on their performance with peers or in a one-on-one writing conference with the instructor. In doing so, learners develop editing and revision strategies that will support them as they progress toward more advanced tasks in formal or professional settings that demand more linguistic accuracy and complexity. These types of strategies will not necessarily feel as natural or meaningful to lower-level learners who have not yet developed their internal knowledge banks, so more time will need to be allocated to lower-level learners.

- Strategy types
    - Cognitive strategies
        - *Rehearsal and repetition:* Learners repeat the sound of the symbol/character aloud after first hearing it. Learners can repeat the sounds under their breath when they encounter the character or letter again.
        - *Imagery:* Learners associate letters or characters with other images to facilitate retrieval.
        - *Context clues:* Learners practice using context clues from other surrounding language to guess the meaning of unknown words or characters.
    - Metacognitive strategies
        - *Reflection:* Learners identify and evaluate their own learning processes as they learn to strengthen future learning.
        - *Organization:* Learners group new sounds/letters/characters in ways that facilitate retrieval.
        - *Descriptions:* Learners describe what strategies they are using to remember new sounds/letters/characters.
    - Social strategies
        - *Developing appreciation:* Make learning characters more engaging by highlighting cultural connections or other "fun facts" and ask learners to trade facts with each other. A cultural appreciation for new alphabets and/or writing systems has been linked to an enhanced ability to acquire new vocabulary.

10.4.2 The Art of Supporting Students in Acquiring Unrelated Languages

- Scaffold text-based resources.
    - In languages like Hebrew and Arabic, texts designed for L2 learners who are just beginning to develop their literacy skills often present shallow orthographies, meaning that the vowels are marked. The marking is thought to help novice learners make the sound–symbol connections that are necessary for reading. These markings are gradually removed as L2 learners progress until they can read authentic texts with deep orthographies (i.e., vowels that are not marked).
    - If available in the language you teach, some learners may find it helpful to use the Roman-based script (e.g., pinyin for Chinese) to help remember how to

Figure 10.4 Explicit instruction of unfamiliar features. Learners benefit from explicit instruction to understand features of the L2 that do not exist in their L1. Image by: Elizabeth Zonarich

pronounce characters (with tone markings, see Figure 10.4), even writing pinyin in the margins of a reading to help recall this information.
- Offer individualized and tiered instructional support:
  - Be familiar with the language backgrounds of your language learners in your class. Collecting this information and understanding what languages your learners bring in the classroom can help you tailor your instruction. When teaching, encourage your language learners to find similarities and differences between their L1(s) and the TL.
  - Use explicit instruction when writing systems are vastly different. For beginning language learners, dedicating a portion of each class to the intentional and explicit development of knowledge (e.g., character radicals) can help support character learning efforts and facilitate language learning strategies during other portions of the class. Research has also suggested that when instructors are able to help learners develop an appreciation for radicals and investigate how characters are formed, the learners are more likely to recognize these words in later instances. When choosing between which radicals to teach first, research suggests that instructors should begin first with the radicals that learners are most likely to encounter in the genuine resources used in class, not necessarily those that might be considered the "simplest."
  - Use exit tickets to learn about which character or letter learning strategies learners are using in your class and which ones you might need to help learners develop in future classes (see Figure 10.5). The act of filling out the exit ticket also supports self-reflection processes that help learners become more self-aware learners. For higher-level learners, you could also challenge them by having them respond

Figure 10.5 Strategies for mastering a new writing system. Exit tickets provide quick ways to check in with learners about the strategies they are using to progress toward course goals. Image by: Elizabeth Zonarich

to a prompt using the TL. The benefit of this is that teachers can assess learners' written production of target grammar, identify common themes among the learners, and select appropriate error correction strategies (see Chapter 3).
- Facilitate opportunities for literacy development in various ways throughout the class period.
- Sensory-motor connections have been shown to be facilitative of character recall.

10.5 Troubleshooting: How the Science Informs the Art

Mrs. J is an Arabic teacher in a high school that also offers French and Spanish. Mrs. J has been the only Arabic teacher since the addition of the language to the school's World Language Department several years ago and often feels like she's on her own, even though she has regular curriculum planning meetings with her very friendly colleagues. Most of the professional development that is offered by her district is geared toward Romance languages that use a writing like the English writing system. As such, she feels her department and administration does not provide her appropriate instructional support and feedback.

Mrs. J is correct in noticing the differences between language writing systems, and how those differences may in turn shape instructional strategies. "Best practices" for developing literacy for L1 English speakers learning French may not apply to L1 English speakers learning Arabic. This is because the learners will not be able to rely on the Latin alphabet skills they used to develop their literacy in their L1 (English) in their L2 (Arabic). While Mrs. J may be able to learn from these professional development sessions she attends with her French and Spanish teacher colleagues, she would likely find a sense of community in professional development sessions geared toward Less Commonly Taught Languages (LCTLs). Mrs. J might look for programs in her area that link teachers of LCTLS and consider developing a peer group where strategies specific to teaching Arabic can be shared.

For example, the target proficiency level for French and Spanish level I courses is Novice High in all modes of communication (interpretive listening/reading, interpersonal communication, presentational writing/speaking). Mrs. J is usually able to get her learners to Novice High in interpretive listening and interpersonal speaking tasks, but her learners usually only make it to Novice Mid in presentational, interpretive, or interpersonal tasks involving reading and writing. As a result, her student performance scores indicate she is underperforming compared to her colleagues in the department. However, a simple comparison of end-of-year proficiency scores doesn't take into account the amount of time and effort put forth by Mrs. J's learners to learn a new script (not a Roman alphabet) and manner of writing/reading (right to left instead of left to right) before even beginning to work on higher-order literacy skills.

Because of differences in language proximity between English and the languages offered at Mrs. J's school, certain allowances must be made for end-of-year scores. In this scenario, French and Spanish are both considered Group I languages, i.e., relatively similar to English, whereas Arabic is considered a Group IV language, or very different from English. Group IV languages require approximately twice as much class time as Group I languages to achieve comparable proficiency levels for the average English L1 learner. Assuming all three languages in Mrs. J's district follow similar school schedules, it is unreasonable to expect learners taking the languages to progress at the same pace. Mrs. J and her colleagues should adjust the target proficiency level accordingly so that the Mrs. J and her learners' hard work is celebrated, instead of interpreted from a deficit perspective. This would be disheartening for both learners and teacher.

Mrs. J wonders if there is a way to compensate for learners' difficulties learning the new script and manner of writing to expedite the task of acquiring novice literacy skills in Arabic. How can Mrs. J facilitate learners' acquisition of the new script? Should she initiate a conversation with her department regarding expected proficiency targets as it relates to reading and writing? How can she present her situation to her administration without them perceiving her to be "lowering the bar" relative to her other language teaching colleagues?

Because of the differences in scripts and writing conventions, Mrs. J will likely find it helpful to incorporate more explicit activities around these differences. While French and Spanish learners will be able to leverage their previous literacy knowledge, her Arabic learners will not. Her learners likely already perceive Arabic to be a more challenging language. Mrs. J should be sure to acknowledge this and encourage learners to view their progress in different terms than the progression of their friends in French and Spanish classes. In conversing with her colleagues, Mrs. J might consider leading an introductory activity for them so they can better understand the challenges of working with a new writing system. If her colleagues only have ever learned languages with Latin alphabetic scripts, they are likely unaware of the challenges facing her learner population. Mrs. J can also think of other ways that can demonstrate student progress throughout her course. She could consider using alternative assessment, like portfolios, where learners can compile collections of their best work throughout the course. In this way, Mrs. J can show her administrators (who may be unfamiliar with the cognitive loads of learning different languages) their progress, even though it may be at a slower rate than Romance languages.

10.6 The Science: Points to Remember

- The difficulty of learning a new language may be influenced by individual factors such the language learners' L1 backgrounds, motivation, and language learning aptitude. Depending on these factors, different languages will need different amounts of instructional time to achieve the same levels of proficiency.
- Learners will experience crosslinguistic transfer, where their understanding of the system of one language will apply when learning the TL. There is positive transfer, which facilitates acquisition, and negative transfer, which can cause interference. Regardless of differences between learners' L1 and TL, studies have shown that language learners will go through universal stages of development.
- Research has suggested that the more different a writing script is from the learner's L1, the more challenging it will be for them to learn. Teachers can support language learners by incorporating and modeling strategies, including cognitive strategies, metacognitive strategies, and social strategies as discussed in this chapter.

10.7 Questions to Consider

1. Think back to your own language learning experiences in formal or casual settings. Which languages were easier for you to learn? Which languages felt more difficult? Why?
2. If you are currently teaching (or have taught) a language class, what L1s do your language learners have? In what ways have you seen examples of positive or negative transfer from their L1(s) into the TL?
3. What are some ways you can draw upon language learners' L1 backgrounds to help them learn the TL?
4. If you are Mrs. J, what are some ways you might incorporate technology to help your learners acquire a new script?

10.8 The Science of Language Learning: The Research Supporting the Points Made in This Chapter

Cysouw, M. (2013). Predicting language-learning difficulty. In L. Borin & A. Saxena (Eds.), *Approaches to Measuring Linguistic Differences* (pp. 57–82). De Gruyter Mouton. https://doi.org/10.1515/9783110305258.57.

Cysouw identifies various factors that can be used to differentiate between languages, which include geographic and genealogical separation between languages, differences in writing systems, and structural differences in grammar. These differences can contribute to the difficulties that the learners experience when learning a second language. Cysouw examines the extent to which these factors pose difficulties for language learners and then describes models that can be used to predict language learning difficulties for learners.

Everson, M. E. (2011). Best practices in teaching logographic and non-Roman writing systems to L2 learners. *Annual Review of Applied Linguistics, 31*, 249–274. https://doi.org/10.1017/S0267190511000171.

In this article, Everson summarizes research developments on how second language learners become able to read in languages with non-Roman alphabetic scripts (such as Chinese, Japanese, Hebrew, and Arabic). He demonstrates how prior research findings have informed best practices in second language pedagogy. Some pedagogical strategies that he addresses include when and how to introduce non-Roman scripts to language learners, and the role of writing in supporting the second language learning process.

Osborne, C., Zhang, Q., & Zhang, G. X. (2020). Which is more effective in introducing Chinese characters? An investigative study of four methods used to teach CFL beginners. *The Language Learning Journal, 48*(4), 385–401. https://doi.org/10.1080/09571736.2017.1393838.

In this study, researchers investigated the impact of four different instructional approaches on beginning adolescent Chinese language learners' familiarity with Chinese characters. These learners were divided into four groups. One group was a control group and did not receive a specific instructional approach. The other three groups were taught through rote memorization, delayed character introduction, and character color-coding, respectively. Immediate and follow-up assessments indicated that rote memorization was most helpful in enhancing learner performance on the immediate assessments. Character color-coding was shown to support learners in mastering the tones of the new characters. The delayed character introduction did not advance this group of learners' familiarity with these characters. Overall, these results confirm the challenges of learning a new writing system and call for more investigation on how different instructional approaches may uniquely contribute to learners' linguistic growth.

For more resources, including more sample lesson plans, videos, and other ideas, visit our companion website: www.cambridge.org/BryfonskiMackey.

PART III

TEACHING THE SKILLS

11 How or when should I teach grammar?

KEY QUESTIONS
- **The Science: How is grammar acquired by language learners?**
- **Where do learners' grammatical errors come from?**
- **The Art: How and when should I teach grammar in my classes?**
- **Is explicit grammar instruction necessary?**
- **Do grammar drills work?**

11.1 Voices from the Classroom

Mrs. E teaches English university courses designed for learners who plan to move to predominantly English-speaking countries after graduation. The learners enrolled in her courses demonstrate an A2 or Intermediate Mid level of proficiency. Given the immediacy and specificity of her learners' language needs, Mrs. E tries to incorporate lots of real-life scenarios and authentic resources into the curriculum so that her learners are prepared for when they move abroad after graduation. Over the past two years, she has deemphasized the importance of grammatical rules and removed weekly verb conjugation quizzes from her curriculum entirely. Since Mrs. E has made these curricular changes, she believes she has noticed her learners' confidence increase! They speak much more fluently (i.e., speaking more quickly, with fewer pauses and less repetition) at the end of the semester than at the beginning of the semester, but she is worried that the accuracy with which they speak and write has not changed very much. Mrs. E is concerned that given the professional nature of her learners' linguistic aspirations, a low degree of accuracy could compromise the opportunities they might have in the future. Could more explicit grammar instruction help Mrs. E's learners' linguistic accuracy improve? She is worried that more grammar instruction would not only be boring for her learners but also make them nervous about using the language. How can she best support her learners?

11.2 The Science: What the Research Says

Many people who have taught or learned a second language in a classroom setting have had the experience of attempting to memorize conjugation patterns, complex grammar rules, and their exceptions. But what *is* grammar? And how and when should it be taught in a language class to facilitate acquisition?

First, the term "grammar" is typically used when we mean to say **syntax** – the order and structure of words and phrases. For example, English has the syntax order Subject-Verb-Object, but many other languages (e.g., Japanese, Turkish) have Subject-Object-Verb order. "Grammar" also commonly refers to **morphology** rules in a language – the internal structure of words and the way they are formed. Some common morphological rules we teach in a second language (L2) classroom include pluralization, gender agreement, manipulating prefixes and suffixes, and the like. Usually, when people talk about "teaching grammar" they are not referring to pronunciation and vocabulary. For this reason, we address pronunciation and vocabulary in Chapters 12 and 14 respectively.

Grammar instruction has been the subject of much debate in both language teaching and second language research, mostly surrounding questions like *Where do grammar errors come from? How much or how little grammar instruction is enough? Which instructional techniques work best? Is it best to structure a class around the most important grammar to learn?* and even *Should grammar be taught at all?* Teachers might wonder whether learners must be explicitly taught grammar in order to acquire it or if they can simply absorb the grammar from instruction implicitly. Before diving into these questions, it is important to first understand how these terms are used to describe three concepts: (1) the type of knowledge learners develop, (2) the type of instruction the teacher provides, and (3) the learning process as a whole.

11.2.1 Types of Grammar Knowledge

The terms **implicit learning** (unconscious, unintentional) and **explicit learning** (conscious, intentional) describe processes that learners experience in the classroom. For example, learners might acquire a new structure without intending to after hearing that structure used in a real-life situation. This would be an implicit learning process. On the other hand, a learner might explicitly study a conjugation table to learn how to conjugate a new structure. This is an example of an explicit learning process. The result of learning is knowledge, which can also be categorized as implicit or explicit. **Implicit knowledge** is procedural, automatic, quickly accessed, and internalized. If a teacher observes a learner spontaneously and fluently using targeted linguistic structures in natural conversation, that learner likely has some amount of implicit knowledge about that structure. **Explicit knowledge** is declarative, comprised of facts, controlled, and requires planning. If a learner can explain why and when to use a targeted linguistic form, that learner likely has some amount of explicit knowledge about that structure.

11.2 The Science: What the Research Says

Just because a grammatical form is learned implicitly doesn't necessarily mean it will become implicit knowledge. Similarly, just because a grammatical form is learned explicitly doesn't necessarily guarantee that it will become explicit knowledge. Finally, **implicit instruction** and **explicit instruction** describe the types of strategies teachers use in class. These terms do not necessarily describe what kind of learning takes place or what type of knowledge is created. In this case, implicit and explicit just describe what sort of instructional practices a teacher is using. For example, in implicit grammatical instruction, teachers might provide learners with lots of comprehensible input (e.g., watching video clips) in the hopes that they will internalize the patterns that they hear (e.g., past tense verb forms) without conscious effort. In explicit grammatical instruction, teachers might provide learners with structured activities intended to draw learners' attention to a linguistic feature, guide learners in identifying a pattern, and provide them with opportunities to examine that pattern, like filling in missing verbs in sentences or playing a matching game involving verb ending (see Table 11.1 for a summary of these terms).

Regardless of which type of instruction a teacher might use, it is important to reiterate that the kind of instruction does not necessarily describe the kind of learning that will take place. In other words, a teacher could be providing implicit instruction in class, yet some of her learners could still be developing explicit knowledge. Because of this, researchers cannot make any claims about what kind of instructional methods will generate what kinds of knowledge. Explicit instruction could lead to explicit or implicit learning. Similarly, implicit instruction can lead to explicit or implicit learning. This is because the learning processes activated during instances of instruction are controlled by the learner (even if they don't realize it!). For example, a teacher might be engaging in a "picture walk"

Table 11.1 Terms for talking about grammar instruction and learning

Concept	Descriptor	Definition
Learning	Implicit	An unconscious process
	Explicit	A conscious process
Knowledge	Implicit	Procedural knowledge that learners have internalized and can access quickly. When using implicit knowledge, communicating feels automatic and is done unconsciously.
	Explicit	Declarative knowledge that requires time and effort to access. When using explicit knowledge, learners need more planning time.
Instruction	Implicit	Teaching strategies that are focused on meaning-making and that aim to help learners "get" grammar without being aware they are trying to learn it.
	Explicit	Teaching strategies that are focused on activating learner awareness of specific linguistic features.

(guiding the class through the illustrations of a book without reading) supported by some translated target vocabulary on the whiteboard. While the teacher might not be calling attention to the pronouns used to describe people in the picture, the learner might consciously think to herself, "The teacher is using 'él' when she talks about the boy in the picture and 'ella' when she talks about the girl. 'Él' must be for talking about boys and 'ella' must be for talking about girls." This internal monologue points to the learner having developed explicit knowledge about the Spanish pronouns *él* and *ella* despite her teacher using an implicit instructional approach.

11.2.2 Approaches to Teaching Grammar

If, how, and when to teach grammar is one of the most studied and debated issues in second language acquisition (SLA) research and practice. *If* grammar should receive any type of instruction will depend on the theoretical/instructional approach taken by the program, curriculum, or teacher. If some attention is paid directly to teaching grammar at any point, researchers refer to this as **form-focused instruction** (see Figure 11.1). Some programs organize their entire curricula or syllabi around grammatical topics (learn more about teaching approaches in Chapter 16), where each unit highlights a particular grammatical form. In this approach, grammar is presented in an isolated context that is separate from a larger communicative task. Teachers typically use explicit instructional approaches in an effort to facilitate explicit learning processes that lead to the development of explicit knowledge. Teachers plan their lessons around the grammatical form, or forms, of the unit/week/day and students are expected to master them incrementally. This approach to teaching grammar is called *isolated form-focused instruction*, and research suggests that it builds explicit metalinguistic knowledge and awareness about the target language (TL). However, this approach assumes that language learning happens piece-by-piece, one grammar component at a time, in a linear manner. Researchers have found that language learning is actually much more dynamic and cyclical. Sometimes learners might

Form-Focused Instruction (FFI)

Integrated FFI → Implicit Instruction, Explicit Instruction

Isolated FFI → Explicit Instruction

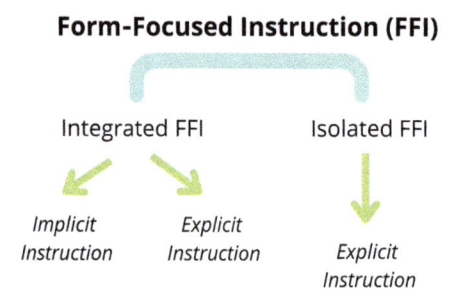

Figure 11.1 Form-focused instruction in the classroom. Form-focused instruction can manifest in a few different ways, depending on the degree to which it is integrated into communicative tasks.

seem to master a part of grammar but then suddenly start to make errors again. Other research has shown that learners pass through some universal stages of development and no amount of isolated form-focused instruction will help them acquire a form they aren't developmentally ready to acquire. We will return to this point momentarily.

In programs that organize their curricula around communicative tasks, grammatical forms are more likely to be presented in an integrated manner as they relate to real-life skills that learners are developing in the TL. Though teachers might still use explicit instructional approaches to draw learners' attention to key linguistic features, the goal of their instruction is not for learners to develop explicit knowledge of how to form the future tense, for example. Rather, the teacher is using explicit strategies to help learners make form–meaning connections so that they may successfully accomplish the targeted task (for more on communicative tasks, see Chapter 17). This type of approach is called *integrated* form-focused instruction. Through this approach, learners are encouraged to think critically, deducing linguistic patterns as they learn to express themselves in more complex ways as they tackle increasingly difficult tasks. Forms are highlighted, through either explicit or implicit teaching strategies, exactly at the moment they are most needed for communication (see Figure 11.2).

Aside from learner- and program-specific factors, the type of grammar feature itself has also been shown to impact how quickly or easily learning occurs. Internal properties of certain grammar features influence the kind of support or intervention learners may need. Certain grammar features seem to pass through universal stages of development. This means that grammar instruction, no matter how it is delivered, may not be able to alter the developmental order of acquisition. This has been found to be the case regardless of the first language(s) of the learners. For example, in English, third person -*s* has been shown to be a late-acquired

Two Types of Focus-on-Form Instruction (Target Form = Past Tense)

Implicit Focus-on-Form Instruction
(Target grammatical item presented in context)

Explicit Focus-on-Form Instruction
(Target grammatical item presented independently)

Figure 11.2 Integrated vs. isolated FFI. Two approaches to FFI for the past tense. In the figure on the left, the past tense forms are integrated as a part of meaningful reading. In the figure on the right, the past tense forms are presented in isolation to be learned explicitly. Image by: Elizabeth Zonarich

Table 11.2 Developmental sequences of English as an L2

"-ing" ending	I like <u>swimming</u> and <u>dancing</u>.	Earliest acquired
plural -s	We see <u>flowers</u>, <u>rabbits</u>, and <u>butterflies</u>.	
"be" copula	They <u>are</u> excited.	
"be" auxiliary	They <u>are</u> celebrating a birthday.	↓
a/the	I want <u>a</u> dessert. I want <u>the</u> cookie.	
irregular past	You <u>went</u> to the post office.	
regular past tense	He <u>walked</u> to the store.	
3rd person -s	She <u>travels</u> every summer.	
Possessive -'s	That is the <u>dog's</u> bone.	Last acquired

grammatical feature by all English language learners, meaning if a learner is not developmentally ready, they will not acquire third person -s. Table 11.2 describes the well-studied developmental sequence for English language learners.

The list in Table 11.2 contains just a few common grammatical features for a single language, English, and can't be used as a roadmap for all features in all languages. However, these orders have also been found in other languages and other grammatical features, such as question formation and negation. What causes learners from a variety of language backgrounds to acquire these features in this order? Much of the order of developmental sequences can be attributed to the frequency in which a feature appears, as well as how regular its formation is. More common, regular features may be faster and easier for learners to master and do not necessarily rely on explicit knowledge to be mastered, especially if they are similar to features in the learners' L1 (see Chapter 10 for more on language difficulty). By contrast, unfamiliar and more irregular linguistic features may cause learners more trouble, requiring explicit instruction and practice opportunities. To master new grammatical features, research shows that learners need to first pay attention to these forms when they come across them in the input (e.g., in written text, spoken conversation). In most instances, learners may pay attention first (and often exclusively) to the meaning of what they just heard because it takes so much effort to attend to meaning, especially for low-proficiency learners. If learners can "juggle" paying attention to both meaning and form of linguistic input, they may be able to pick up grammatical forms without explicit instruction or effort. If they cannot, it is not likely they will pick up grammatical form and instead will require explicit instruction. Grammatical features that learners cannot easily distinguish using a "bottom-up" observational approach (i.e., more implicit instruction) may necessitate a "top-down" processing approach (i.e., more explicit instruction) so that learners can better perceive the qualities of more challenging features. One linguist created the criteria in Figure 11.3 to help identify features that language learners might find more challenging so that appropriate intervention/instruction strategies could be applied.

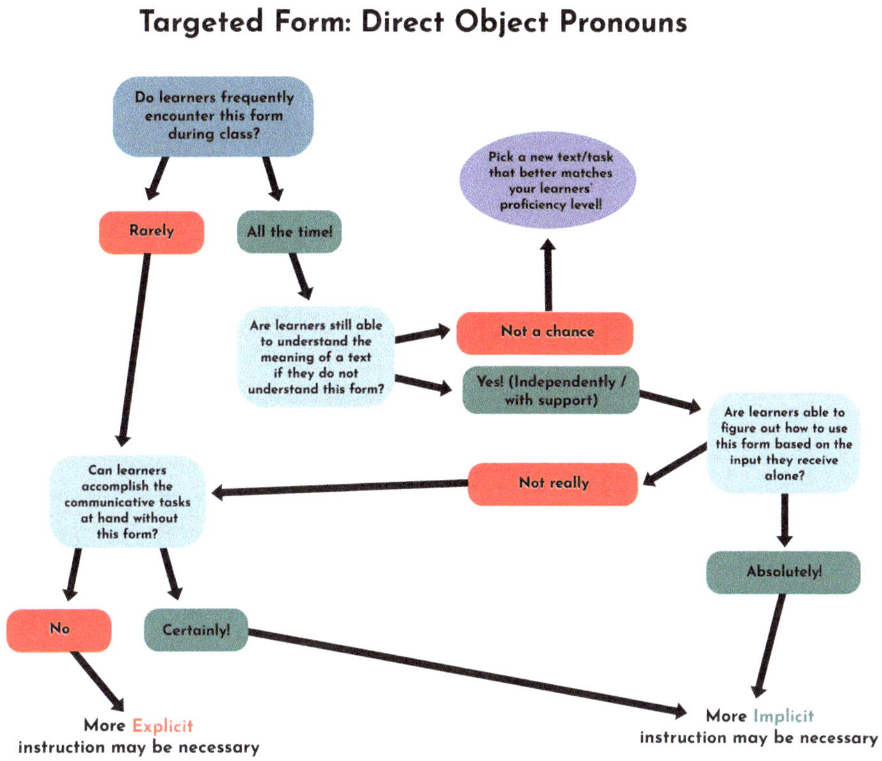

Targeted Form: Direct Object Pronouns

Figure 11.3 Explicit versus implicit instruction. Ask yourself these questions to determine what type of instruction may be most beneficial for your learners.

Research into types of grammar instruction has mostly investigated different instructional strategies to compare how a group of learners who receive one type of instruction perform in comparison to a group of learners who receive another type of instruction. From these studies, findings suggest that instructional techniques that direct learners' attention to certain grammar structures, patterns, or features that are important for completing a task are more beneficial in comparison to using purely meaning-based interventions or drills that are devoid of meaning attached to the forms. In other words, a sort of "middle ground" between entirely implicit instruction and entirely explicit instruction has been shown to be the most effective.

Oral or written corrective feedback targeting grammatical errors (which we covered in Chapter 3) has also been the focus of many studies. As we discussed in that chapter, when learners' attention is drawn to grammatical errors through feedback, they are more likely to notice gaps between their own production and the correction. So, the question is not figuring out if learners will benefit from making form–meaning connections. Instead, the question is to what extent and how frequently to draw learners' attention to form–meaning connections based on factors including learner age, proficiency level, and the goals of the language program.

11.2.3 Role of Age in Grammar Instruction

Not all learners will approach grammar instruction in the same way. Younger learners have been shown to benefit more from implicit and meaning-based instructional techniques because they have more difficulty defining and describing language patterns explicitly. However, adolescent and adult language learners are less likely to make these kinds of important form–meaning connections on their own. For these adolescents and older learners, if they aren't noticing linguistic features, they are not going to be able to acquire them, even when provided with lots of exposure to those features (see Chapter 1 for more on the importance of noticing). For example, explicitly pointing out grammatical errors has been shown to be effective for lower-proficiency learners and older learners, as well as for complex errors. In comparison, implicit corrective feedback, such as recasts, has been shown to be more effective for younger learners, higher-proficiency learners, and less complex grammatical errors. In order to incorporate new linguistic features into their communicative ability, some sort of form-focused instruction will be necessary. However, just because some learners need explicit instruction to master grammatical features does not mean they must be in the form of grammar drills. Grammar drills usually present grammar points in multiple, repetitive ways outside of a meaningful context or task. Drills are an explicit instructional approach that use explicit learning processes with the expectation that learners will develop explicit knowledge. While some learners who are able (perhaps due to excellent aptitude or working memory abilities, see Chapter 9) will transfer this explicit knowledge practice to communicative situations, other students will be unable to do so. Additionally, grammar drills usually focus on developing learners' accuracy in the use of grammar forms. The ability to accurately reproduce grammar forms during drills may or may not transfer to more communicative contexts.

BOX 11.1 The Science! Points to Remember

- The terms *implicit* and *explicit* can be used to categorize the learning process, knowledge, and instructional strategy.
- The type of instructional strategy (implicit and explicit instruction) does not necessarily describe the kind of learning that takes place. For example, explicit instruction doesn't always lead to explicit learning and implicit instruction doesn't always lead to implicit learning.
- In order to acquire new grammar features, learners must first notice it in the input and pay attention to meaning and form.

11.3 The Science: What's Missing?

This area of research is greatly complicated by the fact that researchers do not agree about the role explicit knowledge plays in language acquisition. Whether explicit knowledge serves as the initial building block of the development of implicit knowledge or whether it plays no role in the ultimate development of implicit knowledge at all remains hotly contended between theorists.

Assuming the perspective that explicit knowledge *does* play a role in language acquisition, perhaps in the case of older learners in particular, research still doesn't tell us with certainty how to best support its development. In pursuit of finding the "most effective" form-focused instructional approach, researchers have used different methods for measuring learner performance, and so it is difficult to compare their findings to gain a more complete understanding of which instructional approach is superior. Because of this, current research does not conclusively rank one form-focused instructional strategy above another in terms of its effectiveness in supporting learners in acquiring target linguistic features. Moreover, individual differences between learners certainly play a role in which kind of instructional strategies are ultimately most beneficial. These differences are discussed in more detail in Chapters 7 and 9.

The experimental conditions that researchers often use in their studies examining the effects of form-focused instruction are often quite different from classroom realities, which limits the extent to which the findings can inform language pedagogy. In many form-focused instruction studies, the learners already had some degree of familiarity with the targeted grammatical structures. There are fewer studies that explore the ways in which different instructional strategies influence learners' experiences working with entirely new grammatical structures, which is a common occurrence in lower-level language classrooms. Studies are generally unable to provide the number of instructional content hours that learners would experience over the duration of an academic course. They are also usually unable to measure learner performance with the frequency that teachers can over long periods of time (i.e., over the span of a year, or even several years depending on the nature of the language program). This makes it difficult for researchers to arrive at any conclusive understanding of the language learning process as teachers and learners experience it in classrooms.

11.4 The Art: Research-Based Strategies to Try

11.4.1 The Art of Incorporating Focus-on-Form Strategies

- Provide learners with *enriched input* or *input flooding* (see Chapter 17 on task-based language teaching) where targeted linguistic structures are added to increase the frequency with which they appear in the text/audio.
  - Outcome: Learners "accidentally" notice the target structure (attracted **attention**) (see Figure 11.4) and so are thought to acquire it more easily.
- Provide learners with *enhanced input* where learners receive enriched input as well as advice to pay attention to the target linguistic instruction (either verbally or with signs like bolding or underlining).
  - Outcome: Learners are instructed to notice the target structure (*directed attention*) and so are thought to acquire it more easily.

Figure 11.4 Enhanced input texts. Enhancing the linguistic forms you want learners to notice may help attract their attention as they read. Image by: Elizabeth Zonarich

11.4.2 The Art of When to Incorporate Form-Focused Instruction

- An important decision in teaching grammar forms is *when* to teach them during a lesson. Typically, teachers have three options.
    - Teach the grammar form at the very start of a lesson.
    - Teach the grammar form when learners encounter issues with it during an activity or task.
    - Teach the grammar form at the end of a lesson after learners have already done some activities where they might have encountered it.
- There are a few caveats to each. First, teachers should consider what kind of knowledge they aim to build in their learners. Are your learners continuously making errors on this form even though you've taught it before? In that case, explicit instruction may be necessary if that is your goal or the goal of your curriculum. Are you hoping your learners will be able to use the structure during an activity that is primarily based on meaning-making? Then implicit instruction might be best. Your choice of when to introduce the structure and focus on it explicitly will impact how learners engage with it. Let's take each of the three options listed above:
    - *Before:* If you start off a lesson explicitly explaining a grammar pattern, and then ask learners to do a communicative activity like a role play, they may focus explicitly on the structure during the communicative activity. So you will most likely be targeting explicit knowledge construction and not implicit meaning-making.
    - *During:* If you ask learners to do a primarily communicative activity, and then notice they are making errors with the target structure (or any other structure that is critical to the activity), you may choose to draw learners' attention to

the form in the moment. In this incidental style of focus on form, you might use corrective feedback or short conversations to highlight key grammar points that are essential to learners' success in the activity. Or you may decide to stop the activity and give a brief explicit explanation of the structure and then send learners back to the activity. In this way, they will get implicit communicative practice and may then focus on the form explicitly after learning more about it.
    - *After:* Finally, you could let the learners complete activities and then wait until after the activity is completed to explicitly teach a target form or to highlight other errors you noticed during the activity. In this way, you allow most engagement with the form to be implicit and raise learners' attention afterward. The hope here is that they have built some implicit knowledge that they can later apply to other communicative situations.
- There is no right or wrong way to focus on grammatical forms in a class; the decision should be made based on the goals of the class and the needs of the group of learners. However, see Chapter 17, which advocates for a task-based approach that includes an incidental focus on form (during the task).

11.5 Troubleshooting: How the Science Informs the Art

Mrs. E teaches English university courses designed for learners who plan to move to predominantly English-speaking countries after graduation. The learners enrolled in her courses demonstrate an A2 or Intermediate Mid level of proficiency. Given the immediacy and specificity of her learners' language needs, Mrs. E tries to incorporate lots of real-life scenarios and authentic resources into the curriculum so that her learners are prepared for when they move abroad after graduation. Over the past two years, she has deemphasized the importance of grammatical rules and removed weekly verb conjugation quizzes from her curriculum entirely.

It sounds like Mrs. E is transitioning from a synthetic curriculum (organized around discrete grammar points) to a more task-based curriculum (organized around real-life linguistic needs of learners). The role of grammar in these two curriculum types is very different. Synthetic curricula typically use an isolated form-focused approach to instruction. Task-based curricula use an integrated focus-on-form approach to instruction.

Since Mrs. E has made these curricular changes, she believes she has noticed her learners' confidence increase! They speak much more fluently (speaking more quickly, with fewer pauses and less repetition) at the end of the semester than at the beginning of the semester, but she is worried that the accuracy with which they speak and write has not changed very much. Mrs. E is concerned that given the professional nature of her learners' linguistic aspirations, a low degree of accuracy could compromise the opportunities they might have in the future.

As Mrs. E recognizes, proficiency relates to a speaker's accuracy, complexity, and fluency when communicating. This is important to keep in mind so that teachers can help shape balanced development. While these three components (accuracy, complexity, and fluency) do not necessarily develop at the same rate as each other, it is critical that Mrs. E provide her adult learners (who are not likely to make the same form–meaning connections as children) with support in attending to features so that their language use does increase in accuracy. Accuracy plays an increasingly important role as learners need to communicate more complex themes in high-stakes interactions (i.e., job interviews or business meetings). Using an integrated form-focused approach, Mrs. E can highlight key grammatical issues learners face when accomplishing the tasks. She might do this by providing more, and more targeted, corrective feedback during or after they complete activities in class. Integrating more presentations into her activities will also help develop learners' accuracy. Research shows that when learners know they will have to present information, for example, after having a small group discussion, they are more likely to focus on the accuracy of their production.

Could more explicit grammar instruction help Mrs. E's learners' linguistic accuracy improve? She is worried that more grammar instruction would not only be boring for her learners, but also make them nervous about using the language. How can she best support her learners?

It sounds as though Mrs. E is conflating form-focused instruction with "fill-in-the-blank" exercises that are prevalent in explicit, isolated form-focused approaches. Mrs. E should consider other kinds of form-focused instruction that encourage learners to view grammatical features as a way of making meaning within the context of real-life activities and resources. An integrated form-focused approach will ensure Mrs. E's learners get the instruction they need to continue to improve their accuracy without diminishing the premium Mrs. E has placed on communication and authentic language use.

11.6 The Science: Points to Remember

- In order to master a linguistic feature, learners will first need to notice it and make a connection between how it looks (the form) and what message it communicates to the listener/reader (the meaning).
- It is easier for learners to make form–meaning connections for linguistic features that appear often, carry important messages, and follow predictable patterns.
- When it is difficult to make form–meaning connections, more explicit instructional strategies help teachers direct learners' attention toward the targeted linguistic forms; however, this does not mean the features will necessarily be acquired.
- Individual differences (age, proficiency level, aptitude, learning differences) play a role in whether a learner finds it easy or difficult to make form–meaning connections.

- Remember, providing learners with direct, explicit instruction (i.e., the rules for question formation) does not mean that the learners leave your lesson with that information stored as implicit knowledge. Or even explicit knowledge!

11.7 Questions to Consider

1. Consider the underlying structure of your current curriculum. How would you describe the role of grammar in your curriculum?
2. Is your curriculum centered around grammatical points or is it centered more around tasks and themes?
3. What are some ways you provide form-focused instruction in your classroom right now? How would you characterize the type of form-focused instruction you provide?
4. What do you expect learners to do with the grammatical/linguistic knowledge they have?
5. To what extent do your expectations for how learners use grammatical knowledge align with your current instructional practices?

11.8 The Science of Language Learning: The Research Supporting Points Made in This Chapter

Li, S., Ellis, R., & Kim, J. (2018). The influence of pre-task grammar instruction on L2 learning: An experimental study. *Studies in English Education*, *23*(4), 831–857. http://dx.doi.org/10.22275/SEE.23.4.03.

This experimental classroom-based study compares three classes of adolescent English language learners in China. Each class received a different type of grammar instruction as they learned about the passive voice construction. One class received explicit instruction and completed a communicative task, another class completed only the communicative task, and the final class served as a control group (with no unique teaching strategy) to measure the impact of the instructional approaches on learners' development. Results suggested that the explicit instruction advanced learners' explicit knowledge more than the other instructional approaches but did not support the development of learners' implicit knowledge any more than the other strategies.

Long, M. H. (1998). Focus on form in task-based language teaching. *University of Hawaii Working Papers in ESL*, *16*(2), 35–49.

This article compares three different approaches to teaching grammar: focus on forms, focus on meaning, and focus on form. In a "focus on forms" approach, the curriculum centered around a sequence of linguistic constructions, with learner progress measured by the extent to which they master these constructions at the end of the year (e.g., simple past tense, the past progressive tense, and the past perfect tense). In a "focus on meaning" approach, the curriculum is about the subject matter and not the language at all. Programs that use this approach are immersion programs or content-based programs. It is assumed here that learners naturally and subconsciously acquire linguistic forms from all the input they receive. In a "focus on form" approach, the curriculum is centered around communicative tasks that learners will encounter outside of the classroom. Linguistic constructions are discussed as they become relevant for learners to understand to complete the communicative tasks, which are the main objectives of the course (e.g., navigating a new subway system, buying a cup of coffee, writing a resume). After reviewing each approach, Long advocates for the "focus on form" approach to grammar instruction within a task-based language classroom.

Spada, N., Jessop, L., Tomita, Y., Suzuki, W., & Valeo, A. (2014). Isolated and integrated form-focused instruction: Effects on different types of L2 knowledge. *Language Teaching Research, 18*(4), 453–473. https://doi.org/10.1177/1362168813519883.

This study compares how two groups of learners respond to two different instructional strategies. In both Isolated Form-Focused Instruction (FFI) and Integrated FFI, the primary focus is on meaning-making while drawing the learner's attention to a particular grammatical feature. While Integrated FFI attempts to do this during a communicative task, Isolated FFI does this either before or after a communicative task. The participants in this study were adult English language learners who were enrolled in intermediate-level community classes. Both classes were working on passive voice in English, a new and difficult grammatical form, but while one class received Isolated FFI, the other received Integrated FFI. Assessments at the end of the unit showed that both groups made progress toward mastering this form; however, they had gained different kinds of knowledge. While the class with Isolated FFI demonstrated higher levels of explicit English knowledge, the class with Integrated FFI demonstrated more implicit English knowledge.

For more resources, including more sample lesson plans, videos, and other ideas, visit our companion website: www.cambridge.org/BryfonskiMackey.

12 Is there a "best" way to teach pronunciation?

KEY QUESTIONS
- **The Science: Is it "worth it" to spend class time focusing on target-like pronunciation vs. comprehensibility?**
- Should I ask my students about their goals in pronunciation?
- Why aren't my students improving in pronunciation skills as quickly as other language areas?
- **The Art: Is there a "best" way to teach pronunciation? What strategies should I use?**
- Are there pronunciation learning strategies I can teach to my students?

12.1 Voices from the Classroom

Mr. Z teaches a Mandarin class for business students at the university level. Through a partnership with his university's Business School, the Foreign Languages Department organizes an annual study abroad program for business students taking Mandarin to practice their language in a professional setting. The business students meet with students from a partner university in China and do activities together like networking parties, formal dinners, product pitches, and mock business negotiations. The program has been a huge success over the years and has grown in size and popularity. While Mr. Z is proud of the program's development, he finds that many of his students have a hard time being understood by their Chinese counterparts and frequently revert to English when misunderstandings occur. On more than one occasion, Mr. Z has had to step in during a meeting to clear up a miscommunication when a student's pronunciation was so incomprehensible to the Mandarin native speakers that the meeting ground to a halt either due to the confusion or because a team member inadvertently conveyed the wrong message to their Chinese counterparts. Though his students have high proficiency in all of the requisite language skills, he fears he may need to circle back to drilling tones and pronunciation before the trip, just to be safe. Additionally, many of his learners have told him they want that explicit practice. How can he improve his learners' pronunciation over the long term?

12.2 The Science: What the Research Says

Pronunciation is one of the first aspects of someone's speech that we notice when interacting with another person. Even native speakers of the same language have different ways of pronouncing the same word depending on region and dialect (see Table 12.1). Can you think of multiple ways you have heard the words below pronounced in conversations you've had with friends or coworkers, or maybe even on TV?

Sometimes these pronunciation differences among native speakers cause comprehension issues. *Every person has an accent*, whether it is in their L1 or in a language they learned later in life. Based on prior research in this area, we don't believe eliminating accents is possible or necessary, and we don't advocate accent reduction as a main goal of language teaching and learning in general, unless the learners themselves have a specific reason for this and seek out a dedicated program. We believe most language learning professionals would agree that in general language learning, teachers and learners should prioritize improving **comprehensibility**, or being understood, and developing communication strategies, incorporating more targeted pronunciation exercises if difficulties that arise in pronunciation impede communication.

To provide context for how research has considered phonological development, or the development of sound systems for second language (L2) learners, it is important to first begin with a summary of what we know about how people learn sounds in their L1(s). There is evidence that babies are born already with an awareness of some sound patterns in the language(s) they will learn. This is because even in the womb, fetuses are being exposed to the patterns of sounds in the language spoken around them. They may not hear individual words, but they pick up stronger sounds like vowels and **intonation** curves, or the rising and falling pitch in speech. We know this from studies where babies suck on a pacifier that is wired to a computer and measures the changes in sucking patterns as babies hear different sounds (see Figure 12.1).

During their first months, babies' brains take note of complicated statistical distributions of the sounds they hear around them, essentially attending to all sounds in their environment. Between 8 and 12 months old, babies begin to "specialize" their perception, focusing exclusively on the sounds that are relevant to them in their language environments. Even before their first birthdays, babies' ability to differentiate between similar sounds that aren't important in

Table 12.1 Variation in pronunciation

English	Spanish	Portuguese	Mandarin
jaguar	mangonada	leite	动画片 (cartoon)
caramel	España	telefone	闻 (to smell)
park	gracias	quente	博士 (doctor/PhD)
aunt		dois	

12.2 The Science: What the Research Says

Figure 12.1 Researching phonological development. Researchers have measured babies' sucking patterns to examine what sounds they perceive. Image by: Elizabeth Zonarich

their native language(s) begins to decrease. Research has shown that at only one year old babies become *language-bound listeners*, meaning that they can no longer easily hear the differences between sounds that are not used in their surroundings. In other words, once language-bound, people cannot automatically differentiate the subtle differences between all the different units of sounds used across the languages of the world. For example, English speakers can easily differentiate between the English "r" and "l" sounds in words like *rake* and *lake*. However, in Japanese, these two sounds are *not* distinct and so L1 Japanese speakers often cannot easily perceive the difference between these two words. As a result, producing that difference in their own speech is also a challenge. This ability to hear the differences between sounds in other languages lessens as we age, which is why accents persist even in language learners that have been immersed in their L2 for many years.

What happens, then, when people learn language later in life, after young childhood? After early childhood, it becomes increasingly difficult, but not impossible, to acquire new sound patterns. Research has shown that targeted drills or exercises may help learners of any age improve their ability to hear and produce difficult sounds in an L2. How difficult the new sounds or patterns are may depend on how different they are from those in the learners' L1(s) (recall the discussion of language difficulty in Chapter 10). For some difficult new sounds, learners will pronounce them like the next "closest" sound present in their L1. For example, when English speakers learn Spanish and are sometimes unable to pronounce the characteristic "rolled -r" or "trill" sound in *perro* (dog), they will usually use an English *-r* instead. This typically doesn't cause too many comprehensibility issues in Spanish. Many pronunciation errors fall into this category and might warrant only minimal attention by learners and instructors given the relatively lower likelihood that learners will be able to fully acquire the sound system of the new language as opposed to the grammar or vocabulary. However, other pronunciation errors can cause comprehension issues and learners might want to practice them.

12.2.1 How Can We Teach Pronunciation?

What kinds of pronunciation instruction strategies are backed by research? Here it is important to consider two aspects of pronunciation: **segmentals** and **suprasegmentals**. Segmentals are individual sounds in the target language (TL) like consonants and vowels. Suprasegmentals – or features "above" (*supra-*) the level of the sound segment – include the rhythm, intonation, tone, and stress patterns of the language. Both are important to consider for pronunciation instruction. However, research suggests that having the proper pronunciation of consonants is more important to ultimate comprehensibility than the proper pronunciation of vowels. Findings like this suggest that if teachers decide to dedicate time to pronunciation instruction, they should consider focusing more on segmental consonant sounds than vowel sounds or other suprasegmental features.

There is also a variety of research that has investigated the strategies learners use for pronunciation, and research has found that learners who employ strategies tend to have more spontaneous speech. Strategies that learners use include noticing mistakes, adjusting facial muscles, and seeking help on pronunciation. Other researchers have divided pronunciation strategies into types (see Box 12.1) and found that learners who received instruction focusing on pronunciation learning strategies were able to improve their pronunciation after a four-month course.

BOX 12.1 Types of Pronunciation Strategies (Based on Sardegna, 2009)

Prediction

Prediction: Using strategies to make predictions about the right pronunciation of words and phrases. For example:
- Using a pronunciation rule
- Using spelling patterns
- Looking at facial diagrams or videos

Production

Production: Using strategies to improve the ability to correctly articulate new words and phrases. For example:
- Practicing word pairs
- Recording speech
- Repeating phrases after listening to a recording

Perception

Perception: Using strategies to aid in the comprehension of spoken language. For example:
- Listening to how proficient speakers produce sounds and words
- Watching videos of others speaking
- Asking for help or feedback from others

Images by: Elizabeth Zonarich

12.2 The Science: What the Research Says

Another area that has received a lot of attention is corrective feedback for pronunciation errors (see Chapter 3). Researchers who have studied how different types of feedback support pronunciation development found that more implicit feedback, like recasts (see Chapter 3), are potentially more effective for correcting learners' phonological errors than more explicit forms of feedback. This is thought to be due to an aspect of short-term working memory that is activated when input is received called the **phonological loop**. The phonological loop allows people to "replay" or rehearse in their minds sounds, words, phrases, and even numerical sequences that they hear. Sometimes people might even whisper the sound under their breath to facilitate the phonological loop (Figure 12.2).

In sum, the phonological loop is what allows learners to use all of the strategies to remember a new sound. When other information distracts a learner from that rehearsal, the sounds will become harder to remember unless they get stored in long-term memory. One of the more effective types of feedback for pronunciation is a recast because it doesn't interrupt the phonological loop; learners can hear their own pronunciation and immediately juxtapose it with the corrected pronunciation. However, as discussed in Chapter 3 on feedback, lower-proficiency learners may not benefit as much from recasts as they have to allocate attention to more basic processes (e.g., figuring out the meaning of an unfamiliar word) and will therefore be less likely to notice if their teacher or conversational partner has provided them implicit feedback on pronunciation. As a result, when providing feedback to a lower-proficiency learner, more explicit feedback might be necessary, keeping in mind that only those pronunciation errors that impede comprehensibility need correction with these learners. The same is true for suprasegmental features like tone as well.

Figure 12.2 Activating the phonological loop. Support learners in activating their phonological loop when they are learning more complicated or unfamiliar sounds. Image by: Elizabeth Zonarich

Another factor that impacts an instructional strategy's effectiveness is how long the pronunciation training lasted. In many studies, learners needed hours of drills to make small differences in their perception or production of difficult sounds. Theories of speech learning predict that learners must first perceive the differences in pronunciation (auditory detection) before they are able to produce those differences (articulatory ability). That means if instructors are hoping to change how learners produce sounds in the TL, they should first work to ensure learners are distinguishing the sounds. Some common methods that have been studied include showing learners visuals of the mouth to help them understand how to position their tongue to produce the sound or using annotations to show how pitch or intonation contours change over the course of a word or phrase. One recent study even used an ultrasound machine to show language learners how to move their tongue to produce particular sounds. In that study, the ultrasound wand was placed below the jaw, directly underneath the tongue so that the tongue's movements were visible on the computer monitor. In this way, the study participants were able to compare how their tongues moved while making the "r" and "l" sounds and how their adjustments affected their pronunciation. Another approach is high variability phonetic training, which exposes learners to multiple speakers to increase the variation in TL pronunciation they experience. This approach tries to account for diversity of accent in L2 speakers as well as provide rich pronunciation data for the learner's developing internal language system. Research on the impacts of this type of training suggests that it may help learners better perceive and produce the sounds of the TL, but the differences are often minimal.

12.2.2 Comprehensibility versus "Nativeness"

As discussed above, all speakers of all languages have an accent based on a variety of variables including where we grow up, the dialect our family and friends speak, and the other languages we come into contact with across our lifetimes. It is unrealistic to think that language learners will be any different in their L2s. Given the constraints on language acquisition based on age, most people who learn a language will have a recognizable "accent" based on factors like their L1, the length of time immersed in the language, and their proficiency level. As a result, most will never obtain a phonological system that is equivalent to a speaker who grew up speaking only the TL. Indeed, many researchers and practitioners have argued that a so-called "native-speaker ideal" is particularly harmful and impractical in the context of pronunciation. Prioritizing or elevating the native standards emphasizes a monolingual superiority that is not only unrealistic but also harmful to multilingual communities. Additionally, there can be racial and ethnic biases entangled in this "native-speaker ideal" because it makes a judgment call about who language learners should *want* to sound like.

As a result of these issues, many argue that the onus should not be on language learners to change their accents. Recently, there has been a push to educate and train people who routinely interact with multilingual individuals to try to better understand the variety of accents they encounter rather than pushing language learners to adjust their accent to accommodate or impress their interlocutor. Despite this push, many language learners face communication challenges and discrimination due to perceptions of foreign language-accented speech. Some evidence from the United States has demonstrated that individuals with non-US English accents are less likely to be considered for employment after an interview. For these reasons and others, many L2 speakers are driven to "improve" their accent through accent modification or other techniques, and it is critical for these populations to have access to research-based practices. As a field, we must be active allies of our learners and advocate for what they actually need, keeping in mind the impact accent would have on them; a student who is learning Russian at their home university to fulfill graduation requirements and who has no intent to use the language except while on holiday would likely suffer few consequences if they were to make pronunciation errors. However, an immigrant to Germany navigating the healthcare and education system in their L2 may face more serious consequences if they were to make pronunciation errors or fail to be comprehended (see Figure 12.3).

None of this means that instructors should avoid pronunciation altogether. Pronunciation instruction can be important to learners and their goals for their language learning. Pronunciation can improve the intelligibility and comprehensibility of learners' spoken production, and, for some learners, it is a personal goal to sound a particular way in their L2 (e.g., adopt the pronunciation of a particular group of speakers of the L2).

Lower stakes of L2 pronunciation errors

Higher stakes of L2 pronunciation errors

Figure 12.3 The importance of pronunciation across communicative tasks. Pronunciation errors can sometimes interfere with comprehension, but not all circumstances require the same degree of accuracy. Image by: Elizabeth Zonarich

> **BOX 12.2 The Science! Points to Remember**

- Though babies are born with the ability to perceive every sound in human language, within their first 8 to 12 months, they become language-bound listeners that are primed to pay attention to the sounds of their first language(s). At age one, babies begin to lose the ability to differentiate sound contrasts from other languages that are not essential to their survival.
- A learner's ability to achieve "native-like" pronunciation in a second language depends on how phonetically similar that language is to the first language.
- Holding learners to a "native-like" standard privileges particular speakers of the second language, which runs contrary to the multilingual goals of many world language programs and may subconsciously impact how learners perceive community members who speak their target language with a strong accent.
- Language teachers who are committed to a communicative approach to language instruction should prioritize learners' comprehensibility over their approximation of a particular accent or other pronunciation pattern.

12.3 The Science: What's Missing?

> There is no agreed upon system of deciding what [pronunciation features] to teach, and when and how to do it. (Darcy et al., 2012)

It's true! There is no one way that research has definitively shown to be the "best" way to improve learners' pronunciation. There are several reasons for this. As always, generalizing the findings of controlled, laboratory-based studies on phonological development to naturalistic or classroom-based contexts is problematic. Many laboratory studies ask participants to provide a **controlled response**; in other words, they are asked to practice listening to or producing a single specific feature of interest, like the English "r." This often draws an unusually large amount of learner attention to one phonological feature. This intensity of focus on one particular sound or pattern does not mirror how student attention is directed in real communicative interactions or in classroom contexts. Therefore, these studies cannot reveal whether learners would be capable of producing this phonological feature outside of a laboratory context. In other words, student phonological performance on a targeted test or exercise for specific sounds cannot be assumed to automatically translate to their performance in a more communicative interaction. This notion of phonological transfer between laboratory and classroom contexts is currently a popular area of inquiry for linguistics.

While this area is under investigation, even if these laboratory-based studies were to find effective ways to train learners to pronounce specific phonological features of their L2, the ways in which these changes were brought about are often not practical or realistic to replicate in classroom or immersion settings. For example, it is unlikely for a teacher to have the time in class to offer all learners intensive and controlled drills or the same amounts of individualized corrective feedback. Even if there were the time, dedicating such a large portion of time to pronunciation would detract from time spent developing other areas of language competence. Other studies have used specialized tools like an ultrasound to show images of the tongue. However, this kind of tool is unlikely to be found in a traditional language classroom and therefore has limited applicability (as of now).

Most of the studies that have examined the extent to which instructional interventions impact learners' phonological development focus on adolescent or adult learners (over the age of 13) whose L1 is English or who are learning English. As a result, there is not much research on a broader age range of learners and on learners of other languages. Furthermore, most studies on phonological development have not been designed to collect data on the long-term effects of instructional interventions related to pronunciation. Therefore, it is unknown whether any learner modifications of their pronunciation based on pedagogical interventions would stand the test of time, or whether learners would lose the ability to perceive and produce the targeted L2 linguistic features after some time has passed.

Finally, individual differences are suspected to play a large role in an L2 learner's pronunciation and reaction to instructional strategies. Specifically, research has highlighted phonological working memory, phonological awareness, perceptual abilities, and even musical abilities as all important skills when it comes to efforts related to advancing phonological development. More research is needed to explore to what extent individual differences like these (and of course the usual ones: age and proficiency level) influence the impact of pronunciation-specific instruction.

12.4 The Art: Research-Based Strategies to Try

BOX 12.3 Start Here!

When considering whether or how to address pronunciation challenges that arise in your class, it is important to first identify the type of phonological feature that is causing trouble for your learners. Ask yourself the following questions:
- Is the pronunciation error segmental (sounds or sound combinations)? Or suprasegmental (tonal, pitch, intonation)?
- Do they make the error all the time or only in specific contexts?
- Can learners tell there is a difference between their pronunciation and the target pronunciation?
- Do they know how to physically form their mouths to produce target pronunciation?
- What strategies do learners already know for dealing with pronunciation errors?

Now you can choose from the tips below!

- *Survey learners:* Start by surveying your learners to ask them to what extent they view pronunciation as an important aspect of their language learning. What issues do they see as relevant for their own pronunciation? What goals do they have for their learning and how does pronunciation play a role in reaching those goals?

- Ask if they agree or disagree with the following statements adapted from a research study conducted by Sardenga et al. (2017):
    - I can communicate better if I practice pronunciation.
    - I believe more emphasis should be given to proper pronunciation in class.
    - I start to panic when I have to read aloud or speak in front of others without having rehearsed before.
    - Focusing on my pronunciation when I speak is distracting.
    - It is a pain to correct my pronunciation in the L2.
    - I get nervous when someone corrects my pronunciation mistakes.
    - I look for useful materials to practice my L2 pronunciation on the Internet.
    - I am satisfied with my pronunciation progress this last year.
    - I feel confident that people understand me when I talk.
- *Teach strategies:* Equip learners with the three different research-backed strategies for pronunciation: prediction, production, and perception. Use Table 12.2 (adapted from Sardenga et al., 2017) to see which strategies fall into each category and some ideas for how learners could think about the strategy.

Table 12.2 Prediction, production, and perception strategies

Strategies for improving your SOUNDS before you talk and while you talk:	Strategy type
I look up difficult sounds in a dictionary and hear them pronounced.	prediction
I rely on phonetic symbols (e.g., /æ/) to determine which sound to produce (e.g., Say /æ/ in *cat*).	prediction
I apply spelling rules to determine what sounds to produce (e.g., Say a 'ch' sound when "ure" follows a "t" as in *nature, culture*).	prediction
I predict the right articulation (where to place my tongue, what to do with my lips) right before I say the sound.	prediction
I use descriptions, charts, facial diagrams, video recordings to help me understand difficult sounds.	prediction
I practice word pairs (e.g., *low* vs. *row*; *bad* vs. *bed*).	production
I practice linking sounds by adding one sound at a time.	production
I practice using repetition.	production
I use a mirror to practice my mouth movements.	production
I listen to online/recorded materials.	perception
Strategies to improve your ability to STRESS individual words accurately.	**Strategy**
I look up long words and compound words in the dictionary to find out which syllable receives the main stress.	prediction
I use spelling rules to decide which syllable to stress in a word.	prediction
I draw stress markings on top of words to remind me which syllables receive main stresses.	prediction
I consult pronunciation materials (textbooks, online resources, software programs) to decide how to stress words.	prediction

12.4 The Art: Research-Based Strategies to Try

Table 12.2 cont.

I practice word stress alternations (*commúnicate* vs. *communicátion*) following stress rules.	production
I practice word stress alternations using gestures.	production
I record myself saying long words to assess and/or correct my pronunciation.	production
I read aloud long words and compound words repeatedly in order to improve them.	production
I use difficult words in conversation so that I can improve how I pronounce them.	production
I listen to recorded words (e.g., from electronic dictionary/pronunciation materials).	perception
Strategies to improve your ability to produce the correct stress and intonation in phrases or sentences.	**Strategy**
I divide my sentences into meaningful units or phrases before I read them aloud.	prediction
I apply pronunciation rules to figure out the intonation of a phrase.	prediction
I follow my intuitions to figure out the intonation and primary stress of a phrase.	prediction
I decide the intonation and primary stress of a phrase based on meaning.	prediction
I repeat phrases after a teacher/native speaker, or a recording from TV/podcasts/websites.	production
I practice intonations and/or primary stresses on my own by reading aloud sentences or dialogs.	production
I practice with the help of rhythmic gestures or an object (e.g., pen, stick) that marks rhythm beats.	production
I record myself saying phrases to assess and/or correct my pronunciation.	production
I practice reading aloud with an audience in mind.	production
I self-correct my pronunciation while speaking.	production
I listen to native/proficient speaker production.	perception
I request native speakers'/teachers' feedback on my pronunciation.	perception
I ask someone for help when pronouncing difficult words or phrases.	perception

Other useful tips for integrating pronunciation into your classroom include:

- *Use visuals:* Visual props and strategies may help some learners understand how to move their tongues, lips, mouths, and jaws to better pronounce sounds in the TL. The age of the student should guide the degree of phonological detail provided in these visually supported activities. The proficiency level of the student should guide the selection of featured sounds.
    ○ Tools to help learners see themselves: mirrors, videos

- Tools to help learners see pronunciation models: pitch contour indications, ultrasound or MRI images (easily obtainable online!), intonations contours (word and sentences level), etc.

- *Vary pronunciation input:* Try incorporating different kinds of speakers (varied by gender, age, origin, etc.) into the genuine audio/video resources in your curriculum. As you may have noticed in your L1, everyone has a different accent! Even within the same region, speaker's inflections and tones may vary. Hearing a variety of voices pronounce sounds in the TL may help your learners distinguish new sounds more easily.

- *Practice communication breakdowns:* Equip your learners with negotiation strategies that they can use when they find themselves engaged in a misunderstanding with another speaker. Providing learners with the skills they need to navigate interactions in the TL may strengthen their confidence and willingness to converse in the TL. Even if learners do not need to use these strategies to make themselves understood in their L2, they will likely find themselves in a conversation with an L2 speaker of their first language. Having experienced firsthand the challenges of communicating in another language may make them more sympathetic and supportive conversation partners in these types of circumstances.

12.5 Troubleshooting: How the Science Informs the Art

Mr. Z teaches a Mandarin class for business students at university level. Through a partnership with his school, the Foreign Languages Department organizes an annual study abroad program for the business students taking Mandarin to practice their language in a professional setting. The students meet with students from a partner university in China and do activities together like networking parties, formal dinners, product pitches, and mock business negotiations.

It is wonderful that Mr. Z coordinates an event where his learners get to participate in the types of interactions they will encounter after they graduate and enter the field of international business. If he is not already organizing his curriculum around the tasks that arise during this event, Mr. Z should use the target tasks (participating in a networking event, conversing at a formal dinner, delivering product pitches, and negotiating in a mock business meeting) to structure his course. See Chapter 17 for more information on how to develop a task-based syllabus.

The program has been a huge success over the years and has grown in size and popularity. While Mr. Z is proud of the program's development, he finds that many of his students have a hard time being understood by their Chinese counterparts and frequently revert to English when misunderstandings occur. On more than one occasion, Mr. Z has had to step in during a meeting to clear up a miscommunication when a student's pronunciation was so incomprehensible to the Mandarin native speakers that the meeting either ground to a halt or a team member was inadvertently offended.

Given the more advanced age of his learners and the fact that they are native English speakers who likely have difficulty even perceiving the differences in sounds in Mandarin, it is plausible that they will always struggle with pronouncing certain words and phrases. Some learners, who may have experience with other tonal languages or have a higher aptitude for phonological awareness due to individual differences, may be able to learn to perceive and produce these new sounds. However, other learners may never be able to accomplish this. Dedicating a substantial amount of class time to skills that will be exceedingly difficult (and maybe impossible) to master may discourage learners from speaking at all. Instead of drills, Mr. Z should consider introducing language-based negotiation skills from the "Research-Based Solutions" section so that when his learners experience a pronunciation-based misunderstanding with another Mandarin speaker, they have conversational strategies they can use to resolve the issue in the TL without feeling as unsettled by the misunderstanding. Additionally, Mr. Z can focus explicit teaching on just those very common pronunciation issues that he notices lead to the most (and the biggest) communication breakdowns in his learners.

Though his students have high proficiency in all of the requisite language skills, he fears he may need to circle back to drilling tones and pronunciation before the trip, just to be safe. How can he improve his students' pronunciation over the long term?

Remember, no empirical evidence has revealed a "tried and true" method of improving learners' pronunciation during communicative tasks across long-term learning environments. While intensive drilling might help a learner produce a new sound in isolation and after much targeted practice, no research has concluded that the same learner would be able to successfully produce that sound while engaged in a communicative interaction, when they have more linguistic and social demands to juggle. Because Mr. Z's learners have many immediate professional needs for Chinese, their language development would be best served with more structured opportunities to engage in the types of real-world tasks they will be performing after graduating. Mr. Z can provide ample recasts on his learners' pronunciation errors during class time and encourage them to use strategies such as private rehearsal to continue to practice the pronunciations that seem to result in the most comprehension issues.

12.6 The Science: Points to Remember

- In order for language learners to produce a sound, they first need to be able to perceive it. Drills may help some learners perceive the key differences between sounds, but there is no guarantee.
- For many language learners who begin later in life (adolescence and beyond), "native-like" pronunciation is not a realistic goal and insisting on it may serve to demotivate and/or discourage learners.

- Addressing discrepancies in language learners' pronunciation becomes important when it interferes with their ability to make themselves understood to their target audience.
- Providing learners with the communication tools to successfully manage the inevitable instances when they find themselves in a miscommunication is a more effective use of class time than drilling proper pronunciation.

12.7 Questions to Consider

1. Why does pronunciation matter to you? Why does it matter to your students? Does it matter to any of the other program stakeholders?
2. What are your (or your program's) ultimate pronunciation goals? If your goals center on the pronunciation of monolingual native speakers, what are the ways in which that goal influences student and teacher experiences in the classroom?
3. What are the minimum meaningful and perceptible units of the language that you teach that students need to be able to say in order to successfully communicate?
4. How does pronunciation show up on your rubrics or in your grading system? Does it align with your (and your students') communicative values?

12.8 The Science of Language Learning: Research Supporting the Main Points in This Chapter

Levis, J. M. (2016). Research into practice: How research appears in pronunciation teaching materials. *Language Teaching, 49*(3), 423–437. https://doi.org/10.1017/S0261444816000045.

This article describes how linguists have come to understand L2 phonological acquisition and how the current research perspectives have supported language pedagogy. The author focuses on two research areas that have been underrepresented in language education spheres and may help inform the development of future curricular materials. The first area is called high variability phonetic training (HVPT). HVPT has been found to help language learners perceive differences between key sounds in the TL. During HVPT, teachers are encouraged to use varied voices, dialects, and genders from both native and nonnative speaker models. The second area the author believes to be of importance to language learners is intonation. Research has highlighted how intonational differences can advance conversational purposes and contribute to meaning-making. Key literature on both these topic areas are reviewed for educators' consideration as they select teaching resources and design their courses.

Levis, J. M., Derwing, T. M., & Sonsaat-Hegelheimer, S. (Eds.). (2022). *Second language pronunciation: Bridging the gap between research and teaching.* John Wiley & Sons.

This book features fifteen chapters, each written by an expert in subfields of pronunciation training in the L2 classroom. Care is taken throughout the volume to demonstrate how teachers can use the results of research to inform their practices. Importantly, discussion is centered around issues of technology, including how teachers can integrate pronunciation instruction into curricula for younger learners.

O'Brien, M. G. (2021). Ease and difficulty in L2 pronunciation teaching: A mini-review. *Frontiers in Communication*, 5, 1–7. https://doi.org/10.3389/fcomm.2020.626985.

This article offers an accessible overview of the popular perspectives of teaching pronunciation in world language classrooms. O'Brien provides advice for educators seeking to define pronunciation priorities within their courses from a comprehension-oriented framework. Next, both research-based and classroom-based approaches to tracking learners' pronunciation progress are presented. Proficiency level, language background, motivation, type of input, and length of training are also identified as factors that may influence L2 learners' phonological development. General research findings related to visualization techniques, feedback approaches, and computer-based "games" that may support learners seeking to target specific sounds in their L2 outside of class hours are also discussed.

Saito, K. (2013). Reexamining effects of form-focused instruction on L2 pronunciation development: The role of explicit phonetic information. *Studies in Second Language Acquisition*, 35, 1–29. https://doi.org/10.1017/S0272263112000666.

The experimental study examines the impact of explicit phonological support within a form-focused instructional approach for adult Japanese learners of English. The author hypothesized that explicit pronunciation exercises would be an effective and efficient way to aid learners in producing difficult sounds across both familiar and unfamiliar task contexts. Results showed that learners who received explicit phonological support had greater performance gains and that they were able to generalize their new pronunciation knowledge more widely than those who did not receive explicit phonological support. Based on these findings, the author recommends that teachers consider adding a "noticing" phase, where explicit phonological information is shared; an "awareness" phase, where learners can interact with the targeted sounds in "real life" contexts; and finally a "practice" phase, where learners can continue to demonstrate their ability to produce target sounds in communicative tasks. However, the author does note that individual differences (like learner age, proficiency level, and language learning aptitude) as well as course characteristics (like amount of class time and proficiency goals) should guide the amount of explicit phonological support that teachers want or need to provide their learners.

For more resources, including more sample lesson plans, videos, and other ideas, visit our companion website: www.cambridge.org/BryfonskiMackey.

13 How can I incorporate literacy skills in the target language?

KEY QUESTIONS
- The Science: Can learners transfer their reading and writing skills from their first language to their second language?
- What are the main components of literacy?
- The Art: How can I incorporate literacy skills in the target language?
- How can I support my struggling readers and writers?

13.1 Voices from the Classroom

Ms. W is a French teacher who works in a school for high school learners who have struggled academically in the past, or had discipline issues or frequent absenteeism. Many of the courses offered involve intensive remediation and small class sizes to help the learners to catch up and attain the skills they need to be successful in the workforce or in a college/university program. As a result, one of the core instructional goals of the school is literacy: how to decode unfamiliar words, be a resilient reader, read for varying depths of comprehension, and communicate ideas clearly. Ms. W wants to incorporate literacy strategies more intentionally into her instruction but is unsure where to start. Many of the learners are still developing literacy in their first language (L1) and she fears they wouldn't be ready to start applying the same techniques from the L1 to the second language (L2). How can she learn from and adapt the strategies being used in the learners' L1 classes (not just literature, but also math and science) to reinforce and support their developing French L2 literacy? What kinds of tasks and feedback are most useful for developing beginning literacy in an L2?

13.2 The Science: What the Research Says

Developing literacy, or the skills of reading and writing in a language for some type of social context, is quite different from the development of oral communication skills. Everyone who is provided access to input from a young age will achieve oral fluency in their L1(s), even without formal instruction (except, of course, in cases of certain developmental disabilities that profoundly impact oral communication and severe cases of abuse or neglect by caregivers). Literacy development, on the other hand, typically begins when children first enter school and is a slow, complex, and nonlinear process. Studies show that language teachers perceive the process of teaching learners to write in the L2 to be challenging and to require lots of time. This perception is exacerbated by the fact that many L2 teachers receive little training on how to develop their learners' L2 written literacy and that, in many circumstances, the learners themselves have only developing L1 written literacy. In some cases, especially with young children, learners are simultaneously developing literacy in their L1 and L2. In other cases, learners are acquiring an L2 after having already developed strong literacy skills in their L1. We tackle each of these possibilities below.

13.2.1 What Are the Components of Literacy?

Literacy is a social skill that encompasses reading and writing and situates them in a greater social context, where the relationship between the authors and audience influences the interpretation of the text. Literacy development is not just important for engaging with texts; there is evidence that strong literacy skills also facilitate other important L2 skills. For example, research shows that the more learners notice aspects of the L2 like grammar patterns or new vocabulary, the more they will acquire. Learners can be trained to notice these features in what they read by adopting reading strategies themselves (e.g., keeping a list of what they notice in the margins of printed readings) or a teacher could purposefully enhance a text by bolding key words or phrases to draw learners' attention to those elements. Some studies have shown that learners with higher literacy are also better able to recognize corrective feedback (see Chapter 3) during oral interactions than learners with low literacy. This cross-modal positive impact means that reading helps learners develop strong listening and comprehension skills that they can use in oral conversations.

Some basic components of literacy are summarized in Figure 13.1 and Table 13.1. Note, however, that literacy development progresses differently in alphabetic versus non-alphabetic languages, so not all the literacy components listed will apply

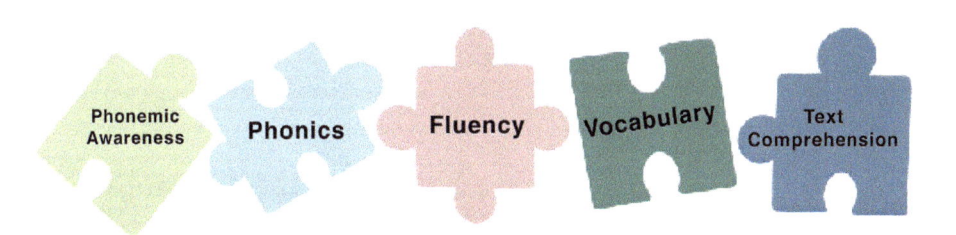

Figure 13.1 Literacy subskills. Breaking down literacy into its subskills can help inform instructional choices in the classroom. Image by: Elizabeth Zonarich

Table 13.1 Components of literacy

Literacy Component	Description
Concepts about print	• Understanding that printed language is symbolic; that the meaning of words/characters does not change, and words contain messages. • Understanding how to hold a book, the direction text is read, how punctuation functions in the language. • Understanding why people read or write. • Understanding different genres. • Understanding how to develop/organize a piece of writing. • Understanding basic writing conventions (e.g., beginning-middle-end in storytelling).
Phonemic/phonological awareness	• Understanding that words can be broken down into individual sounds. • Ability to break down words into their individual sounds. • Ability to substitute and manipulate the individual sounds in a word (e.g., rhyming).
Sound–symbol correspondence	• Knowing which sounds correspond to which letters/symbols/characters.
Word/character identification	• Ability to recognize common words or characters in a language (e.g., common "sight words" in English).
Decoding	• Varies by language. Ability to blend letters/symbols together while reading to pronounce written words orally.
Fluency	• Ability to read or write words with accuracy in a given time frame.
Vocabulary/morphology	• Ability to choose the right word or fill in the right word that is missing in a sentence. • Correct use of morphology (if applicable in the language); for example, use of prefixes/suffixes/infixes.
Comprehension	• Ability to answer questions about what was read. Ability to retell or summarize.
Spelling	• Varies by language. Knowledge of spelling rules/conventions.
Use of reading strategies	• Ability to make predictions based on what has been read or based on images/illustrations. • Ability to visualize/imagine what is read. • Ability to make connections between what is read and prior knowledge. • Ability to use context clues to infer meaning or fill in knowledge gaps. • Ability to answer comprehension questions about a text.
Cultural and pragmatic knowledge	• Choice of most appropriate vocabulary for a range of situations or genres. • Ability to interpret pragmatic contexts from reading. • The inclusion or understanding of culturally relevant/important messages.

to all languages in the same way (see Chapter 10 for more about cross-language differences and their contribution to language learning difficulties). Since literacy development is nonlinear, this list does not imply an order that learners must follow. In fact, learners often develop in several of these sub-components at once when they are presented with authentic reading and writing tasks to complete (see Figure 13.2).

13.2.2 Literacy Development in Younger Multilingual Learners

Rather than causing confusion in literacy development, there is evidence that children who are exposed to multiple languages from a young age develop basic understandings about literacy earlier than monolingual children. This might be because the experience of being exposed to multiple languages enhances children's awareness of the structures of language. Research has also demonstrated that children learning to write in their first language or in multilingual learning environments transfer their developing literacy skills between languages. Knowledge, skills, and attitudes toward literacy in one language can influence developing literacy in another language. When learners are acquiring literacy in their L1 and their L2(s) simultaneously, they benefit from the transfer of knowledge of those developing literacy skills. For example, acquiring phonological awareness and concepts of print have been shown to be particularly important to developing literacy. Phonological awareness in any language has been shown to facilitate reading skills for all languages, even languages in which children aren't receiving direct literacy instruction. Research has tied vocabulary size to writing ability. As we cover in Chapter 14, when both languages are considered,

Literacy Skills

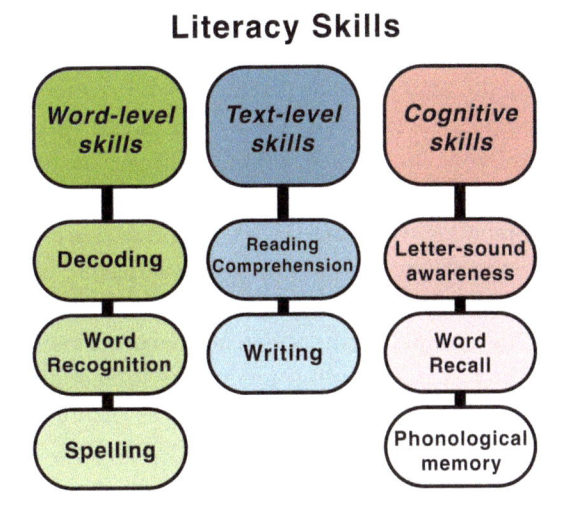

- Word-level skills
  - Decoding
  - Word Recognition
  - Spelling
- Text-level skills
  - Reading Comprehension
  - Writing
- Cognitive skills
  - Letter-sound awareness
  - Word Recall
  - Phonological memory

Figure 13.2 Literacy skills hierarchy. Understanding the skills that are required for successful reading can also help learners track their literacy progress in the L2. Image by: Elizabeth Zonarich

multilingual children tend to have larger vocabularies than monolingual children, though they might have smaller vocabularies in each individual language. Therefore, multilingual writers might engage in more **translanguaging**, or switching between languages, as they write and may require more support in developing their vocabularies to support their burgeoning writing skills.

13.2.3 Literacy Development in Older Language Learners

For L2 learners, literacy is always a multilingual process in which they are drawing upon all the literacy skills they have in all their languages. Many L2 learners, especially older language learners (e.g., those who have already had some years of formal schooling), will arrive at their language classroom with some level of preexisting literacy skills in their L1(s). Compared to young children developing literacy skills for the first time, older L2 learners typically exhibit different linguistic and processing abilities, including different amounts of grammatical and vocabulary knowledge, as they continue to develop their L2 literacy skills.

While we know that L1 literacy skills can facilitate L2 literacy skills, learners bring a wide range of preexisting literacy skills to the classroom. For example, learners might already be highly literate in their L1(s) when they start learning the L2 (e.g., university learners enrolled in a world language course), writing in a variety of genres and reading fluently for school or pleasure. On the other hand, some learners might just have basic concepts about print or some knowledge of the writing process, but not feel comfortable yet reading or writing in their L1. Some learners, like those coming from indigenous backgrounds, might may speak an L1 without a formal writing system or have limited access to print materials in their L1. Any preexisting literacy skills can be leveraged from the learners' L1s to benefit literacy development in the L2. For example, the skill of decoding (see Table 13.1) has been shown to transfer across languages. If a learner who can already decode in their L1 struggles to decode a word in the L2, it might be because they don't know the word yet orally in the L2.

A variety of research-based strategies can be employed with learners who are still developing literacy skills. First, it's important to elevate any/all existing literacy practices of your learners. This prior knowledge needs to be activated in any literacy-building work done in the language classroom. Many learners without a strong literacy foundation in their L1 will need to be explicitly taught to use cognitive and metacognitive strategies to read texts (see Chapter 5 and below for more ideas). For example, learners may need explicit instruction in how to approach a text in the L2 before, during, and after reading as illustrated in Figure 13.3.

Embedding any strategy instruction as demonstrated above into authentic uses for reading or writing (as supported by task-based language teaching, see Chapter 17) will further enhance the benefits for L2 learners by encouraging them to develop literacy skills for real-world purposes. Finally, for all language learners, but especially those with developing literacy skills from traditionally marginalized backgrounds, researchers like Nelson Flores advocate for avoiding the dichotomy between "academic" and "non-academic" language, which often serves to further

13.2 The Science: What the Research Says

Time	Strategy instruction	Benefits for L2 learners
Pre-Reading	How to preview the book (looking at the table of contents, illustrations, front and back matter, etc.) and make predictions about what they will read.	Activating prior knowledge and making connections to preexisting ideas, which will facilitate learners' comprehension later.
During Reading	How to revisit predictions and update them, if necessary, adding new predictions along the way as needed.	Facilitates learners' monitoring of their own comprehension as they read.
Post-Reading	How to return predictions and decide if they were right or wrong and provide reasoning.	Induces learners to engage in summarizing, identifying key pieces of evidence, and other reading skills shown to facilitate comprehension and literacy development.

Figure 13.3 Reading strategies

cement a deficit perspective of multilingual learners. Instead of pointing out how learners' language is "non-academic" or "improper," Flores and others suggest teachers reframe to encourage learners to recognize the cultural and linguistic skills they already possess and how those skills can be successfully applied to academic texts. Invite learners to see themselves as "language architects" who make critical choices about the language they read, write, and interpret. To do this, conduct activities that encourage learners to analyze the language they encounter in written text. How does the language used help advance the author's message?

13.2.4 Literacy Development for Learners with Strong L1 Literacy

Even when learners arrive at the language classroom with strong preexisting L1 literacy, they must still develop a variety of new literacy practices in their L2. These might include understanding new cultural expectations or differences between L1 and L2 writing norms or encountering new genres. In any case, learners will certainly use writing and reading to reinforce or learn new L2 grammar or vocabulary. For these learners, it's important to start by first discussing the purposes and communicative functions of reading and writing in the L2.

To maximize literacy skill development, learners should engage in frequent conversations around the goals of their literacy activities, different learning strategies that can help them achieve those goals, and the type of inferences between their prior knowledge and the literacy tasks they face. Some strategies teachers can use include:

- Intentional incorporation of a variety of genres across traditionally academic (book reports, journal articles) and other genres (social media posts, emails). Varying genre will help learners develop literacy skills appropriate in multiple contexts (see Figure 13.4).

Figure 13.4 Real-world literacy needs. (1) Genres used in professional contexts: emails, briefs, reports, conference schedules, journal articles, slide decks. (2) Genres used in travel contexts: text messages, product reviews, menus, street signs, blog posts, bus schedules, housing/hotel listings. Image by: Elizabeth Zonarich

- Explicit instruction of reading and writing strategies. Much like the strategies discussed above for lower-literacy learners, these strategies help learners practice advanced cognitive skills involved in literacy, like inference-making, perspective-taking, and comprehension-monitoring. Depending on the learners' L1 and L2, an L2 learner may be taught how to leverage cognates to help with comprehension and production in literacy-based activities.
- Breaking down texts into sub-components to encourage careful reading. Research shows that learners process more language when they read slowly and carefully. Similarly, breaking down the writing process into simple steps can help scaffold learners with limited writing experience to be able to access a wider variety of genres.
- Providing time for brainstorming or planning before writing or reading tasks. Research shows that when learners have time to think or plan before engaging with a text, they produce more complex ideas and language.

A few different models for writing instruction for learners with preexisting literacy have been proposed in previous literature. **Genre-based pedagogy** has been shown to help developing L2 writers better understand the communicative purposes of literacy. In genre-based approaches, language is presented contextualized within a variety of different genres like argumentative texts, persuasive essays, cover letters, etc. (see Figure 13.5). Situating texts based on their intended audience, as well as within larger social contexts may further engage L2 writers, drawing their attention to different linguistic forms and styles of a range of genres.

Another approach is **extensive writing**. An extensive-writing approach can be defined as an approach that allows learners to (1) write as much as possible, (2) write on a wide range of topics, (3) write for different reasons and in different ways, (4) decide what they want to write about, (5) write at a variety of speeds.

Figure 13.5 Genre-based pedagogy. Introduce learners to the writing conventions of specific genres they will encounter outside the classroom. Image by: Elizabeth Zonarich

Some research has investigated blogging as a genre that facilitates extensive writing. This research indicates that integrating blogging into the language classroom can encourage learners to develop their writing proficiency while partaking in authentic and meaningful communication. Through regular blogging, learners can improve their writing mechanics and organization. Additionally, the "open" nature of genres for extensive writing, like blogging, encourages learners to review and revise their writing without teacher interference, thereby promoting learner autonomy over their literacy development.

BOX 13.1 The Science! Points to Remember

- Language skills are all related, so working on strengthening literacy skills, like reading and writing, can help advance speaking and listening abilities.
- Learners can draw on first language literacy skills when developing their second language literacy skills.
- A learner's vocabulary size impacts their development of reading and writing skills.
- Becoming a strong reader or writer requires explicit instructions on the mechanics and strategies for reading and writing.
- Learners with and without prior literacy skills can benefit from cognitive and metacognitive strategies to promote effective reading and writing practices.

13.3 The Science: What's Missing?

There are a variety of gaps in the research in L2 literacy development. First, low- and nonliterate populations are underrepresented in SLA research, which usually relies on university students with well-established literacy skills because these are a relatively easy population to recruit for research. Without research focused on the L2 acquisition and L2 learning processes of low-literate and nonliterate populations, our collective understanding the development of L2 literacy skills (and the potential influence of L1 skills to L2 skills) is incomplete. Individual differences may also play a role here, as in other areas of language learning (see Chapters 6, 7, 8, and 9 for more on learner differences), but the role of these differences in literacy development in low-literate populations is not well explored. Because literacy skills have long been considered a window into learners' language processing, the absence of low-literate language learners from these studies also negatively impacts how we understand language to be cognitively represented in individuals with limited or no formal schooling.

In addition, there is a paucity in terms of longitudinal studies, which means we lack an understanding of the long-term impact of different instructional practices on the development of literacy skills. For this reason, we cannot say with certainty if one type of writing or reading instructional approach (e.g., genre-based) is definitively better than others for promoting literacy development in the long run. We also cannot make definitive claims about how different strategies for promoting reading and writing skills impact the development of other language skills, like speaking or listening. We can only emphasize that they are interrelated in the populations and educational contexts represented in SLA research.

Thus far, there is inconclusive research about whether the frequency of writing (e.g., in personal journals or blogs) or reading will lead to literacy development. This lack of a clear answer is because many of the studies looking at reading and writing frequency define "improvement" in widely different ways (e.g., organization, use of mechanics, grammatical accuracy, the complexity of vocabulary, or how fluently learners write), meaning we can't make a clear "apples-to-apples" comparison across studies. Another important caveat is that some aspects of improvement are difficult to measure – older learns might develop new strategies to engage with reading or writing that are difficult to detect or quantify, and yet these skills will facilitate their ultimate language learning. It is important for teachers to recognize the various and sometimes incremental ways leaners may demonstrate literacy development as they reflect on the effectiveness of their instructional approaches.

13.4 The Art: Research-Based Strategies to Try

Literacy is a social skill that serves personal purposes and so developing literacy skills should also include social components. Bring in resources that highlight all the different ways written communication occurs in the TL and TL communities, including a variety of different genres such as fiction, nonfiction, digital media, poetry, news coverage, classic texts, etc.

13.4 The Art: Research-Based Strategies to Try

For the strategies below, we first address literacy components that promote reading development, including reading aloud to learners, asking learners to read independently, guiding learners through the reading process, and promoting reading strategies. We then cover strategies for writing instruction and end with literacy assessment. Many (if not most) classrooms include learners with a mix of literacy levels in the L2 or their L1(s). One way to account for mixed abilities while promoting literacy development is to set up literacy stations. Allow learners to pick which stations they want to work on to differentiate learning. Stations could include comparing texts from two different genres, reading restaurant reviews to decide where to eat, or reading and discussing comprehension questions with a partner. For younger learners, some stations for reading development could include reading a book to a stuffed animal, reading a book in an audio message, or playing a phonics game in small groups (see Figure 13.6).

Figure 13.6 Literacy stations. Literacy stations can help learners practice reading and writing skills. Image by: Elizabeth Zonarich

13.4.1 The Art of Structured Read-Aloud and Independent Reading Time

- Pick books intentionally. For beginning readers and/or learners of a low-proficiency level, consider selecting books with predicable plots or familiar plots to build confidence and encourage learners.
  - Predictable books: rhyming, repetitive lines/words/phrases so readers can "predict" what words/sounds/phrases they will next encounter or participate actively during a read-aloud activity.
    - If doing a read aloud, ask learners to listen for key vocabulary and raise a finger when they hear it. Or have learners read along with you with individual copies of the book. This encourages careful reading, which has been tied to literacy and language development.
  - Familiar books: learners are already familiar with the characters or plot. These may be popular books translated from the learners' L1 to their L2. They may also be books that the teacher creates for the learners, using inside jokes from class, commonly known places, etc.
- For young or developing readers, introduce your learners to the "five-finger rule" when they choose texts to read independently. If they begin reading a text and realize they do not know five words on a page, the text will likely present challenges to read without external support and scaffolding. Empower learners to recognize what kinds of books will be right for their level, but also push learners to read slightly outside of their comfort zone. Not knowing every single word is ok! What words can they figure out using context clues?
- Encourage older learners who are working on developing their read-aloud ability to record themselves reading and listen back for key characteristics like speed, intonation, and pronunciation. This may help learners develop confidence and become more autonomous in their learning processes.

13.4.2 The Art of Incorporating Reading Strategies

- Consider integrating instruction in reading strategies before, during, and after engaging with a text.
  - *Pre-reading* activities can develop and/or activate the prior knowledge needed to participate in a literacy-based activity. Some pre-reading activities can include making predictions, journaling about the topic of the book, discussing the purposes of different genres, or instruction on the key vocabulary or content that will be important to know for the reading.
  - *During-reading* activities can help learners monitor their comprehension. Some activities include practicing re-reading difficult sections for more context clues, revising predictions, reflecting on what was just read, practicing reading aloud, or making a connection to the story they are reading (see Figure 13.7). Learners might be encouraged to maintain a list of the vocabulary or grammar they notice while reading. Noticing has been tied to language development in a variety of research studies and is one of the many ways literacy development facilitates language acquisition.

13.4 The Art: Research-Based Strategies to Try

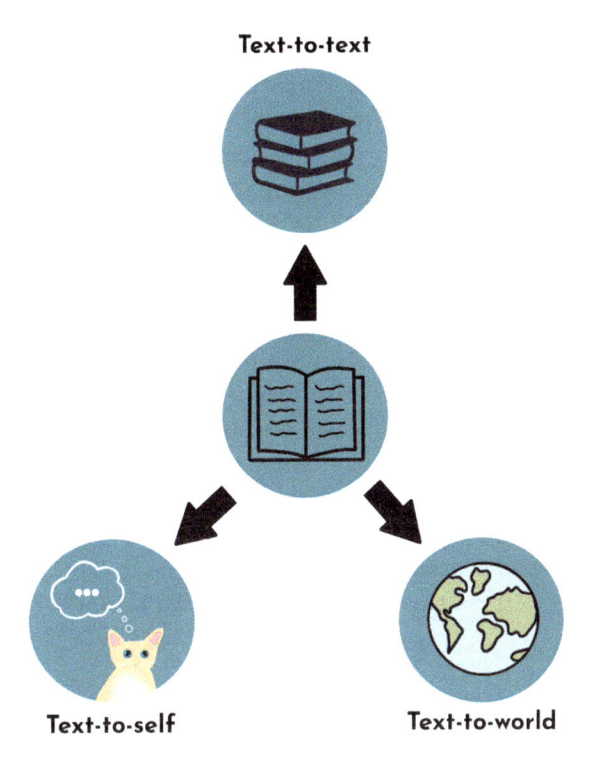

Figure 13.7 Text connections. Reading strategies can also include text connections to promote learner engagement and comprehension. Image by: Elizabeth Zonarich

- *Post-reading* activities help learners focus on language, content, or other aspects of literacy development. Some activities include analyzing some aspect of the text like the characters, plot, or genre. Learners might respond to what they read with a creative writing assignment or analyze the language they encountered.
- It is important to note the following:
  - Learners with little to no literacy experience in their L1 will need more scaffolding and support as they begin to develop literacy in an L2.
  - Consider the prior knowledge necessary to understand a written text. Background knowledge about the plot or organization of a text/genre can help learners fill in the linguistic gaps in their knowledge.

13.4.3 The Art of Scaffolding the Writing Process

- Consider structuring writing around the steps of the writing process. Learners at all levels can benefit from structured steps toward writing in their L2 just as they might in their L1.
  - Pre-writing: Thinking, brainstorming, researching, searching
  - Drafting: Writing, sketching
  - Revising: Re-reading, restructuring, reorganizing
  - Editing: Correcting, proofreading, spellchecking

- Publishing: Finalizing, printing, illustrating, polishing
  - Share the "final products" of student-authored work in the classroom. Encourage learners to read each other's work. Not only will student writing be comprehensible with familiar themes, but it will also help the student authors feel a sense of accomplishment and ownership over their writing products and help to legitimize their identity as writers.
  - Finding time in class for learners to share their writing orally to further support the authentic social nature of the writing process.
- Develop "mini lessons" based on what learners need to implement that unit in their writing. Mini lessons are short (5–10 minutes) moments of direct instruction or modeling on some writing technique. Some examples to get you started include:
  - How to brainstorm what to write with a web-diagram
  - How to create and use an editing checklist to correct your work
  - How to find evidence to support an argument in a research paper
  - How to properly cite sources for a particular genre
  - How to separate ideas into paragraphs
  - How to craft a narrative story by including a beginning, middle, and end (maybe by filling in a graphic organizer)

13.4.4 The Art of Measuring Literacy Development

- Some teachers might want to assess their learners to better understand what kinds of literacy skills they have when they start the school year or semester, or first join their language class. Alternatively, a teacher might suspect a literacy difficulty that a learner is exhibiting and want to learn more. Use Table 13.2 for some assessment options that correspond with the components of literacy discussed earlier in this chapter.

Table 13.2 Diagnostic assessments

Literacy component	Possible assessments
Concepts about print	• Observation of book handling skills including turning pages, following along with fingers. • Writing sample.
Phonemic/phonological awareness	• Phonemic awareness test: Ask learners to say out loud the sounds in a given word. E.g., "what are the sounds in *cat*?" "/k-æ-t/. What about *sing*? /s-i-ŋ/."
Sound-symbol correspondence	• For alphabetic languages: a phonics survey. Point to letters and ask learners to say out loud what sound the letter makes (not its "letter name" for languages like English where letter names differ from sounds).
Word/character identification	• Use flash cards and ask learners to say the word aloud as fast as they can. • Make games with cards with words on them. For example, spread out a group of sight word cards on the floor. Say a word and ask learners to hop onto the word or toss a coin to land on the right card.

Table 13.2 Continued

Literacy component	Possible assessments
Decoding/Fluency	• Fluency tests like running records can be used to calculate learners' reading fluency. Time learners reading target texts and note down reading errors.
Vocabulary/morphology	• Use cloze tests (i.e., reading passages with key vocabulary words missing) to find out more about learners' current vocabulary knowledge. • Check the language used in a writing sample from various genres.
Comprehension	• Ask learners to read a passage and retell you what they just read. • Ask learners to summarize something they just read. • Ask learners comprehension questions based on a text they just read.
Spelling	• Use a spelling inventory (i.e., a type of spelling test that systematically samples the spelling of common patterns in the L2).

- Outside of diagnostic assessments, you might wish to include writing as a form of formative or summative assessment of a learner's ability in the TL. One option is to bring together all the different literacy development activities in an ongoing portfolio so that learners (and you!) can see their progress. You can combine the creation of a portfolio with other self-reflection tools as alternative assessment measures. Learn more about this option and the research that has been conducted on assessments in Chapter 20.

13.5 Troubleshooting: How the Science Informs the Art

Ms. W is a French teacher who works in a school for high school learners who have struggled academically in the past, or had discipline issues or frequent absenteeism. Ms. W wants to incorporate literacy strategies more intentionally into her instruction but is not sure where to start. Many of her learners are still developing literacy in their L1 and she fears they wouldn't be ready to start applying the same techniques from the L1 to the L2.

Research on the transfer of L1 knowledge to L2 knowledge has yet to identify a definitive point where learners are "ready" to start applying knowledge acquired in one language to another. What we do know is that encouraging learners to make connections between whatever linguistic resources they have (from their L1s or L2s) can positively impact their development, when their progress is measured in a fair and reasonable way. Because of cognitive differences, some learners will start to transfer their L1 abilities to their L2, regardless of their level or the amount of teacher support. Others may never have this inclination. Ms. W can support all her learners' growth by providing clear, explicit guidance on literacy strategies. She might want to start by surveying her class for their interests and then choosing reading materials from a variety of genres based on those interests. Starting from a place where students can apply their prior knowledge will foster engagement in the L2 literacy development process. Ms. W can then leverage that engagement by integrating purposeful reading strategy instruction, like pre/during/post-reading activities, for genres or topics students are less familiar with.

How can Ms. W learn from and adapt the strategies being used in the learners' L1 classes (not just literature, but also math and science) to reinforce and support their developing French L2 literacy? What kinds of tasks and feedback are most useful for developing beginning literacy in an L2?

Because L1 literacy and L2 literacy are so closely related, Ms. W should reach out to her colleagues in math and science to identify techniques that they are using in their courses. This may also help her tailor her expectations for learners' progress accordingly. For example, if learners are learning how to identify the supporting details in a five-paragraph essay in their science courses, which are taught in the learners' L1, she may not be able to expect them to perform similar tasks in the French classroom, but she can encourage them to apply their new skills to French texts. Learners may need to first focus on identifying words they recognize in shorter texts, like advertisements or social media posts, before moving on to more complex French texts.

Tasks that teach Ms. W's learners how to notice key grammatical patterns or vocabulary that are important for meaning-making will be most immediately helpful in supporting learner autonomy. Because Ms. W's learners are adolescents, they may feel frustrated or get disheartened with such seemingly simple tasks. Ms. W can combat this by sharing the various components of literacy discussed in this chapter, encouraging learners to track their own progress, and selecting texts and resources about themes that interest her learners (rather than texts that are intended for much younger children). Ms. W can offer feedback to learners by encouraging them to chart their own progress. Using some of the assessment strategies suggested above, learners can keep track of their reading fluency rates, number of sight words, or other benchmarks. In this way, progress can be celebrated by students and Ms. W alike. For feedback on writing, Ms. W can refer to some of the feedback suggestions provided in Chapter 3.

13.6 The Science: Points to Remember

- Literacy involves a variety of interrelated subskills like sound–symbol correspondence, phonemic awareness, form–meaning mapping, and vocabulary knowledge.
- Language learners with limited or informal schooling and literacy background will need more support and scaffolding when developing literacy in their L2.
- Research suggests learners will make the most L2 literacy gains when they are encouraged to draw on all their linguistic knowledge and literacy resources, including those

from their L1. Some learners may do this naturally, whereas others may need more explicit guidance from the teacher.
- Introducing reading and writing strategies may help increase learners' motivation and sense of autonomy, prompting them to seek out more literacy opportunities that provide them with more input, which is one of the four main ingredients for language development (see Chapter 2).

13.7 Questions to Consider

1. Think about your own experiences learning second languages (if any) or encountering a second language in the world (e.g., a menu in another language). What literacy skills did you find you could leverage from your L1 and apply to the new language?
2. What (if any) literacy skills have your learners mastered? What (if any) skills are they currently working on in their other classes?
3. What attitudes do your learners have toward reading and writing?
4. What kinds of literacy practices do your learners engage in during your class periods?
5. What kinds of real-world literacy practices will your learners likely encounter outside of your classroom?
6. Do your learners have scaffolded opportunities to develop literacy skills in age-appropriate, real-world situations during your class?

13.8 The Science of Language Learning: Research Supporting the Points Made in This Chapter

Allen, H. W. (2018). Redefining writing in the foreign language curriculum: Toward a design approach. *Foreign Language Annals, 51*, 513–531. https://doi.org/10.1111/flan.12350.

This article addresses the lack of time and energy often devoted to writing skills (in comparison to speaking, listening, and reading) in foreign language classrooms. The author contextualizes the important role that L2 writing plays in a learner's linguistic development and advocates for a design approach to writing instruction. Within a design approach, writing skills are integrated into the curriculum within communicative, real-world tasks. In this way, learners are applying their writing skills to gain and share new knowledge rather than simply writing for the sake of writing. The advantages and potential challenges of this approach are discussed and the author concludes with recommendations for educators considering adopting a design approach in their own classrooms.

Kim, Y. S., & Piper, B. (2019). Cross-language transfer of reading skills: An empirical investigation of bidirectionality and the influence of instructional environments. *Reading and Writing, 32*, 839–871. https://doi.org/10.1007/s11145-018-9889-7.

This empirical study compares the development of literacy skills in primary schoolchildren who are learning to read in Kiswahili (an official language of Kenya) and English. Some groups of children received explicit instruction designed to improve their phonological awareness and phoneme–grapheme correspondences and others did not. Data was collected to explore the extent to which the students' literacy skills in one language impacted their progress in the other. Results suggest that all students did transfer their reading skills between their two languages, but that students who received more explicit instruction on the subskills involved in literacy (like letter sounds) had more instances of transfer than the students who did not receive any explicit instruction. The authors conclude that intentional, explicit instruction can help facilitate beginning and advanced reading skills in an L2.

Troyan, F. J. (2014). Leveraging genre theory: A genre-based interactive model for the era of the Common Core state standards. *Foreign Language Annals, 47*(1), 5–24. https://doi.org/10.1111/flan.12068.

This article offers a comprehensive overview of how a genre-based approach to writing instruction can be used in K–12 (primary and secondary) world language classrooms. Several common genres that surface in these settings are presented and discussed from a genre-based pedagogical perspective. Troyan applies this pedagogy to the development and introduction of presentational writing tasks via a genre-based interactive model. This model comprises four mandatory stages (preparation, comprehension, interpretation/discussion, and creativity) and a fifth, optional, stage: extension. The application of this model with a sample writing task is included, complete with activities that readers can try out in their own classrooms.

For more resources, including more sample lesson plans, videos, and other ideas, visit our companion website: www.cambridge.org/BryfonskiMackey.

14 When or how should I teach vocabulary?

KEY QUESTIONS
- **The Science: What does it mean to know a word? How much vocabulary do my learners really need to know?**
- **The Art: How or when should I teach vocabulary?**
- **What percentage of the vocabulary words should my learners be able to understand during a reading or listening activity?**
- **What is a reasonable amount of vocabulary to introduce to my learners each class/unit?**

14.1 Voices from the Classroom

Mrs. L's high school language program recently made the decision to abandon the traditional textbook that formed the foundation of their curriculum. Mrs. L is excited to co-create a new curriculum with her learners, one that is centered around their needs and interests. She has decided not to pre-make vocabulary lists because she wants learners to bring in the words and phrases that are meaningful to them. However, after the first unit in her Spanish III class, Mrs. L noticed that while her learners often looked up new words during each class period, their performance on the final project felt more repetitive and stilted than in years past. She is worried that she did not provide enough structure related to unit vocabulary. Because she allowed each student to develop a more personalized vocabulary list, she feels she may not have held them each accountable for learning and incorporating all these new words. As she plans for her next units, what should she do to make sure that she is effectively teaching vocabulary to her learners?

14.2 The Science: What the Research Says

Having a large and varied vocabulary is a key ingredient to being a successful communicator in a second language (L2). Even an excellent command of the L2 grammar, sound system, and culture will not make up for a lacking vocabulary when it comes to meaningful L2 interactions. In other words, knowing how to structure a grammatical sentence but not knowing the word for the concept that needs to be expressed in that sentence greatly limits interaction. Building a robust L2 vocabulary has many benefits for learners. Research shows that a larger vocabulary is associated with not only more fluent speaking and writing, but also an increased comprehension ability in reading and listening activities. When many people think of learning vocabulary in a second language, they imagine memorizing word lists using flash cards. However, L2 vocabulary acquisition is actually an incredibly complex process that involves much more than pure memorization. The bank of vocabulary words learners have acquired is called their **lexicon**. Depending on the age learners started learning their L2, or other individual differences, their first language (L1) and L2 lexicons might be stored differently in their memory. Building up an L2 lexicon requires learners to connect new L2 words, and their associated meanings, to word–meaning pairs in their L1. Usually, the connections between words in the L2 lexicon are not as strong and stable as they are in their L1, which is why, for many learners, new words are harder to remember and use. It is only after repeated exposure and practice that learners are able to strengthen the bonds of their L2 lexicon. Some researchers (Cook, 2002) visualize this progression along a continuum. The spectrum in Figure 14.1 is based on Cook's (2002) interpretation of an L2 user. On the far left, learners' L1 and L2 lexicons are completely separated. They might even think of a slightly different prototypical meaning or image (the two types of mice) in each of their languages. In the middle, there is interconnection between the two where learners link their L2 lexicon to their L1, translating from one to the next. On the far right, the L1 and L2 lexicons are integrated, and learners might switch frequently between languages and have a single concept (mouse) for both.

14.2.1 What Does It Mean To "Know" A Word?

At a shallow level, "knowing" a word may mean simply recognizing it as a familiar word while reading a passage or listening to story. At a deeper level, "knowing" a word might mean translating the word or even providing additional information

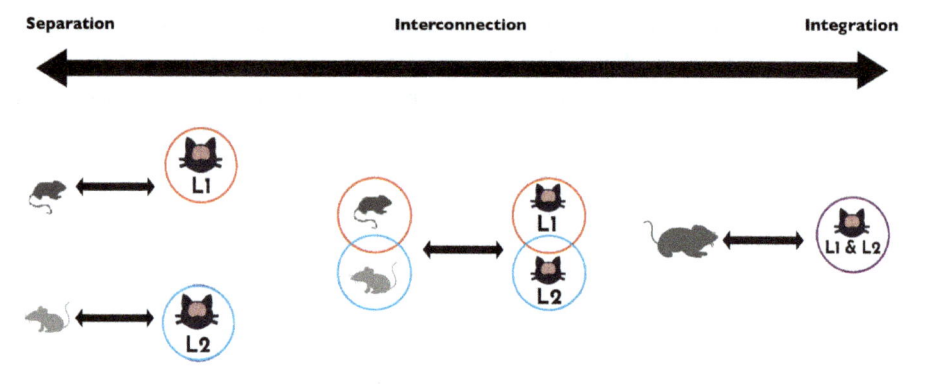

Figure 14.1 The spectrum of L1 and L2 lexicons. This spectrum shows the progression from separation to integration between L1 and L2 lexicons (Cook, 2002). Image by: Elizabeth Zonarich

14.2 The Science: What the Research Says

Recognition   **Form–meaning connection**   **Production**

Figure 14.2 Receptive and productive word knowledge. The cat begins to recognize the word *stop*, strengthening the form–meaning connection, and ultimately allowing the cat to produce the new word in context. Image by: Elizabeth Zonarich

about its origin and functions. Vocabulary knowledge can also be broken down into **receptive knowledge** (words that a learner might recognize and understand but be unlikely to produce) and **productive knowledge** (words a learner produces during communication) (see Figure 14.2).

Early studies in vocabulary acquisition suggest that learners develop receptive knowledge prior to productive knowledge and that it is easier for them to recognize a newly learned word than it is to describe its meaning or use it in a new context. But word knowledge is more than just recognition and production. Word knowledge can be further broken down into separate components: knowledge of word form, knowledge of word meaning, and knowledge of word use. Research shows that the more interconnected these components are for learners, the more successful they will be at processing and using vocabulary. These connections are thought to be strengthened after repeated exposure, which builds associations to prior knowledge and contextual knowledge, and increases memory of the word and its meaning. If the connections are low quality, for example if a learner has internalized the incorrect spelling or pronunciation of a word, it might be harder for them to form strong connections within their L2 lexicon and understand the word when they hear or see it in context.

While reading and writing can support vocabulary learning, it's important to keep in mind that knowing vocabulary for the purposes of speaking and listening is different from being able to read and write vocabulary, as literacy is a separate set of skills in L2 learning (see Chapter 13 on literacy for more details).

14.2.2 How Is Vocabulary Learned?

Language learning is a continuous process and vocabulary learning is no different. Research suggests that as speakers learn more vocabulary, that vocabulary can be leveraged to help understand, process, and learn new words. When learners know more words in a text, they can use those words to figure out new words (see Figure

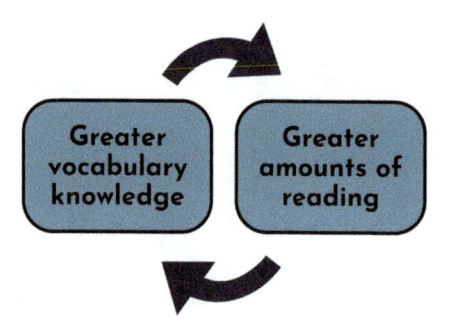

Figure 14.3 The cycle of vocabulary acquisition. The more learners read, the more vocabulary words they will learn. The more vocabulary words they learn, the more they will be inclined to read. Image by: Elizabeth Zonarich

14.3). Because of this, learners with larger vocabularies tend to learn more new words through reading than learners with smaller vocabularies.

The process of learning vocabulary is often broken down into two types: **incidental learning** or **intentional learning**. When researchers describe incidental learning, they are describing the process of learning words in context, indirectly, and without intention. An example is learning new words while reading a novel. This contrasts with intentional vocabulary learning, where the goal is to learn new words. An example is studying flash cards of words to remember (see Figure 14.4).

Research has identified advantages and disadvantages to each type of learning (see Box 14.1). The extent to which the advantages or disadvantages outweigh the other is dependent on contextual and learner-specific factors. Given the extraordinarily large vocabulary size needed for independent comprehension and the limited number of contact hours in a typical language classroom, many linguists (and teachers) are particularly interested in how to support incidental vocabulary learning.

Figure 14.4 Incidental and intentional vocabulary learning. The cat on the left is learning new vocabulary words incidentally, through independent reading, while the cat on the right is learning new vocabulary intentionally, through flash card practice. Image by: Elizabeth Zonarich

BOX 14.1 Incidental and Intentional Vocabulary Learning: Strengths and Critiques

Incidental Vocabulary L2 Learning		Intentional Vocabulary L2 Learning	
Strengths	Critiques	Strengths	Critiques
• Rich knowledge • Retention rate	• Inefficient • Slow • Requires prior vocabulary knowledge	• Practical • Quick	• Decontextualized knowledge • Difficulty applying vocabulary in interaction

What factors impact incidental vocabulary learning? Research has uncovered several important variables, the first being the frequency and length of exposure to target words. Words are thought to enter a student's vocabulary after repeated exposure. The more often a student encounters a word, the more likely that student is to add that word to their vocabulary. The amount of time a learner sees a new word is often dictated by the length of time spent either reading or listening to texts in the target language (TL). However, the amount of time learners spend in their language classrooms is finite. Research has shown that learners who take efforts to read, listen, and interact in the TL outside of class experience greater vocabulary gains than learners who do not. For example, findings suggest that English language learners who watch movies and TV shows in English have a larger vocabulary than their L2 English peers who do not.

But how many times does a learner need to encounter a new word in order to learn it? In research studies that examine frequency, learners are divided into groups, and then each group is exposed to the targeted words on two, four, six, etc. occasions in reading passages. Next, all learners take the same tests to measure whether they have learned the target words. These types of studies have had mixed results. Some researchers found that a single exposure is sufficient for a student to be able to identify a target word. Others claim eight exposures are necessary, and still others say twenty! What could account for these differences? Two individual differences could be at play: age and proficiency level. Findings indicate that older or higher-proficiency learners stand to experience greater benefits from repeated exposure to vocabulary than younger or lower-proficiency learners. This finding is independent of the learners' existing vocabulary knowledge. Researchers suggest that this is because older learners have developed more effective reading strategies and literacy skills than younger learners. Also, the type of text learners read and the method of testing their vocabulary development can also impact how often a word needs to be encountered before it is acquired.

Interestingly, most standard textbooks do not align with these ideas about vocabulary learning. Textbook analyses have revealed that the vocabulary within one textbook unit is usually quite specific and generally distinct from the vocabulary featured in the next unit. Learners then do not have a chance to read, hear, or produce vocabulary once they have completed each unit. This contrasts with the research, which has identified frequency of exposure as an influential variable in vocabulary development. However, the details about how much repetition and how other factors (age, proficiency level, motivation, working memory) impact the "ideal" amount of repetition remain unknown.

Another factor impacting vocabulary development is the use of multiple, simultaneous modes of input. This refers to learners reading a text while listening to it read aloud, or learners viewing a picture while listening to a description of it being read aloud. This could be any combination of reading, listening, or viewing visuals. Studies exploring how receiving multiple modes of input affects vocabulary learning have argued that access to the additional, simultaneous input makes it easier for lower-level learners to build form–meaning connections (i.e., figure out what new words mean). Listening to a passage being read aloud was hypothesized to relieve learners of the burden of figuring out how words might sound. With this extra attentional capacity, they might be able to focus more on the meaning of the words they are hearing and reading. Research findings also suggest that the characteristics of written text may influence learners' vocabulary learning. The characteristics that researchers have investigated, including presence of contextual clues (illustrations), genre, and length, could impact the extent to which learners are able to extend their vocabulary knowledge. For example, context clues like bolded words with definitions or examples with pictures have been shown to support vocabulary learning.

14.2.3 How Much Vocabulary Knowledge is Necessary?

The amount of new vocabulary a learner needs to have in order to understand and communicate varies based on several factors, including the number of **cognates** between the L1 and the TL and the presence of other contextual clues that could support comprehension. The table in Box 14.2 shows how cognates appear across a variety of languages.

BOX 14.2 Cognate Pairs

English word	Cognates	Languages
daughter	daughter- دختر [doxˈder]	English-Farsi
desert	desert- desierto	English-Spanish
foot	pie- पैर [pɒː]- paira	French-Farsi-Hindi
tooth	donti- diente	Greek-Spanish

14.2 The Science: What the Research Says

For young learners (e.g., ages 10–12), the similarity between words (whether or not the TL word looks/sounds like its counterpart in the learner's L1) has been shown to have a large influence on whether learners incorporate that word into their growing knowledge bank. How salient a word is also important for vocabulary development. Words described as "salient" are words that stand out to learners for any given reason. Studies suggest these salient words may be more easily learned than less salient words. The characteristics of words affect how salient they will be for learners. Research shows that word characteristics like frequency, part of speech, and whether or not the word is a cognate are qualities that may play a large role in determining whether learners perceive certain words to be more salient than others. Concrete words that describe tangible or observable things (e.g., cat, tree) are also usually more salient than abstract words (e.g., freedom or happiness). The frequency of a word will affect how easily a learner will form connections between form and meaning. Is the word likely to be heard or read multiple times in a variety of contexts? Or is it a technical term that is used mostly in academic contexts? Or maybe the word isn't technical, but it's really uncommon and it's unlikely the learner will hear it too often. "Function" words like articles, prepositions, and conjunctions are some of the most frequent words (e.g., in English: *the, to, of, and, a, in* …), whereas technical words, for example *diphthong* (when two vowels combine in a single syllable, as in *coin*) are uncommon (for non-linguists) and may require more frequent exposure for successful learning.

Research on vocabulary sizes and comprehension indicate that to completely understand a text with no external support (i.e., no dictionaries, no visuals, no notes), learners should already be familiar with about 98 percent of the words in the passage (1 unknown word in 50). In other words, in order to understand a variety of material (magazines articles, cartoons, museum plaques, novels, children's movies, etc.) at the level of a highly proficient or native speaker, research suggests that an individual must have a vocabulary of at least 8,000 word families (see Figure 14.5). However, in language classrooms learners have access to many resources that they

How large a vocabulary is needed to understand…?

Written texts	Aural passages	TV shows & movies
8,000-9,000 word families ⬇ 98% coverage	750-3,000 word families ⬇ 90-95% coverage	3,000 word families ⬇ 95% coverage

Figure 14.5 Vocabulary size. Research indicates that the following word family sizes are required for learners to read independently and without any outside support (e.g., peers, dictionaries, notes). Image by: Elizabeth Zonarich

can and should be encouraged to use to make the input they receive more comprehensible. Teachers can also structure pre-, during-, and post-reading activities to support learners in meaning-making even when they encounter words they do not yet know (see Chapter 13 for more on literacy). Therefore, this 8,000 word families number does not mean that students should resort to memorizing vocabulary lists and interacting with highly simplified resources until they have incorporated a "sufficient" number of words in their vocabularies.

When linguists talk about word families, we are talking about derivational word families, or groups of words that share a common root. This is a slightly different interpretation of word families from those that are used for teaching phonics (see Figure 14.6).

There are some important caveats to consider when we think about "how much" a learner needs to know. First, these numbers do not mean that learners should be shielded from the types of materials listed above until they have learned "enough" words to communicate. On the contrary, repeated exposure to these materials and chances to use words from these situations in meaningful communicative interactions will support learners' ongoing vocabulary development. Also, there are a variety of reading strategies that can be developed when learners encounter texts that are not yet entirely comprehensible (see Chapter 13 on literacy development for sample ideas).

14.2.4 Connections to Practice: Technology and Vocabulary Learning

Game-based learning is a more recent area of interest for researchers investigating L2 vocabulary acquisition. Since we know that the more exposure to and interaction with the TL the better the L2 development, using technology to increase the potential for encountering the TL "in the wild" (i.e., not the classroom) increases learners' exposure substantially. Given that higher levels of motivation and engagement are associated with greater learning (see Chapter 8), online games, videogames, and other digital tools have received considerable attention as potential language learning tools, as they tend to be highly motivating ways to engage learners. Findings so far show that digital games can

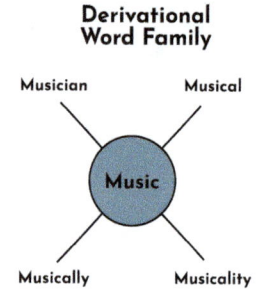

Derivational Word Family

Musician, Musical, Musically, Musicality — Music

Rhyming Word Family	
-ap word family	
cap	rap
clap	tap
lap	snap
map	tap

Figure 14.6 Word family visualizations. An example of a derivational word family and a rhyming word family. Image by: Elizabeth Zonarich

support vocabulary development among language learners. Researchers have examined how variations like age, proficiency level, technology (computer vs. phone), play time (one or multiple sessions), and type of game influence the extent to which participating in a digital game affects learner vocabulary. Studies on elementary-aged learners found that learners who played five or more computer games in the TL knew and used more vocabulary words than their counterparts who did not. Another study found that young language learners (11- to 12-year-olds) who gamed five hours or more per week knew more vocabulary than those who played less often or didn't play at all. More research is needed to figure out how to incorporate and structure these games to maximize their educational potential across different learner groups. Other studies have looked at how virtual reality (VR) impacts vocabulary learning. This research points out that the immersive experience that VR provides can allow for greater vocabulary growth and engagement for L2 learners.

Another digital tool that has been popular for vocabulary development is the use of corpora – large, searchable databases of language in context. Tools like these allow learners to search for key words in context from a huge number of sample contexts to see how they are commonly utilized. The image in Figure 14.7 shows a screen shot of one tool.

For more on why digital games and other technological tools may be so valuable to language learning, refer to Chapter 19.

Left context	KWIC	Right context
any and all work displayed on this website (unless	otherwise	indicated).</s><s>Please do not copy or use it withou
alone) for us, on us, in us, and through us.</s><s>	Otherwise	(in another "wisdom") we serve (work together with) a
ɔressure, it appears the devs relented and decided	otherwise	.</s><s>PUBG Season 9 is just around the corner an
ely,</s><s>Notifications</s><s>Unless you choose	otherwise	, the system will tell you about replies in your threads.
ctor of the potential view available in 2014, which is	otherwise	obscured by trees.</s><s>Centred looking to the wes
aim at making Canada thoroughly British."</s><s>	Otherwise	Buller reported favourably on the character, actions, a
ook the step of embedding the texture file, 'baked',	otherwise	all I got was a black blob on the desktop full screen :-)
ack Your Trades (TYT) simplifies completion of the	otherwise	tedious federal Schedule D (Capital Gains and Losses
practice of artists in the context of revolutionary or	otherwise	politically-motivated acts.</s><s>Indonesian artist Tita

Figure 14.7 Corpora example. Key word in context for *otherwise*, from sketchengine.eu concordance finder.

BOX 14.3 The Science! Points to Remember

- There are two types of vocabulary knowledge: receptive word knowledge and productive word knowledge.
- New words are added to learners' vocabulary through incidental or intentional learning practices.
- The frequency and length of exposure to words are the two main instructional factors that dictate whether a word will be added to learners' vocabulary. Age and proficiency level are also important variables to consider.

BOX 14.3 (Continued)

- Learning strategies, like looking for cognates or connecting word families, can help learners maximize their comprehension and grow their vocabularies.
- Learners who engage with the target language in a variety of ways (reading, listening to music, playing video games, watching TV), both inside and outside of class time, are more likely to develop a large vocabulary than their peers.

14.3 The Science: What's Missing?

Though vocabulary acquisition is a topic that has been well researched in the field of applied linguistics, there are still several notable areas that have yet to be explored. Recent studies suggest that receiving multiple, simultaneous sources of input is beneficial to vocabulary learning; what remains unclear is what combinations of input sources are best suited to advancing learners' development. Currently, researchers speculate about this, but there is no concrete, empirical evidence capable of explaining the processes. For example, a few studies have explored whether listening to music in the TL is a strategy to develop student vocabulary knowledge. The results have been contradictory, with some studies finding no relationship between the two and one finding a positive relationship. More research is needed to examine the extent to which listening to music supports vocabulary development and how listening to music may complement other types of input, like reading a newspaper article.

There is also no research-backed "magic" number of words to teach per week that language teachers should abide by. Some researchers have suggested twenty words per week will support vocabulary development in most learners, but it is difficult to say for certain because there are so many factors that differentiate language classrooms, including how often the language class meets and for how many hours. Even if there were an agreed-upon ideal number of words, how to best support learners' growth is still debated. Though some studies suggest that receiving multiple, simultaneous sources of input is beneficial to vocabulary learning, what remains unclear is what combinations of input sources are best suited to advancing learners' development. We also do not know if all types of words are acquired in the same way (e.g., nouns vs. verbs vs. adjectives, monosyllabic vs. multisyllabic words). Most of the research on vocabulary development has focused on nouns. It remains unclear whether the reading/listening strategies and processes described in this chapter would also apply to other parts of speech, like prepositions or adverbs.

Within the studies that have examined learners' acquisition of nouns, there is not much research on the process of vocabulary development (e.g., whether certain learning strategies are better suited when learners are encountering words for the first time vs. when they have some familiarity with the words). More research is needed on the sorts of activities and guidance L2 learners could benefit from as they extend their receptive knowledge to productive knowledge (e.g., the ability to independently use words in written or spoken communications). Research has shown that textual enhancement strategies (underlining, bolding, or circling targeted words) can help draw learners' initial attention to vocabulary; however, conclusive empirical findings on the extent to which these textual enhancement strategies facilitate long-term vocabulary learning across varied environments (i.e., reading a word in a book in class and then understanding that word three months later in a verbal interaction) are underdeveloped. When it comes to measuring learners' mastery levels, how fluency (what speed of recall or speed of production learners demonstrate) relates to the underlying strength or quality of vocabulary knowledge in spoken/writing contexts is relatively understudied, especially among K–12 learners.

Finally, we know that learners do not acquire a language in a vacuum and that individual, social, and contextual factors play a role in learners' vocabulary development. A lot of the research centers on participants from similar backgrounds, learning in a similar type of classroom environment with similar linguistic goals and resources available to them. Most of the research on vocabulary learning has focused on university-aged learners, who are often already intermediate or advanced speakers of the TLs. Findings from this population cannot be generalized to younger learners, or learners at the novice level. Within this university-aged population, most of the research has focused on learners of English, rather than learners of other languages like Arabic, Korean, or Persian. Given the global prevalence of English, the options for out-of-class interaction for L2 learners of English are usually much greater than the L2 learners of other languages, who may not have many opportunities to get TL exposure outside of the classroom, apart from moving to a new country. Studies on how vocabulary learning happens have taken very different approaches in their research designs, and so their findings may not be comparable. They may vary in how they measure learners' vocabulary gains and when they measure learners' vocabulary gains. There are also not many longitudinal studies in vocabulary learning, so researchers do not have much evidence supporting how certain instructional strategies might impact learners' linguistic development long term. More research is needed to learn about how (and if) learners retain vocabulary over time.

14.4 The Art: Research-Based Strategies to Try

14.4.1 The Art of Tracking Vocabulary Growth

- Incorporate regular opportunities for confidence ratings into your class periods, where learners can share either publicly or privately how confident they feel about key words or phrases within a unit. Confidence ratings help teachers and learners quickly assess whether or not they have the language they need to complete a task at hand. For example, a teacher might show a series of pictures representing target words and have students give a physical indication (like thumbs up or thumbs down) about whether they have the vocabulary to describe the picture or whether they need more support.

- Keep a cognate word wall to help learners recognize similarities in words across languages. This does not have to be a physical wall in your classroom! Older learners can be prompted to keep a page in their notebooks where they add cognates that they find. Class websites or blogs can also provide space to keep a digital "word wall" that teachers and learners are responsible for updating together. Learners can access online repositories of common words at home, or even after the course ends.
- Make a vocabulary mural that combines text and images. This could be a mural that learners add to throughout the entire year, or it could be a mural that corresponds to a particular unit. After each authentic text (newspaper article, storybook, interview, movie, TV show, map, etc.) that learners encounter, ask each learner to design a graphic representation of a word or phrase they learned. This can also be done in small groups. Encourage learners to refer to the murals throughout the unit. If you do not have a classroom space that you can decorate, vocabulary murals can be created online just like the cognate word walls.
- Host a vocabulary word class challenge. Within a set time frame, like a week or a semester, depending on learners' age and course meeting schedules, challenge learners to keep track of how often they hear, speak, or read certain words in the TL. The class can decide on the challenge words together, or the teacher can pick which words are featured, based on the vocabulary learners will need to successfully complete communicative tasks that are important to them (see Figure 14.8).

	Name: _____		
Vocabulary Challenge: Week 3			
Word/Phrase	**How often did you hear it?**	**How often did you use it?**	**Give an example!**
To walk	IIII IIII	II	I used this word in class on Wednesday.
The gymnasium	IIII	III	I saw this word on the campus map.
Competition	II	IIII	I used this word in my journal entry on Thursday.
They won!	III	I	I watched a soccer game and I heard the announcer say this at the end of the game.

Figure 14.8 Vocabulary scavenger hunt tracker. Learners can complete this vocabulary scavenger hunt throughout the week, track their progress, and share back with the class.

14.4.2 The Art of Maximizing External Resources

- Reading is an important activity for L2 vocabulary development, but sometimes learners can get discouraged if they encounter lots of new words or phrases. Use of external support (like dictionaries) or the incorporation of communicative activities (like pre-/post-reading activities) can help learners navigate the vocabulary they encounter in texts.
    - When presenting learners with external resources, it is important to teach them how and when to use them. For example, dictionaries can provide definitions or translations. Thesauruses are useful for finding synonyms and antonyms. A corpus tool gives examples of word use in context.
        - TESOL International hosts a directory of corpora tools for vocabulary learning and teaching that is available on its website.
- As learners find new words during independent reading opportunities, encourage them to make lists of unfamiliar language to bring to class. Together, learners can design their own picture-based dictionaries or semantic maps (see Figure 14.9), which in turn can be resources learners rely on throughout the rest of the course.
    - Semantic maps might include the following components. This can be created as a whole class, in small groups, or individually, depending on learners' developmental and proficiency levels.
        - Add words or phrases that correspond with a central word.
        - Add pictures.
        - Add other commonly associated words.

14.4.3 The Art of Recycling Vocabulary

- Research shows that learners need to encounter words and phrases many times to acquire them, but in a classroom environment it can be hard to naturally create this kind of environment without resorting to rote drills and exercises. Instead of drills,

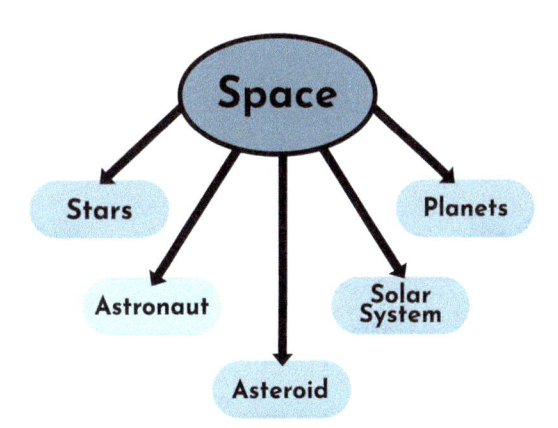

Figure 14.9 Semantic map. A semantic map can capture all the different associations a learner has with a certain word. The example above is a semantic map for the word *space*. Image by: Elizabeth Zonarich

think about maximizing the ways in which learners could interact with the same type of input in class. The goal is novel repetition!
- Jigsaw activities: Divide the class into small groups. Each group will get a different paragraph from the same text. The groups need to read and understand their own assigned paragraphs first. Then, form new groups where each member has read a different paragraph. Now the learners are responsible for reporting what they learned from their paragraph to their classmates. This kind of jigsaw structure has learners interacting with the passage vocabulary in several different ways, all of which can help build their knowledge and familiarity (see Figure 14.10).
    - Problem-solving or opinion-exchange activities: Give the class the first half of a text, but do not share the ending or resolution! After they read the first half of the text, divide the class into groups. In their groups, learners need to decide how to resolve the conflict or issue from the text. Then the groups must present their decision (this can be written or spoken, with or without graphics) to the class. The class can vote on the ending they think is most creative, plausible, or entertaining. Then provide the class with the real ending of the text. In creating opportunities to problem-solve and share their opinions, learners get to interact with the vocabulary in the text more often than if they had simply read the entire text in one sitting.
    - While popular language learning apps might not a silver bullet for language fluency, there is evidence that apps are useful for vocabulary development and review. Oftentimes, they provide spaced learning conditions, which research shows are more effective than massed learning conditions. In a spaced learning condition, words that have been identified as more difficult to master are shown more frequently (see Figure 14.11). For more on how to incorporate technological resources, see Chapter 19.

14.4.4 The Art of Assessing Word Knowledge

- Being able to translate words from the L1 to the L2 (or vice versa) is only one dimension of vocabulary knowledge. As we discussed above, knowing a word might mean actively being able to produce the word, or being able to recognize the meaning passively. The chart in Box 14.4, based on Laufer and Goldstein (2004), shows some

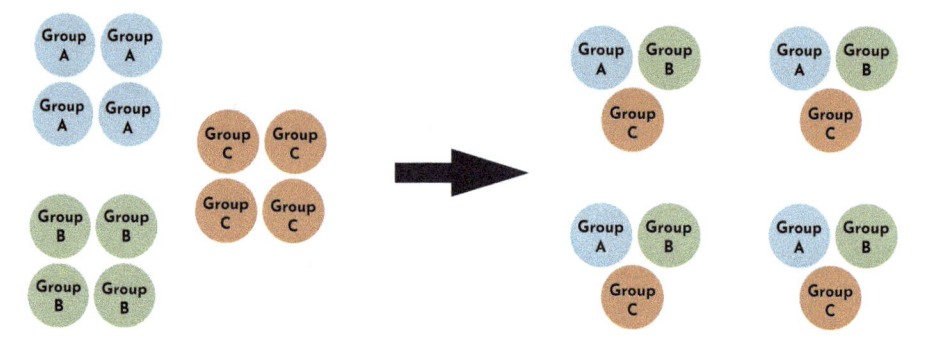

Figure 14.10 Jigsaw groups. Learners can be grouped and regrouped in varying configurations to share new knowledge with each other. Image by: Elizabeth Zonarich

14.4 The Art: Research-Based Strategies to Try

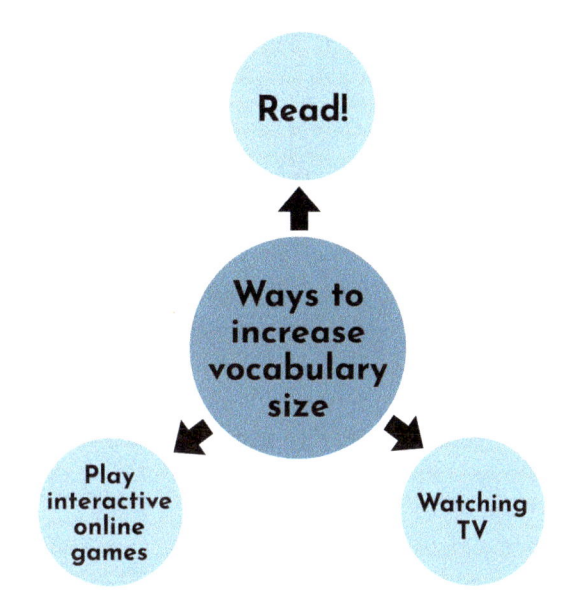

Figure 14.11 Growing your vocabulary. The best-researched ways to increase your vocabulary are through reading, watching TV, and playing interactive online games. Image by: Elizabeth Zonarich

BOX 14.4 Approaches to Assessing Vocabulary

Level of vocabulary knowledge	Assessment example
• Active form recall: Can the learner produce the word in the L2 when given the meaning in the L1?	• Ask the learner to translate back and forth from the L2 to the L1 (orally or in writing). E.g., "how do you say *alfombra* [rug] in English?"
• Passive meaning recall: Can the learner give the definition or meaning of a word in the L2?	• Show a picture and ask the learner what that word means in the L2. E.g., [pointing to a picture of a rug] "What is this thing in the picture? What do you do with it?"
• Active form recognition: Does the learner know the L2 word based on its definition?	• Lay out flash cards of L2 vocabulary words. Show the learner a picture and ask them to find the word that goes with that picture. E.g., [shows a picture of a rug] "Can you find the English word that goes with this picture?"
• Passive meaning recognition: Does the learner know the meaning of an L2 word?	• Lay out flash cards of images. Ask the learner to find images that correspond to words in the L2. E.g., "Can you find the picture for *rug*?"

ways a simple flash card activity could assess multiple levels of passive and active vocabulary knowledge.

14.5 Troubleshooting: How the Science Informs the Art

Mrs. L's high school language program recently made the decision to abandon the traditional textbook that formed the foundation of their curriculum. Mrs. L is excited to co-create a new curriculum with her learners, one that is centered around their needs and interests. She has decided not to pre-make vocabulary lists because she wants learners to bring in the words and phrases that are meaningful to them. However, after the first unit in her Spanish III class, Mrs. L noticed that while her learners often looked up new words each period, their performance on the final project felt more repetitive and stilted than in years past. She is worried that she did not provide enough structure related to unit vocabulary.

There is a lot to consider when moving away from a textbook-centered curriculum, but the idea of centering it around student needs and interests is supported by research (see Chapter 17 for more on this). Rather than moving from isolated unit to isolated unit, Mrs. L should consider ways she can weave common sets of vocabulary throughout many units so that her learners have regular opportunities to hear/read these words. Without frequent opportunities to hear, see, and produce vocabulary, learners will not master the new words and phrases, even if they are meaningful to them. If Mrs. L is finding that her learners are overreliant on a small collection of words in their final projects, it may be because learners are not making cross-unit connections. Mrs. L might also find that her learners need more practice and encouragement throughout the semester to draw on their own vocabulary banks rather than resort to the basic words they already feel comfortable with. This might include offering more planning or revision time where learners can return to their notes to make sure they are incorporating rich, descriptive language.

Because she allowed each student to develop a more personalized vocabulary list, she feels she may not have held them each accountable for learning and incorporating all these new words. As she plans for her next units, what she should do to make sure that she is effectively teaching vocabulary to her learners?

A challenge for classroom learning is supplying learners with enough input. The more often learners encounter the same words, the more likely they are to add them to their own vocabulary. However, the time allotted to Spanish class in Mrs. L's high school puts a limit on what can be accomplished. Mrs. L should encourage learners to engage with the TL outside of class across a variety of different modalities. For example, Mrs. L might ask learners to spend some time independently reading and logging vocabulary they notice in journals. In addition, moving forward Mrs. L might consider dedicating more time in class to helping learners reflect and track their own progress with some of the strategies described in Section 14.3. This can build accountability and remind learners of just how much they know. A personalized vocabulary list is a great idea! This is a learning strategy that help learners become more autonomous and engaged. Mrs. L can challenge learners to find words from their vocabulary list in the "real world" and bring them into class to share with their peers.

14.6 The Science: Points to Remember

- Repeated and varied exposure to vocabulary in meaningful contexts helps learners develop strong productive and receptive knowledge of words' definitions and uses.
- Vocabulary development is a continuous and cyclical process, just like language learning, so learners should be supported in leveraging their existing vocabulary knowledge to access new words and phrases.
- Characteristics of effective learning environments including multiple, simultaneous modes of input, clear form–meaning connections, repeated vocabulary encounters, and scaffolded support.
- Many variables, both instruction- and learner-related, impact vocabulary acquisition, which makes it difficult for research to conclude the most effective strategies for teaching new words.

14.7 Questions to Consider

1. How often do your learners have the opportunity to repeatedly encounter *unknown and/or partially known* words in your courses?
2. Over the duration of a semester or year, how often do your learners have the opportunity to repeatedly encounter the same words in new contexts?
3. What strategies do you teach (or do you observe your learners using) to build their vocabularies? How do these strategies change as learners age or advance?
4. Think about how (if!) you test your learners' vocabulary knowledge. What kind of knowledge are you testing? Do they only need to recognize a word in context? Do they need to recall a word independently? Do they need to translate a word?

14.8 The Science of Language Learning: Research Supporting the Points Made in This Chapter

Hobson, V., & Schmitt, N. (2019). A review of current research on second language vocabulary learning. OASIS Summary of Schmitt (2008) in *Language Teaching Research*. https://oasis-database.org/concern/summaries/h989r323x?locale=en.

This summary reviews a 2019 article about research on L2 vocabulary learning. Using a bulleted structure, the authors clearly present key findings on how L2 learners learn and use new words. Intentional and incidental learning strategies are discussed and reviewed in terms of their ability to support learners in growing the size of their vocabulary quickly. The research concludes that the most effective way to strengthen learners' knowledge is to provide them with as many sustained opportunities for engagement with the targeted words as possible.

Puimege, E., & Peters, E. (2019). Learners' English vocabulary knowledge prior to formal instruction: The role of learner-related and word-related variables. *Language Learning, 69*(4), 943–977. https://doi.org/10.1111/lang.12364.

This study explores incidental vocabulary acquisition in adolescent English language learners. The authors are specifically interested in how learners' participation in out-of-class (or "extramural") English-related activities impacts their vocabulary size. The study also examines how the type of word (e.g., whether it is a cognate) impacts learners' mastery. Findings suggest that word-specific factors do predict whether or not a word is incidentally learned during extramural English activities. The frequency, cognate status, and concreteness of a word all impacted the extent to which a word was incorporated into learners' vocabulary. Authors also found that the learners' reading comprehension ability in their L1 impacted their ability to recognize and learn L2 cognates.

Suárez, M. M., & Gesa, F. (2019). Learning vocabulary with the support of sustained exposure to captioned video: Do proficiency and aptitude make a difference? *The Language Learning Journal, 47*(4), 497–517. https://doi.org/10.1080/09571736.2019.1617768.

In this article, researchers explore how videos influence vocabulary acquisition and content comprehension in groups of adolescent and university-aged English language learners. Over the course of an experimental study spanning the entire academic term, some learners watched TV episodes with captions and other learners watched TV episodes without captions. Researchers found that for the younger, adolescent learners, the group that viewed the captioned content scored higher on vocabulary assessments than the group that did not. However, for the university-aged learners, there was no difference in assessment performance between the with-caption and without-caption groups. These findings support previous research which indicated that multimodal and varied types of simultaneous input is especially beneficial for younger or lower-proficiency learners.

For more resources, including more sample lesson plans, videos, and other ideas, visit our companion website: www.cambridge.org/BryfonskiMackey.

15 What are some strategies for teaching learners about politeness, register, or other pragmatic skills in the second language?

KEY QUESTIONS
- The Science: What is pragmatics, and why is it an important element of second language learning?
- What are the stages of pragmatic development, and how can these stages inform how I teach?
- The Art: Should I teach pragmatics in my language classroom?
- How does teaching pragmatics support a communicative approach to language teaching?
- Why does learning pragmatics matter for my students?
- What are some strategies for teaching learners about politeness, register, or other pragmatic skills in the second language?
- How can technology be used to teach pragmatics?

15.1 Voices from the Classroom

Ms. X just moved to Japan from the United States and is excited to begin her first year of teaching debate at an English-only international high school. Ms. X has spent a lot of time and energy planning topics for small-group discussions for the first few days of the term as a warm-up for the larger-scale debates she has in store. However, from the very first class, her anticipation turns to confusion: in the ten minutes allotted for the first discussion activity, she is surprised to find that most of her groups, rather than diving into her carefully selected discussion prompt and engaging in animated conversation, have instead spent the first five or so minutes deciding how and when each student will have their speaking turn. Ms. X is perplexed that instead of organically dividing themselves into groups according to their personal opinions and stances, the learners have arranged themselves in a hierarchical order based on grade level and age. She hears many of her oldest learners continuously offering points to support both sides of the argument rather than prioritizing one side and providing supporting evidence to make the case that their *argument is stronger; what's more, many of the younger learners seem to be consistently agreeing with the older learners, regardless of the topic. With only a minute left to spare, the groups' informal leaders then promptly began to wrap up their discussions by briefly summarizing all the points that had been made. In the end, when most of the groups reported to the whole class that they were not able to reach any conclusion about which argument was the strongest, Ms. X could feel herself deflating. What has Ms. X missed? How can she modify her lesson plans going forward?*

15.2 The Science: What the Research Says

Consider the following scenario: You are sitting in a room on a hot summer's day with another person who is sitting near a closed window. Which of the following requests would you use to ask the person to open the window? "Would you mind opening that window, please?" or "Open that window," or "My, it's hot in here, isn't it?" or something else? Now consider if the person was your friend. Your boss? A child? How would your relationship impact your choice of words? Even though the delivery is quite different, each of these phrases may (or may not) result in the person opening the window. Your choice of words might also impact whether or not the person thinks of you as polite or rude, or demanding (see Figure 15.1). Meanings are not only just attached to words and letters in a one-to-one relationship. Research has demonstrated how meaning is generated and understood (or misunderstood!) in a particular context. The set of skills that determines what and how all language users modify their communication style (verbal and nonverbal) to fit the conversational context is called pragmatic competence. Researchers who examine **pragmatics** try to understand the kinds of choices that people make in conversation given the specific circumstances of the environment, including in relation to other people. In other words, pragmatics is how people decide *how* to say *what* to whom and *when*. Consider the different communication styles needed for a job interview, chatting with a friend at a coffee shop, asking a university advisor for help, navigating a customer service interaction over the phone, or a high-stakes situation like being questioned by a police officer on the side of the road or being treated for a medical condition at a hospital. Each scenario would

Figure 15.1 Pragmatics and requests. The light gray cat demonstrates three different ways someone might communicate the same message. Which would you choose? Image by: Elizabeth Zonarich

require different decisions about word choice, phrasing, and other linguistic features to ensure the communication is smooth and successful (and, in some cases, safe!). If the goal of language learning is to learn how to communicate effectively with others, then pragmatics – and teaching pragmatics – is an essential piece of the puzzle.

What Ms. X experienced in the story above is based on a famous study of intercultural communication. The researcher, Deborah Tannen, analyzed video-taped conversations of fifteen to twenty minutes in length between groups of American and Japanese people in a school setting. Her study illustrated some of the differences in expectations about how people should organize, lead, and navigate group discussions. Ultimately, her findings helped deepen researchers' and educators' understanding of how pragmatic behaviors vary across cultures, pointing out that there is no one "right" way or "wrong" way to communicate. Instead, the speakers' interactional choices vary along a continuum of pragmatic **appropriateness**, all of which depends entirely on the social context of a given situation, environment, and group of people.

15.2.1 Pragmatic Competence

Researchers have defined two main types of pragmatic knowledge (or pragmatic competence), and both are critical to understanding how pragmatics can be learned and taught. The first is **sociopragmatic competence**, or the knowledge about what is or isn't appropriate in a certain social situation. When someone draws on their sociopragmatic competence, they might ask themselves questions like:

- What is normal and acceptable in this situation?
- Who deserves respect or deference? Who is my equal?
- How do my gender, age, or status affect how I talk to someone? How about the gender, age, or status of the person I'm talking with?
- What is considered a small favor, and what is considered a huge imposition in this situation?

Individuals who have not been raised in the target culture – for example, many second language (L2) learners – may find it challenging to navigate the unknown waters of what is considered "polite," "rude," or "normal." As educators, it's essential to be mindful of the different cultural, linguistic, and sociopragmatic backgrounds that learners bring to the classroom – and how those might differ from the norms of the target language (TL) and culture. Teaching sociopragmatics would involve discussions with learners about how different variables, such as the relationship between speakers, the context of a conversation, or other cultural norms, impact language use.

The second type of knowledge is **pragmalinguistic competence**. If sociopragmatic competence encompasses the social rules that we aim to live by, then pragmalinguistic competence refers to the specific ways we *use* language to follow (or break!) these rules. For example, have you ever started to write an email and paused to consider what kind of greeting or opening you should use? Or when you formulate a suggestion, might you use modals (e.g., *would, could, can*), if-clauses, or expressions such as "Would it be possible …?" or "I was just wondering …?" While sociopragmatic competence concerns all the factors that would determine the atmosphere and the expected conventions of an interaction, pragmalinguistic competence refers to the specific language and linguistic tools needed to get the job done. When someone draws on their pragmalinguistic competence, they might ask themselves questions like:

- How can I make this sound more or less polite?
- Which words would make my point clearer?
- What phrases would make this more or less direct?

Teaching pragmalinguistics would involve discussions about how different word choices or grammatical patterns impact how messages are received.

As shown in Figure 15.2, sociopragmatic competence and pragmalinguistic competence combine to encompass the overall level of pragmatic competence. Pragmatic learning has traditionally received less attention than other topics in second language acquisition (SLA) research and language teaching circles. However, there is ample evidence that learners can (and should) benefit from pragmatic instruction in their language classes, especially as they become older and more advanced language users.

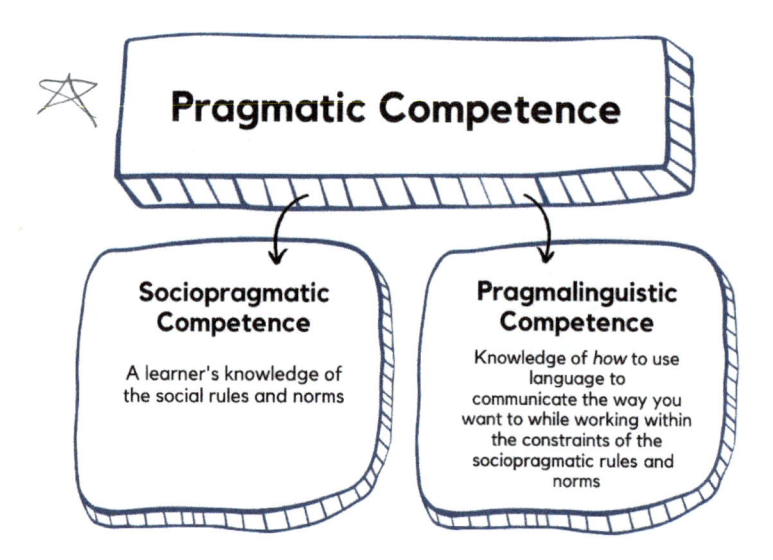

Figure 15.2 Components of pragmatic competence. Understanding the two components of pragmatic competence can help inform instructional approaches and resource development efforts. Image by: Kris Cook

15.2.2 Stages of Pragmatic Development

What happens as learners start to acquire pragmatic knowledge about the L2? Research shows that, much like other forms of language, pragmatic knowledge develops in a predictable order. A lot of research in L2 pragmatics has investigated how learners acquire language used for specific communicative actions, also known as **speech acts**. Some common speech acts include requests, apologies, refusals, suggestions, and more. Research on pragmatic development revealed five stages that L2 learners generally experience.

Using Table 15.1, we can see that pragmatic development does not happen all at once. Instead, teachers can use this framework to identify the stages their learners

Table 15.1 The five stages of pragmatic development

Pre-Basic Stage	There is no adjustment of language toward different individuals because learners have lower proficiencies – they are making the best of what they have and will use whatever linguistic (and even nonlinguistic) means necessary to get their message across.
Formulaic Stage	Learners produce very simple language (such as high-frequency phrases or very simple verbs), so while there may be a basic form of politeness (e.g., *thank you*, *please*), it may be applied universally, with no adaptation to different environments, situations, or conversation partners. Some preliminary understanding of basic honorifics or differential pronoun usage (e.g., *tu* versus *vous* in French) might begin to emerge, but any situations deviating from those learners have previously memorized could result in anxiety or pragmatic missteps.
Unpacking Stage	At this point, learners are able to use longer expressions with some variation. Learners are still learning the sociopragmatic rules and building their pragmalinguistic competence toolboxes, so they may still have some trouble producing or understanding complex speech acts. However, they are learning to adjust their language expressions according to social context factors (e.g., the closeness of the relationship, the importance of "power," and "solidarity"). For example, at this stage, learners may start using indirect language when formulating requests (*Could you …?*).
Pragmatic Expansion	As learners' proficiency levels increase, so does their repertoire of pragmalinguistic options and (ideally, but not always) their understanding of sociopragmatic norms. For example, in this stage, learners tend to have higher levels of L2 proficiency and may become overconfident in their pragmalinguistic knowledge despite persistent gaps in how they apply that knowledge. Although there may still be mismatches and miscommunications from a lack of knowledge, overall, the learners' speech act productions become more complex and nuanced. Learners at this stage can attain higher politeness levels and, further, make more effective decisions about how to shape their language to match their situations context by context.
Fine-tuning	At this stage, learners' understanding of pragmalinguistic and sociopragmatic tools is mostly accurate. Learners continue to adapt their nuanced language use (verbal and nonverbal) to fit their conversations.

are currently in and the types of pragmatic knowledge they currently possess. With this information, teachers can better understand what kinds of pragmatic instruction learners are developmentally ready to engage in.

15.2.3 Pragmatics and Intercultural Communication

Pragmatics is more than knowledge about a culture and what is or isn't considered polite. Every speaker comes from a unique background, which impacts their dialect and their **conversational style**. Conversational style varies within a culture and includes how people take turns in a conversation, how they tell stories and jokes, and even how long they pause before they continue talking. Conversational styles might differ by language, dialect, or region. For example, depending on one's conversational style and the sociopragmatic norms of one's cultural background, there may be a preference for more direct or indirect language. Overlapping speech – when people talk at the same time – might be considered rude for some but might signal engagement, understanding, and solidarity to others. In all cases, it's important to recognize that conversational styles vary widely, that no one way is right or wrong, and to provide multiple examples when discussing pragmatic variation in class. For example, if a Japanese language teacher wants their learners to explore how Japanese speakers engage in refusals during a conversation, the teacher might ask their learners to watch a few video clips from popular Japanese TV shows with refusals. The teacher can have their learners discuss the interactions from the clips and analyze what, where, how, and why the particular language forms were being used in that way. During the class discussion, the teacher could point out that factors such as the differences in the perceived status of the speakers play a role in how refusals are constructed. After raising the learners' awareness, the teacher could replay the video clips for the learners.

15.2.4 Benefits of Teaching Pragmatics with Technology

Recently, there has been a surge of technology-related pragmatics research, reflecting a wide range of possible instructional and interactional mediums through technology-mediated environments. This includes everything from social media, digital gaming, virtual environments (e.g., *Gather*, a gamified video chat platform designed to make virtual interactions "more human"; www.gather.town/), video conferencing apps (e.g., Zoom, Skype, etc.), text-messaging apps (e.g., WhatsApp, WeChat, HelloTalk), virtual reality (VR), augmented reality (AR), blogs, and more. In light of the COVID-19 pandemic, video conferencing has had a particularly large impact on language learning as large numbers of learners began taking language classes online. Zoom interactions can impact the pragmatics of conversations, such as negotiating for a turn to speak, accidentally talking over someone else, or forgetting to unmute. There is some early research in this area that shows that language learners can be taught how to navigate this new territory to smooth digital interactions.

Such technological platforms and spaces can allow learners to cross vast differences to interact with users of the TL, often in cases where they may not have otherwise had the opportunity to do so. In the case of digital gaming and AR or VR, learners can further interact in immersive virtual environments, which typically prompt learners to experience many different kinds of roles and tasks in diverse social settings and simulations. Furthermore, when learners participate in these virtual, computer-mediated, or game-based interactions, they can see how their pragmatic choices may impact others in their virtual environments. This experience may further increase their noticing of sociopragmatic rules and pragmalinguistic tools, which may, in turn, shape everything from their future linguistic actions to their interpersonal relationships and self-identity construction.

Not only do the new technological developments expand educators' options for teaching pragmatics, but they also help researchers and teachers alike deepen our understanding of the processes and procedures of L2 pragmatic development – concerning both "in-person" contexts and technology-driven mediums.

BOX 15.1 The Science! Points to Remember

- Pragmatic competence comprises *sociopragmatics* (the norms that govern our interactions) and *pragmalinguistics* (the linguistic tools we use to navigate social contexts).
- Pragmatic competence develops in stages that relate to learners' other developing linguistic skills (speaking, reading, writing, listening, metalinguistic knowledge, etc.).
- Speech acts are language utterances that perform some communicative action, such as requests, apologies, refusals, suggestions, humor, advice, invitations, turn-taking, and persuasive arguments.
- Pragmatic preferences during speech acts may vary based on age, gender, race, region, or even power dynamics of the individuals involved.

15.3 The Science: What's Missing?

Second language pragmatics is still a relatively new area of research for SLA researchers. In the past, researchers have focused more on learning grammar, vocabulary, and sounds than pragmatic norms. This may be partially due to the wide range of pragmatic norms across and within languages, cultures, and people. As a result, many questions are not yet answered. For example, more research is needed to know what specific mechanisms drive pragmatic development and the type of background knowledge on pragmatic norms teachers need in order to teach pragmatics effectively. In addition, we do not yet know exactly how pragmatic competence changes in response to developments in technology. Nevertheless, research in this fascinating area is increasing.

15.4 The Art: Research-Based Strategies to Try

Research in L2 pragmatics has shown that explicit teaching is generally more effective than implicit teaching. This means that learners can benefit more when they are explicitly told about the different types of forms associated with different pragmatic meanings and when and how to use them rather than just learning them from context. Learners can practice pragmatics in the TL both receptively and productively. Learners will benefit most when a combination of receptive and productive practice is included.

15.4.1 The Art of Utilizing Receptive Practices to Teach Pragmatics

Receptive practice can measure learners' sociopragmatic competence or, in other words, assess how well learners know what is or isn't appropriate in a certain context. Below are several examples of ways in which L2 teachers can help facilitate receptive pragmatic development.

- Prepare learners to act as natural language analyzers. To teach pragmatics is to foster critical interpersonal skills by encouraging learners to study the social, interactional, and linguistic practices of a given community. Researchers in the field have stressed the value of helping learners analyze authentic conversations and extract patterns (e.g., phrases, intonations, words, expressions, and nonverbal gestures) that they can use themselves. Naturally, the practice and implementation of this will vary greatly according to learners' proficiency levels, but the goal of deepening one's understanding of natural language in authentic contexts should remain constant. One idea is to create an opportunity for learners to share if they've ever had moments of intercultural miscommunication and what they've learned from their experience. Another idea is to ask learners to analyze the speech or constructed conversations produced by artificial intelligence (AI) chat bots to identify any pragmatic patterns that expose the language as being artificially created.
- When introducing a lesson on a particular speech act, first engage learners in a discussion where they can talk about how speech acts are performed in their own local contexts. Having this initial discussion can prime your learners to see the similarities and differences in the performance of speech acts in other cultures when introducing input such as video clips.
- Ask learners to form small groups and act out a skit from a script. The rest of the class will watch their skit and evaluate what was appropriate or inappropriate. For example, if the skit demonstrates a request between a student and a professor, you could have the class vote on how appropriate the learner's request is. This could then lead to a discussion about what variables impacted their decision about the appropriateness of the request.
- Find a list of video clips of popular TV shows or movies that show speech acts in context. First, you can play these clips in class. You could lead a class discussion highlighting similarities and differences in how the speech act was used and received.

After bringing the learners' attention to variables such as the relationship between the speakers, level of formality, and context, you can replay the video clips for your learners.

15.4.2 The Art of Utilizing Productive Practices to Teach Pragmatics

Productive practice can measure learners' pragmalinguistic competence or their knowledge of how to use language in a specific context.

- Have learners complete written and spoken discourse completion tasks. A discourse completion task includes a script of an interaction with a key aspect missing for the learners to fill in. For example, in a script where someone is letting a friend know that they can't attend an upcoming event they had planned on going to together, the line where the friend says they can't come will be left blank for the learners to fill in. For example, invite your learners to brainstorm *how they would tell their friends they can't attend an event anymore.* (See Figures 15.3 and 15.4 for more examples.)
- Have learners practice using role-play cards. Give out scenarios and roles for small groups (or partners) to act out. Switch roles often so that learners can judge what to say when they are in a variety of different positions in a social context. This can also be an opportunity to incorporate technology by having learners create a video acting out their given scenario. In class, learners can share their videos, and teachers can facilitate the class discussion about their language use.

15.4.3 The Art of Teaching Second Language Pragmatics: A Sample Lesson

Second language pragmatics can be taught using a combination of implicit and explicit teaching techniques to maximize effectiveness and model the largest range of possible situations.

- Start with an input flood. In an input flood, learners are presented with many examples of the target feature. These examples could be videos of people navigating a particular situation, written dialogues, or other types of examples. An input flood

Figure 15.3 Pragmatic practice in declining an event. Role-playing different types of conversations allows learners to experiment using a variety of conversational moves. Image by: Elizabeth Zonarich

Discourse Completion Task

Scenario: You made plans with your friend, Jennifer, to attend your 10-year university reunion tonight. You know she has been looking forward to this event for a long time. However, this morning you encounter an unexpected emergency at work, and your boss expects you to stay in the office to resolve the issue. You can no longer attend the reunion with Jennifer.

Write a text message, or a series of texts, to Jennifer explaining that you can no longer attend tonight's event:

Figure 15.4 Discourse completion task example. In addition to role plays, learners can also benefit from writing out how they would respond to different interpersonal situations.

will raise learners' awareness of a pragmatic norm even if they are just watching and listening. They can also see a few different options for how a conversation could be resolved.

- ○ Example: Learners are learning about the speech act interruptions. Play video clips of various people interrupting one another. These can range from in-person conversations, interviews, and Zoom meetings. YouGlish (https://youglish.com/) is a website where you can easily search for YouTube clips with target words and phrases (in a variety of L2s) to find many examples of interruptions. One caveat to consider with YouTube clips is that clips from TV shows generally require "fairly strong listening comprehension" skills (intermediate level or higher), so if you choose to engage your learners with TV show clips, you should supplement with more examples from other sources that are more level-appropriate.
    - After the input flood, ask learners to identify where on a spectrum particular phrases and expressions, fall. You can even make visual posters of these continua and have learners post their ratings on the continuum using Post-it notes, like in Figure 15.5.
      polite/formal ⟵⟶ simple/informal
      appropriate ⟵⟶ inappropriate
      unfamiliar interlocutor ⟵⟶ familiar interlocutor
      higher level (power) ⟵⟶ same/lower level (solidarity)
    - Then, have the learners engage in a discussion about why they made the ratings they did for each example.
- Following the input flood and continuum discussion, ask learners to practice interrupting each other to try out some of the phrases that they heard. One way to do this is with a spot-the-difference task. Give out pictures to partners that differ in selected ways. Without looking at one another's pictures, assign one learner the role of the describer and one the role of the interrupter. The describer tells their partner

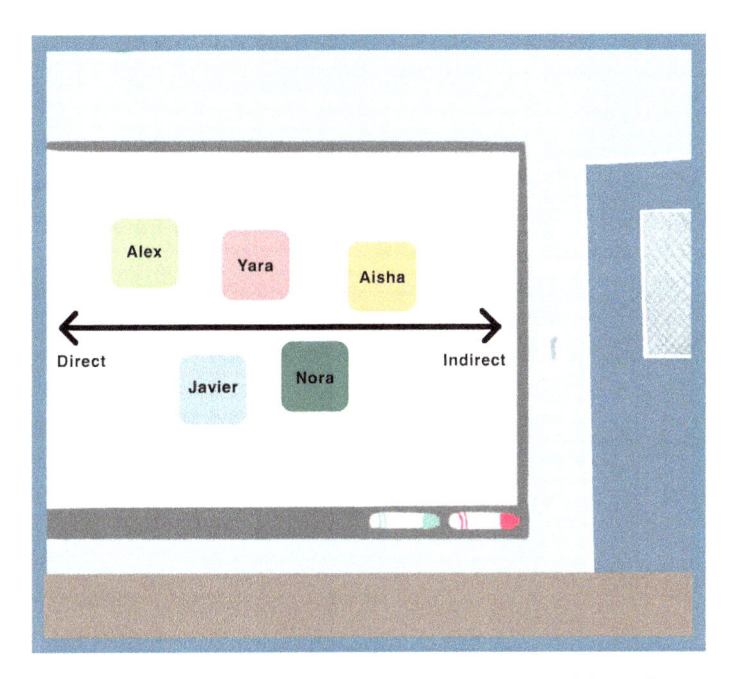

Figure 15.5 Spectrum activity with pragmatic decisions. Spectrum activities offer an interactive way for students to discuss what pragmatic choices they observe or would make and why. Image by: Elizabeth Zonarich

what they see in their picture, and the interrupter stops them when they hear a difference. Then have the partners switch roles.
- Follow up this partner task with an explicit whole- or small-group discussion about the phrases used to interrupt and how they vary by politeness with more explicit practice if necessary. This cycle can be repeated with different tasks, speech acts, or situations like service encounters, phone calls, or email writing.

15.4.4 The Art of Integrating Technology to Teach Pragmatics

Integrating technology can maximize the benefits of pragmatics teaching by introducing more common contexts for learners to navigate. Below are some tips for integrating technology into pragmatics instruction.

- *Use technology to diversify the examples you use to demonstrate pragmatic language use.* Raising learners' awareness of pragmatics may be the first necessary pedagogical step to increase learners' understanding of the kinds of differences possible between different contexts of communication. In other words, it is important to utilize technology to increase learners' exposure to multiple conversational styles (i.e., not just your own) so that they can continue to expand their pragmatic competence repertoire as well as their intercultural communication skills. By using YouTube clips, telecollaborative learning opportunities, or video games, learners will gain greater access to a wide range of conversational and pragmatic norms. These may include how to appropriately apologize, take turns, interrupt, or disagree as they either see these conversational moves surface in authentic video clips or encounter them in "real time" in interactive virtual environments.

- *Use technology to facilitate collaboration with learners living in different parts of the world.* You can collaborate with other teachers living in different countries so that their class of learners can practice their intercultural communication skills through video calls. For example, learners from both classes might engage in the same discourse completion task assignment focusing on a particular speech act before the video call. Learners can ask questions to each other during the video call about common pragmatic norms. After the video call, teachers can have further discussions with their classes to discuss what they have learned through their interaction with learners from a different country. Another idea is to have learners complete a project where they work in groups to record a video of themselves doing a skit of a particular speech act. These videos can be created through platforms including FlipGrid, Padlet, and even through email. You can collaborate with the teacher in a different country in order to complete the same video assignment and then have learners exchange videos. They can watch each other's videos while also evaluating the appropriateness using the visual spectrums listed in Figure 15.5.

15.5 Troubleshooting: How the Science Informs the Art

Ms. X is perplexed that instead of organically dividing themselves into groups according to their personal opinions and stances, the learners have instead arranged themselves into a hierarchical order based on grade level and age. She hears many of her oldest learners continuously offering points to support both sides of the argument rather than prioritizing one side and providing supporting evidence to make the case that their argument is stronger; what's more is that many of the younger learners seem to be consistently agreeing with the older learners, regardless of the topic. With only a minute left to spare, the groups' informal leaders then promptly began to wrap up their discussions by briefly summarizing all the points that had been made. In the end, when most of the groups reported to the whole class that they were not able to reach any conclusion about which argument was the strongest, Ms. X can feel herself deflating. What has Ms. X missed? How can she modify her lesson plans going forward?

We now know that the disconnect between Ms. X's expectations and her learners' expectations of how small-group discussions should operate derived from a lack of shared pragmatic knowledge about the social rules constraining their conversations. Ms. X had been planning her classroom activities according to one set of sociopragmatic expectations (e.g., overlapping speech, high-involvement strategies, direct conversational style, less-structured turn-taking, overt stances, and sharing of opinions, etc.). Meanwhile, her learners were following a different set of sociopragmatic rules in which they demonstrated respect by arranging and following a social hierarchy based on factors such as grade, age, experience, and so on.

How could Ms. X have structured her debate class differently in considering these pragmatic differences but also exposing her learners to a range of pragmatic and cultural norms?

It sounds like Ms. X is asking learners to jump in and engage in productive practice without properly scaffolding learners for the debate. Before engaging in productive practice, Ms. X can raise learners' awareness by introducing receptive activities. From the beginning, it is important for Ms. X to familiarize herself with the local culture and expected norms in Japan. For example, when introducing debates, she could first ask learners how opinions and arguments are presented in the local culture. Through this warm-up discussion, she might learn about the role of perceived social status in expressing opinions, which can inform how she assigns learners into separate groups. She can then assign specific roles for each student, so they are familiar with what they are expected to share with the class at the end of the activity.

15.6 The Science: Points to Remember

- Pragmatics is an area of language that studies how languages relate to the "real world" in given social contexts.
- Be mindful of how pragmatics is presented in your curriculum. Educators should strive to be open to multiple frameworks of pragmatic competence and be explicit about the context-specific pragmatics frameworks that are taught. It is also important to be sensitive to the pragmatic backgrounds that learners bring to the classroom.
- As described in this chapter, learners go through stages of pragmatic development. These stages can inform teachers' curricula and instructional choices.

15.7 Questions to Consider

1. Think back to Ms. X's first day of class. Have you ever had an experience in which your learners operated according to a sociopragmatic framework that was different from what you'd expected?
2. What are some ways you can use social media to teach pragmatics to learners?
3. Where else might you find resources that you can use to provide an input flood to learners?
4. How might you modify your teaching of pragmatics to accommodate learners with lower proficiency?

15.8 The Science of Language Learning: The Research Supporting the Points Made in This Chapter

Culpeper, J., Mackey, A., & Taguchi, N. (2018). *Second language pragmatics: From theory to research*. Routledge.

In this book, the authors combine their areas of expertise in general pragmatics, second language research methodology, and pragmatics research to expand the theoretical knowledge base of L2 pragmatics through the use of cutting-edge research methodology. This book begins with a general historical overview of L2 pragmatics research. It then provides conceptual overviews and a range of data elicitation methods that can be applied to understanding pragmatics production and learners' comprehension and awareness. The authors also explain the conceptual overview and data elicitation methods that focus on L2 pragmatic interaction.

Ishihara, N., & Cohen, A.D. (2021). *Teaching and learning pragmatics: Where language and culture meet*. Routledge.

This book is a practical guide for language educators that is aimed at bridging the gap between theoretical pragmatics-based research and classroom practices. It provides its readers with insights into the possible causes of learners' errors while engaging in intercultural communication. Language educators can find ideas for designing curricula, assessments, and culturally sensitive instructional strategies to help language learners develop their intercultural communication skills. In addition, this book also provides language educators with guidance on ways to incorporate technology in their teaching approaches.

Roever, C. (2021). *Teaching and testing second language pragmatics and interaction: A practical guide*. Routledge.

In this book written for second language teachers, test designers, and curriculum designers, Roever explains how one's pragmatic competence is developed and what language teachers can do to teach and test pragmatics in the classroom. The author provides readers with a brief foundational overview of pragmatics and then provides examples of teaching and testing techniques that teachers can use with learners of various proficiency levels. This book also provides a curriculum structure that teachers could use when implementing pragmatics instruction. In addition, the author describes the future of pragmatics teaching and testing and suggests ways that technology can be incorporated to enhance instruction.

For more resources, including more sample lesson plans, videos, and other ideas, visit our companion website: www.cambridge.org/BryfonskiMackey.

PART IV

LESSON AND UNIT PLANNING

16 What are some of the most popular language teaching methods?

KEY QUESTIONS
- **The Science: Which models of language teaching are based in research?**
- **The Art: How can I adapt teaching methods for my teaching context?**
- **What are the main differences between different teaching methods?**
- **How should I pick a teaching method?**
- **What if I have no choice (e.g., my curriculum specialist or school insists I use one approach, but I prefer a different one)?**

16.1 Voices from the Classroom

Ms. Q is a novice teacher about to start her first job as a Spanish teacher in a high school. Though she completed a teacher preparation program as part of her university degree, she was one of just a few future language teachers and was usually lumped in with future history or literature teachers. As a result, most of her coursework was geared to humanities taught in the first language (L1), not for language teachers supporting learners' acquisition of a second language (L2). During her student teaching apprenticeship with a local master teacher, she observed her mentor teach in what she called a "textbook-communicative hybrid" approach. Her mentor was required to use the textbooks the school had onsite but also incorporated many resources, activities, and projects that went beyond the scope of the textbook and were more focused on communication and negotiation for meaning rather than learning grammar. Ms. Q loved observing her mentor implement this approach but feels she should develop her own teaching style. As a result, she started researching language teaching methods online and quickly became overwhelmed by the number of resources available, all touting their methods as the "best" way to teach languages. How should she pick the approach that is right for her and her learners? If she finds out that she must follow a particular approach when she starts her new job, how can she adapt it to her own needs and strengths?

16.2 The Science: What the Research Says

Popular approaches to teaching languages have changed regularly over the years with new methods gaining traction while others fall out of favor. The goal of this chapter is not to introduce the latest trend, but to highlight the various ways in which approaches to language teaching vary, and what that means according to research into how languages are learned. Most teachers will find that they must strike a balance between their own teaching style and the guidelines mandated by their school district or program. This chapter will point out ways in which each approach can be adapted to better align with practices from applied linguistics research. Most approaches to language teaching can be thought of as somewhere on a continuum from grammar-based approaches to naturalistic approaches.

In grammar-based approaches to language teaching, curricula, syllabi, and lessons are organized around grammar points (e.g., "In Unit 4 we will learn about the near future tense" or "In Unit 4 we will learn the target structures *I will [INFINITIVE], You will [INFINITIVE],* and *S/He will [INFINITIVE]*"). This method of teaching – sometimes also called a "focus on forms" approach – assumes that learning happens piece by piece in the order presented by the teacher or textbook. Perhaps the most recognizable version of a grammar-based approach is the **grammar–translation** approach, where most of the teaching occurs in the learners' native language and focuses on *learning about* the language, rather than on how to *use* the language. In a grammar-based classroom, activities often take the form of fill-in-the-blank worksheets focusing on grammar patterns, translation exercises, and memorizing word lists. Any language class that is primarily organized around grammar points (e.g., the future simple tense, superlatives, prepositions of place, etc.) would be considered a grammar-based classroom.

There can be a number of advantages to a grammar-based approach. First, this method of instruction encourages learners to make explicit connections between their L1(s) and the L2. This tends to be helpful for older learners who already understand how the grammar works in their L1(s). Grammar translation is also typically easier for teachers to execute because most textbooks are already organized around grammar and so teachers don't have to produce their own materials. Finally, grammatical approaches can be efficient for learning complex grammar patterns. This approach can be especially helpful for learners with learning difficulties (e.g., dyslexia, ADHD, see Chapter 7), who often have trouble noticing grammatical patterns on their own and struggle with implicit learning. However, there are also several significant disadvantages. When language is presented in a decontextualized or isolated way, learners are less likely to retain and be able to use what they have learned outside the classroom. If too much of the class occurs in the L1 of the learners (e.g., explaining in the L1 how the L2 grammar works), learners have limited L2 input and opportunities to generate written and spoken/signed production, which we know is important for language learning. We also know that most language learning does not occur grammar point by grammar point in an orderly, linear way but is instead learned in chunks that develop regardless of how a textbook or teacher presents them. Another disadvantage is that when these approaches are used with young children, they are less likely to be effective because children cannot easily leverage the explicit language study skills that adults have to memorize grammar rules and vocabulary.

The opposite end of the spectrum provided in Table 16.1 involves naturalistic approaches to L2 learning, sometimes also called "meaning-focused" approaches. In a purely naturalistic classroom, there is no focus on grammar instruction at all. Instead, learners listen to lots of L2 input or engage in activities where they are exposed to input that has been made *comprehensible* (by way of gestures, images, changes in volume or tone, etc.) or has been *simplified* (by way of only omitting any vocabulary and/or grammatical features that learners already know). In this approach, learners are believed to learn their L2 much like they acquired their native language in infanthood. All (or most) of class time would be spent in the

Table 16.1 The ends of the L2 teaching approaches spectrum

Grammar-based approaches	Naturalistic approaches
• Organize teaching around grammatical points and vocabulary chosen by the teacher (or determined by the textbook used) ahead of class time. • Use class time to explain and practice grammar. • Use a linguistic/lexical syllabus. • Assume a linear, synthetic approach to language learning. • Rely primarily on explicit learning.	• Organize teaching around what the students need and like to do or talk about (as in an immersion program or content and language-integrated learning [CLIL] program). • Spend class time hearing and using the L2. • Use a procedural syllabus. • Assume an analytic approach to language learning. • Rely primarily on implicit learning.
Advantages: • Generally easy to plan for because there is a definite, predetermined set of linguistic features. • Efficient way to ensure all learners (regardless of aptitude or learning differences), at a minimum, have access to patterns in L2 forms. Disadvantages: • Do not provide many opportunities for learners to rely on their own linguistic resources to communicate on topics that matter to them (because the focus is on supplying correct forms). • Many grammar-based syllabi try to force learners to learn (i.e., memorize, recall, and apply) complex grammar before they are ready.	Advantages: • Student-centered. • Focused on meaning. Disadvantages: • Inefficient because students will not have a sufficient number of "contact hours" (and, therefore, not enough linguistic input) to make meaningful gains in their communicative ability. • Assume all students will be able to independently and intuitively detect and analyze the rules of grammar.

L2 in a naturalistic-based classroom, so there is plenty of access to important language input. The advantages to this approach are that learners get lots of exposure to the L2 and that learning is allowed to happen in an order that is natural and in line with whatever developmental stage learners are currently in. Additionally, many of the ingredients we know to be necessary for successful second language acquisition can be found in naturalistic L2 classrooms, including opportunities to interact with other learners and produce the L2, negotiation for meaning, and more. However, there are also disadvantages to purely natural approaches, especially for older children and adults. Research suggests that as we age, we are less able to learn quickly and efficiently from the kind of implicit information a naturalistic classroom provides. This shift from a preference for implicit learning in childhood to explicit learning in adulthood can result in a mismatch of needs versus practice in purely naturalistic classrooms.

Additionally, as discussed in Chapter 2, learners need to *notice* features and patterns in their new language in order to acquire them. The rate at which learners notice patterns varies tremendously, with some learners able to quickly notice linguistic features, while others require additional time and support in order to notice them. Some learners who are never explicitly told to focus on a grammatical feature or vocabulary term will simply not notice and not acquire them, thus limiting their language development. This presents a problem for equity of access in the classroom, as typically only those learners who are already able to learn implicitly will excel in a purely naturalistic setting. Another issue with naturalistic approaches is that research suggests that when language is simplified to be made comprehensible, acquisition is limited. Simplified oral language often strips resources of natural conversation features, relies on the standardized forms of the L2 (which often does not represent the rich linguistic diversity of the L2 community), and minimizes learners' opportunities to learn to interpret visual/contextual clues to assist in the meaning-making process. If learners only ever interact with simplified language in class, they are unprepared to navigate the reality outside of a classroom and the authentic language used there. For example, solely using the most frequently used verbs in the classroom might make learners comfortable with those verbs (sometimes called the "Sweet 16" verbs), but purposely avoiding synonyms of these verbs or constraining classroom discourse so that these verbs can be maximally used will not effectively prepare students for conversations with speakers of the L2 who do not limit their production in this way. This is not to say that young or novice learners should be presented with full length novels or radio talk shows. Research has shown there are more effective ways than simplification to make input comprehensible, such as pausing (to provide learners with time to process what's been said/signed), repetition, and rephrasing content. See Chapters 5 and 18 for some of these strategies.

Bridging the gap between these two ends of the spectrum are **communicative approaches** that blend communication goals while not ignoring the grammar or vocabulary that it is necessary to know to be able to communicate. In a communicative classroom, class is held in the L2 (as much as possible), and learners spend the majority of class time engaged in communication-driven tasks or activities where the goal is to successfully accomplish the task or activity goals rather than to use a specific grammar form or vocabulary word. However, teachers or the task itself will draw learners' attention to the grammar or vocabulary that is necessary for achieving the task goals. The key is to choose the tasks that align with students' communicative or curricular needs and use those tasks as building blocks for your curriculum rather than organizing lesson plans around grammatical or vocabulary points.

In a communicative classroom, learners have many opportunities to engage in meaning-making, negotiate for meaning, hear and read authentic L2 texts, engage in written and spoken production of their own, and receive corrective feedback from peers or their teacher. As discussed in Chapters 1, 2, 3, and 4, these are the key ingredients of successful language acquisition and therefore these are the approaches most backed by current research in applied linguistics.

Communicative language teaching (CLT), or a **communicative approach**, is really an umbrella term used to describe a variety of popular methods including proficiency-based, task-based, and content and language integrated instruction. What differentiates these approaches is how they organize curricula, syllabi, units, and lessons. Task-based classrooms are organized around the meaningful tasks that learners indicate they need to be able to do in their L2 and the resulting language necessary to accomplish those tasks. Proficiency-oriented or proficiency-based language teaching is organized around proficiency goals or benchmarks that represent what learners are able to do in the L2. Content and language integrated instruction includes classes where content such as science, math, art, history, etc. are taught in the L2. We cover **Task-Based Language Teaching (TBLT)** in detail in Chapter 17 because there has been a lot of recent research into how TBLT aligns with research about how languages are learned. Also, teachers using any approach may benefit from considering how activities can best support language outcomes by considering what makes an activity a communicative "task" versus a grammar exercise (see Chapter 17).

Communicative classrooms enjoy a blend of the advantages from grammar-based and naturalistic approaches. They are also advantageous because they are typically learner-centered, which tends to be motivating for learners since they may be able to envision a use for their new language skills. Classes built around communicative goals address learners' real-life needs for their language abilities, like applying to a study abroad program, interviewing for a job, or speaking with their grandparents. Furthermore, because communicative language teaching is "the best of both worlds," it allows all learners to develop a positive self-image as a language learner regardless of their age or aptitude. Expecting adults to learn their L2 in the same way they learned their L1 may lead to frustration and may result in learners viewing themselves from a deficit perspective, which is not conducive to any kind of learning, language or otherwise. Research shows that as people age, they develop more learning strategies that can be leveraged in language learning contexts. Communicative approaches to language teaching encourage adult learners to leverage new skills they didn't have during L1 acquisition, which may increase learner motivation, confidence, and ultimate "buy-in" to the language learning process.

> **BOX 16.1 Avoiding Grammar Exercises in Disguise!**
>
> One common issue we see teachers facing when designing activities for communicative language classroom is that their communicative activities are actually grammar exercises in disguise!
>
> **Read the exercise below. Why is this NOT communicative?**
>
> > *Complete the dialogue with either "will" or the correct form of "to be going to" and perform it with a partner.*
> >
> > CHARLIE: What are you _____ to do over the weekend?
> > SELENA: My family and I _____ drive to the beach.
> > CHARLIE: That sounds like it _____ very fun.
> > SELENA: What are you _____ to do?
> > CHARLIE: My friends _____ watch a soccer game. I think I _____ watch with them.
> > SELENA: That sounds like it _____ be very fun too.
> > CHARLIE: I think so too.
> > SELENA: I hope you have a good time!
> > CHARLIE: Thank you. I _____ see you on Monday.
>
> Keep in mind …
>
> - Just because learners are talking to each other does not mean that activity is communicative! Here they are just reading from a script.
> - Just because there is a topic that learners can theoretically relate to (we all talk about our weekend plans) does not mean that learners feel the "need" to talk about that topic. Moreover, the language is so stilted and repetitive here that the conversation is quite different from how a real-life conversation would occur.
> - How could this be adapted to become a communicative, meaning-based activity? One option would be to plan a trip to a dream destination next weekend with a partner. In order to accomplish the task, learners must decide together where to go, what to do, and where to eat. They finish the activity by presenting on their choices to the class. This activity will most likely also elicit the future tense from the learners, and the instructor could point out usage of the future tense during presentations to ensure learners are all noticing its correct usage.
>
> **Read the exercise below. Why is this NOT communicative?**
>
> > In a paragraph, describe three–four specific features of your dream house and why they are important to you. You should use at least ten words from the Unit III vocabulary list. You should also use at least three prepositions of location and three examples of the future tense.
> >
> > When you've finished writing, exchange your paragraph with a partner. Circle their vocabulary words and underline the prepositions.
> >
> > _____
> > _____

> **BOX 16.1 (Continued)**
>
> Keep in mind …
>
> - Just because there is a fun or creative prompt does not mean learners are engaged in authentic language use. How often do people journal and try to use a certain number or type of words in their writing?
> - Just because learners are exchanging work and reading a peer's responses does not mean they are "communicating." Here, the interactive component is framed as a metalinguistic exercise where learners must identify parts of language. They are not asked to do anything meaningful with the content of the paragraph.
> - How could this be adapted to become a communicative, meaning-based activity? Learners could use this same prompt ("design your dream house"), but instead be provided with a budget and a list of prices for some common household items. Then learners could sketch models of their dream house and list the features they will prioritize in their budget with reasons why. Then they could work in pairs or small groups to share their opinions and debate why certain features were worth including over others. This will still certainly draw on key vocabulary and preposition usage; however, now grammar and vocabulary are integrated into a meaningful communicative activity.
>
> For more ways to adapt grammar exercises, see Chapter 17 where we provide more detail on how to ensure activities can be designed to best approximate real-world tasks where language will authentically be used!

The main disadvantages of communicative approaches are that they are more time-consuming to design and implement. In a communicative-based classroom, there is a focus on meeting the individual needs of the community or learners in a given context with customized teaching materials. Therefore, it is hard to rely solely on a one-size-fits-all textbook. Also, textbook activities are often grammar drills in disguise (see Box 16.1), which have been shown to be ineffective for long-term acquisition (and are difficult to implement with younger learners). Because of this, teachers or programs seeking to implement a communicative teaching approach must take on the responsibility of finding resources and creating appropriate tasks and activities. However, the work of designing and implementing communicative language classroom is worth the effort, as these practices are grounded in research about how languages are learned. There are also places where teachers and programs seeking to incorporate more communicative instruction can also find support. More and more teachers are sharing resources and materials on both free and subscription-based online platforms. In many contexts, even those districts or programs where there are mandated grammar-based textbooks, resources can be supplemented, and activities can be adjusted to foster negotiation for meaning and communication.

> **BOX 16.2 The Science! Points to Remember**
>
> - Most teaching approaches fall on a continuum from grammar-based to naturalistic approaches. There are pros and cons of all teaching approaches that vary based on a number of learner, teacher, and programmatic factors.
>   - In grammar-based approaches, the syllabus is structured around discrete grammatical points and vocabulary lists. It is expected that learners master these in a prescribed order.
>   - In more naturalistic approaches, the L2 learning environment is designed to replicate (as much as possible) the L1 acquisition.
> - Communicative approaches fall between grammar-based and naturalistic teaching approaches. The curriculum is centered around what a learner wants or needs to do with the L2.
>   - Task-based language teaching (TBLT) is one kind of communicative approach. With TBLT, specific linguistic features may be addressed explicitly if learners need to use them to complete a meaningful, real-world task.

16.3 The Science: What's Missing?

There is no research that definitively says what the "best" method of language teaching is for all learners in all contexts. For teachers or programs interested in pursuing more grammar-based approaches, the research does not tell us about how (or when) explicitly learned metalinguistic information transfers to spontaneous, fluent use across different learner populations (if it will at all). For teachers or programs interested in pursuing naturalistic approaches, the research does not tell us exactly how much (per hour, per class period) input is necessary to further language acquisition across different learner populations. While there is research noting that some instruction is better than no instruction, there is no one method or approach that has been "proven" to be most successful in facilitating language learning. There will always be situation- or learner-specific reasons why one approach is better received than an other or some approaches cannot be implemented at all. For example, in some educational contexts, learner-oriented approaches are in conflict with cultural norms around teaching. In some schools or programs, teachers are simply not given a choice about what approach they want to use and are instead mandated to follow a district-wide curriculum or textbook. Given the absence of conclusive empirical evidence in support of one approach over another and the diversity among learners, language programs, and teacher expertise, teachers should consider weighing the advantages and disadvantages of each approach as they decide how to structure their classes. For teachers who find that their preferred approach conflicts with the district or program visions, we offer some advice below.

16.4 The Art: Research-Based Strategies to Try

16.4.1 The Art of Transitioning to a Communicative Approach

If you or your program currently uses a grammar-based approach:

- *On a curricular level:* Think about the grammatical features that your syllabus is currently structured around. Brainstorm the different real-world functions that these grammatical features serve (e.g., we often use the command form of verbs when we are giving instructions). Which of these real-world functions relate best with your learners' concrete needs and interests? How can you organize classes so that the tasks are the focus rather than the grammar or vocabulary point? See Table 16.2 for an example of how to translate a grammar-based syllabus into communicative target tasks.

Table 16.2 Restructuring a grammar-driven curriculum

What your grammar-based curriculum says to teach …		Task ideas to use instead
Grammar forms	**Vocabulary**	
Question formation Give & follow directions (commands)	Cardinal directions City sights/locations Transportation methods	Target task: **Asking for and giving directions when navigating a new city** Example: How do I get to the museum? Walk two blocks south and catch the red metro bus.
Opening and closing statements Conjunctions Spelling and punctuation Abbreviations and contractions	Colloquial lexicon (i.e., conversational fillers) Academic vocabulary	Target task: **Write an email in a professional/academic context asking for a letter of recommendation** Example: I hope this message finds you well … I look forward to hearing from you.
Present tense Transition words (*first, then, last*) Cause & effect	Body parts of an insect Natural/outdoor vocabulary Color Size	Target task: **Explaining the life cycle of a butterfly** Example: Then, the caterpillar eats lots of leaves so that it can grow big.
Expressing opinions Prepositions of place Future tense	Household items Colors Sizes Shapes	Target task: **Plan decorations for a new space (e.g., classroom, bedroom, office space)** Example: I think I'll want to put the table next to the small window.
Modals Conjunctions Past tense	Daily routines Body parts Foods	Target task: **Give advice to a younger classmate/colleague on school/work balance** Example: You should always get 6–8 hours of sleep each night. When I was in your grade …

- *On a daily level:* Plan to spend the first five–ten minutes of each class getting to know learners' hobbies, interests, opinions, etc. This can be done with a variety of speed dating/summer camp-type games. These games will help learners feel more comfortable about talking openly and will also help you learn about them, which is information you will need as you redesign your curriculum.

If you or your program currently uses a naturalistic approach:

- *On a curricular level:* Reflect on your current course structure to identify recurrent types of interaction or themes that arise in class (e.g., the weather, what learners ate for lunch). How can you develop these themes into more cohesive units that involve learners completing real-life tasks and referencing authentic resources? What forms do learners need to know to accomplish these tasks? How can you raise learners' awareness of these key grammar or vocabulary items? Can you provide more corrective feedback?
- *On a daily level:* Begin bringing more authentic resources (more on these in Chapter 18) into class. Because your learners will likely be more accustomed to working with simplified input, you will need to teach them how to approach authentic texts so your learners have the skills they need to tackle unfamiliar language.

16.4.2 The Art of Finding Materials for a Communicative Classroom

- Many resources can be repurposed as class materials, but they might not always be what first come to mind when you're lesson planning. Here are some items that can lend themselves to the communicative classroom (and see Chapter 18 for more details about authentic resources).
  - Maps (street-level, public transportation)
  - Menus
  - Street/traffic signs
  - TV shows/movies
  - School/university schedules
  - Vlogs
  - Magazines and newspapers (any kind)
  - TripAdvisor reviews (in the L2)
  - Airbnb accommodation and reviews (in the L2)
  - Reddit posts and threads
  - Food labels
  - Recipes
  - Paperwork (passport forms, bank applications, mock voting forms)
  - Visit a location where the L2 is spoken (or ask a friend to do so for you) to take pictures of menus, maps, street signs, public transportation options, etc.
  - Request videos from friends or community members of their day-to-day experiences

16.4.3 The Art of Designing Curricula for a Communicative Classroom

- Think about delving deeper into the activities and tasks you have already developed to ensure that learners are getting the most from the rich resources and language you present them with. By building on activities and tasks you already

have, you can save time and ensure that learners are getting the repetition they need as language learners.
- For example, start by showing a video of different tourist attractions in a place where the L2 is spoken. Then, lead a whole group discussion where learners recall what attractions they saw featured. This short 15-to-20-minute activity can inspire follow-up activities that vary based on who the learners are talking to (individual, small group, whole group) and how they are communicating (speaking vs. writing). For example, students could pick their own tourist destination and present on the key historical facts or things they would recommend a tourist to see if they visited. Chapter 17 will explain in more detail how to develop and structure tasks and activities in the classroom.

16.4.4 The Art of Navigating between Different Teaching Methods

- Learners who may have had previous language learning experiences that do not align with a communicative approach may be wary of the new expectations and activities they encounter in your classroom. If this is the case, it may be helpful to give them a mini "crash course" (age-appropriate, of course!) in their first language to explain why you teach the way you do, what they can expect out of you as a teacher, and what you expect out of them (see Figure 16.1 for some ideas).
- If your preferred teaching approach conflicts with your school's or district's approach, investigate what approach your district/program is taking; which one of the approaches above does it best approximate? How can small day-to-day changes bring you more in line with your preferred method?
- If you must use a district/program-mandated textbook, are you able to alter the activities to make them more communicative? Can you restructure how you present the items in the text so they are in a thematic or task-based order, rather than organized by grammar points?
- Go back to Chapter 1 and focus on integrating the main ingredients for successful SLA: access to authentic, quality input, opportunities to produce output,

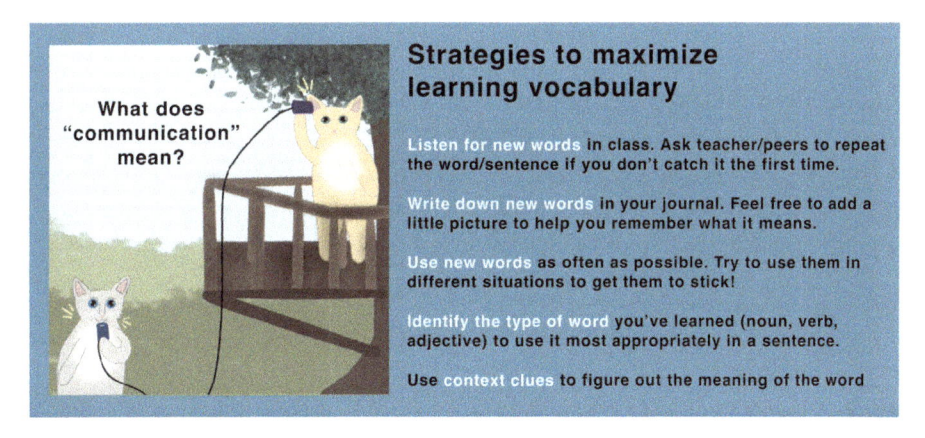

Figure 16.1 Strategies to maximize learning in a communicative classroom. Learners who are not familiar with a communicative classroom may benefit from an introduction to how to navigate the new environment. Image by: Elizabeth Zonarich

opportunities to negotiate for meaning and receive corrective feedback. Even if the structure of your course is predetermined, ensuring these ingredients are present in every lesson will ensure your teaching is aligned with best practices from research.
    - For example, if a textbook asks you to have learners repeat a dialogue about a restaurant, instead have two learners perform the dialogue for the class, then ask learners to act out their own restaurant situations in small groups. Ask them to introduce realistic "problems" into ordering food, for example, when there is nothing they like on the menu, or they have a food allergy. This will still be on the same topic as presented in your text, but instead of decontextualized memorization of a dialogue, learners are able to communicate authentically to achieve the same goal.
- While some amount of sampling from each approach is encouraged and may be necessary depending on your teaching context, some ways of styles "mixing and matching" do not work as well as others. Here are some pairings that do not support learner linguistic development and may confuse or demotivate learners:
    - Using a naturalistic approach and grammar-driven assessments or placement tests (and vice versa).
        - For example, many standardized language assessments (TOEIC, Advanced Placement, SAT II, IELTS) call upon extensive amounts of metalinguistic knowledge. Therefore, when passing one of these tests is the only (or main) goal, class instruction should be designed in a way to ensure that learners get the metalinguistic knowledge they need to perform well on these tests (e.g., more explicit grammar instruction may be necessary).
    - Using a naturalistic approach during class time and scoring learner performance with a grammar-based rubric (and vice versa).
        - Learners should not be assessed in a manner different from the way they were taught (see Chapter 20 on assessments for more details). This will advantage learners who naturally perform well on grammar-based exercises and disadvantages those who don't and never practiced in this manner during class. Task-based or performance-based assessments will better align with a communicative or naturalistic-based classroom. For example, learners who learn about travel interactions can "perform" the skills in a final assessment where they book a trip (in a role-play scenario) and leave a written review on attractions they visited.
- When comparing the different approaches to language teaching that you encounter in conferences or professional development workshops, use the graphic organizer in Figure 16.2 to consider how they view the process of language learning.

16.5 Troubleshooting: How the Science Informs the Art

Ms. Q loved observing her mentor implement this approach but feels she should develop her own teaching style. As a result, she started researching language teaching methods online and quickly became overwhelmed by the number of resources available all touting their methods as the "best" way to teach languages. How should she pick the approach that is right for her and her learners?

16.5 Troubleshooting: How the Science Informs the Art

How does the teaching approach describe…

	Approach #1: _____	**Approach #2:** _____
The kind of input learners receive?		
Who learners receive input from?		
The kind of output learners are expected to produce? What (if any) supports are provided when learners produce output?		
How written/spoken errors are addressed (if at all)?		
The role of grammar in the curriculum? How do linguistic features surface in class (if at all)?		
The order and nature of the course syllabus? What determines the sequence of the units?		
The goals of language learning? How are they articulated? How is progress towards them measured?		

Figure 16.2 Investigating teaching methods. This graphic organizer can help teachers gather information about new teaching approaches they encounter in professional development workshops. Image by: Caitlyn Pineault

Despite what Ms. Q may have found on the Internet, there is no research that has ever concluded that one teaching method is the "best" method for teaching all languages, to all students, in all classrooms. The language learning process is too complex, and there are simply too many important contextual and learner-specific factors that impact the success of one method over another to make such a general claim.

Research does show, however, that learners need to get input, produce output, receive feedback, and have opportunities to negotiate meaning to make progress in a world language classroom. As Ms. Q transitions into her own classroom and begins to develop her own approach, she should keep in mind these four components and tailor her instruction to maximize the extent to which each component occurs in her classroom. Communicative approaches such as task-based and project-based curricula that integrate content and language tend to include the elements known to support successful SLA more often than grammar-based approaches, which tend to promote short-term memorization of grammar and vocabulary that is difficult for learners to apply to real-world contexts.

If she finds out that she must follow a particular approach when she starts her new job, how can she adapt it to her own needs and strengths?

It is likely that when Ms. Q begins her new job, the language program will already have a teaching approach, and possibly even a textbook, that they would like her to follow, complete with curriculum, supplementary resources, and required assessments. If Ms. Q finds that the program's approach is more like a grammar–translation approach, Ms. Q can supplement the scripted exercises with more authentic interactions between students based on their needs and interests. Ms. Q should also consider participating in conferences or workshops to get inspired about what other teachers are doing in their classrooms. While not all their ideas may align with her approach to language teaching, this is a great way for Ms. Q to begin to develop her own repository of resources and activities.

16.6 The Science: Points to Remember

- Most teaching approaches fall on a spectrum ranging from "least" grammatically driven to "most" grammatically driven.
- There is no one, undeniably superior, research-backed approach to teaching world languages.
- Teacher, learner, and environmental contexts influence which teaching approach may work "best" with any given class.
- The ideal teaching approaches maximize learner opportunities to engage in meaning-making, negotiate for meaning, hear authentic L2 output, produce output on their own, and receive corrective feedback from peers or their teacher.

16.7 Questions to Consider

1. How did you learn your L2(s)? Did the instructional approach your teachers use "work" for you? Why or why not?
2. Where do you feel your own teaching approach falls on the spectrum of "grammar-based" to "naturalistic"?
3. What factors have influenced your current teaching approach?

4. What about your current teaching approach works well for you and your students? How do you know?
5. What about your teaching approach is more challenging for you and your students? After reading this chapter, how might you adapt those elements?
6. To what extent does the structure of your curriculum align with your program's mission? With your learners' own language goals? With your goals for your learners?
7. Pick a unit from your curriculum and conduct a brief analysis on its structure with the following guiding questions:
   a. What resources are included in this unit?
   b. What must learners accomplish to be successful in this unit?
   c. How is progress measured?
   d. Is the instructional focus more on talking about the L2 or using the L2 to communicate about other topics and themes?
8. Return to the exercises presented in Box 16.1. How could you alter these exercises to make them more communicative?

16.8 The Science of Language Learning: Research Supporting the Points Made in This Chapter

Butler, Y. G. (2011). The implementation of communicative and task-based language teaching in the Asia-Pacific Region. *Annual Review of Applied Linguistics, 31*, 36–57. https://doi.org/10.1017/S0267190511000122.

In this review, Butler examines the successes and challenges of adopting CLT and TBLT across several countries in the Asia-Pacific region. In this region, CLT and TBLT were introduced to replace grammar–translation and audiolingual methods of instruction that were not helping students achieve communicative competence outside their classrooms. While CLT and TBLT have both become popular approaches, they have also presented new challenges for teachers and administrators. The implementation trends identified in this article can guide stakeholders in other educational contexts who also seek to adopt CLT and TBLT approaches in their own language programs.

Gass, S. M., Behney, J., & Plonsky, L. (2020). *Second language acquisition: An introductory course* (5th ed.). Routledge.

While not strictly an L2 teaching methodology manual, this text represents one of the most complete and nuanced resources available on SLA research and provides readers with the essential terms and concepts needed to interpret SLA research as it relates to L2 teaching. This edition (the fifth since its original release in 1994) also provides pedagogical tools and connections to the classroom context that both SLA researchers and L2 teachers will find helpful.

Littlewood, W. (2014). Communication-oriented language teaching: Where are we now? Where do we go from here? *Language Teaching, 47*(3), 349–362.

The article discusses the history of CLT, drawing connections to other popular instructional approaches over the last forty years and looking forward to what "best practices" for teaching may hold. Littlewood presents the original motives for developing a communicative approach to language teaching and explores the ways CLT has been interpreted differently over the years. The challenges of implementing CLT across a variety of teaching contexts and educational needs are also addressed.

For more resources, including more sample lesson plans, videos, and other ideas, visit our companion website: www.cambridge.org/BryfonskiMackey.

17 Content, form, and activities: How do I select activities, tasks, and projects?

KEY QUESTIONS
- The Science: Why do tasks lead to more language learning?
- The Art: How can I design and incorporate tasks into my classes?
- How do I find out what the learners in my class need to learn?
- How do I select and sequence activities, tasks, and projects?
- How do I balance language form and content so my learners learn both?
- How do I know what tasks will be easy or difficult for my learners?
- Can I use task-based methods if my learners need to pass standardized assessments mandated by my school, district, or program?

17.1 Voices from the Classroom

Ms. B has been teaching a beginner class for English as a second language (ESL) learners for ten years in a high school vocational program in the United States. Her learners come from a wide range of language backgrounds and home countries. Most are recent immigrants who enroll in her class prior to seeking employment opportunities in a range of fields. Her learners are interested in learning about how they can make their language "better" and how the grammar of English works, and as a result her class often focuses on grammar and grammar exercises. Learners seem most engaged with language when they are quietly working on worksheets and exercises. Despite meeting the desires of her learners, Ms. B has heard from former learners that upon entering the work force, her former learners often cannot perform the job duties asked of them in English. They seem to do well at all the activities they complete in class and always ask questions and study and understand the grammar given to them. The learners' language improves in accuracy as they complete the worksheets and activities Ms. B provides in class. Why can't her learners seem to understand and use their English outside the class? How can Ms. B make her English classes more useful to her learners?

17.2 The Science: What the Research Says

How is it possible for learners to succeed in class, become better at grammar, get excellent grades, yet fail to apply those skills in the "real world"? How often do we hear learners say things like: "I took ten years of Spanish in school, but I couldn't even order coffee when I visited Madrid," or similar stories? This common problem has plagued language teachers and learners in second language (L2) learning contexts of all varieties worldwide. Research on L2 learning provides insight into why this is such a common complaint. Traditional approaches to language teaching, like the one Ms. B uses in the real-life example, organize their teaching around grammar points and vocabulary. They usually use a textbook that starts with "easy" interactions like *introductions* and "simple" vocabulary lists like *around the house*. Learners hear the teacher present the grammar and vocabulary, they practice with worksheets or activities and then are assumed to "know" those words and structures, and the class moves on to the next chapter. This classic method of language teaching is called the **Presentation, Practice, Production (PPP)** model, and it is found being used in classrooms of various languages around the world. But how well does this way of teaching align with what we know about how second languages are actually learned and used?

As we discussed in Chapter 11, one important research finding about how people of all backgrounds learn languages is that there is an order, or series of stages, that learners pass through on their way to acquiring the grammar of any language. This subfield of second language acquisition (SLA) is known as **developmental sequences research**. We now know unequivocally that learners do not necessarily acquire the structures in the order they are presented by the teacher or textbook but, rather, proceed through natural stages of acquisition that are largely determined by things like a structure's frequency and resemblance to similar structures in learners' first language(s), L1(s). In light of this information, organizing a language syllabus or class around predetermined grammar points could come into conflict with the developmental stage of the learners and limit or slow down acquisition. Instead, teachers must first accept that language is acquired in an internal order, and then organize our syllabi around what language learners need to be able to *do* with their language in the real world.

One approach to language teaching that has integrated these research findings is called **Task-Based Language Teaching (TBLT)**. In a TBLT classroom, the teacher, admissions staff, or program administrators might first conduct a **needs analysis**, often through a survey or by asking learners (or if they are children, parents or other teachers) what tasks they want to be able to accomplish using the L2. In Ms. B's vocational program, learners might want to be able to write a resumé in English, fill out a job application, or complete a job interview in English (Figure 17.1). If so, these would be some of the tasks that Ms. B would design her syllabus around instead of grammar points. Ms. B would then use those tasks

17.2 The Science: What the Research Says

Figure 17.1 Real-world task examples. Language learners come to class with real-world tasks in mind that they would like to accomplish in the L2. Image by: Elizabeth Zonarich

Figure 17.2 Task deconstruction sequence. Once teachers identify the target tasks learners want to accomplish, they can break down these larger tasks into smaller sub-tasks that can be explored in the classroom. Image by: Elizabeth Zonarich

to determine which linguistic forms, grammar, and vocabulary learners need to know to accomplish their tasks.

Ms. B would include a series of related tasks where learners interact and receive feedback and the tasks become gradually more complex until they approximate the **target task**, or the skill learners need to do in their L2, like *apply for a job*. In order to do this, the target tasks need to be broken down into their sub-components, or sub-tasks (see Figure 17.2). Then learners will complete **pedagogic tasks**, which are the activities they will complete in the classroom. Pedagogic tasks are related to the target task but might include different content or be altered in such a way to make them appropriate for classroom-based activities and interactions. For example, if one of the sub-tasks for the target task of *applying for a job* is to navigate websites to find job opportunities, a pedagogic task could be navigating websites to find a vacation location and hotel, sharing findings with classmates, and saying why they are or are not appropriate for a vacation with the class. In this way, the pedagogic task approximates the skills needed to accomplish the target sub-task. For younger or lower-proficiency learners, these target tasks might be broken down further into "building-block" tasks, which are further abstractions from the target task but still involve the same skills. For example, if a target task is to identify and describe habitats for different animals, a pedagogic task might be providing half the class with pictures of animals and the other half with pictures of habitats. Learners need to describe their animal or habitat to their peers until they find a match. A building-block task might ask learners to work with a partner to draw and label the habitat of an assigned animal. With incremental practice on similar tasks, the learners will build the skills they need to perform the sub-task and eventually the target task.

While learners perform the pedagogic tasks, the teacher would differentiate her feedback to each learner so they would get reinforcement of the language they need to complete tasks. She would focus on meaning (how well are learners making themselves understood?) rather than accuracy in her feedback, and encourage this from other learners as she encourages them to interact with each other. The objective would be for the learners to accomplish the tasks they set out to do (or the best approximation of those tasks).

Within research on task development, linguists have found that changing elements of the task (like whether it is in in pairs or in small groups) has an impact on the type of language that learners experience. Therefore, teachers need to think about how changing key elements of a task can affect how difficult a task is for their learners. Different types of tasks also affect how much learners in a group interact. Here are some examples of elements that change how difficult tasks might be for learners:

1. *Planning time:* Learners have a chance to plan out what they will say before a mock interview (easier) or do not have time to plan (more difficult).
2. *Familiarity:* The task is familiar for learners, like giving directions in their own neighborhood (easier), or the task is unfamiliar, like giving directions in a new city (more difficult).
3. *Content:* The task has only a few elements, like a simple map (easier) or many elements, like an authentic map copied from Google Maps (more difficult; see example in Figure 17.3).
4. *Form:* Learners must discuss present-tense ideas (easier) versus talking about past ideas (more difficult).
5. *Solutions:* The task has only one solution, like making a decision about a group project (less interaction, one solution), or has an open-ended conclusion, like a discussion of top project ideas (more interaction, multiple solutions).
6. *Information:* All the learners in a group have the same information to discuss (less interaction), or learners need to share information with each other (more interaction).

Easy Version

Difficult Version

Easy in this example might mean the map has *fewer* elements or roads to navigate, the map might also be of a *known* area like the learners' neighborhood.

Difficult in this example might mean a map more closely approximating a *real-world* map. To make this more complex this map could be from an *unfamiliar* region like a new city to the learner.

Figure 17.3 Map task. Tasks can be adjusted to become increasingly difficult as learners gain confidence and linguistic skills. Image by: Elizabeth Zonarich

17.2.1 Aligning with the Research

TBLT aligns with what the research says about language learning because learners proceed through their own stages of development, are motivated by target tasks that align with their real-world language needs, interact often, and receive feedback, their learning is differentiated, and success is assessed based on what learners can do with their language skills. However, not just any classroom activity promotes the types of behaviors and experiences that facilitate language development. To determine whether an activity qualifies as an L2 task, researchers have compiled four criteria for effective tasks. These criteria are presented as questions in Box 17.1 to guide task development for researchers and teachers alike.

BOX 17.1 Evaluating a Task

Is my activity/task/project a "task"?
1. Is the task *focused on meaning-making* (not language or grammar)?
2. Are learners *working and interacting* together to *find out something* they don't already know?
3. Will learners have to rely on their *own language skills* (rather than all the language being provided for them) to solve the problem/do the task?
4. Does the activity have a *clear communicative outcome* (i.e., not just accurately using language/grammar)?

If you answer "yes" to all four questions, your activity will meet the criteria for being a task that strongly promotes language learning (see Figure 17.4). The first two questions in Box 17.1 both encourage learners to interact while completing a task. They also ensure that learners are focused on meaning-making rather than manipulating grammatical patterns in isolation. We know from the research discussed above that interaction is critical to L2 learning and that emphasizing form–meaning connections maximizes learner development. The third question asks if learners must rely on their own language skills to solve the task. But where do these skills come from? In some methods of designing a task-based curriculum, each new unit starts with a "flood" of information from authentic resources with examples of successful task completion from the "real world." For example, the learners might watch videos of people asking and answering questions in job interviews. Chapter 18 discusses how and why these resources are critical in language learning. Then learners have a chance to interact and engage in the tasks. Ideally, learners will first engage in supported practice of the target task, where they work with the teacher and then in small groups before trying the task alone. This way, learners will have learned some language and vocabulary through observation and practice before they participate in the task on their own. Finally, learners reflect on their own learning during the tasks. One way to encourage reflection is to video record learners doing tasks and asking them to watch the video back and report what they noticed.

From Exercise to Task

EXERCISES	ACTIVITIES	TASKS
✗ Primary focus on meaning?	? Primary focus on meaning?	✓ Primary focus on meaning?
✗ Some type of "gap"?	? Some type of "gap"?	✓ Some type of "gap"?
✗ Learners use their own linguistic resources?	? Learners use their own linguistic resources?	✓ Learners use their own linguistic resources?
✗ Non-linguistic outcome?	? Non-linguistic outcome?	✓ Non-linguistic outcome?

Good for...
- Developing metalinguistic knowledge
- Examining complex linguistic patterns
- Drawing connections between the L1 and the TL

Good for...
- Practicing specific grammar forms and vocabulary
- Scaffolding more advanced language and communicative functions

Good for...
- Connecting linguistic form and function
- Providing high quality, comprehensible input
- Supporting language development

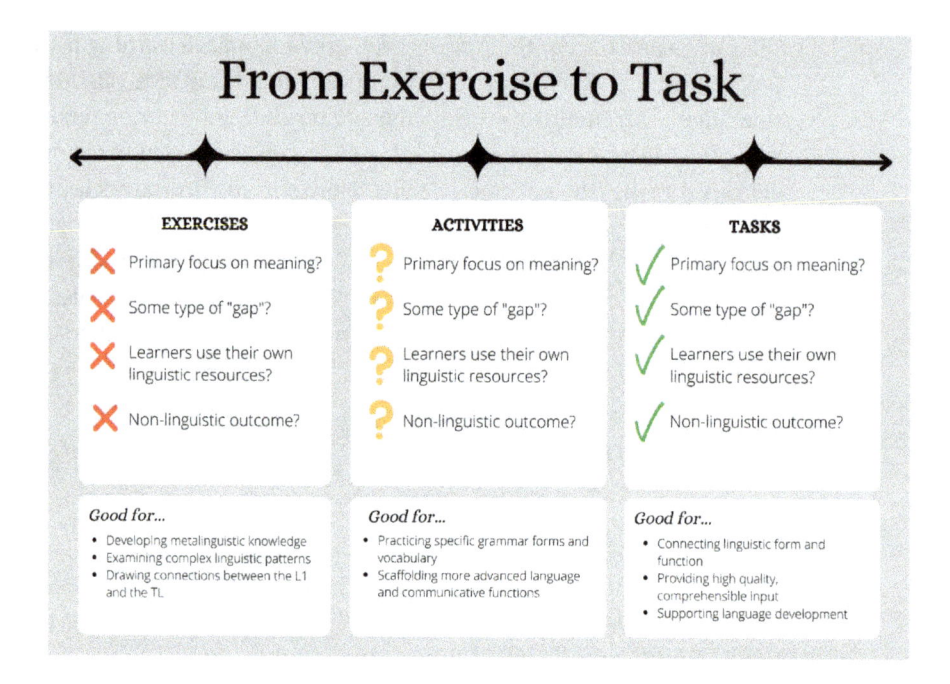

Figure 17.4 Defining task characteristics. Exercises, activities, and tasks have different defining characteristics and serve different purposes in the language classroom. Image by: Caitlyn Pineault

17.2 The Science: What the Research Says

While investigating the impact of tasks on learners' linguistic development, researchers have identified several different main types of tasks that contribute to learners' progression through proficiency levels. The tasks that are most facilitative of language development promote comprehension of input, include feedback on production, and offer opportunities to negotiate for meaning. For example, tasks that require a two-way exchange of information, like group problem-solving tasks, have been shown to naturally provide more opportunities to negotiate meaning than one-way tasks where one learner has information and supplies it to another learner.

One task categorization approach looks at the interaction requirement outcome options for a task. This approach asks: "is interaction necessary to complete the goals of the task?" and "is there one solution to the task or are there many different possible outcomes?" The answers to these questions typically result in five main types of tasks: *jigsaw tasks*, *information-gap tasks*, *problem-solving tasks*, *decision-making tasks*, and *opinion-exchange tasks* (see Figure 17.5). While there is no single task that has been identified as the "best" for language learning, this framework empowers teachers to consider how the task design influences the types of language learners will (or won't) use.

Regardless of the task types that teachers choose, it is important to reflect on the different conceptual and communicative demands that a task requires and the cognitive resources that learners will need to meet those demands. The variables that researchers have studied as they explored how certain task features impact learners' performance include whether they require learners to use prior knowledge, more complex reasoning, or multiple authentic resources. When working through a complex task, for example on a topic they are unfamiliar with or that has lots of moving parts, researchers have found that learners' focus on meaning-making, which may mean that they prioritize the fluency of their speech (e.g., rate of talking, number of pauses) rather than the accuracy of their language. While proficiency scales like those of ACTFL and the Common European Framework of Reference (CEFR) do not prioritize accuracy at the lower levels of proficiency, as learners become more advanced they will be expected to recognize and produce complex linguistic structures more consistently. Therefore, the tasks

Task Types

Jigsaw — Information-Gap — Problem-solving — Decision making — Opinion Exchange

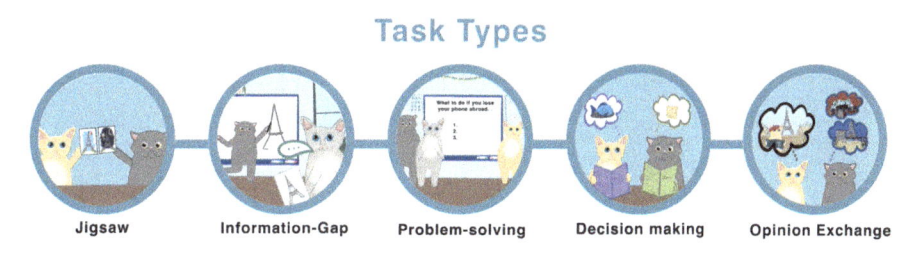

Figure 17.5 Task types. There are five primary types of tasks that vary based on who has the information, who needs the information, and what is done with the information. Image by: Elizabeth Zonarich

in advanced language classrooms should create a communicative need for linguistic accuracy. Some scholars have recommended incorporating a "reporting" stage within a task to accomplish this. Whether individual or group, written or spoken, these final presentations are expected to be more formal and polished.

> **BOX 17.2 The Science! Points to Remember**
>
> - Learners' language needs are central to designing and developing the syllabus.
> - Learners learn by doing.
> - Learners are motivated to learn when they are focused on meaning.
> - Learners should receive differentiated feedback to meet their individual needs.
> - In-class activities should resemble the tasks learners want to accomplish with the second language.

17.3 The Science: What's Missing?

Second language learning and teaching involves many different variables, unique contexts, and situations. This means that it is difficult to say for certain which teaching method will always be best for language learning outcomes in every context. Even though we have every reason to think that TBLT, which is supported by theory and research in the field, will be successful, it is still a relatively new approach and more research is needed. There have been a few large-scale evaluations of task-based language programs that demonstrate success for this approach (e.g., in Belgium), but questions like whether TBLT is better than **Task-Supported Language Teaching (TSLT)** (tasks used to supplement a pre-designed curriculum that is organized around discrete grammar), content and language integrated instruction, or other popular methods (see Chapter 16) remain unanswered. At this point, we only know that TBLT *aligns* better with findings about language learning in general and learner psychology when compared to other methods. Some teachers may find it useful to adopt some aspects of TBLT while keeping some aspects of their existing teaching methods like the ones described in Chapter 16.

While TBLT provides a framework for organizing a language course, it does not specifically say how every teacher should develop every aspect of their course. There are a lot of different options to choose from within the stages of TBLT, from whether and how to do needs analysis (for some school settings this won't be possible or necessary) to choosing sub-tasks and designing assessments to work out what's been learned. The tips and tricks in Section 17.4 provide some ideas to get teachers started but should be seen as a starting point, not as an exhaustive implementation guide. We provide a list of resources for where teachers interested in this approach can go for more information. Instructors are always best equipped to know and say what works best for their own language learners in their teaching context.

Finally, one of the largest challenges that has emerged in research on implementing TBLT in language programs is the amount of time it takes for teachers to develop enough tasks for their curriculum. While materials development is daunting, there are resources available to support teachers looking to move toward a TBLT approach, such as those provided in this chapter and on our website.

17.4 The Art: Research-Based Strategies to Try

17.4.1 The Art of Conducting a Needs Analysis

A needs analysis is a first step in designing a task-based course (see Figure 17.6). As noted above, in many contexts where tasks are used as more of a support for existing curricula (or in programs with mandatory curricula), a full needs analysis might not be necessary. However, this step is important for those who wish to implement a true task-based curriculum, as the results of the needs analysis will uncover the tasks the students want or need to be able to do in the target language (TL). There are multiple ways to do needs analyses. Some common methods include conducting surveys, interviews, and focus groups of relevant stakeholders (e.g., learners, parents/caregivers of younger learners, program administrators, former students of the program), or even by reviewing reports on learners from similar backgrounds or demographics. Using all these methods in a single needs analysis is likely not feasible for busy classroom teachers, but it is advisable to combine information from at least a few sources. For example, course designers

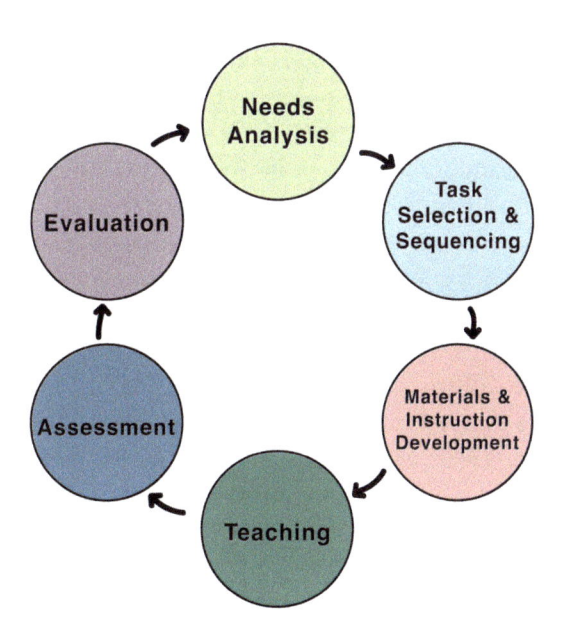

Figure 17.6 TBLT implementation cycle. The cyclical approach to TBLT adaption and evaluation follows a series of stages that assess the planning, teaching, and learning processes. Image by: Elizabeth Zonarich

could interview administrators and community members, and then send out a survey to enrolled students. In the case of Ms. B's high school classroom, it may be helpful for her to reach out to places that have hired her learners in the past to see what skills they require in English and how those former learners meet or fail to meet the language expectations.

For younger learners, a needs analysis might take the form of parent–teacher interviews about learners' backgrounds, family language policies, and even interests in hobbies or activities. Learners as young as 11–13 years of age may already be thinking about preparing to take standardized tests in their chosen L2 and may have needs more aligned with school norms. Adolescent learners may have needs more associated with employment, higher education, or specific industries. Questions on any surveys or interviews should change to reflect the diverse needs of these populations. In other cases, language departments may mandate a curriculum, in which case a needs analysis will simply gather information about learners' interests and anxieties that can help the teacher design tasks that are motivating.

17.4.2 The Art of Selecting and Designing Tasks

Once target tasks are established, teachers can design simplified versions of target tasks for learners to engage with in the classroom. When designing the pedagogical tasks, some criteria should be kept in mind to ensure that learners are interacting and making meaning; for example, if the task only entails asking "yes" or "no" questions, or filling in blanks on a worksheet, then interaction will be limited and the activity will not be considered a "task." There is a useful, simple framework for determining if your task meets the criteria for a "task." Assess your task by asking the questions listed in Box 17.1.

A practical example: Ms. B has identified *job interview in English* as a target task for her learners. After watching YouTube videos of some example interviews, she determines that learners will need to be able to ask and answer background questions. She decides to create an interactive task where learners can try out this skill. She divides her learners into groups of three. She gives each learner a background sheet she has prepared containing information about themselves that they need to share. One learner is assigned as the interviewer. The interviewer must decide between the two candidates who gets the job based on some provided criteria. The learners switch roles, so that each has the opportunity to be the interviewer and the interviewee. Ms. B knows this task meets the four criteria for a task because (a) the task must be accomplished via interaction, (b) there is a gap because each student has different information they must provide to the interviewer, (c) the learners are not provided with a vocabulary list or a prescribed set of forms to use in the interactions, and (d) the goal is to be hired by the interviewer. In this way, learners get the language they need to complete the task from videos, info sheets, feedback, and the reflection session, but not from a grammar or vocabulary list.

17.4 The Art: Research-Based Strategies to Try

17.4.3 The Art of Sequencing Tasks

When working toward a target task like *applying for a job*, there will be many different sub-tasks involved. It is through the deconstruction of target tasks, using a backwards design framework, that a task-based syllabus is created. Box 17.3 outlines how a teacher could hypothetically navigate this process for a group of adult language learners.

BOX 17.3 Building a Task-Based Syllabus for Adults

Steps	Example
1. **Determine target tasks**	• Ms. B works in a vocational program with adults, so she could survey her learners directly to find out what their needs are. She does this informally with a survey and discussion as part of a welcome packet at the start of the academic year. She will use this information to identify main themes that she can tailor to her particular group of learners. While needs analyses can be far more robust than this example, Ms. B has limited time and is the only teacher in her program.

2. **Sequence target tasks** based on their relative difficulty and importance for learners	• Ms. B found that her learners are all working toward the target task *applying for a job*. Based on her experience working with these learners, she knows *applying for a job* is really a collection of several different target tasks including:
	  ◦ writing a cover letter,
	  ◦ creating a resumé,
	  ◦ navigating job listings online to find appropriate opportunities,
	  ◦ sending and replying to emails regarding job opportunities,
	  ◦ scheduling interviews,
	  ◦ interviewing for the job, and
	  ◦ negotiating a job offer.
	• Mrs. B decides to order her syllabus in the natural order of the job application sequence listed above because these tasks become more high stakes as learners get closer to being interviewed, increasing the complexity and anxiety for learners.

3. **Design pedagogical tasks for each target task**	• Ms. B decides to further break down the first target task, writing a cover letter, into sub-tasks. Ms. B designs a sequence of several sub-tasks to address all aspects of cover letter writing, including letter introductions, highlighting personal strengths for a job, aligning the cover letter to a particular job opportunity, letter closings, and basic letter formatting. She uses these sub-tasks to design the pedagogical tasks which learners will complete in the classroom. • In one of these pedagogic tasks, learners work in pairs to read examples of introductions from a variety of pre-written cover letters and discuss the aspects they like or dislike about each and why. At the end of class everyone votes on which cover letter introduction they liked best and defends their point of view.

BOX 17.3 Continued

Steps	Example

4. **Focus on form**: Identify the key vocabulary, phrases, and other linguistic forms that emerge during task performances that learners need to focus on to successfully accomplish the target task	• While learners are working on their pedagogic task of analyzing letter introductions, Ms. B circulates the classroom and discusses some key language issues that arise with her learners. Some language that seems critical to task performance for her learners included:
	  ○ Pragmatically appropriate openers: *Greetings, To whom it may concern, Hello, Dear manager*, etc.
	  ○ Progressive verb forms: *I'm writing to ..., I'm applying for ...*, etc.
	  ○ Vocabulary to highlight skills: *adaptable, hard-working, punctual, leadership experience*, etc.
	• Ms. B highlights these forms as they arise during the task performance by offering feedback during and after the tasks.

Target tasks for younger learners will look a little bit different from target tasks for adult learners, who have more "real-life" language needs. For younger learners, whether they be students in a bilingual program or a world language program, their needs may frequently parallel the communicative, social, or literary goals in other subjects. Because of this, task-based language teachers are often able to collaborate with their teacher colleagues in interdisciplinary ways to share resources and instructional strategies. In other instances, language programs for younger learners must align with government learning standards. Box 17.4 outlines how a teacher could develop a task-based syllabus within pre-established curricular parameters.

BOX 17.4 Building a Task-Based Syllabus for Younger Learners with a Preexisting Curriculum

Steps	Example
1. **Determine target task**	• Mr. L is a 2nd grade teacher in an elementary bilingual school that uses a preexisting curriculum. Mr. L needs to draw from that curriculum to identify tasks for his learners. For example, his language arts curriculum includes learning objectives like *learners will be able to identify and explain the key differences between fiction and nonfiction texts* and *learners will be able to make and evaluate predictions about a text*.

2. **Sequence target tasks** based on their relative difficulty and importance for learners	• This unit is all about exploring genres. Mr. L uses his curriculum objectives to identify and sequence target tasks that he knows will be meaningful to learners while also covering the goals of his curriculum like *identifying the features of fiction texts*. He identifies and sequences the following target tasks:
	  ○ Making predictions about what will happen in a book and telling a friend
	  ○ Evaluating if your predictions were or were not correct and why
	  ○ Sharing the story of your favorite fiction book with a friend
	  ○ Writing a letter to the author of your favorite fiction book

BOX 17.4 Continued

Steps	Example
	• Mr. L sequences these target tasks in such a way that learners will circle back to repeat previously learned skills such as retelling and summarizing orally and in writing until they can accomplish the most complex task of *writing a letter to an author*, which will combine all of these tasks.
3. **Design pedagogical tasks for each target task**	• Mr. L breaks the target task, *sharing the story of your book with a friend*, into a series of sub-tasks including summarizing the story's beginning, middle, and end, identifying the main characters of the story, identifying key plot features in the story, and retelling a story orally. • Guided by one of the sub-tasks, Mr. L designs a pedagogic task for learners to complete in the classroom. In one of these pedagogic tasks, learners work in small groups and each group member is assigned a different character from a fiction book and the other group members must try to figure out which character and book they are describing. While one group member describes the character, the others take notes and organize the key features of the characters on a graphic organizer. The learners have to ask and answer questions about the characters in order to work out which character and which book their partner is describing.

4. **Focus on form**: Identify the key vocabulary, phrases, and other linguistic forms that emerge during task performances that learners need to focus on to successfully accomplish the target task	• While learners are working on their pedagogic task of *describing characters*, Mr. L circulates the classroom and discusses some key language issues that arise with the learners. Some language that seems critical to task performance for the learners included:
	  ○ Adjectives to describe characters: *little/big, mean/friendly, young/old*.
	  ○ Question formation:
	    ▪ *What does your character look like?*
	    ▪ *Where does your character live?*
	    ▪ *Who is your character's friend?*
	    ▪ *What happened to your character?*

17.4.4 The Art of Leading a Task

Teachers should also consider the individual differences of the learners in a group when organizing tasks. For example, if a task has learners working in groups, interpersonal dynamics may impact the group's ability to complete the task just as much, if not more, than their linguistic abilities. For that reason, a teacher may want to consider the following questions when reflecting on how to lead group tasks:

- What is the relationship between the group members?
- Are they friends, or did they just meet?
- Do the learners seem to be similarly motivated?
- Is one learner anxious to interact?

These individual differences may influence how much language learning occurs during each task. Teachers should incorporate a variety of pairings and groupings throughout class to investigate all the different ways learners work together and identify the ways they work best as a group. For more details, see Chapter 4 on the benefits of peer interaction and how to group learners of different proficiencies.

17.5 Troubleshooting: How the Science Informs the Art

Ms. B has read about task-based language teaching as an alternative approach to the way she teaches her current ESL class, and she did a short professional development training where it was introduced. However, she is used to a teacher-centered style of language teaching. She worries she will lose control of her large and tightly managed class if she moves to a student-centered approach. Will TBLT work for her?

In some parts of the world, learners and teachers are more accustomed to a teacher-fronted style of classroom language teaching and may find it uncomfortable to transform their classrooms completely to a TBLT style. In this case, teachers might consider moving more gradually toward a task-based approach, perhaps by first conducting a needs analysis and including some tasks aligned with those needs. As discussed above, teachers can also adopt aspects of TBLT to best suit their own context, like using interactive tasks to support their existing curriculum. Research findings show that even a task-supported curriculum has advantages over traditional language teaching styles. Over time, Ms. B may find it easier to manage a class that is learner-driven and find that learners are actually more engaged and better behaved when they are motivated to complete activities that are meaningful to their own language needs.

Ms. B has started to develop tasks aligned with her learners' language needs. She notices they are excellent at accomplishing the tasks in class. However, when she gives her learners her traditional grammar test at the end of the semester, many learners still fail. What is going on? Are her learners not learning after all? And where can she look for more information about assessing whether her learners have learned anything from the tasks? What if her learners need to pass a state- or school-mandated standardized assessment at the end of the year?

An important step in any class – task-based or otherwise – is to assess student learning. Learners should be assessed on what they have learned, and in this case, it will be how well they can accomplish the tasks they practiced in class. In Ms. B's old approach of testing discrete grammar points using fill-in-the-blank verb conjugations, her learners would likely fail the test because they would be assessed on what they haven't learned and in a way they haven't learned it. Ms. B needs to design a task-based assessment, probably in the form of a portfolio (see Chapter 20 for research-based approaches to assessment, where we describe state-of-the-art approaches to assessing language learning, and how to do it). Learners being assessed via tasks "perform" their target task and receive feedback. They are assessed on how well they accomplished the task rather than on how many grammatical errors they made or vocabulary words they know. The best form of a task-based assessment is an authentic one, where learners leave the classroom and do their task in the real world.

One issue with task-based teaching that many teachers face is what to do if the school, district, university, or program mandates a standardized test that learners must pass to indicate they have reached a required proficiency level. Some examples of these levels are ACTFL's proficiency scale, the CEFR for language scale, or the Interagency Language Roundtable (ILR) scale. Teachers attempting to innovate within their classrooms by adding a task-based component may still face the reality that learners must pass a mandatory standardized test that is not task-based, but grammar-based and misaligned with the way they prefer to teach. If learners are exposed to a wide variety of task types at various levels of complexity and receive meaningful, frequent feedback on their own language production, TBLT may still be enough to prepare these learners. However, if a teacher finds that task-based-trained learners fail to meet the demands of a standardized test, it might be necessary to include test preparation alongside the otherwise task-based elements of the course. This might be in the form of practice tests with feedback so that learners are exposed to the type of content on the standardized test before they take it. While most standardized tests do not align with what the research says about the nature of L2 development, they are the reality of most language programs worldwide, and teachers should do whatever they deem necessary to prepare learners for success.

17.6 The Science: Points to Remember

- Task-Based Language Teaching is an approach to language teaching that uses tasks, not grammar, to organize a curriculum or syllabus.
- Sub-tasks are the topic of each lesson.
- Task-Based Language Teaching aligns with research about how languages are learned.
- A needs analysis gathers information about what language learners need to do in the L2 through multiple methods and by investigating multiple sources.
- Tasks should be designed to promote interaction in the L2, push learners to use the skills they already have in the language, and accomplish a specific outcome.
- Tasks can be ordered based on how easy or difficult they are, how much learners need to interact to succeed in the task, and around learners' individual differences.
- In task-based courses, learners are assessed based on how well they can accomplish the target task, not on the accuracy of their grammar.

17.7 Questions to Consider

1. What are some strengths of task-based language teaching's approach to language teaching? What are some weaknesses of TBLT?
2. Would TBLT work in your context? Why or why not?
3. What will be the challenges of implementing TBLT in your context (if any)?
4. What are some needs of your current language learners? How do they compare to your own experiences in language learning? How do they compare to the experiences of your friends or family members?
5. Take, for example, the target task of designing a zoo and justifying where the animals should live and what their habitats should look like. What is a simple version of this task? A complex version? How would you assess this task?
6. Select an activity that you already use in your curriculum and review it against the task checklist in Box 17.1. Which criteria does it meet? Which criteria are not satisfied? What adjustments can you make so that the activity becomes more "task-like"?

17.8 The Science of Language Learning: Research Supporting the Points Made in This Chapter

Ellis, R., Skehan, P., Li, S., Shintani, N., & Lambert, C. (2019). *Task-based language teaching: Theory and practice.* Cambridge University Press.

This recent addition to the task literature provides a history of TBLT with recent developments and issues in the field. This book provides in-depth overviews of key pedagogic elements such as syllabus design and lesson planning. It also includes critiques of TBLT and directions for future research.

Long, M. (2014). *Second language acquisition and task-based language teaching.* John Wiley & Sons.

This book offers full, in-depth coverage of the history, theoretical issues, key elements, and future directions of TBLT and how it relates to SLA research. This book is key for anyone who wants more details about a specific element of TBLT or wants to read the foundational theories that ground this approach to language teaching. For language teachers, we suggest finding the specific chapter that relates to your context or needs.

Van den Branden, K., Bygate, M., & Norris, J. (2009). *Task-based language teaching: A reader.* Amsterdam: John Benjamins.

This book is an edited collection of articles in the field of TBLT research and practice. It begins with historical perspectives on TBLT issues and moves on to discuss all the key elements of TBLT in detail. Readers who are interested in the key studies that form the basis of suggestions in this chapter, for example on complexity, pre-task planning, or assessment, will find this book useful. There are also chapters on the role of the teacher in TBLT.

17.8 Supporting Research

For more resources, including more examples of task-based lesson plans, samples of task rubrics, and assessment ideas, visit our companion website: www.cambridge.org/BryfonskiMackey. There are also places where teachers and programs seeking to incorporate more communicative instruction can also find support. More and more teachers are sharing resources and materials on both free and subscription-based online platforms. One example of a free platform where communicative lessons plans are shared freely is the IRIS repository of instruments and materials. Another is Indiana University's TBLT Language Learning Task Bank. More information on these repositories is offered on the website!

18 Menus and maps: How can I make my classroom more authentic in terms of materials and practices?

KEY QUESTIONS
- The Science: What role does authentic input play in language acquisition? Why is authenticity important in input and output?
- The Art: How can I make my classroom more authentic in terms of materials and practices?
- How can authentic resources be used to teach culture?
- What does "linguistic landscape" mean and how should I tailor the linguistic landscape of my classroom for my learners?

18.1 Voices from the Classroom

Ms. T is an Arabic teacher in a middle school. Her school was recently renovated, adding on more classrooms for the world language program. Ms. T is excited because she will finally have a room to herself! In years past, Ms. T has had to conduct her Arabic classes in several other classrooms that were primarily her colleagues' spaces. As a result, she could not hang up posters with helpful words or phrases, or pictures from Arabic-speaking countries. Now that she has her own space, she wants it to be filled with resources that will inspire her learners and encourage them to speak more Arabic. She has collected some realia (artifacts from the target language community) and purchased charts and posters from language teaching conferences over the years. In planning for the new year, Ms. T is now feeling unsure. In having her own space, Ms. T hopes to use more realia in her classes because she believes it will make her courses more authentic. However, she is unsure whether some of her materials, especially the magazines and books, are comprehensible enough for her learners. How can she use the materials she has collected over the years and incorporate them into the curriculum in a way that is beneficial for her learners?

18.2 The Science: What the Research Says

In addition to the many posters, worksheets, books, and websites teachers use in their second language (L2) classrooms, many teachers also collect **realia** like menus, brochures, and even food wrappers so that their learners interact with real things produced using the L2. The idea, for many teachers, is that interacting with real objects made by and for L2 speakers will help prepare their learners to use these objects in real-world L2 situations beyond the classroom. Sometimes, however, the appropriate materials are inaccessible or simply don't exist for a particular topic, language, or context. At other times, teachers find themselves overwhelmed with the variety of resources available online or already in their schools and wonder which are most appropriate for specific proficiency levels or groups of learners. Research suggests that learners obtain the same, if not more, linguistic, social, and cultural benefits from using authentic resources instead of over-simplified pedagogic resources in their classrooms. This chapter will first explore why the research considers authentic resources to be better for learners than simplified resources. Then we share some research-supported strategies for incorporating authentic resources into the L2 classroom.

18.2.1 Defining Authenticity in the Language Classroom

Authentic materials, sometimes also called realia, refer to any materials that were *not* created for educational purposes. Traditionally, realia are defined as being created "by and for" native speakers; however, the fields of both language education and linguistics have been moving away from centering native speakers as the gold standard for language use. Therefore, we could say authentic resources are resources made to serve a communicative purpose outside of language education by an individual who is proficient in the target language (TL). These authentic resources are contrasted with texts that were created specifically for language learners. Therefore, an important characteristic to keep in mind when evaluating a resource is the original purpose of its development (see Figure 18.1).

It's also important to consider that labeling a resource as "not authentic" carries negative associations that might disrespect or undermine the time, money, or effort that went in to creating that educational resource. Thoughtfully presented educational resources can still have a place in a language classroom. To legitimize and elevate the resources that they have produced, some teachers and curriculum developers might label their own resources as "authentic" because they were made for a specific classroom and learner population. Basically, use of the label "authentic" has evolved away from a purely descriptive term to become more of a value judgment component, where it is often used in L2 teaching circles to mean "useful," "rigorous," or "worthwhile" rather than the circumstances that led to its initial creation. These multiple and conflicting uses of "authentic" highlight the subjectivity of the label and underscore why it is important to move beyond the

Figure 18.1 Resource selection questions. The three questions above can help teachers identify the defining features of a targeted resource. Image by: Elizabeth Zonarich

dichotomy of authentic/inauthentic to understand how, why, and when certain texts may be better suited for learners' linguistic development than others.

Because of the challenges with the labels of authentic and inauthentic, one linguist proposes using the terms *learner-centered texts* and *non-learner-centered texts*. These terms point to why the texts were created, namely the extent to which a language learner was considered as the end user of the text. Learner-centered texts are those that are created specifically with language learners in mind, while non-learner-centered texts are those created for proficient or native speakers and not specifically for teaching purposes. The terms do not ask teachers or researchers to take a stance on the perceived authenticity of each text, which may vary from person to person depending on how they judge authenticity. Another linguist preferred to use the terms *genuine* vs. *pedagogic* to describe written and spoken texts for the same reasons. Similarly, these labels refer to the purposes that the original authors of the texts intended them to serve, with genuine resources created to serve interactions outside of the language classroom and pedagogic resources created to serve interactions within language classrooms. We encourage you to engage in critical reflection and discussion within your own teaching communities as you decide how you wish to refer to resources and why. Because second language acquisition (SLA) research shows both kinds of resources are useful and needed to varying degrees (and for different goals) in the L2 classroom, we do not support abandoning one or the other entirely. Additionally, in our estimation, the *genuine–pedagogic* terminology carries fewer value judgments than other terms, so these will be used throughout the rest of the chapter (see Box 18.1 for an overview of these terms).

BOX 18.1 **Resource Descriptors**

HOW TO TALK ABOUT CLASSROOM RESOURCES		
Classroom-based	VS.	Authentic
Educational		Realia
L2 learner-centered		Non-learner-centered
Pedagogic		Genuine

18.2.2 The Role of Authentic Resources in Language Acquisition

Genuine texts provide learners with samples of language as it exists "in the wild." These resources are realistic and reliable representations of the kind of language learners would encounter if they were to travel abroad or interact with communities that speak the TL. In comparison, the language that appears in simplified pedagogic resources, like example dialogues, is often quite different from the language used in the "real world." Research has shown that the input provided by simplified resources is not a trustworthy example of how individuals use the TL to communicate. Sometimes examples of language use in educational materials are so oversimplified that they no longer reflect a true example of the L2 at all! Take the example in Box 18.2 from an English textbook published in 2006 (*New Horizon English, Course 1*, pp. 42–43) and approved for a large school district in Japan. Consider how this interaction compares with your own fast-food service encounters:

BOX 18.2 **Fast Food Interaction**

1	Mike:	Two hamburgers and two colas. Please?
2	Worker:	Large or small.
3	Mike:	Large, please?
4	Worker:	For here, or to go.
5	Mike:	To go.
6	Worker:	Here you are. That's five hundred and forty yen. Please?
7	Mike:	Thank you.

As we mentioned in Chapter 2, access to input is one of the essential ingredients for language learning, but research shows that not all input is created equally. If language learners are not engaging with the TL as it is used in the real world when they are in the classroom, they will not be equipped to communicate outside of the classroom (see Box 18.3). To prepare learners to use the TL in the real world, it is important that they encounter genuine resources during their studies.

BOX 18.3 **Resource Comparison**

HOW RESOURCES DIFFER	
Genuine	**Pedagogic**
Rich input	Stilted, impoverished input
"Real life" model of target language and culture	Recycled grammar patterns
Slang/dialectal expressions	Limited set of vocabulary
Variety of sentence lengths and constructions	Short sentences
Not targeted to a particular proficiency level	Targeted to a particular proficiency level

18.2.3 Incorporating Genuine/Authentic Resources

Teachers sometimes worry that learners are ill-equipped to handle the linguistic diversity and complexity of genuine, authentic, real-world texts. They worry that learners will feel overwhelmed and that these negative emotions toward the TL will detract from their learning potential. However, genuine texts need not be daunting with proper scaffolding and developmentally appropriate tasks. There are many research-backed strategies that have been shown to be effective to help learners process genuine resources. When handling genuine texts, there are several main decisions a teacher must make about HOW they decide to incorporate them into a lesson. Their decision can be condensed into three options: whether they will present the *genuine* version of the resource (unaltered), a *simplified* version of the resource (altered to remove certain linguistic features while adding others based on learners' proficiency level and the course syllabus, essentially transforming it into a pedagogic text), or an *elaborated* version of the resource (altered to maximize comprehensibility without altering the linguistic integrity of the original resource). Box 18.4 presents several options that teachers may find helpful in their classrooms.

In the elaborated versions, the genuine version is retained but includes added redundancy that is more in line with how input would be elaborated in a genuine conversation or text. Rather than removing the genuine vocabulary, as was done in the simplified version, repetition, redundancy, and elaboration are used to increase comprehensibility. Research studies that compare learners who read or hear simplified versus elaborated texts have shown that learners understand elaborated texts about as well as the simplified versions and more than the genuine version. Teachers can further modify to remove some redundancy and keep texts short without simplifying them, as shown in the modified elaborated example. As learners develop, the elaborations can be slowly removed until learners are able to comprehend the genuine version.

BOX 18.4 Resource Analysis

DESCRIBING HOW RESOURCES ARE ALTERED

Term	Definition	Example	Possible issues
Authentic input *found in "genuine" resources made by and for L2 speakers*	Created for real-world interactions and purposes, without the goal of including certain vocabulary words or linguistic features. e.g., TV shows, email, Twitter threads, poems	"The bees had likely only **taken up residence** at the house for about a week and a half." —*Washington Post* article	Unless learners are advanced, these might be linguistically overwhelming or developmentally inappropriate.
Simplified input *found in pedagogic resources*	Designed with specific vocabulary, grammatical structures, and expressions in mind based on the intended audience's proficiency level. e.g., graded readers, role plays, textbook reading passages	"There were some bees. Bees are insects that fly. Bees make honey. The bees live in the house. The bees moved into the house two weeks ago."	Unrealistic examples of language prioritize comprehension over acquisition.
Elaborated input *found in genuine and pedagogic resources*	Involves altered communication patterns but ultimately does not change the input itself. It often involves lots of repetition, synonyms, and informal definitions. Occurs with genuine resources, when the conversational partners have different ages, amount of knowledge about a topic, or proficiency levels.	"The bees had likely only moved in recently having **taken up residence** at the house for about a week and a half."	Elaborations increase the length of text and the time they take to read/hear and sometimes alter the original meaning.
Modified elaborated input *found in genuine and pedagogic resources*	Like elaborated input, but shorter sentences due to more repetition and scaffolding as necessary.	"The bees had likely only moved in recently. They have **taken up residence at the house** for about a week and a half."	—
Bimodal input *found in genuine and pedagogic resources*	Involves two sources of input provided simultaneously. For example, watching a move with subtitles, listening to an audiobook while reading along.	[While watching a video of the news clip] Subtitles: "The bees had likely only taken up residence at the house for about a week and a half."	—

It's important to point out that just because a resource is genuine doesn't mean that it will be used in a genuine communicative way in the classroom. For example, a real email could be used for a game where learners are given the email sentences out of order and asked to arrange them. Or the email could have key vocabulary or grammar endings removed and learners are asked to fill in the blanks. In this example, while the text (i.e., the email) was authentic, the activities were not. These types of language-focused activities are not likely to lead to the kinds of knowledge associated with long- term retention and use of language (see Chapter 17 for ideas of how to turn this example into a communicative task).

18.2.4 The Benefits of Authentic/Genuine Resources

Finding genuine resources, preparing them for class by including elaborated input, and designing communicative activities is more time-consuming than simply selecting the next level of graded reader off, the bookshelf. However, research shows that the hard work involved in curating a collection of genuine resources within a course curriculum pays off, as linguist Mike Long points out in the quote shown in Figure 18.2. A study comparing learners who received genuine resources with learners who received equivalent pedagogic resources found that the group that worked with genuine materials scored higher on a pronunciation test and a vocabulary test than the learners who worked with the pedagogic materials. This finding aligns with early studies examining how noticing features of language can facilitate acquisition. By working with genuine resources, learners are provided with realistic and natural linguistic input which they will be more likely to notice and thus acquire themselves. Apart from gains in vocabulary, other studies have also shown that learners who interact with genuine resources in class are more aware of the pragmatic elements of the TL, which often get excluded from pedagogic resources (see Chapter 15 for more on pragmatics). Studies in which learners were guided to notice how certain features of language were used to convey interpersonal messages in a genuine resource found that these learners remembered their observations as they participated in communicative tasks themselves.

Some of the benefits of genuine resources arise from the fact that learners generally report being more engaged with the content of genuine resources. This has been

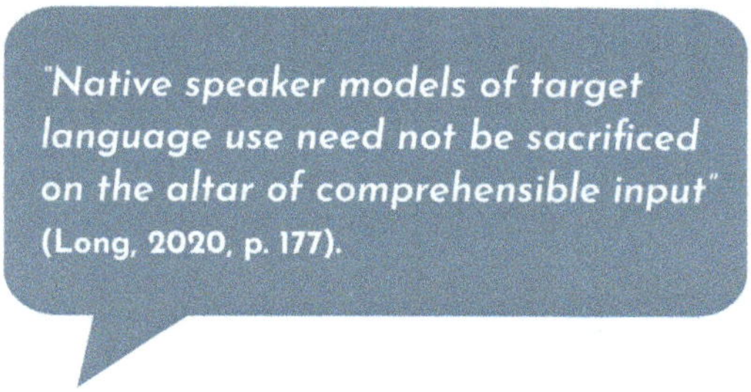

"Native speaker models of target language use need not be sacrificed on the altar of comprehensible input" (Long, 2020, p. 177).

Figure 18.2 On target language models. According to linguist Professor Mike Long, learners should not be shielded from real-life target language use.

found to be especially true among heritage language learners (HLLs). When working with a curriculum that featured pedagogic resources, this population felt disconnected and unengaged in class activities because they did not necessarily see themselves, their language variety, or their culture represented in course material. Other studies with younger HLLs underscore the importance of including these learners' existing linguistic and cultural knowledge in class activities to foster engagement and support learning. Often, pedagogic resources represent a limited view of the TL, culture, and speakers, which could ostracize certain groups of learners.

BOX 18.5 The Science! Points to Remember

- It is more important to consider *why* a resource was created, rather than who created it or who was intended to be its end recipients.
- All types of resources can be useful in a language classroom, but they all serve different purposes.
- Genuine, or authentic, resources provide models of how language is used in real-world communication, which educational texts typically do not.
- In addition to vocabulary or grammatical structures, resources also offer learners a window into pragmatic and cultural norms of the target language communities.

18.3 The Science: What's Missing?

The research on learner responses to different kinds of input (genuine, simplified, elaborated vs. modified elaborated) and how these types of input impact comprehension and language development is still growing. Most of this research has focused on university-aged learners of English. These learners tend to be older and more advanced. There is not much research about how other populations of learners respond to these three approaches to providing input. However, we can use what we know about individual variation in language learning to hypothesize that there will be some differences. Because elaborated input is typically longer and more complex than simplified input, younger learners (who may be just learning to read or who have shorter attention spans) or neurodivergent learners (who may also find longer passages of text more challenging to process, see Chapter 7) may interact with elaborated input differently from the populations that have been featured in studies in this area of research so far. It is possible that the sheer volume of text on the page, or the length of a spoken utterance may be daunting to younger or lower-proficiency learners, increasing anxiety or limiting motivation. For these reasons, elaborated input can be modified as described above based on the teachers' knowledge of the learners, their individual differences, and their teaching context.

Studies have already revealed differences between how children and adults learn when they receive similar input. In a meta-analysis (a study that combines the results of many similar studies) that compared incidental learning (see Chapter

11 for more on incidental learning) of vocabulary in activities featuring spoken input, adult L2 learners performed better than child L2 learners. Differences like these indicate that more research is required to understand how learners of different ages interact with types of input. For example, to successfully process elaborated input, research has shown that learners will need to use skillsets they have likely encountered in other subject areas. University learners (the featured population in many existing studies) are typically more familiar and comfortable with these academic strategies, whereas younger learners may still need prompting and support to use these learning techniques on their own. While the research continues to investigate these areas, there are some tips and tricks provided in the next section that can help teachers with younger or lower-level learners equip their learners with the skills necessary to reap the benefits of elaborated input.

While it is advisable that all teachers try to bring in as many genuine resources as possible, given the available research in this area and the many variables at play, this chapter cannot advocate for the exclusive use of one kind of resource over another. There may be advantages and disadvantages to any resource. Therefore, it is critical that teachers understand the "why" behind resource selection and modification for language acquisition. Only with this conceptual understanding will teachers be able to confidently make informed decisions around activity design and curriculum development from class to class.

18.4   The Art: Research-Based Strategies to Try

18.4.1   The Art of Gathering Authentic Resources

- Cultivate what is known as a *linguistic landscape* in your own classroom and teach your learners to identify linguistics landscapes around them. A linguistic landscape can be defined as the ways language appears publicly. For example, a region with a multilingual population might have street signs, emergency exits, supermarket signs, menus, or other public messages displayed in multiple recognized languages. These linguistic landscapes provide a window into how classrooms, communities, or governments value or recognize particular languages (see Figure 18.3).
- In a classroom, a linguistic landscape might look like resources labeled with the TL and the L1s of the learners in the classroom. Or it could look like labels with multiple possible words for the same object depending on dialect differences (e.g., *bolígrafo, boli, pluma, lapicero,* and *lápiz* can all mean "pen" in Spanish, depending on the dialect or region). In classes with many heritage speakers, this helps your learners see that their home language varieties are valued and recognized.
- In many immersion education settings, the linguistic landscape also encompasses school-wide messages in the L2, such as morning announcements, posters advertising school events, calls for participation in clubs or teams, and other school-related activities.
- The linguistic landscape does not just refer to written messages – it describes the entire language environment (e.g., oral, signed, written language) as well as cultural

18.4 The Art: Research-Based Strategies to Try

Figure 18.3 Multilingual environment. Multilingual environments recognize the value of using multiple languages to communicate. Image by: Elizabeth Zonarich

materials that contribute to the presence of the L2 (e.g., reproductions of artwork made by speakers of the L2). These environmental components can play an important role in a program's pedagogy because they demonstrate for learners the ways in which their language learning is being supported by their teachers (e.g., the linguistic supports made available to them in class) as well as the tangible ways in which language can be used outside of the classroom.

- If beginning a collection of classroom realia, or genuine resources, seems daunting, ask your learners to help. Encourage them to be on the lookout for examples of the TL outside of the classroom. Learners could physically bring in language that they find printed on snack labels, they could take pictures of signs they see around the community, or they could even use their phones to record commercials or advertisements they come across at home.
- If your language program has mandatory pedagogic resources (e.g., textbooks, readers) that you are not able to substitute for genuine resources, you can supplement with genuine resources instead.

18.4.2 The Art of Presenting Authentic Resources to Lower-level Learners

- Genuine resources do not have to be text heavy! When bringing in authentic resources to classrooms of lower-level learners, start with photo-based resources like advertisement campaigns, traffic signs, or even popular hashtags trends (see Figure 18.4).

Figure 18.4 Authentic resource examples. Interacting with the authentic resources above requires some literacy skills, but also provides visual and contextual support for lower-proficiency learners. Image by: Elizabeth Zonarich

Figure 18.5 Literacy framing questions. Providing learners with framing questions helps to prepare them for the content and language they may encounter in authentic or genuine resources. Image by: Elizabeth Zonarich

- The following questions can help novice learners think critically about cultural practices, products, or perspectives that are often reflected in authentic resources (as also shown in Figure 18.5):
    - What do you see?
    - Are there any words or phrases you recognize?
    - Where do you think you'd find this resource?
    - What about this resource looks familiar to what you'd expect?
    - What about this resource looks different to what you'd expect?
- Remember that elaborated texts are usually longer than genuine and simplified texts, but the added length does not necessarily mean they are more complex. Lower-level learners working with elaborated texts for the first time (or learners unfamiliar with elaborated texts) may benefit from exploring them first within whole-class activities where they learn to break down the elaborated texts into more manageable sections so they do not feel overwhelmed.

18.4 The Art: Research-Based Strategies to Try

- General rule of thumb: When working with a new or challenging resource, *simplify the task* and *elaborate the input*. See Chapter 17 on ways to simplify tasks without simplifying input.
- Besides elaborating written texts to improve their comprehensibility, teachers can also provide interactionally modified texts. With interactionally modified texts, learners have opportunities to ask clarification and confirmation questions to their peers and/or teachers.
- Structure activities with genuine resources so that learners have an opportunity to converse with a partner or a larger group of classmates if they get stuck. If the learners are much younger, consider leading these activities as a whole class so that learners can develop critical reading and listening strategies.
- Use the strategies in Figure 18.6 for more ideas for how to increase comprehensibility without removing genuine input from resources.

HOW TO INCREASE COMPREHENSIBILITY	
Strategy	**Example**
Build schema	Before a writing activity where 1st graders write letters to pen pals about their hobbies, they brainstorm different hobbies as a class on a mind map to activate prior knowledge.
Pre-teach vocabulary	Before a primary school science unit on endangered animals, key words (endangered, species, habitat, environment) are added to the class word wall after they are introduced so they can be referenced as the unit progresses.
Provide visual aids	Learners in a primary school classroom use images to track daily weather as a morning routine.
Explain unfamiliar grammatical features	As primary school learners write a letter to a pen pal about their hobbies, they struggle with progressive endings. The teacher, after noticing this, provides a short mini-lesson on *-ing* endings and learners return to writing.
Gloss or translate unfamiliar vocabulary	She only **caught a glimpse** of the driver. (She just saw him for a moment.)

Figure 18.6 Increasing comprehensibility. Several additional strategies for maximizing the comprehensibility of authentic or genuine resources.

18.4.3 The Art of Presenting Authentic Resources to Advanced Learners

- Remember that elaborated texts do not remove the genuine input from the original text! Encourage more advanced learners to see if they can find the genuine input that was expanded upon. This type of encouragement supports learners in noticing the "real-world" linguistic features instead of just relying on the synonyms or repetition to understand the overall themes.
- Use the basic framework of a "spot the difference" game to encourage older or more advanced learners to notice linguistic features. Provide one partner with the genuine version of a text and the other partner with the elaborated version of the same text. Neither partner can see the other's text. They must work together to extract the main information from the text and then use it to complete a task together. Or, if learners perform scripted role plays of a workplace interaction, have learners also watch workplace interactions from TV shows. Have learners identify phrases, body language, or different items from the conversations between characters. Encourage learners to incorporate what they notice into the scripted role play provided in the textbook series to make it more representative of "real-life" language use.
  - This type of activity can also benefit mixed classes, where some learners are at a higher proficiency (for whatever reason) than others. In mixed pairs, provide the more advanced learner with the genuine text and the other with the elaborated version so that both can communicate equally in the activity. Structuring an activity in this way ensures that learners will provide each other with lots of input as they negotiate meaning.
- The examples in Box 18.6 from Long (2020) show the differences between genuine, simplified, elaborated, and modified elaborated versions of the same sentence.

BOX 18.6 Traffic Accident Sentences

Version	Sentence (bolding indicates key vocabulary)
1. Genuine	The only **witness** just **caught a glimpse** of the driver as he **fled the scene**, so she could only provide the police with **a rough description**.
2. Simplified	A woman was the only person who saw the accident. She saw the driver for only a moment. The driver did not stop. He immediately drove away fast. The woman could only tell the police a little about him.
3. Elaborated	The only person who saw the accident, the only **witness**, was a woman. She only **caught a glimpse** of the driver, just saw him for a moment, because he **fled the scene**, driving away fast without stopping, so she could only provide the police with **a rough description of him**, not an accurate one.
4. Modified elaborated	The only person who saw the accident, the only **witness**, was a woman. She only **caught a glimpse** of the driver, just saw him for a moment, because he **fled the scene**, driving away fast without stopping. As a result, she could only provide the police with **a rough description** of him, not an accurate one.

Teachers of older or more advanced learners can use elaboration strategies like those in versions 3 and 4 to make input more comprehensible without eliminating the genuine input of the original, authentic sentence. Teachers can compare the length of the sentences in each version as well as how many sentences are included to compare the possible alterations.

18.5 Troubleshooting: How the Science Informs the Art

Ms. T is an Arabic teacher in a middle school. Her school was recently renovated, adding on more classroom dedicated for the world language program. Ms. T is excited because she will finally have a room to herself! In years past, Ms. T has had to conduct her Arabic classes in several other classrooms that were primarily her colleagues' spaces. As a result, she could not hang up posters with helpful words or phrases, or pictures from Arabic-speaking countries. Now that she has her own space, she wants it to be filled with resources that will inspire her learners and encourage them to speak Arabic more. She has collected realia (artifacts from the target culture, not from a "teacher store") and purchased charts and posters from language teaching conferences. In planning for the new year, Ms. T is now feeling unsure how much to hang up. Is it possible to have too much input in the "linguistic landscape" of the classroom?

Individual learner differences will determine what amount of input is "too much" input. For the learners that are more easily overwhelmed, the words and pictures on the wall will "blur" together and will not be processed. For learners who are not overwhelmed, the additional visual input could help support their linguistic development. However, as Ms. T decorates her classroom, she should remember that hanging up posters with words and phrases (an implicit instructional strategy) does not mean that learners will necessarily incorporate those words into their vocabulary. If there are certain posters with phrases that Ms. T expects her learners to use regularly (e.g., a poster with survival expressions, like those discussed in Section 1.4), Ms. T should be sure to explicitly draw learner attention to these graphics. One way to do this would be to design an activity or task around them at the beginning of the class. This increases the possibility that learners will process the input from the posters and incorporate into their own developing understanding of the TL.

In having her own space, Ms. T hopes to use more realia in her classes because she believes it will make her courses more authentic.

Ms. T should remember that authenticity is assigned not to the item itself but for the reason it was created, and how the intended audience interprets it and how it is used contributes to communicative interactions. By simply hanging realia on her walls, Ms. T is leaving much of that interpretation up to her learners and she has not constructed any sort of task that invites her learners to meaningfully engage with the printed input (e.g., pictures, labels, street names, etc.). For learners to reap the benefits of interacting with genuine resources, Ms. T will have to intentionally incorporate them into the lesson plans and take steps to make sure that the input from the realia is made comprehensible through textual or visual elaboration when necessary.

However, she is unsure whether some of her materials, especially the magazines and books, are comprehensible enough for her learners. How can she use the realia she has collected over the years and incorporate them into the curriculum in a way that is beneficial for her learners?

There are many ways in which Ms. T can incorporate her realia, or genuine resources, into her classes, regardless of the learners' proficiency levels. For print or written resources, she can use elaboration techniques, like adding repetition, synonyms, antonyms, or informal definitions. Techniques like this will help maximize redundancy, increasing the frequency of the important words or phrases. This will help learners notice the language that is carrying the primary messages. It may be daunting for Ms. T to provide this kind of elaboration for her entire repository of realia because it requires a lot of careful thought and planning. However, if Ms. T makes it a goal to add elaboration to several pieces of realia per unit, over the course of several years, she will eventually have created a collection of realia that can be easily adjusted for learners of all different proficiency levels.

18.6 The Science: Points to Remember

- Authentic, or genuine, resources are those created to fulfill real-world (non-educational) communicative purposes.
- Pedagogical resources are those created with language learners and language classrooms in mind.
- Teachers and language learners can use elaboration strategies to increase the comprehensibility of genuine texts without compromising the richness of the input.
- Learners will likely be more engaged and motivated when working with a curriculum supported with authentic or genuine texts because they help strengthen the connection between their current selves and their ideal L2 learner selves.
- When looking for genuine resources, it is important to include material created by diverse populations for a range of purposes to provide learners with a wide sampling of how the TL is used (e.g., across different ages, countries, genders, contexts).
- Some textbooks do include excerpts of genuine texts. Teachers who do not have the resources to find authentic resources on their own can use textbooks to pick texts. However, they may choose to design their own activities and tasks rather than use the textbook-provided activity, which may be a grammar-based exercise.

18.7 Questions to Consider

1. How do you and your colleagues describe your resources (authentic, genuine, pedagogic, learner-centered, something else)? Do you all use the same terms? What aspect of the resource do these terms refer to? If you and your colleagues have different ways of describing resources, is it possible to reach mutual agreement on terms to streamline future collaborative efforts?
2. Review your upcoming unit. How many simplified resources do you have? Genuine resources? Elaborated resources? How can you maximize the number of elaborated or genuine resources in this unit?
3. In your next class, ask your learners why they are enrolled in your course and what they hope to be able to accomplish as L2 users of the TL. Do the resources you include in your curriculum help your learners meet their goals? Why or why not?

18.8 The Science of Language Learning: Research Supporting the Main Points in This Chapter

Gilmore, A. (2011). "I prefer not text": Developing Japanese learners' communicative competence with authentic materials. *Language Learning*, *61*(3), 786–819. https://doi.org/10.1111/j.1467-9922.2011.00634.x.

This study compares the development of two groups of university-aged English language learners over semester-long course. One group of learners interacted with educational resources (a textbook) and the other group interacted with authentic resources during class and homework assignments. At the end of the semester, both groups took a series of assessments that measured their communicative competence. The learners who received the authentic resources performed better than those who received the textbook ones on five of the eight assessments. Researchers recognize the challenges of creating courses designed entirely with authentic resources but emphasize the value and impact of using rich, genuine resources in the classroom.

Gorter, D. (2018). Linguistic landscapes and trends in the study of schoolscapes. *Linguistics and Education*, *44*, 80–85. https://doi.org/10.1016/j.linged.2017.10.001.

This piece concludes a special issue published by the journal *Linguistics and Education* focusing on the issue of linguistic landscapes and the study of linguistic landscapes within educational settings, termed "schoolscapes." Shoolscape research is a developing field, but initial findings have indicated that they can be influential in most (if not all) education settings because they can serve as pedagogical tools embodying the perspectives of L2 speakers as well as an indication of how teachers in the environment position their learners to the L2. The piece summarizes much of this recent research and provides suggestions on how learners might be mobilized and involved in creating their schoolscapes.

Helmer, K. A. (2014). "It's not real, it's just a story to just learn Spanish": Understanding Heritage Language Learner resistance in a southwest charter high school. *Heritage Language Journal, 11*(3), 186–206.

This study follows the classroom experiences of adolescent Spanish HLLs in their Spanish language classes over two years. The Spanish class relied heavily on a textbook and its accompanying resources (e.g., video series) in the curriculum. Through extensive class observations and interviews with learners, the researchers find that the HLLs have negative reactions to the educational resources used in their class because they perceive it to be uninteresting and infantilizing. Moreover, these resources do not provide examples of the TL or culture that resonate with how the learners experience the language or culture in their families and larger communities. As a result, these learners feel alienated from class and act accordingly. Researchers encourage teachers to draw from local communities so that their learners receive rich and accurate linguistic input capable of supporting learners' communicative abilities, increasing their motivation, and creating positive attitudes toward language learning.

Long, M. (2020). Optimal input for language learning: Genuine, simplified, elaborated, or modified elaborated? *Language Teaching, 53,* 169–182. https://doi.org/10.1017/S0261444819000466.

In this position paper, Long describes the different types of input that may appear in a language classroom and how they may (or may not) support language learning. While unaltered genuine, or authentic, resources provide rich and exciting language to bring into communicative classes, they may present challenges to young or novice language learners. To make genuine resources suitable for these groups of language learners, Long advocates for modified elaborated input and the incorporation of multimodal resources that offer the same dynamic and accurate language without compromising learners' overall comprehension. He believes that genuine resources that have been modified to elaborate on key linguistic features are best suited to helping learners notice important linguistic patterns as they focus on meaning and achieve larger communicative goals.

For more resources, including more sample lesson plans, videos, and other ideas, visit our companion website: www.cambridge.org/BryfonskiMackey.

19 How could/should I best use technology in the language classroom?

KEY QUESTIONS
- **The Science: Can technology enhance language learning? How can I leverage language-based technologies to support my learners' learning?**
- **The Art: How could/should I best use technology in the language classroom?**
- **Does watching movies or TV shows in the target language help my learners advance their second language development? What about virtual/augmented reality, gaming, or apps?**
- **How should I decide when (if!) my learners access online translation tools?**

19.1 Voices from the Classroom

During the COVID-19 pandemic, Mrs. D's middle school closed its physical campus and transitioned to fully online education. Each student was provided with a laptop and teachers were required to do all instructional activities using applications that were accessible on the student laptops. Mrs. D digitized many of her existing materials and incorporated games, videos, and other collaborative activities into her lessons. Some of her learners' favorite activities were the competition games she used to review material before a test; learners would work in teams to recall vocabulary items and compete against each other for points. Mrs. D also used the laptops for collaborative writing and brainstorming activities, asking the learners to do the same pair and group work she would ordinarily have used paper worksheets for, just in a digital workspace. Though her school is no longer fully virtual, Mrs. D wonders which of her new digital resources she should keep using and which ones she might be better off eliminating. She wonders whether technology can continue to enhance the learning in my language classroom and if so what tools and resources should she focus on?

19.2 The Science: What the Research Says

With worldwide health crises potentially driving language learners across the globe into virtual classrooms, the increasing popularity of language learning applications, and the growing accessibility of tools like virtual reality headsets, technology has become ubiquitous for language learners and language teachers alike. Recognizing the importance of *interaction* to the language learning process (see more in Chapter 1 on the four key ingredients for language learning), researchers have primarily investigated whether learners who engage in meaningful, technology-based communication have similar (or more) language development as learners engaging in "traditional" face-to-face communication. For example, researchers want to answer questions such as are language classes conducted on video conferencing platforms (e.g., Zoom, Microsoft Teams, Skype, Google Meet) as effective as in-person ones? Do learners notice corrective feedback in text messages in the same way they do when corrected orally in a classroom?

As digital tools have advanced, researchers have also begun to explore the many dimensions of virtually based activities, games, and other tasks that would otherwise be inaccessible or impossible to recreate without technological support. While language learning and teaching can still be successful without the use of technology, the reality of modern life means that learners will likely interact at some point with technology using their second language (L2). They might take part in an online or virtual conference, read restaurant or Airbnb reviews, use a rideshare app to hail a cab, send text or audio messages, or play a game in the L2 (see Figure 19.1). Teachers can leverage the well-researched benefits of technology for language learning while simultaneously preparing learners to engage and interact with a variety of platforms in their L2.

Researchers who study how technology influences language learning or, **Computer-Assisted Language Learning (CALL)**, are mainly interested in finding out how technology impacts learning or how technology can be leveraged to support L2 pedagogy. At first, research focused on how technology could be used to supplement teacher input and feedback during student practice via

Figure 19.1 Technology-supported language learning. Many online activities involve literacy components and interactive exchanges that facilitate language development. Image by: Elizabeth Zonarich

technology-based games and exercises, and through automated feedback software. Some teachers still use technology for these purposes today, for example using technology to review vocabulary (e.g., Quizlet, Blooket) or grammar (e.g., Kahoot quizzes), or directing learners to sites like Grammerly.com to receive feedback on their writing. Later, computer software for language study started to become popular. CD-based, and then internet- based, courses were developed so that learners could skip ahead in the material and have additional freedom to practice the structures/vocabulary/games they wanted to practice. This practice is still relatively intact today with commonly used programs and apps like Duolingo, Rosetta Stone, ABCMouse, Mango, Muzzy, LingQ, and FluentU (as well as less commonly used programs like Babbl, Busuu, Little Pim, PetraLingua, DinoLingo, and others) focusing primarily on grammar and vocabulary but offering a degree of flexibility in the order and extent of practice. Today, CALL has blossomed into an even more powerful tool for communication. Learners might encounter and engage with a variety of languages while navigating social media and the Internet. Many language programs now use virtual reality, MMOs (massively multiplayer online games), adventure and role-playing games, and more to connect L2 learners to L2 communities around the world.

Much of the research on technology has investigated how much it allows learners to access the four key ingredients for successful second language acquisition (SLA) (opportunity to produce output, access to input, and the ability to engage in negotiation of meaning and receive corrective feedback, see Chapter 1) compared to traditional face-to-face communication. With technology in general and online-based technologies in particular, researchers have pointed out the increasing opportunities for language output. Learners might be exposed to (input) and use language (output) through a variety of different platforms to, for example, instant message, email, social media, and pop culture. Learners might quickly scroll through TikTok and Twitter feeds and comment on posts from around the world. They can engage in multiplayer video games with players with diverse linguistic repertoires. They might also be immersed in digital fandoms and be writing blog posts. With online-capable technology, the possibilities for practicing the target language (TL) by producing output are endless. The key to taking advantage of these opportunities to best develop an L2 is to push learners to produce output and interact with other language users.

19.2.1 Technology as a Support

Researchers have compared **Synchronous computer-mediated communication (SCMC)**, where learners interact live, like on Zoom, FaceTime, text chats, or audio phone calls, and **asynchronous computer-mediated contexts (ACMC)**, where there is some delay in the interaction, as in email or message board posts. In SCMC contexts (see Figure 19.2), researchers have investigated how interacting live can help L2 learners develop grammatical, sociolinguistic,

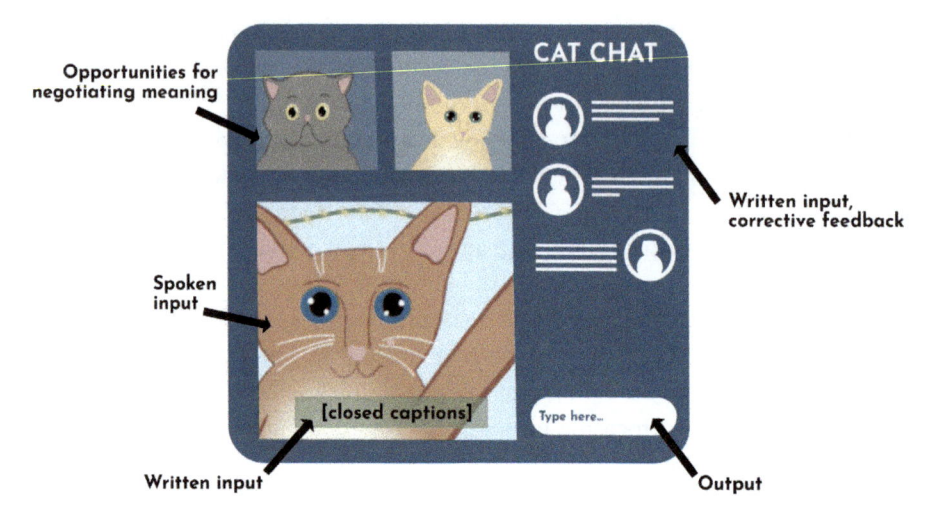

Figure 19.2 Facilitative components of video-chats. The communicative nature of video-chats naturally provides an environment that includes the four key ingredients for language learning. Image by: Elizabeth Zonarich

strategic, and discourse skills necessary for successful communication. Studies have revealed that SCMC environments, like text chats, are less stressful and reduce anxiety, thus encouraging learners to be more active and produce more output than they otherwise would have in more potentially embarrassing face-to-face interactions. In this way, learners take more risks that help them develop their understanding of how to use the TL to communicate information that is important to them. Another interesting context in which interaction has been studied in SCMC environments has been in online multiplayer team video games like *World of Warcraft*. Several studies have investigated how participants use their L2 (e.g., English, German) with a variety of teammates to accomplish missions within the game. Research teams have analyzed a variety of components of participants language use, including accuracy, pragmatic development, fluency, vocabulary, and more, but the consensus was clear: the interactions learners participated in had a positive impact on their L2 development. A survey of studies examining SCMC suggests that computer-mediated instruction may also provide learners with more time to process the input they receive and plan what to say next because of the normalcy of lags in SCMC interactions as well as modality factors like typing being slower than speaking/signing. The additional time has been hypothesized to allow learners more opportunities to notice different features of language. A comparison of the effectiveness of corrective feedback in different conversational interactions found that feedback provided over computer-mediated contexts was just as, if not more, supportive of language development as feedback provided in face-to-face interactions for similar reasons.

For ACMC contexts like writing emails or blog posts, software or other applications with text formatting options have been shown to help learners develop literacy skills and content knowledge. Some tools present text in shorter lines to facilitate comprehension and potentially draw student attention to targeted linguistic forms, thereby enhancing noticing. Some research suggests that written mediums, like text messaging, email, and blogging, may even be more beneficial than speaking/signing, since those mediums provide a visual representation of language that allows learners to reread and process input as well as plan and revise output. Researchers have also examined how the use of social media platforms impacts development. An experimental study investigated whether the incorporation of Facebook (via a class group page) led to a greater quantity of student writing in weekly tasks in comparison with learners completing the same writing tasks with pen and paper. While the Facebook learners did write more than the other learners on the majority of tasks, there was no difference in the quality of the writing. This research points out how technology can enhance learning but also shows that it's not necessarily a "fix-all" for every instructional concern language teachers might have.

19.2.2 Technology as a Task or Activity

CALL research has also examined the different ways in which technology could be incorporated into classroom settings. Technology might be used as a tutor (i.e., offering translation or editing services) or it might be used as a tool (i.e., offering extensions of face-to-face activities, like researching a tourist destination page online). When technology is used as a tool, it can be leveraged to give learners more opportunities to engage with the TL community that they wouldn't have access to without the technology. When it is used as a tutor, learners can continue to correct errors or refine existing skills, essentially expanding practice and feedback beyond what the teacher can offer by themselves and offloading some of the teacher's instructional labor. Task-Based Language Teaching (TBLT, see Chapter 17) has been identified by researchers as a curricular approach particularly well-suited to the incorporation of technological resources because technology is a common real-world tool learners need to use to accomplish tasks using the TL.

BOX 19.1 An Example of a Technology-Mediated Language Learning Lesson Plan

Objective: *Learners will be able to articulate and defend their opinion in Spanish.* To achieve this goal, use a task where the focus is on successfully sharing their opinion, and the target language then becomes a tool for negotiating meaning.

Pre-task: Learners watch the Disney movie *Encanto* in Spanish. This movie is about the Madrigals, an extraordinary family who live hidden in the mountains of Colombia in a charmed place called the Encanto where every child is born with a gift. After having watched the movie, learners discuss their thoughts and opinions about the characters in Spanish in small groups.

During-task: After discussing in small groups, learners choose their own gift – one that none of the characters from the movie had – and justify why they chose that power. Learners then explain how they

> **BOX 19.1 Continued**
>
> would use the power to help others, just like the other members of the Madrigal family from *Encanto*. The learners share their opinion in a written blog or discussion board post or orally in a recorded video. This is a pedagogical choice the teacher should make based on which language skill they are hoping to work on with their learners. Throughout the process, teachers can help learners as they work to complete the different stages of the task as well as provide corrective feedback.
>
> **Post-task:** Learners could post their blog or videos to a class webpage and leave comments for one another in Spanish debating which gifts or powers would be most useful. This stimulates output and negotiation of meaning surrounding a current pop culture phenomenon (a movie) in the target language through technology (blogs/videos).

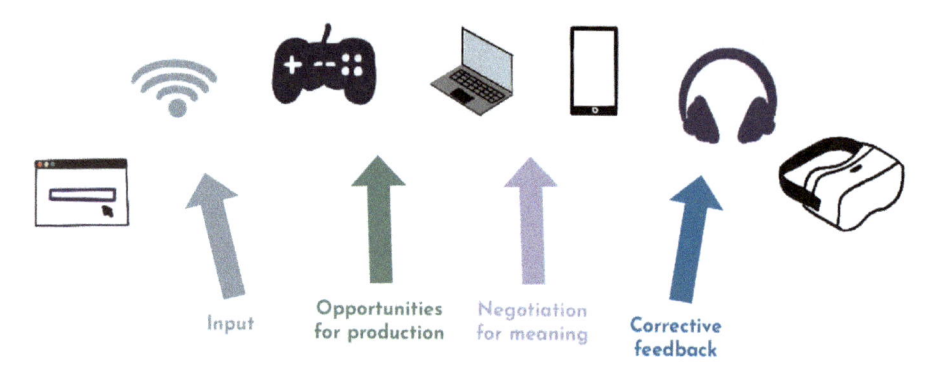

Figure 19.3 Relating technology and language learning. Technological tools can help enhance the quantity and quality of the four key ingredients for language learning. Image by: Elizabeth Zonarich

The sample lesson in Box 19.1 incorporates each of the four ingredients for successful language acquisition: input, output, opportunities to interact and negotiate meaning, and chances to receive and respond to corrective feedback, all while using technology to facilitate these opportunities (Figure 19.3). While watching TV shows and movies are useful ways to obtain input, the teacher needs to provide opportunities for learners to go beyond only processing the input. In TBLT, technology should be applied to tasks where learners are pursuing a meaningful objective with real-world implications beyond just the practice of language. For more on what constitutes a task, see Chapter 17.

19.2.3 Technology as a Teaching Resource

Technology is also being used to transform teaching practices, with some teachers migrating their existing physical materials onto digital platforms. For example, teachers in virtual or face-to-face classrooms might organize content and key resources in a virtual classroom or learning management system (e.g., Google Classroom, Canvas, Blackboard, Moodle), offer learners digital brainstorming spaces (e.g., Google Jamboard, Padlet), digitize presentations (e.g., VoiceThread, Flipgrid, Vimeo, YouTube), or gamify memorization and recall (e.g., Quizlet, Kahoot, Blooket, Duolingo). Teachers might also compile lists of websites that would be helpful to their learners like dictionaries (e.g., WordReference, ReversoContext), cultural/social resources, news articles, videos, music, and photos of TL-speaking people and places. Learners can be trained to use reference resources such as online dictionaries or translation services (e.g., Google Translate) at times when it is most appropriate. While many teachers may want to ban automatic translators altogether, research shows that they are nearly unavoidable – almost all learners use them at some point. With this in mind, teachers may want to think critically about how to teach learners to use them in ways that are active and useful, rather than passive and avoidant. For example, typically, the errors made by translators are in the grammar due to speaker identity (e.g., in gendered languages), issues of style (e.g., mistranslating colloquial expressions), or pragmatic issues (e.g., problems with word choice or degrees of formality and appropriateness). One amusing way to demonstrate these pitfalls is to have learners translate a text into multiple languages and see how it is warped from translation to translation. A teacher using this as an example in class might pre-select a few texts with a variety of common issues (like those listed above) and use learners' translations to guide a whole-class discussion of what happened to the meaning and coherence of the texts. While there is no definitive evidence that using a translator tool will have negative effects on learners' development in the long term, if learners blindly translate texts, they might be less likely to notice features of the language and may fail to be able to integrate them into their own output. For this reason, teachers might limit the use of translators to specific tasks where they can be used to supplement or edit a preexisting piece of student writing or used as feedback. A classroom environment where mistakes are encouraged and meaning-making is valued over accuracy will help learners see that they don't have to use translators in order to learn and be successful.

BOX 19.2 The Science! Points to Remember

- Technology can serve as a tutor or a tool for language learners for all ages and proficiency levels.
- To best support language learning, technology must be integrated thoughtfully and critically in a way that advances the overarching learning goals.
- When used in this way, technological resources can boost learner motivation and engagement, improve the cultural and linguistic representation within course materials, and reduce language learning anxiety.
- Translation tools may be useful in helping learners communicate their message quickly and efficiently in a high-stakes, real-world situation, but in a classroom context they might distract learners from engaging in the productive learning behaviors that facilitate language learning.

19.3 The Science: What's Missing?

With rapidly changing technological resources and new technologies constantly being developed, it can be difficult for researchers to keep up. This means teachers need to take care when anyone – researchers included – tout a program or platform as "the next big thing." A platform that was identified in a study to be highly effective in, for example, facilitating interpersonal writing tasks might be soon outperformed by ten new platforms that all boast similar capabilities. Teachers should judge the potential utility of any technology with the needs of their learners, teaching context, and community in mind. For example, a survey of learners' caretakers showed that attitudes toward technology-based language learning vary greatly, with some expressing concerns about the dangers of extended screen time and fears about the potential of technology-based games and artificial intelligence (AI) to replace human interaction. This research points out where technology may not always be the right fit for a given community. For these reasons, teachers should be wary of lists or rankings of specific virtual tools over others and instead use a combination of research and their own best judgment when deciding to employ technological tools in their classrooms.

Some research findings examining the impacts of CMC have been mixed. For example, research that investigated how different types of tasks translate into online settings (*jigsaw* versus *information-gap* versus *decision-making gap* tasks; see Chapter 17 for more information about these task types) has been inconclusive, with one study finding that jigsaw tasks facilitated more negotiation of meaning and another finding that decision-making tasks resulted in more negotiation of meaning. This research area has mostly only investigated the immediate effects of participating in computer-mediated interaction on learner development. So, we don't know what the lasting impacts of digitally based activities are for language learning. Many researchers and teachers want to know if there is any sort of equivalence between time spent interacting online or playing online games and number of words learned or proficiency levels advanced (e.g., do learners who watch five hours of Spanish language TV programming each week have greater vocabulary knowledge than learners who do not? How much or little time is necessary?). While we know the use of technology and time spent interacting in the TL online does offer benefits, as we discussed above, there is no specific amount of improvement or learning that can be expected, since there is so little research that has tracked learners interacting with technology over long periods.

Finally, there are many external factors that have been shown to impact learners' growth such as their proficiency level, the context where they are learning, the supports provided, how learning is measured, etc. For example, a study that investigated how learners used captions when they watched videos in the TL found that learners' behaviors differed depending on the language they were learning, their current proficiency level, and the instructional methods used. Any promises a particular tech tool makes about learning outcomes is likely glossing over nuances that may be very relevant to teachers and their learners.

19.4 The Art: Research-Based Strategies to Try

Owing to the fast-paced nature of developing technologies, we avoid providing tips here about any one specific type of software or material. We also recognize that not all programs can offer the same kinds of technological resources. The tips below can be used with a variety of technologies, and teachers are encouraged to recommend or use the ones that best match their learners' and community's needs.

- When considering how you might incorporate more technology into your classroom, you might find it helpful to think of the modes of communication that these technological resources require. Different online tools lend themselves to inspiring and developing different linguistic skills. It is important to ground the new technology in the language skills you want to target to ensure you are not just bringing in technology for technology's sake and are instead incorporating technology in a way that maximizes language learning. Teachers might aim to mix activities from various modes of communication as shown below:
  - *Interpersonal mode* → Collaborative tasks with pen pals via emails, synchronous chat platforms, or shared discussion boards on class websites.
    - Online platforms are uniquely equipped to allow participants to join or form communities where they can engage in problem-solving and information exchanges as they wrestle with "real-world" tasks.
    - Interpersonal mode offers the advantage of immediate feedback.
  - *Interpretive mode* → Multimodal texts or videos with or without captions, presented at different speeds.
    - Learners can use the technology to focus on comprehension without worrying about responding.
    - Interactive components can be used (i.e., embedded comprehension questions, reaction emojis, etc.) to check comprehension.
  - *Presentational mode* → digital storytelling opportunities for learners to share their projects (video, audio, images, pre-recorded).
    - Learners have a chance to plan what to say or write without the pressure of immediate feedback like in interpersonal mode.

19.4.1 Technological Tools

- *Tools for encouraging student output and noticing of corrective feedback:*
  - Video-conferencing tools offer opportunities for synchronous interaction where learners both receive input (written, spoken, signed) and provide output (written, spoken, signed). Even if learners are having an in-person language class, they could use these tools to connect with peers for homework or group assignments or interact with pen pals across the globe.
  - Zoom, Google Meet, Skype, Facetime, WhatsApp, Microsoft Teams
- *Tools for encouraging written student output and feedback:*
  - Other digital tools allow for asynchronous activities that give learners more opportunities to engage with course content. With these tools, there are

numerous ways to save student media entries so that the teacher (or peers, if learners are more advanced) can provide feedback in addition to the teacher.
  - Examples: Google Docs, class blogs (Weebly, Wix, WordPress, etc.), VoiceThread (a site for uploading presentations where learners can leave text, audio, or video comments), FlipGrid (a place where learners respond to questions with short videos), class social media pages.
- *Tools for encouraging meaning-focused interactions:*
  - Digital games may engage learners in the target outside of their class responsibilities, allowing them to experience interactions "in the wild" as they engage in simultaneous gameplay with one or many other speakers of that language. There is a variety of interactive digital games.

  Examples: sporting competitions, virtual pet care, simulation, role-playing, action/adventure games.
  - Survey learners to find out how to tailor gaming suggestions to their specific interests.

19.4.2 Teacher-Centered Tools

Still other tools allow teachers to modify existing material (YouTube videos, articles, slide decks) so as to better engage learners as they read or listen independently. Some web-based tools or software, like PearDeck and EdPuzzle, allow instructors to build in comprehension checks or provide elaborated input to improve learners' interactive experience. Because these resources are for learners to use independently, they are free to pause, rewind, or rewatch as many times as needed based on their own learning differences.

There are also tech tools that allow teachers more opportunities to check in with the learners about how class is going. These tools allow for quicker and anonymous feedback to help teachers make sure they are meeting all learners' needs. Some of these web-based platforms, like Mentimeter and Slido, display poll questions that learners can complete simultaneously as they interact with another resource (e.g., watching an advertisement and answering a question about whether or not the product is appealing). Other tech tools are embedded within software, like the Zoom "Poll" feature. Still others, like GoogleForms, can be used to complement in-class learning and offer learners more extended and detailed room to share their experiences.

When trying out a new online platform with their class, whether you are using it as a tool, activity, or task, researchers recommend getting your learners' feedback on it afterwards, as a number of individual differences may be impacting their reactions and the effectiveness of the new platform. This could be done with individual exit tickets, a quick Google Forms survey, a group conversation, or a thumbs up/down check-in. Asking them to share whether they felt any changes in their motivation, engagement, learning, or enjoyment when working with a new technological resource can help you adjust your future lessons accordingly.

19.5 Troubleshooting: How the Science Informs the Art

During the COVID-19 pandemic, Mrs. D digitized many of her existing materials and incorporated games, videos, and other collaborative activities into her lessons. Though her school is no longer fully virtual, Mrs. D wonders which of her new digital resources she should keep using and which ones she might be better off eliminating. Can technology continue to enhance the learning in her language classroom, she wonders, and if so what tools and resources should she focus on?

As Mrs. D reflects on the technological resources she uses already, she should keep in mind the four key ingredients for language acquisition. As she weighs up the pros and cons of each resource, they can guide her thought process in the following way. Did the technological resource:

- strengthen the quantity or quality of input learners received during class?
- allow learners more opportunities to produce output?
- provide opportunities to negotiate meaning that could not otherwise be provided?
- relate to real-life needs learners may encounter when working with the target language?

If the answer to each of the questions is yes, it sounds like that would be a great resource to keep in class next year!

Mrs. D might consider polling her learners about which technological resources they found to be most helpful and why while classes were being taught online. This information, along with her own perspectives as the teacher, can motivate Mrs. D's decisions about what technology she continues to utilize as class transitions to in-person learning once again. If her learners like a resource simply because "it was fun," but Mrs. D herself did not find the resource to support the four ingredients for language acquisition, she may consider keeping this resource (like a vocabulary-based online flash card game) as an extension activity to be used sparingly. If her learners' reflections indicate that they felt more motivated, more engaged, or more willing to take risks with the TL, then it might be a resource that is worth incorporating in future years. Mrs. D has a great instinct to reflect and reevaluate the technology resources in her room. New technological resources are developed rapidly, and it can be challenging to stay up-to-date on all the options available to teachers and learners. Through regular reflection, even when her mode of instruction does not change, Mrs D. will ensure that the technology in her class elevates her pedagogy.

19.6 The Science: Points to Remember

- There are no "short cuts" or "silver bullets" in language acquisition, and technological resources are no exception to that!
- Research shows that technological resources can be used to enrich the learning experiences through improving the quantity and quality of learners' access to language learning opportunities.

- In particular, technological resources have been found to successfully encourage learners to reflect on corrective feedback they receive and inspire learners to pursue additional meaning-focused interactions in the TL outside of regular class hours.
- Some technological resources are better suited to advancing certain linguistic skills over others, so it is important for technology users to be aware of the linguistic skills that they are targeting in their classes so that they can choose a technological resource wisely.

19.7 Questions to Consider

1. What technological resources are your learners using in their everyday lives? How can the types of communicative tasks that your learners complete with these resources be incorporated into the language curriculum?
2. How can the technological resources in your school or program be leveraged to help your learners envision themselves successfully speaking the TL and/or integrating into the TL community?
3. What sort of technological resources might leaners have to navigate when they travel abroad, or within the TL communities? What sorts of tasks can be designed to prepare learners for success in the tech-mediated future situations they may encounter after they leave your class?
4. As you try out different technological resources in your curriculum, how will you know if they are elevating your classroom pedagogy? What signs will you look for?

19.8 The Science of Language Learning: Research Supporting the Points Made in This Chapter

González-Lloret, M. (2020). Collaborative tasks for online language teaching. *Foreign Language Annals, 53*, 260–269. https://doi.org/10.1111/flan.12466.

This article discusses the opportunities and challenges that arise in online teaching environments. Researcher González-Lloret emphasizes the importance of critically examining the type of interaction that technological tools promote when contemplating how to design tasks with more technological components. The collaborative learning opportunities that are afforded through technological platforms are of particular interest to researchers, teachers, and learners alike because they provide learners with the opportunity to build relationships and encourage understanding of the context, culture, and language of study. Through using technology-mediated tasks, learners have more opportunities to participate in meaningful problem-solving and decision-making tasks, which have been shown to promote language growth. Several exemplar tasks are described.

González-Lloret, M., & Rock, K. (2022). Tasks in technology-mediated contexts. In N. Ziegler & M. González-Lloret (Eds.), *The Routledge handbook of second language acquisition and technology* (pp. 36–49). Routledge.

19.8 Supporting Research

This chapter covers the history of technology as an integrated component of TBLT and synthesizes high-impact research published in this burgeoning subfield of SLA. The authors discuss the impact of task type, task sequencing, and task-based assessments in technology-mediated TBLT. By providing a bird's-eye view of technology in TBLT, this chapter serves not only as a concise introduction to the field but also as an indication of where technology-mediated TBLT might be headed in future research.

Michel, M., & Smith, B. (2017). Measuring lexical alignment during L2 chat interaction: An eye-tracking study. In *Salience in second language acquisition* (pp. 244–268). Routledge.

SCMC has been shown to increase the salience of input, enabling learners to more easily notice patterns. This study investigated whether written SCMC had any impact on participants' *lexical alignment* – mirroring the words of one's interlocutor. The authors hypothesized that because participants' written messages stayed on the screen throughout the interaction, this would lead them to mirror one another's language use more often than they otherwise would have. This study involved six advanced L2 speakers of English who worked together in pairs over the course of six weeks on an academic abstract (a genre of academic writing that summarizes the main points of a paper). Using eye tracking, screen recording, and corpus linguistics methods, the authors examined what participants seemed to notice, attend to, and align with throughout their chats. Analysis of the eye gaze patterns, chat transcripts, and resulting abstracts revealed that learners participating in SCMC do lexically align with their conversation partners while completing tasks, but it happens less frequently than might be expected from a simple reading of the chat transcript alone.

Sundqvist, P. (2019). Commercial-off-the-shelf games in the digital wild and L2 learner vocabulary. *Language Learning & Technology*, 23(1), 87–113. https://doi.org/10125/44674.

This study explores how noneducational computer programs and other technological software that learners may use outside of the classroom impact their linguistic development, in particular, the size of learners' vocabulary as measured in vocabulary tests and an essay. Spanning three years, this researcher compares the linguistic growth of a group of adolescent English language learners based on how much time they spent playing video games in English during their free time. Results suggest that the amount of time learners play English-based computer games can predict the size of their vocabulary. The type of computer game (single player vs. multiplayer vs. massively multiplayer) also impacts linguistic development; however, additional research is needed to better understand how different types of games contribute to the development of specific linguistic abilities.

Ziegler, N. (2016). Taking technology to task: Technology-mediated TBLT, performance, and production. *Annual Review of Applied Linguistics, 36,* 136–163. https://doi.org/10.1017/S0267190516000039,

This article explores areas of overlap between TBLT and CALL. The author advocates for the integration of technology into task-based classrooms in order to strengthen learners' digital literacy and develop twenty-first-century technology skills that will serve learners both inside and outside the classroom. Through reviewing the theory of TBLT and the features of CALL as explored in previous research, the author explains how these two fields can support the other to improve learners' classroom experiences and maximize their growth. In particular, the ability to negotiate meaning and notice linguistic features are two skills that have been shown to be enhanced when technological resources are incorporated into class. To guide the integration process, five criteria are recommended for researchers and educators alike. After explaining these criteria and the theoretical foundation, the article concludes with recommendations for how to further examine how technology impacts language learning.

For more resources, including more sample lesson plans, videos, and other ideas, visit our companion website: www.cambridge.org/BryfonskiMackey.

20 How do I assess language learning?

KEY QUESTIONS
- The Science: How is language learning most efficiently and accurately measured? How do the types of assessments differ from each other?
- The Art: What are the best ways to track learners' progress in my classroom?
- How do assessments and proficiency levels relate?
- Why should I be thinking about conducting formative and summative assessments?

20.1 Voices from the Classroom

Ms. U's high school Spanish department recently made a transition from a grammar-based, textbook-oriented curriculum to a more proficiency-oriented curriculum where each instructor is encouraged to create their own activities for the shared thematic units. However, even after two years of developing and implementing a new curriculum, the department still uses its old grammar-heavy midterm and final assessments for each level. The learners have complained that these assessments are difficult. Ms. U thinks to herself, "midterms and finals are supposed to be challenging, right?" Ms. U's colleagues say that even with the new teaching approach, the expectations for what learners should know at the end of each level are the same, so using the old assessment is not an issue. Ms. U is not quite sure how to respond. What should she keep in mind as she considers how to assess her learners? Should the entire department consider developing new assessments?

20.2 The Science: What the Research Says

Assessment is the process of gathering information about a learner to determine the extent to which learners have learned what teachers have taught, monitor learners' progress in reaching curricular objectives, place learners into courses based on prior experience, and contribute to other instructional decisions. Assessments can take on a myriad of forms because they can (and should) be used to answer a wide variety of questions. For example, assessing learners can be informal check-ins to evaluate learners' progress, differentiate learning, or gauge if a class is ready to move on to a new topic. Assessments might also be as simple as asking learners informally what they learned or listening in on small-group conversations to hear what kinds of language are being used. Assessments can also include high-stakes standardized exams learners may need for future education or work placements. In general, assessments can help learners, teachers, administrators, and families understand, improve, and celebrate progress within their language classrooms. However, not all assessment methods are equally informative or beneficial. Programs might choose to assess language-related skills, like reading, writing, listening, or speaking, either individually or in combination. Assessments might target specific grammar forms, pronunciation, or vocabulary knowledge. Other assessments might focus on assessing cultural or pragmatic competence. Some programs might examine how well learners *use* language to complete a task or to understand the content.

Regardless of the type of assessment, all assessments should align with teaching pedagogies and program goals and should be developed before classroom tasks or activities. Additionally, assessment needs to be integrated into a program's daily classroom routine, rather than seen as a periodic obligation every semester or grading period. Assessing in an integrated, continual way allows for timely interventions before learners fall too far behind program objectives because of comprehension issues or other learning difficulties. The shorter the delay between recognizing a learning gap and taking action to fix it, the more likely the intervention is to be effective.

20.2.1 Types of Assessments

The first question to ask when considering the type of assessment to use in a program or classroom is: *What is the purpose of this assessment?* Researchers and educators often categorize assessments into two major groups: assessments *of* learning (i.e., summative assessments) or assessments *for* learning (i.e., formative assessments).

Summative assessments offer information on the extent to which a learner has mastered the targeted information (e.g., content) or reached a targeted proficiency level after a certain period of time. Examples of summative assessments include more "traditional" assessments like tests, quizzes, or unit exams. Summative assessments can also include task-based assessments like projects, portfolios, demonstrations, or plays. Formative assessments, by contrast, generate information on learners' ongoing progress toward an objective. Examples of formative assessments might include providing corrective feedback (orally or in writing) (see Chapter 3), asking questions from a variety of learners, asking learners to show answers on whiteboards or scrap paper, exit tickets, homework, short

20.2 The Science: What the Research Says

presentations, or posters (along with many more possibilities). An assessment is only formative or summative based on *how it is used*. For example, presentations could be used regularly and informally as ways to evaluate learners' production, or they could be used as a final presentation of all the material learned in a unit. Assessments provide teachers with data on how each learner is progressing, how they can be supported, or how they can be better challenged. In effective classrooms, both formative and summative assessments are used together throughout the course to provide evidence of learners' evolving abilities.

In addition to these two progress-monitoring assessment types, there are also assessments that can be used for other purposes. For example, an **achievement assessment** is often submitted as evidence that a learner can meet course, level, or program goals and successfully progress to the next degree of difficulty. Another type is a **performance-based** or **task-based assessment** (see Chapter 17). In both performance-and task-based assessments, learners perform a real or simulated task. In some models of performance assessments, learners are asked to demonstrate their knowledge across three modes of communication: *interpretive* (ability to understand and draw on background knowledge to interpret information), *presentational* (ability to prepare a written or oral/signed presentation and give it to an audience), and *interpersonal* (ability to negotiate for meaning in real time without rehearsal). In a task-based assessment, instead of focusing on the language *forms* learners use and evaluating them for accuracy, learners are evaluated on how well they accomplished the communicative components of the task they set out to perform. For example, after a unit on restaurant/take-out ordering, learners could attend a dinner at a restaurant (outside the classroom or simulated) and order their own meals. They could rate themselves and each other and receive feedback from the teacher on how well the interaction went and if they were able to order what they wanted to eat for dinner. Another popular type of assessment is a **diagnostic assessment**. In a diagnostic assessment, a teacher or administrator gathers information about a learner's strengths and struggles in order to tailor future instruction accordingly. Next, placement tests are frequently used to inform decisions around enrollment so that learners are appropriately advised and supported as they sign up for their language course(s).

The final common type of assessment is a **proficiency-based assessment**. These assessments are curriculum-neutral – meaning that they do not align with any particular textbook, program, etc. but, rather, look at whether learners are able to accomplish communicative tasks in the target language (TL). These assessments take a "snapshot" of a learner's general proficiency level at a given point of time and associate their performance with a particular proficiency benchmark (see Figure 20.1 for an overview).

There are several commonly used scales to describe learners' language proficiency. The first is the Common European Framework of Reference (CEFR). This proficiency scale is developed by the Council of Europe and presents language educators and learners with a set of comprehensive proficiency scales used in the

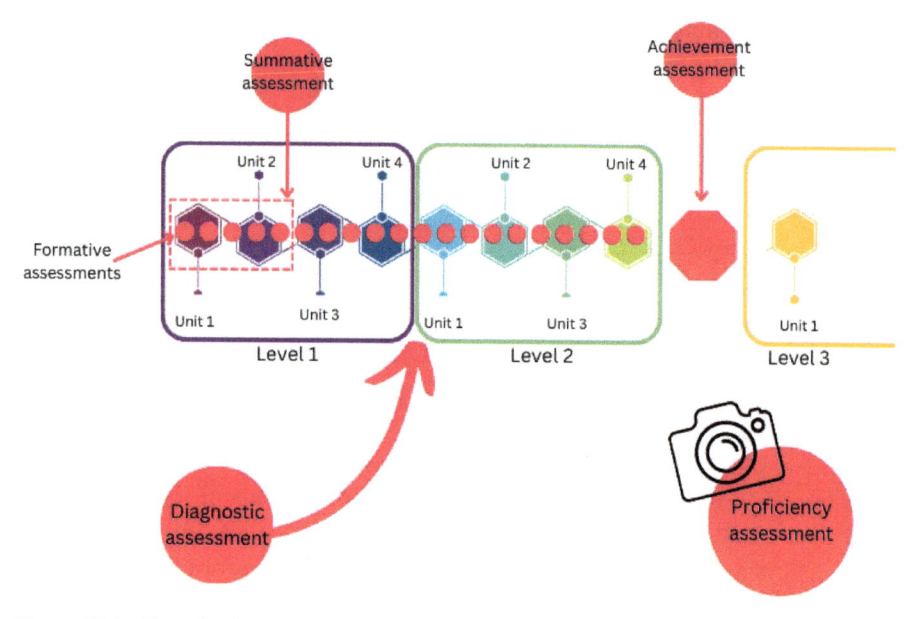

Figure 20.1 When do the types of assessments happen? Assessments should be integrated into the curriculum so that information about learners' language developments is being continually collected. Image by: Erin Fell

design of language syllabuses, curricula, materials, and assessments. The CEFR scale consists of language-proficiency levels from A1 level to C2. Each of these levels has specific descriptors that are defined through "can-do" statements. For example, for vocabulary at the A2 level, learners "can control a narrow repertoire dealing with concrete, everyday needs," and at the C1 level, they "can use less common vocabulary idiomatically and appropriately." Another commonly used framework is the ACTFL Proficiency Guidelines. The scale is divided into five main proficiency levels: Novice, Intermediate, Advanced, Superior, and Distinguished. The first three levels are divided into three subcategories in which each proficiency level is broken down into sub-levels (low, mid, high). ACTFL has its own set of "can-do" statements associated with each level which describe what learners at each level can perform consistently over time. They are designed to be a starting point for performance-based grading, rubric development, and for student self-assessment (see Box 20.1 for an example of a self-assessment). The statements are organized across the interpretive, presentational, and interpersonal modes of communication. For example, three of the ACTFL "novice-low" indicators are:

- Interpretive: "I can identify memorized or familiar words when they are supported by gestures or visuals in informational texts."
- Interpersonal: "I can express some basic needs, using practiced or memorized words and phrases, with the help of gestures or visuals."
- Presentational: "I can introduce myself using practiced or memorized words and phrases, with the help of gestures or visuals."

There are other scales worldwide that might be more appropriate to a particular teaching context. Teachers should use the appropriate resources to help set their regular learning targets for their learners, and schools can use them to set performance targets for their classes or programs.

The benefits of well-planned assessments are clear. Research has shown that timely and high-quality feedback helps maximize an assessment's potential to contribute positively to future learning. When feedback is connected to rubrics or scales and relates concretely to the overarching unit or course goals, studies show that learners will make more progress toward the desired "end goal."

BOX 20.1 How Well Did I Convey My Message?

	(Novice Language Learner)				
	All of the time	Most of the time	Part of the time	Rarely	Never
I achieved the communicative goal of the interaction.	X				
I used memorized phrases and simple sentences.		X			
I asked short, practiced questions to maintain the conversation.			X		

BOX 20.2 Review of Key Terms

- *Achievement assessments* are used to determine whether learners have successfully mastered the skills needed at a certain level, particularly the skills needed to continue on to the next iteration of a language program.
- *Performance-based assessments* require learners to integrate content to create a complex product/response using multiple skills and/or modes of communication.
- *Task-based assessments* require that learners complete a real-life situation to demonstrate their linguistic abilities.
- *Modes of communication* describe how learners can use language to accomplish interpersonal, interpretive, and presentational tasks.
- *Diagnostic assessments and placement tests* inform enrollment decisions and provide concrete information about a learner's progress in specific skills or areas.
- *Proficiency-based assessments* capture the extent to which a learner is communicatively competent in a variety of different situations or contexts. These assessments are not tied to a particular curriculum and provide results aligned with second language proficiency levels (e.g., ACTFL Proficiency Guidelines, CEFR Levels).

20.2.2 Selecting and Designing Assessments

The best assessment practices are *cyclical* – documenting not just an individual learner's performance at one point in time, but also revealing areas of strengths and weaknesses. These data are the most helpful when they enable learners and teachers to create a plan for the future. Assessment practices and classroom instruction should inform one another to advance and guide student development and course curricula. Assessments should also be closely aligned with the goals or objectives of a lesson, unit, or curricular plan. This can be accomplished through a **backward design** to lesson and assessment planning. In backward design, teachers consider goals and objectives and the assessments that will be used to evaluate the extent to which learners met those goals and objectives before designing any associated classroom tasks or activities. In other words, it is essential to teach what you plan to test and vice versa (see Box 20.3 for an example).

BOX 20.3 Two Approaches to Assessment and Lesson Planning

Read the two vignettes below. Which teacher do you think is implementing backward design?

Ms. H, Science class	Ms. A, Literacy class
Ms. H is a second-grade teacher in a bilingual school. She has a peer group of colleagues that get together once a week to discuss best practices and trade ideas about upcoming cross-curricular unit plans. In preparation for an upcoming discussion about a science unit, Ms. H scrolls the pages of her favorite teaching blogs and Pinterest in search of ideas to share. She sees a fun and crafty idea she likes, which has learners use cotton balls to illustrate different cloud formations. Using this idea, she creates a lesson focusing on cloud formations. She decides she will look at each learner's individual cloud diagrams to judge how well they understood the new vocabulary. Her plan is well received by the teaching group, so Ms. H logs back into Pinterest again the next week for more ideas.	Ms. A is also a second-grade teacher in a bilingual school with a peer group of colleagues that meet once a week to co-plan. Each week Ms. A gets out her curricular documents and looks for the overarching goals for an upcoming literacy unit. She sees that one objective is that learners should be able to make a prediction as a pre-reading strategy. She decides that the best way to judge if learners can make predictions is by practicing with the class-guided reading text and then asking individual learners to make predictions about their independent reading books. She looks on Pinterest and some teaching blogs and finds a graphic organizer that will help learners organize their predictions and brings copies to show her colleagues during their weekly meetings.

Ms. H looks for ideas for activities, implements them in her classroom, and uses the results of those activities to judge learning. Ms. A looks for objectives in her curriculum that she wants her learners to be able to accomplish and considers how she will evaluate if they are able to accomplish those objectives. Only then does she plan the activities and finds the resources she will use. Ms. A is using a backward design approach to her lesson planning.

20.2 The Science: What the Research Says

Assessments should allow teachers to identify, incorporate, and evaluate learners' ability to complete age-appropriate and linguistically appropriate tasks. In addition, it is important to consider how well learners' performances on assessments can predict their performances on other similar tasks. In other words, can the ability to perform a certain task (e.g., ordering food at a restaurant) be generalized and transferred to performing related tasks (e.g., ordering food on the phone, on a plane, etc.)? After a unit on applying for jobs, are learners able to compete in the local labor market? This nuanced aspect of performance assessment still calls for further classroom-based research and teacher training. Importantly, implementing backward design enables teachers to integrate their goals, instructional moves, and classroom practices into a cohesive unit moving toward clear, attainable unit objectives. As one teacher once put it: *Teach how you test and test how you teach*.

When designing any assessment, there are four key principles that must be centered: **validity**, **reliability**, **practicality**, and **impact** (see Figure 20.2).

Validity refers to the meaningfulness and appropriateness of what an assessment measures and what interpretations it grants the teacher or test-taker. For instance, if you design a test that intends to measure learners' understanding of cultural aspects of a TL, the test should only measure and allow interpretations for cultural understanding and not anything else, like learners' grammatical proficiency or vocabulary use. Of course, you can always incorporate and measure several skills at once in a single test. However, when considering the validity of the assessment, always ask yourself: *Does this assessment measure what I want it to measure?*

Reliability is how consistent an assessment is regardless of the number of times an assessment or test is administered. An assessment is considered reliable if it produces similar results regardless of interference from outside variables like time of administration, learner (or teacher) energy levels, or mode of assessment. For example, if learners usually take weekly quizzes first thing in the morning, and then one day, due to a change of schedule, they take their quiz at the end of the day and do worse than normal, the test might not be reliable because learners

The Principles of Assessment

VALIDITY	RELIABILITY
Does the test measure what you want it to measure?	Are scores on the test consistent?
PRACTICALITY	**IMPACT**
Is it possible to deliver the test to the intended population?	What will/can these test scores be used for?

Figure 20.2 The principles of assessment. The four concepts above drive the decisions around assessment design and selection.

are scoring differently when the time of the day changed. This change in results might be due to differences in energy or engagement as the school day ends. How questions are formatted (online or on paper) and even how the teacher feels while grading or scoring assessments can all impact an assessment's reliability. While it might not be possible to mitigate every reliability issue that could happen in a classroom assessment, it is important that teachers try to design tests or evaluate learners reliably by minimizing as best they can the factors influencing the way a test is interpreted and scored (see Figure 20.3).

Finally, it's important when designing an assessment to consider how practical it will be and how it will impact learners' academic trajectory. *Practicality* means that the test needs to be logistically possible to administer effectively. If it's too long or too difficult to score, it might not be practical for a particular context. Practicality is often an issue for task-based assessments where the aim is for learners to perform tasks as they would in the real world. In second language (L2) settings, it might be easy to take a class to a local restaurant or to a grocery store and see how well they perform. However, in world language settings, where learners aren't immersed in the TL, it can potentially be difficult (or even impossible) to interact with speakers of the TL. Additionally, no assessment should be undertaken without a clear understanding of its *impact* – will the result of the assessment be used to guide future instruction? to help place a learner in a program

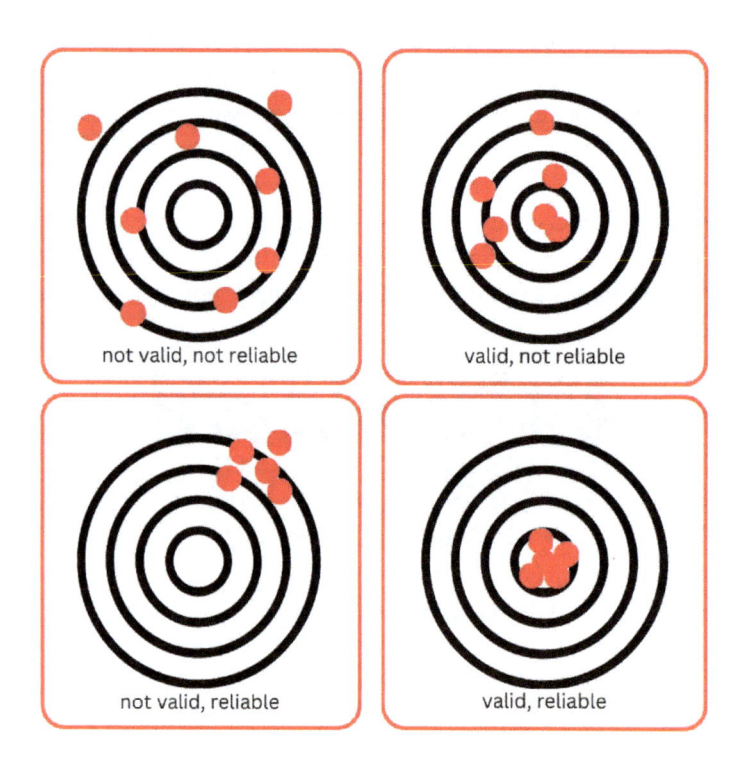

Figure 20.3 Validity and reliability in assessment. Valid assessments measure what's meant to be measured and reliable assessments produce similar results over multiple administrations.

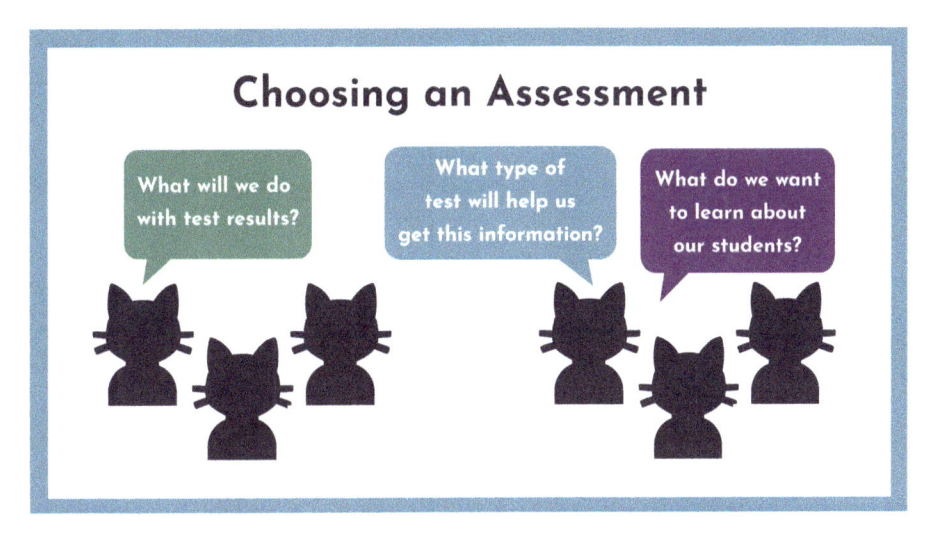

Figure 20.4 Choosing an assessment. Guiding questions like the ones above can inform decisions surrounding assessment selection. Image by: Elizabeth Zonarich

or class? to make university admission decisions? All assessments take time and energy, so attention must be given to how results will be used (see Figure 20.4).

20.2.3 Issues Related to Language Assessments

Language assessment researchers often focus on whether they are measuring what they intend to measure, how assessments relate to proficiency guidelines or other learning standards, and how assessments are perceived by test-users and test-takers. For example, research findings indicate that both learners and educators tend to conflate *proficiency* and *performance* – something that is understandable given how the two terms are sometimes used interchangeably outside of education circles. Within second language acquisition (SLA) research, we understand proficiency to be what a learner can do in the L2 with consistency. On the other hand, performance is a "snapshot" of what a learner can do in a specific task, at a particular moment in time. We can think of proficiency, then, as a big-picture description of what a learner can generally do in the L2, whereas their performance is a more fine-grained look at what they are able to do in a particular situation at a given point in time. Both levels of analysis are useful (and necessary) in L2 teaching and learning and should be accounted for in L2 assessment.

CALF Measures

One of the tools SLA researchers commonly use to assess L2 production is **CALF measures**: *complexity, accuracy, lexis,* and *fluency*. While much L2 assessment has focused on the accuracy component of learners' production, how learners perform with regard to the other CALF measures is an equally useful tool for assessing a learner's L2 development. In research, complexity is usually understood through syntax: How complex are learners' sentences (or utterances, in oral/signed language)? Do they generally stick to simple sentences with a subject, verb, and object, or do they add extra details using adjectives, adverbs, embedded clauses, and the like? Accuracy, for L2 teachers, is self-explanatory: do learners' accurately employ the grammatical rules governing the L2? Lexis refers to the breadth of a learner's L2 vocabulary. Generally, when evaluating for lexis, a difference is made between function words (i.e., articles, pronouns, conjunctions, and other words that don't carry much additional meaning but that are necessary for expression) and content words. Those using and reusing a limited set of content words would be said to demonstrate lower levels of lexical diversity, whereas those who infrequently reuse content words have higher lexical diversity. Finally, fluency is usually understood as the degree of elaboration a learner exhibits in their production. Sometimes this could be the number of words they produce (e.g., the number of words they write in response to an essay prompt) or the number of discrete ideas presented (recall creative fluency in Chapter 9). When assessing spoken or signed L2 production, fluency could also include the number of pauses or reformulations an L2 learner makes while producing the L2.

We bring these assessment concepts up here in this book not because there is any particular rubric, product, or schema we recommend with regards to CALF, but rather because we recommend teachers consider how they might use these tools from SLA research as they develop their own assessments of L2 production. Astute readers may have also noticed that CALF is only really appropriate for assessing production. SLA research has yet to coalesce around a set of similar constructs that can be applied to interpretive and interpersonal tasks.

Assessing Skills

For decades, the dominant practice of L2 assessment was to separate assessment sections by the four "traditional" communicative skills: reading, writing, listening, and speaking. Many older assessment scales (e.g., those used in the Canadian Language Benchmark, the Common European Framework, the Assessment of Language Performance) structure their scoring schema around these discrete skills in isolation, resulting in a score for listening, a score for reading, and so on. SLA research has shown, however, that L2 learners do not silo off their L2 skills; rather, they draw on *multiple skills* to complete a communicative task (i.e., ordering food from a restaurant). Acknowledging this complex skills interplay, newer assessment scales have compensated for this by accounting for the integrative nature of communicative interaction and task completion. For example, a learner may receive points based on the extent to which they engaged in facilitative behavior (e.g., asked follow-up questions to foster a conversation).

Self-Assessment

Research has also explored alternative types of assessments and their potential for shaping classroom practices and learners' L2 experiences. Research on self-assessment (see Figure 20.5) suggests that these types of assessments can be useful

20.2 The Science: What the Research Says

"I can purchase food from a market."

I cannot do this at all. — *I can do this easily!*

Figure 20.5 "Can-do" statements. Meters based on "can-do" statements are simple and efficient ways for students to track their progress on L2 goals.

resources because they involve learners in goal setting and reflecting on their performance. Regularly using self-assessment tools can help learners become more autonomous and self-aware learners (see Chapter 5 for a discussion on strategies). This is not to say that self-assessments should replace performance assessments; research has shown that many learners are not accurate self-assessors and may frequently over- or underestimate their abilities in the L2. Variables like previous academic performance, familial expectations, experience with self-assessment, cultural identity, and more can make a learner an inaccurate self-assessor. Instead, self-assessment should be a strategy that learners are trained in to help them monitor their progress toward L2 goals, improve confidence in the L2, identify gaps in their developing L2 knowledge, etc. This kind of training has been shown to be most effective with higher-proficiency learners (probably due to extensive experience with the L2 learning process) when scaffolded with concrete statements of ability and usually linked to specific real-world tasks.

BOX 20.4 The Science! Points to Remember

- A strong assessment is valid, reliable, practical, and is used to impact the test-taker's language learning experience in appropriate ways.
- When creating or selecting assessments for your courses, use the following questions to guide your investigation process:
  - What do I want to learn about my learners?
  - What types of assessment will help me get this information?
  - How will I score this assessment?
    - What communicative skills are my learners using and how do those skills overlap?
    - Would integrating CALF measures be useful in assessing learners' L2 production in this assessment?
    - Are my scoring criteria centering accurate use of L2 linguistic forms or use of the L2 to reach some communicative end?
  - What will I do with student scores from this assessment?
- There are many types of assessment, and each serves a unique role in measuring linguistic progress.
- Assessments are most effective in furthering learner progress when they align with course content, instructional approach, and learners' end goals.

Portfolios as Assessment

One approach to assessment that is becoming increasingly popular is **portfolio-based assessment**. A portfolio is a collection of work and reflections from a learner that showcases their progress toward individual L2 learning goals. Portfolios are *not* simply folders (physical or digital) that store all the work assigned by a teacher over the course of an academic year. Rather, they are curated selections of a learner's overall experiences – progress, successes, feedback, and self-corrections – that paint a comprehensive picture of what the learner has done thus far with their language and what their future language goals are. Importantly, portfolios are largely driven by learner input (instead of teacher input), with the learner evaluating, selecting, and reflecting on each artifact put in the portfolio. Teachers who implement portfolio-based assessment can set aside time to discuss artifact selection with their learners in class – for example, calling learners to their desk for short one-on-one chats during independent work time – or provide feedback on learners' selections after class. One popular tool for portfolio-based assessment is LinguaFolio (https://linguafolio.uoregon.edu/). With online platform organization tools and integrations with the ACTFL Proficiency Guidelines, LinguaFolio can be a useful tool for teachers new to portfolio-based assessment.

One of the biggest advantages of portfolio-based assessment is that it facilitates a growth-based mindset – an approach that encourages learners to see their language skills as trainable and improvable rather than innate or fixed. Many teaching contexts in recent years have emphasized growth mindsets as a way to help learners become more resilient when they encounter difficulties in learning. Portfolios can also be beneficial for learners who have learning difficulties or test-taking anxiety, as they emphasize the importance of creating a holistic picture of a learners' performance over time in a variety of contexts.

While some teachers who use portfolio-based assessment assign grades to components of the portfolio – either because they are required to report grades or because they consider grades necessary for their learners – many opt for an **un-grading approach**. Like the term implies, un-grading is the practice of not assigning grades to pieces of work learners produce over the course of instruction. Although number or letter grades are not used, this does not mean that teachers do not give feedback in an un-grading approach. Rather, teachers using un-grading provide their learners iterative feedback across activities in an instructional unit, drafts of a formal project, or other language learning artifacts.

20.3 The Science: What's Missing?

Compared to other subfields of education, SLA standards and the associated assessments are still relatively young and limited in scope. As of the writing of this book, the commonly used standards are still developed based on quite a narrow picture of proficiency level – the standards are not yet differentiated by *age* (e.g., how does proficiency manifest in young children versus adolescents versus adults?), *specialized language use* (e.g., using the L2 in school for a required course versus in a professional setting), *neurodiversity* (e.g., what special assets and struggles do neurodivergent L2 learners have?), *heritage language status* (e.g., how does divided language use impact bilingual speakers' proficiency in their languages?), and other important factors that impact how a learner's proficiency can (and should) be assessed. All of this means that when we use assessments and tools like proficiency guidelines (e.g., ACTFL, CEFR), we need to acknowledge that these materials are still being developed and made more inclusive, equitable, and *useful* for all L2 learners.

20.4 The Art: Research-Based Strategies to Try

20.4.1 The Art of Selecting an Assessment

- Reflect on the purpose of the assessment with your instructional team; what skills do you want to assess and what results will be generated by the assessment tasks? With your colleagues, develop your instructional materials *after* you have finalized your assessment tasks and scoring procedures. Follow the teacher maxim *teach how you test and test how you teach* to ensure you are appropriately preparing your learners to be able to accomplish the assessment tasks your team has developed. Several examples of how the modes and skills combine are listed below.
    - An interpretive listening assessment task might involve listening to the automated recording options from a pharmacy phone line and selecting the correct options to get the help needed.
    - A presentational writing assessment task could ask learners to compose a series of social media posts raising awareness about an issue of relevance to the learners (e.g., a local park initiative, advocating for the inclusion of their school in a coalition of internationally minded programs).
    - An interpersonal task could involve learners role-playing a scenario where one learner pretends they borrowed the other learner's laptop and damaged it. Together, these two learners must navigate this uncomfortable situation, determining how to proceed with fixing (or replacing) the fictional laptop and who will pay for the associated expenses, etc.
- Connect with learners who have exited your program to learn about how their language skills have served them since they left your classroom. Make sure that you are targeting these skills in class and that the assessments, when possible, demonstrate learners' growth so that they are prepared for a smooth transition when they use their language skills to communicate outside of your classroom.
- Teachers should incorporate both summative and formative assessments as they track learners' progress in both the short term and the long term. These assessments provide information for educators and administrators too. While formative assessment results can help inform instructional practices, summative assessments can inform program-wide decisions. Box 20.5 includes several examples of each type of assessment.

> **BOX 20.5 Formative Assessment Examples**
>
> - *Informal checks of student progress toward lesson/unit objectives.*
> - Give a thumbs up/thumbs down (thumbs up if you understand, thumbs down if you are still confused, thumb in the middle if you think you understand but would like to double check).
> - Give a "fist to five" (fist indicates "0" or completely unconfident and five indicates five fingers or completely confident; numbers between 0 and 5 indicate varying degrees of confidence).
> - Give a red, yellow, green card (to indicate how "ready" they feel to do a task, or how they felt about their task performance).
> - Use a one-word image (use one word to describe a picture that summarizes what was covered in class).
> - Create a storyboard.
> - Contribute to a living mind map (learners add details to a physical or digital mind map, connecting new information to previously discussed material).
> - Complete exit tickets (three learned concepts, two interesting concepts, one question). Learners must answer a question before leaving class or moving on to the next activity. You collect the data. Who understands and who doesn't?
> - Write a letter to a friend, weekly journal entries (student writes to a friend or keeps a journal of what they've learned in class).

- If you are deciding between several different assessment options and have the resources to do so, give learners a choice in how they demonstrate their knowledge and communication skills. If learners can choose the topic or the modality for their final project or portfolio, they may be more invested and motivated. Similarly, give learners multiple methods for demonstrating their proficiency. For example, allow them to present on a topic of their choosing and then write a news article. This will allow them to demonstrate proficiency with multiple skills (speaking, reading, writing).
- Any assessment type can be modified for younger learners. However, younger learners may need more scaffolding to understand what is expected of them. Young children will most likely not be able to ascribe value to numbers, letters, or percentages, but checking in with the grade-level teachers will be helpful in this regard. Instead, you could teach learners to associate shapes or symbols with your expectations for assignments as shown in Figure 20.6.
- Remember, assessments in your classroom do not need to be just between learner and teacher. As you weigh your options, consider these two types of informal, lower-stakes assessment approaches:
  - Peer assessments: You can provide learners with checklists to help them evaluate and support each other's work.
  - Informal, self-assessments:
    - Charting their confidence in a folder. If you use a folder system in class where students store their work or assessments, consider adding a graph to the inside cover where they can plot their self-assessments over time. This is a

20.4 The Art: Research-Based Strategies to Try

Grading System for Younger Students

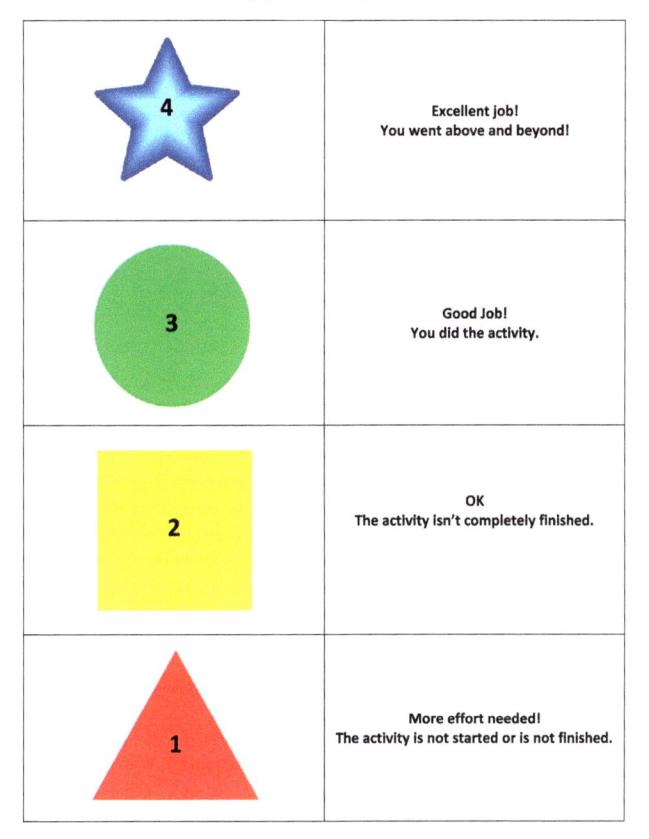

★ 4	Excellent job! You went above and beyond!
● 3	Good Job! You did the activity.
■ 2	OK The activity isn't completely finished.
▲ 1	More effort needed! The activity is not started or is not finished.

Figure 20.6 Grading systems for younger learners. Grading systems with visual components and straightforward language help younger learners understand how their progress is being measured.

I was interested in what we learned today.	😃 😐 🙁
I understood what we learned today.	😃 😐 🙁
I completed all my work in class today.	😃 😐 🙁

Figure 20.7 Exit tickets as formative assessments. Exit tickets can be used as self-assessment tools and help teachers gauge learners' socioemotional orientation to coursework.

great way to reinforce math concepts (e.g., plotting points and lines) as well as to visualize learning.

- Journal exit ticket: Ask learners to keep a journal, and as an exit-ticket, write what their main takeaways from class were with fill-in-the-blanks: "Today in class I learned _____ and it was important because_____." Or for another example, see Figure 20.7.

20.4.2 The Art of Trying Out a New Assessment in Your Program

- Check in with learners after conducting a new type of assessment. Did they feel it allowed them to demonstrate their linguistic abilities? Was your method of providing feedback helpful to them? What else would they like to receive feedback on?
- Rubrics can help both teachers and learners identify expectations. Not every aspect of an assignment needs to be reflected as a grade or point in the rubric. Consider what the most important goals of the assessment were and use only those criteria to complete the rubric. Stick to relatively few levels (between three and five; e.g., *exceeded expectations, met expectations, approaching expectations*). Too many levels become hard for learners to follow and teachers to grade. Similarly, stick to seven or fewer key criteria that will be evaluated in a single rubric (e.g., complexity, accuracy, lexis, fluency). Sometimes criteria can be pulled from a standard or curriculum. A variety of websites can help you generate rubrics from pre-formatted options. For US-based teachers, the Ohio Department of Education, in particular, is a great resource for rubrics.
- The first time you use a new rubric, be sure to review it together prior to the assessment so learners understand the expectations, and after the assessment, so that learners have the opportunity to reflect on your feedback and their own performance. After you have implemented a rubric a few times, consider using samples of previous students' work (anonymized and with consent, of course) to model how the assessment will be graded using the rubric.
- Make time in your planning periods to take a deep dive into the formative assessment data (e.g., learners' scores and results) the first time you use a new assessment tool. There may be other factors at play that are impacting how learners are engaging with that assessment tool, and these could skew their results, obscuring what learners can really accomplish with the TL. For example, what if their comprehension of the instructions is low? You might re-explain using a different approach, model what you mean, model with other learners, explain difficult terms, slow down your pace, use a different order, work with a small group, do more practice activities, and give more examples.
- To learn more about different types of assessments, visit the Center for Applied Linguistics' Foreign Language Assessment Directory, which contains information on over 200 assessments in over ninety languages for learners of all ages and levels.

20.4.3 The Art of Connecting Classroom Practices with Assessment Practices

- Use "can-do" statements at the beginning and end of each unit and/or course. Co-create them with learners to help increase student motivation and ensure that your curriculum is centered around communicative tasks and topics they care about.
  - Throughout the semester, check in with learners about selected can-do statements. Are they relevant? Are they clear? Are they reasonable? Are there additional

tasks/skills that learners want to see included in the "can-do" statements? Make them visible in your classroom and use them to clarify expectations.
- An assessment should not be a big surprise to learners. Provide your learners with exemplar models of how to complete the tasks they will be assessed on. These models can be incorporated into day-to-day classes. Explore them together and help learners break down the communicative components that lead to successful interactions in the TL at their target proficiency level.
- Collect examples of high-, middle-, and low-proficiency work for each of your assignments. This can help tailor future instruction and refine rubrics for your next group of learners. Pass these examples (anonymized) on to teachers you know, or use them in workshops. Examples of learners' work are useful for practicing making rubrics and evaluating and redesigning assessment tools.

20.5 Troubleshooting: How the Science Informs the Art

Ms. U's high school Spanish department recently made a transition from a textbook-oriented curriculum to a more proficiency-oriented curriculum where each instructor is encouraged to create their own activities for the shared thematic units. However, even after two years of developing and implementing a curriculum that is focused on developing communicative abilities rather than metalinguistic knowledge, the department still heavily relies on their old midterm and final assessments for each level.

In this new proficiency-oriented curriculum, how does the department define success? If success is still defined as the memorization and application of discrete grammar points and vocabulary lists, then it makes sense to continue using the old midterms and finals. If this is still how success is defined, the department has not adopted a proficiency-oriented curriculum. However, if the department defines success within a more communicative approach, Ms. U should refer to the standards in their reconstructed curriculum. Then they will want to redesign their assessments, so they are assessing the same way as they are in teaching. These two processes should go hand in hand.

The learners have complained that these assessments are difficult. Ms. U thinks to herself, "midterms and finals are supposed to be challenging, right?"

What is the department's purpose in conducting midterms and final assessments? If a student has worked hard throughout the semester, should the midterms and finals really be a challenge? For performance-based assessments, research suggests that these assessments are most beneficial to learners and educators when expectations about optimal student performance are made clear, and learners have many opportunities to build up to this end goal. Assessments should not come as a shock or surprise to learners. Rather, they should complement the types of activities and tasks that learners are accustomed to seeing in their regular classes.

What do you want to assess?

Modes of Communication

Interpretive   Interpersonal   Presentational

Reading   Writing   Speaking   Listening

Language Skills

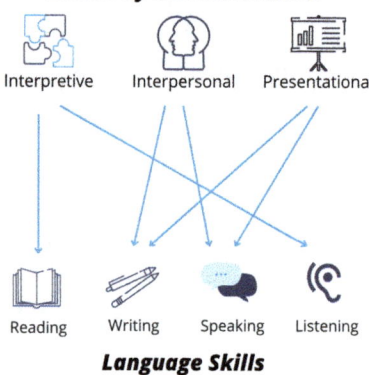

Figure 20.8 Dimensions of assessment. Identifying what communicative and linguistic skills are of interest helps focus the assessment development and selection process. Image by: Caitlyn Pineault

Ms. U's colleagues say that even with the new teaching approach, the expectations for what learners should know at the end of each level is the same, and so using the old assessment is not an issue. Ms. U is not quite sure how to proceed. What should she keep in mind as she considers how to assess her learners? What should she be sure her entire department is considering?

It is concerning that Ms. U's colleagues are under the impression that learners' knowledge will be the same, whether they operate under a more grammar-based curriculum or a communicative curriculum. For more on how these teaching approaches differ, see Chapter 16. She and her colleagues should first make sure they have similar understandings of their methodological approaches. Without solid foundational knowledge, it is very difficult to develop shared tools and resources, let alone align assessments. Once Ms. U and her colleagues are in agreement, they can then use the graphic in Figure 20.8 and the questions in Section 20.7 to guide their departmental conversations around assessment.

20.6 The Science: Points to Remember

- Assessments can provide evidence of learning (summative assessments) or evidence for learning (formative assessments).
- Well-selected and efficiently scored assessments have been shown to support learners' progress toward their language goals.
- When selecting or designing an assessment, language programs should consider the validity, reliability, practicality, and impact of their assessment options.

- Alternative assessments like portfolios may enhance learners' attitudes toward language classes and strengthen their learning strategies.
- Professional development workshops can help advance teachers' language assessment literacy, enabling them to make more informed decisions around tracking and measuring learner progress.

20.7   Questions to Consider

1. Present sample profiles for group discussion around assessment selection.
    a. Example: Ms. X is the coordinator for an elementary school language program. She is looking for a test to identify what skills her students need to have mastered to have a smooth transition between the elementary program and the secondary program. What do you recommend she consider as she embarks on her search?
    b. Example: Mr. Z works in a school district with a transient student body where there are often new learners who enroll partway through the year. He and his colleagues have a difficult time knowing where to place these learners because they do not receive a lot of information about the learners' prior educational experiences. What sort of assessment tools or practices should Mr. Z and his colleagues keep in mind as they consider ways to place new learners into the best-fitting course level?
2. Do the scales or rubrics used in your program position a "native speaker" as the ultimate accomplishment? (How) Might this end goal discourage learners, and what might you do to mitigate this? Do your course standards focus on what a learner *can* do rather than what they *cannot*?
3. Look at your program's mission or vision statement. How do the assessments you currently use support learners in achieving program goals? How do you measure their progress toward these goals?
4. Do your current assessments center around student knowledge of language skills like grammar or vocabulary in isolation? Or do your assessments focus on learners' ability to participate in complex, real-world-based interactions? How well does this align with your instructional practices and/or programmatic goals?

20.8   The Science of Language Learning: Research Supporting the Points Made in This Chapter

Butler, Y. G., & Lee, J. (2010). The effects of self-assessment among young learners of English. *Language Teaching, 27*(1), 5–31. https://doi.org/10.1177/0265532209346370.

This study explores an underexamined area within SLA research, the use of self-assessment tools in primary school language classrooms. Though self-assessment has received a lot of positive attention as an alternative assessment strategy, little empirical research has investigated it in practice with younger language learners.

This project investigates Korean sixth-grade English language learner's ability to effectively complete self-assessments and whether the act of completing self-assessments has an impact on their attitudes toward studying a new language. Results revealed that self-assessments had small but positive effects on the learners' perspectives on language learning. In addition, the learners' responded very differently from class to class, which motivates further exploration of how to support learners in maximizing their use of self-assessment tools to deepen their own learning processes.

Cox, T. L., Malone, M. E., & Winke, P. (2017). Future directions in assessment: Influences of standards and implications for language learning. *Foreign Language Annals, 51*, 104–115. https://doi.org/10.1111/flan.12326.

This article explores how the development and implementation of language standards have shaped the field of language assessment. Beginning with the formation of the ACTFL Proficiency Guidelines and subsequence assessments, the authors explain how the National Standards for Foreign Language Learning in the 21st Century were first conceived in 1996 and how they have shaped the assessments for world language education in the United States since their creation. A review of this literature revealed that not all standards are equally represented in regular assessments. Given that the literature also indicated that a standards-based approach supported language learners' development and strengthened world language program articulation across grade levels, it is important for researchers and educators to reflect on how to equally incorporate all standards into their curriculum. Connections between the ACTFL Proficiency Guidelines and the European standards for foreign language education are also discussed. Authors advocate for more investigation of the alignment between assessment formats and the standards for language learning, which they believe will provide more concrete insights for language instruction.

Malone, M.E. & Montee, M. (2014). Stakeholders' Beliefs About the TOEFL iBT Test as a Measure of Academic Language Ability. *ETS Research Report Series*. 10.1002/ets2.12039.

This research report on the TOEFL constructs a validity argument for the test item types and scoring procedures used to assess test taker's English language proficiency. Additionally, the researchers investigated the extent to which various stakeholders (including sutdents, instructors, and university administrators) reported understanding the ways in which the TOEFL assesses academic English and endorse the test as a useful tool for determining test takers' readiness to participate in English-speaking academic environments.

Norris, J. M. (2016). Current uses for task-based language assessment. *Annual Review of Applied Linguistics, 36*, 230–244. https://doi.org/10.1017/S0267190516000027.

In this chapter, language assessment is explored from a task-based perspective that prioritizes capturing learners' ability to use the TL to complete relevant and meaningful tasks. First presented as an alternative to traditional testing approaches, task-based language assessment emerged as researchers and educators began to center communicative competence, interaction, and authenticity in their work. This article offers an overview of the research that has focused on how best to design and implement task-based assessments to measure learners' linguistic growth. Sample assessment tasks are presented to demonstrate how tasks can address language standards, span linguistic modalities, and serve learners from a range of ages and proficiency levels.

For more resources, including more examples of task-based lesson plans, samples of task rubrics, and assessment ideas, visit our companion website: www.cambridge.org/BryfonskiMackey.

21 How can I make the most of professional development opportunities for language teachers?

KEY QUESTIONS
- **The Science:** How do my teacher identity and past experiences influence my practice? Why should I be engaged in reflective practice?
- **The Art:** How can I continue pursuing professional development? What other teacher training or professional development is important for teachers?
- How do I navigate and make the most of teacher observations?
- What is action research, and how can it help me?

21.1 Voices from the Classroom

Mr. P teaches a Japanese world language class in a high school setting. Because he is a novice teacher (in his first five years of teaching), Mr. P's department chair observes him twice a semester, and his administrator observes him twice a year. Neither his department chair nor his administrator speaks Japanese, and both have encouraged him to seek out external resources as he develops his teaching approach. Mr. P has joined a number of online communities for language teachers. Many of these communities offer for-purchase resources, workshops, and even personalized instructional coaching for their members. While he has gotten a lot of ideas for concrete lesson activities, he also feels as though some of the information distributed in these online professional development communities is contradictory. Some say that learners only need comprehensible input to make linguistic gains. Others stress the importance of providing a strong grammatical foundation. Some claim that class should be led 100% in the target language (TL). Others say that one day each week should be dedicated to the TL. Some say that learners should engage with resources made for native speakers by native speakers. Others say that learners should use graded readers with limited vocabulary and predictable sentence structures. All of them say their practices are backed by research. Mr. P has found the variety of information overwhelming, and this has made it difficult for him to plan longer curricular sequences because he is not sure what best practices and principles he should be following. What can Mr. P do to advance his professional development? How should he process all the information that is available to him?

21.2 The Science: What the Research Says

All teachers engage in some form of professional development during their careers, whether through formal teacher preparation programs, online modules, or informal discussion groups with peer teachers. Professional development may include opportunities for teachers to improve their language skills, their language teaching skills, or both. They may also offer teachers the chance to learn about related fields, including second language acquisition (SLA), multicultural studies, critical pedagogy, or other content areas. With the wealth of information now available online, it can be overwhelming to wade through these opportunities and resources. Teachers may wonder what is worth their time and energy and what will really make a difference in their classrooms. There is a field of research, Language Teacher Education (LTE), that studies these very issues to better understand what types of knowledge and what kinds of experiences language teachers need most during certification programs or other professional development opportunities.

At the core of LTE research are **language teachers' beliefs**, what they know, think, or judge to be true about language teaching and learning. These beliefs have been shown to be among the most powerful forces in how teachers experience professional development. In order for teachers to make any sort of changes to their teaching practice, research has found that teachers must first recognize their existing knowledge and beliefs about language teaching. Because of this, it is recommended that all language teachers seek out and engage in reflective teaching practices that explore the relationships between teachers' identities, their educational contexts, and classroom settings. Making connections between beliefs, identities, and teaching contexts helps ensure that any new information teachers receive is appropriately contextualized. This maximizes the likelihood that teachers interpret and apply the information to their own instructional practices.

Like learner identity (see Chapter 6), teacher identities are context-based and ever-evolving as a result of both internal (e.g., age, language-related identity) and external factors (e.g., classroom experience). Teacher identity may be strongly tied to their relationship with the TL, the TL community, and the school community. Other important factors may include teachers' age, race, gender, years of teaching experience, and their academic or professional background. Research suggests that professional development experiences that build in opportunities for reflection and connection to their prior experiences are more effective in advancing teachers' personal pedagogies and sparking positive change (see Box 21.1).

> **BOX 21.1 Questions for Language Teacher Self-Reflection**
>
> Teachers can consider how the answers to the following questions might impact the beliefs they hold about language teaching and learning and how those beliefs may shape their teaching practices.
>
> What is your relationship to the language you teach?
> - Is it your first language? Your second/third/+ language? Your heritage language?
> - Did you learn the language in school? At home?
> - If you learned the language in school, did you like the teaching approaches your teachers used?
> - How difficult would you say the language learning process was for you?
>
> What is your relationship to the target language community?
> - Do you see yourself as an insider to the target language community? An outsider?
> - Are you a citizen of a country where the target language is spoken? An immigrant? A long-term resident? A visitor?
> - Do you feel a cultural connection to the target language community?
>
> What is your relationship to your school community?
> - Are you new to your school, or have you been teaching there for many years?
> - Do you consider yourself more experienced compared to your teacher peers? Less experienced?

21.2.1 Types of Professional Development Opportunities

All professional development opportunities, either explicitly or implicitly, have made a judgment about what kinds of knowledge teachers need to prioritize. Researchers group teacher knowledge into two categories: *conceptual* and *practical*. Some programs focus on conceptual knowledge, providing pre-service teachers (or teachers engaging in continuing education programs) with a theoretical base in SLA research or other theories about best teaching practices. Other programs will prioritize the practical by including frequent modeling opportunities (e.g., capsule lessons) or a student–teacher experience, connecting teachers with mentors who help them learn about the profession through "hands-on" experiences. Some programs will offer a mix of both. The balance of knowledge you are looking to build should be a factor you consider before investing time (and money) in a professional development program.

Regardless of the type of professional development, teachers should engage in continual reflection and critical evaluation of how their own beliefs and identities interact with the materials. Teachers can ask themselves, *does this resource support or conflict with what I believe about my teaching practice? Why or why not?* It is also important to consider the perspective of the authors, businesses, or funding bodies involved in the resources found online. Teachers can ask, *what are the motivations for advocating for a particular approach or tool? Is there strong evidence from outside sources to support this claim?* Approaching resources with a critical eye helps teachers identify what resources are best matched for their unique teaching contexts and needs.

What about language-specific resources? There are a variety of language-specific teacher associations where teachers from different parts of the world can connect to share resources targeting the same language. These associations host conferences and workshops and often have for-purchase material available as well. Practical constraints, such as time and funding, may hinder teachers from engaging in in-person, extended professional development opportunities. However, professional development need not be limited to formal workshops or trainings, which are frequently contingent on financial and logistic resources. Other methods of teacher-guided professional development include collaborative research, team teaching, peer coaching, or professional learning communities.

Classroom Observations as Professional Development

Most practical, teacher-guided approaches to professional development involve some type of classroom observations with peers, mentors, or administrators. During an observation, educators watch one another as they teach to better understand the strengths and areas for improvement in their teaching practices. There are several benefits to engaging in observations. First, there is evidence that teachers who engage in frequent observations are better able to problem-solve when instructional issues arise and are more skilled in using a range of resources in their classrooms. Watching other teachers' practices can be used as an opportunity to learn and implement new teaching strategies. Teachers might use observations to identify behavioral, linguistic, or interaction trends that occur in the classroom. These may be trends the teacher has noticed and would like to understand in more detail, or they may be trends the teacher has not yet noticed independently. Observations can also establish and sustain mentorship relationships. Strong mentorship relationships have been shown to provide support systems and increase retention, develop problem-solving abilities, foster reflective practice, and develop teacher leaders.

However, observations are also sometimes a source of anxiety for many teachers. In many contexts, classroom observations are treated as performance reviews that determine whether a teacher's contract is renewed for the following school year or whether a teacher qualifies for a pay raise or bonus. Worries around such observations can sometimes be exacerbated if administrators are not familiar with what a well-run language classroom looks like. The high-stakes nature of such observations can lead to a more generalized anxiety around observations, including those between teacher peers (i.e., those not conducted by administrators). Additionally, the logistics of scheduling observations in an already busy schedule can be an inconvenience or even disruptive to a teacher's daily routine. However, there are steps that can be taken to minimize the stress of observations, including giving teachers more autonomy in deciding who will observe them, holding pre-observation meetings so that trust can be built and reasonable expectations can be set, as well as engaging in meta-feedback talk so teachers can ask for the kind of feedback that is most helpful to them. Observations do not have to be stressful; they can be productive opportunities for supportive community building and growth – both professionally and pedagogically (see Figure 21.1).

Figure 21.1 Observation experiences. There are a number of factors that can impact how a classroom observation is perceived and the impact is has on classroom practices. Image by: Elizabeth Zonarich

21.2.2 Action Research as Professional Development

New research is published every year investigating how languages are learned and suggesting how they might best be taught. However, not all this research winds up in the hands of teachers, and even if it does, many teachers don't find research to be immediately useful or practical for their classrooms. A study that investigated how much direct and indirect exposure language teachers get to empirical research found that there were many barriers separating teachers and research, such as subscription access to publications and limited citations of primary research in teacher-facing publications (e.g., teaching magazines, blogs). Some teachers also found applied linguistics publications to be too lengthy or too irrelevant to their day-to-day teaching. Some teachers stated they preferred to learn by doing rather than through exposure to research papers. Why would it be important to understand the science behind art? There is a danger in the "learn-just-by-doing" approach; while teachers might gain experience in the specific teaching situations they encounter in their practical experiences, relying solely on personal, hands-on experience can limit teachers' flexibility when approaching novel issues in different teaching contexts.

One way research has been integrated into teachers' practices is through an approach called **action research**. Action research is classroom-based research that is conducted *by teachers, for teachers* and identifies a classroom phenomenon or teaching strategy of interest and investigates it in a systematic way. Action-research projects are frequently driven by teachers' desires to better understand the inner workings of their classrooms and adapt their pedagogical practices accordingly. Some teacher education programs, including graduate degrees in teaching (e.g., M.Ed., Ed.D.), require action-research projects in the form of thesis work.

21.2 The Science: What the Research Says

However, an action-research study does not have to be complicated or elaborate to be a rigorous and effective project. A simple action-research project might, for example, explore the frequency with which different groups of learners participate in class. A more complex action-research project might investigate whether the incorporation of independent reading time impacts learners' vocabulary size. Because these projects are inspired by and conducted within a particular educational context, the findings of these types of investigations are specific to that educational context and are not meant to be generalized, unlike other types of research.

The steps to carrying out an action-research project include (1) identifying the question or problem you want to investigate, (2) making a plan to observe or collect data to answer your question, (3) carrying out your plan, (4) observing and reflecting on the results, and (5) making recommendations or plans for the next steps (see Figure 21.2). For example, a teacher might wonder if students are more

Figure 21.2 The action-research process. At its core, an action-research project is a cycle of observation, experimentation, and reflection that helps teachers strengthen their practices. Image by: Elizabeth Zonarich

engaged when they are in larger groups versus pairs when doing group work. She plans to investigate this over the course of a week, where some group work tasks will be done in pairs, and others will be in groups of four. Using an observation sheet she designed for this purpose, the teacher circulates during group work noting how often each student participates. After a week of observations, she summarizes the results. She finds that her lowest-proficiency students seem to talk more and be more engaged during pair work than in larger groups. However, there is more engagement overall when all students are considered and when groups are larger. She makes a plan to observe again with different groups of low- and high-proficiency learners to see if she can find the right balance.

By centering teachers, action research has been shown to facilitate teacher empowerment and professional growth. Participating in action research enables teachers to become more flexible, receptive to new ideas that challenge their pre-existing beliefs, and better problem-solvers when issues arise in their classrooms. Engaging in action research is one solution to the research–practice gap because it empowers teachers to investigate the issues that are most important to them, their students, and their teaching context.

BOX 21.2 The Science! Points to Remember

- Professional development can be conceptual, practical, or a combination of both.
- Professional development can be pursued at the group level or at the individual level; it may be an ongoing commitment or a one-time workshop.
- A language teacher's past beliefs and experiences play a large role in how that teacher engages with professional development opportunities.
- Regular reflective practices help teachers maximize their growth and learning during a workshop or training.
- Teachers can engage in action research to investigate the instructional questions they have about their classrooms.

21.3 The Science: What's Missing?

One of the biggest challenges facing research in language teacher education is how to bridge the gaps between (1) what teachers and researchers think about language teaching and (2) what teachers and researchers want to know about language teaching (see Figure 21.3). As we established above, the research shows that information passed to teachers through professional development opportunities is most likely to have long-lasting impacts on teachers' classroom practices if teachers are able to integrate it into their belief systems. However, the research also shows that most language teachers don't engage much with applied linguistics research for a variety of reasons, including lack of time, accessibility, or practicality.

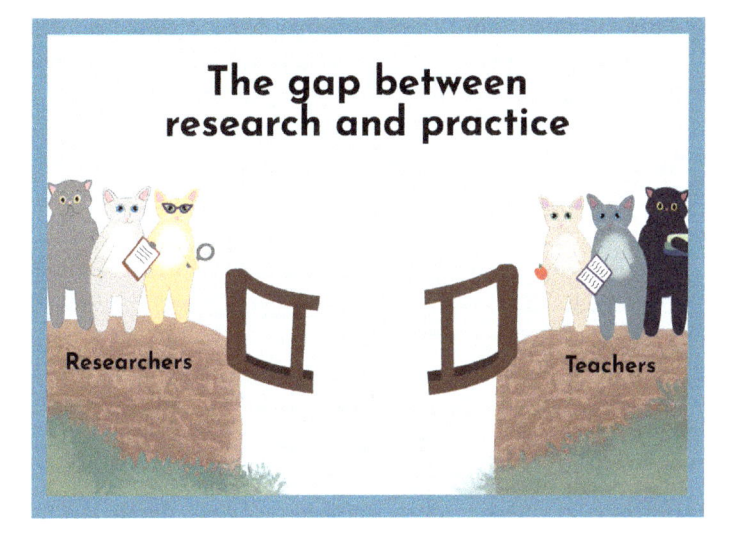

Figure 21.3 Research–practice divide. Both researchers and teachers are concerned with improving how languages are learned, but a number of variables can make it difficult for these two groups to collaborate. Image by: Elizabeth Zonarich

As discussed above, action research is one way teachers can get involved in research, but researchers also need to get involved with teachers. Too often, SLA researchers disseminate their findings in long, dense papers that don't make it clear how their results can be applied to classroom practice. Several initiatives have been created to address this issue, including the creation of platforms like OASIS (Open Accessible Summaries in Language Studies; https://oasis-database.org/), where short summaries of empirical investigations are written in accessible language, and digital communities of practice bring researchers and teachers together to discuss mutual interests.

21.4 The Art: Research-Based Strategies to Try

21.4.1 The Art of Navigating External Professional Development Opportunities

- Attend a wide variety of workshops and trainings organized by different groups to learn about all the different ways to approach language teaching and language learning.
- Interested in reading primary research from applied linguistics, but low on time? Check out OASIS (https://oasis-database.org/). This site aims to make research findings more accessible to a wide audience by asking authors to submit one-page summaries in simple language of their publications.
- Reflect on the teaching experiences and beliefs you bring to a workshop or training and consider how those experiences and beliefs may be impacting how you engage in the workshop. Bring a journal and make a note of emotions you can connect to your own beliefs or identity as you engage in various trainings.

- Bring an open mind to professional development workshops or trainings. There are many different approaches to language teaching because there are many different student and contextual variables. Remember the four key ingredients (access to input, opportunities to produce language, provision of feedback, and ability to negotiate for meaning) to language learning and see if you notice them throughout the training or workshop.
- Even if a professional development training has different understandings of how and why language learning takes place, look and listen for concrete teaching activities or ideas that you can adapt for your own teaching context. Ask yourself, *how can I apply this concept to my own teaching?*
- Just as language teachers strive to make their classes student-centered to maximize learning, professional development opportunities should also be participant-centered. Look for opportunities that involve ample opportunities to engage, reflect, and try out new teaching practices/concepts.
- It is important for teachers, regardless of the subject they teach, to have a sense of agency in their career trajectory and professional development. If you are a teacher trainer or administrator, consider asking teachers what kinds of opportunities they want or need, rather than predetermining programming. There is evidence that giving choices generates better buy-in to the information presented during professional development.

21.4.2 The Art of Engaging in Reflective Teaching Practices

- Write a language learner autobiography. In this chapter, we covered how our past experiences with language learning inform our teaching beliefs and practice. Think back to your own language learning experience and how it shapes your current teaching philosophy. You might ask your students to do the same!
- Keep a teacher's journal/notebook. Write down issues right after class and try to document what works or doesn't work. These can serve as inspiration for action-research topics.
- Set instructional goals for yourself at the beginning of the year or semester. What do you hope to improve and how will you know when you have met that goal?

21.4.3 The Art of Maximizing Observations

- Research shows that teaching observations are most effective when goals are chosen by the teacher who will be observed, rather than by someone in a position of authority. For this reason, schedule a time to meet with the person who will be observing you *before* the observation takes place to discuss the purpose of the observations and how the observation notes will be shared after the fact.
- Negotiate what the outcome of the observation will be so that the teacher can see how they will benefit from the observation.
- If your observer does not have a background in world language education, you might make a list of specific classroom routines or behavior you would like them to look out for during the observation.

- Suggest using a predetermined observation protocol. Observation protocols can be used both in commonplace observations and in observations that contribute to an action-research project. These allow you or your observer to collect data about a particular theme, behavior, or topic of interest during your observation (see the example in Box 21.3). In this observation, the teacher wanted help identifying whether she was providing enough feedback on the areas she wanted to address in her class. She asked the observer to note down all the instances of feedback she provided to students during a twenty-minute lesson. The observer took notes on the linguistic target of the feedback, who the feedback was directed at, and whether the student(s) noticed or disregarded the feedback.

BOX 21.3 **Example Observation Protocol: How Much Feedback Is the Teacher Providing?**

Example #	Feedback target: (Pronunciation, vocabulary, grammar, content)	Directed at: (Whole class/individual student/small group)	Noticed? (yes, no, unclear)
1			
2			

21.4.4 The Art of Conducting Action Research

- Comments and feedback from observations can serve as inspiration for an action-research project. Use the following examples as inspiration for generating questions for your own action-research project:
    - Observation comment 1: Students are not on task during paired activities.
    - Action-Research question 1: Why are students not on task during paired activities?
    - Observation comment 2: It is not clear where students should be directing their attention during class.
    - Action-Research question 2: How can TL input be clearly presented through a multimodal approach during class?
- Outline the plan for your action-research project *before* you begin. It is easy to get lost in the weeds once you have started to collect your data. Know what kind of data you are looking for and how you will analyze it.
- Collaborate with a colleague to conduct an action-research project together to compare how instructional strategies work in your classrooms or to compare how your different groups of learners navigate a new communicative task.
- Invested in action research? Consider collaborating with an applied linguist on your next action-research project.

21.5 Troubleshooting: How the Science Informs the Art

Mr. P teaches a Japanese world language class in a high school setting. Because he is a novice teacher (in his first five years of teaching), Mr. P's department chair observes him twice a semester and his administrator observes him twice a year. Neither his department chair nor his administrator speaks Japanese and both have encouraged him to seek out external resources as he develops his teaching approach. What can Mr. P do to advance his professional development?

Mr. P is lucky to have administrators that encourage him to seek out the professional development opportunities that will be most beneficial for his unique language classroom. As he has already discovered, world language teachers have formed large online communities that can offer support by sharing activities, resources, and other pieces of advice. However, they can also be quite overwhelming. As the "What's Missing?" sections have highlighted throughout this book, there is a lot that researchers do not have conclusive answers for. Many professional development communities claim that their resources or strategies are the most effective, but the truth is that the research has not yet pointed to a conclusive solitary way that languages should be taught in all circumstances. As Mr. P explores the training and workshop options over the summer, he should try out as many as possible, knowing there is no one "best" pedagogy, and keep an open mind about what each option would contribute to his own approach to language learning.

Mr. P has found the variety of information overwhelming and this has made it difficult for him to plan longer curricular sequences because he is not sure what best practices and principles he should be following. **How should he process all the information that is available to him?**

As he does this, he will likely encounter even more contradictory information. To help him navigate this, Mr. P should take an afternoon to reflect and draft several guiding questions that he wants to center in his own teaching journey. For example, this might include a question like, "How can I incorporate more literacy into my lessons?" At each workshop, Mr. P can look for answers to the questions he cares most about at that point in his career. As a novice teacher, professional development opportunities, especially big conferences, can be pretty daunting. This way, Mr. P is just focused on dimensions of his classroom practice he wants to improve the most. These questions will also likely be language agnostic (e.g., not specific to Japanese), and so he may even be able to draft this with his other language teaching colleagues. With these guiding questions, Mr. P can be sure he has a sense of purpose when attending each workshop and will hopefully take away stronger ideas about how to structure his courses.

21.6 The Science: Points to Remember

- Teachers and language programs should be sure to select the type of professional development opportunity that best matches their needs and priorities.

- Because all teachers bring different beliefs and experiences to the workplace, it is possible for two teachers to leave the same training with entirely different conclusions.
- Internal professional development initiatives, like regular observations, should carefully consider what other factors (like power dynamics within a department) may impact the observations and design observation protocols accordingly.
- Action research is a type of professional development activity that can better connect the fields of world language education and SLA, as well as provide concrete ideas for improving classroom practices.

21.7 Questions to Consider

1. In what ways have your teacher identity and past language learning/teaching experiences influenced your teaching?
2. Drawing from your own experiences participating in professional development, what made a teacher training session helpful for you? Why do you think it was helpful?
3. Try to brainstorm at least three issues you notice when teaching your own classes. Devise your own action-research questions. How might you implement your action-research steps?
4. How might you use technology to further your own teacher professional development?
5. Try out an action-research project of your own either independently or with a group of colleagues. You can either follow the steps in Figure 21.2 or use the action-research project outlined below. Check out the website for more detailed steps and how you can connect with the authors and other readers as you conduct your research.

   - The Main Problem
     What action-research question(s) will you investigate?

   - Data Collection Tools
     What methods will you use to gather data to address your question(s)?

   - Data Analysis
     How will you examine your data so that you can draw conclusions?

   - Intervention Design
     What will you do to address any findings from the action research project? Will you make any changes to your classroom or your teaching approach?

   - Final Reflection
     What were the outcomes of your action-research project? What would you do differently next time?

21.8 The Science of Language Learning: Research Supporting the Points Made in This Chapter

Burns, A. (2005). Action research: An evolving paradigm? *Language Teaching, 38*, 57–74. https://doi.org/10.1017/S0261444805002661.

In this article, Burns defines and provides a comprehensive overview of action research within the fields of English language teaching and applied linguistics. She traces the development of action research as a practice and illustrates how action research can be carried out by educators. Burns responds to common concerns about action research and outlines ways in which it can benefit teachers.

Freeman, D., & Johnson, K. E. (1998). Reconceptualizing the knowledge-base of language teacher education. *TESOL Quarterly, 32*(3), 397–417. https://doi.org/10.2307/3588114.

In this classic work, Freeman and Johnson proposed a reconceptualization of the knowledge base of language teachers and put forward a three-part framework: teacher-learner, social context, and pedagogic process. Rather than viewing teacher-learning as stemming from a transmission-based learning approach (i.e., expert transmits knowledge to the passive learner), they argued that language teachers' experiences, accumulated knowledge, and beliefs inform their teaching practices.

Mackey, A. (2017). Classroom-based research. In S. Loewen & M. Sato (Eds.), *The Routledge handbook of instructed second language acquisition* (pp. 541–561). Routledge Handbooks.

The chapter offers an overview of the ways in which classroom-based language research has been conducted over the past several decades. Distinct from laboratory-based research – which is often conducted in a very controlled setting – classroom-based research takes place in real classrooms. While this can make it challenging for researchers to create truly experimental conditions, it honors the complexities and realities of language learning. The primary research techniques used in this type of research, including observations, diaries, and action research, are each reviewed in detail for what they have and can contribute to future research efforts. Several logistical issues that researchers and educators may face when conducting research in language classrooms are also described.

For more resources, including more sample lesson plans, videos, and other ideas, visit our companion website: www.cambridge.org/BryfonskiMackey.

GLOSSARY

Achievement assessment: A type of assessment that is used to measure knowledge or skill and as evidence that a learner can meet course, level, or program goals and successfully progress to the next degree of difficulty.
Action research: Classroom-based research that is conducted by teachers for teachers, and identifies a classroom phenomenon or teaching strategy of interest and investigates it in a systematic way.
Anxiety: The feeling of unease, worry, and nervousness associated with learning or using a language.
Appropriateness: The ability to use language appropriately in different social contexts while considering the social, cultural, and situational norms of the context.
Aptitude: A range of abilities that predict how quickly or easily someone will learn a language compared to others.
Asynchronous computer-mediated contexts (ACMC): Delayed communication mediated by technology/Internet (e.g., email, social media posts, message/discussion boards etc.).
Attention: The ability to focus and concentrate on relevant forms and information in the language learning environment.
Attrition: A gradual decrease in language skills in a particular language.
Automaticity: The ability to produce and process language at a high speed with low error rate.
Autonomous learning: A self-directed learning process where learners take more responsibility for their own learning.
Backward design: An approach to lesson and assessment planning that considers goals and objectives and the assessments that will be used before designing any associated classroom tasks or activities.
CALF measures: A framework of linguistic measurement focusing on the Complexity, Accuracy, Lexis, and Fluency of learners' language production.
Clarification request: A conversational device indicating that what the learner said wasn't understandable and asking them to restate or repeat themselves again to clarify.
Cognate: A word that is related in origin to a word in another language. These two words may share similar meaning, spelling, and pronunciation.

Communicative approach: An approach to instruction that focuses on achieving communication goals while not ignoring necessary grammar or vocabulary. Learners spend the majority of class time engaged in communication-driven tasks in their second language.

Comprehensibility: Speech that is or can be understood by others.

Comprehensible input (CI): Input that is slightly above learners' current proficiency level; includes input that is from authentic "real-world" sources, even if it is not 100% comprehensible.

Computer-Assisted Language Learning (CALL): The study or use of computer-based resources to assist with language learning and teaching.

Computer-mediated communication (CMC): Communicative exchanges between participants using a computer.

Confirmation check: Asking the learner a question about something they said to confirm understanding.

Controlled response: The practice of listening to or producing a single specific feature of interest (usually involves participants in laboratory studies).

Conversational style: An individual's own style of conversing with others. This includes how people take turns in a conversation, how they tell stories and jokes, and even how long they pause before they continue talking.

Corrective feedback: Responses to a learner's non-target-like production.

Crosslinguistic influence: The impact a learner's first language may have on the second language they are learning; when information from one language system transfers to the new system.

Deep orthography: A written system where sounds correspond to multiple symbols/letters.

Developmental sequences: A fixed order of sequences or stages in which grammar features of a language are acquired.

Diagnostic assessment: A type of assessment that is used to inform enrollment decisions and provide concrete information about a learner's progress in specific skills or areas.

Differentiation: Tailoring instruction to meet individual needs/differences.

Engagement: Investment, active participation, and/or emotional commitment to learning.

Executive functioning: A set of cognitive processes (e.g., attention, self-control, mental flexibility) that coordinate other cognitive abilities and behaviors.

Explicit instruction: Instruction with a primary and overt focus on language forms/rules.

Explicit learning: Learning with a conscious intent to identify rules and patterns in the input.

Explicit knowledge: Knowledge *about* language that learners consciously know and can retrieve from memory.

Extensive writing: An approach where learners (1) write as much as possible, (2) write on a wide range of topics, (3) write for different reasons and in different ways, (4) decide what they want to write about, and (5) write at a variety of speeds.

Extrinsic motivation: Motivation driven by external rewards (praise, approval, grades, etc.).

Focused/Unfocused feedback: Corrections on a specific type of error (focused) or on all the errors (unfocused) a learner makes. Typically refers to written errors.

Foreign language settings: Settings where the learner's only exposure to the target language is through the input they receive in their language classroom (e.g., an English speaker taking German classes in the United States).
Form-focused instruction: Instruction that directs learners' attention to forms/rules (grammar, vocabulary, pronunciation) of a language.
Genre-based pedagogy: An approach to instruction where language is presented contextualized within a variety of different genres like argumentative texts, persuasive essays, cover letters, etc.
Grammar–translation: A grammar-based approach to instruction where most of the teaching occurs in the learner's L1 language and focuses on learning *about* the language, rather than on *how* to use the language.
Grammatical sensitivity: A learner's analytical ability regarding grammar. This skill is closely related to noticing because it relies on pattern recognition and inductive reasoning.
Grapheme–phoneme correspondence: The degree to which there is a one-to-one correspondence between the sounds and symbols in a language.
Heritage language learner (HLL): Learner of a heritage language (a language an individual speaks due to family or cultural ties that is not the commonly used language in the surrounding environment).
Ideal self: The possible future self a learner wants to become.
Identity: An individual's sense of self in relation to the language and culture they are learning.
Implicit instruction: Instruction with a primary focus on creating, conveying, and understanding meaning.
Implicit learning: Learning that occurs without any intention or awareness.
Implicit knowledge: Knowledge *of* language that learners unconsciously know but may not be able to verbalize.
Incidental learning: The process of learning in context, indirectly, and without intention.
Individual differences: A variety of factors (e.g., age, motivation, personality, aptitude) that may affect an individual's language learning process.
Input: What a learner hears or reads in the target language.
Instrumental motivation: An individual's desire to learn an L2 to achieve an immediate or practical goal.
Integrativeness: An individual's desire to learn an L2 of a valued community in order to communicate with and/or join that group of people.
Intentional learning: The process of learning with an intention or goal to learn.
Intonation: The rise and fall of pitch in speech.
Intrinsic motivation: Motivation driven by internal rewards (self-enjoyment or satisfaction).
L1/L2: First language (L1); second or learned language (L2).
Language-related episode (LRE): An episode when learners discuss aspects of the language they need to be able to complete whatever task or activity they are working on.
Language teacher beliefs: What language teachers know, think, or judge to be true about language teaching and learning. These beliefs may impact on how teachers experience professional development opportunities and approach their teaching.
Lexicon: The bank of vocabulary learners have acquired.

Metalinguistic feedback: Grammatical explanation of a learner's error.
Modified output: A learner's production of reformulated or self-corrected original utterance.
Morphology: The internal structure of words and the way they are formed.
Native language(s): The language or languages children are exposed to from infancy. See **L1**.
Natural approach: An approach to instruction without any grammar instruction that primarily consists of engaging with second language input. Sometimes referred to as the "meaning-focused" approach.
Needs analysis: An analysis conducted with learners and relevant parties (e.g., parents, teachers, stakeholders) to identify target tasks and design task-based curricula.
Negative transfer: The interference in acquisition of one language by another language.
Negotiation of meaning: Adjustments speakers make to their speech during interaction to repair a breakdown in communication.
Neurodiversity: Natural differences in an individual's brain function and behavioral traits.
Noticing: From "Noticing Hypothesis" proposed by the researcher Richard Schmidt, which is the theory that language learners must notice language features, such as errors in their own production, in order to acquire them.
Ought-to self: The possible future self a learner thinks they ought to become.
Output: What learners produce (write or speak) in the second language.
Pedagogic task: A task related to the target task, but appropriately altered for classroom or instructional settings.
Performance-based assessment: A type of assessment which involves learners demonstrating their skill by performing a real or simulated task.
Phonemic awareness: A learners' ability to distinguish between segments of sounds of a word and put them together to form words.
Phonological awareness: A learner's ability to recognize new sounds, rhyme words, and divide words up into syllables.
Phonological decoding: A learner's ability to apply spelling cues to identify words and retrieve their meanings.
Phonological loop: An aspect of short-term working memory that is activated when input is received that allows people to "replay" or rehearse sounds, words, phrases, and even numerical sequences that they hear.
Phonology: The sound structure of words and phrases.
Positive transfer: One language facilitates the acquisition of another language.
Pragmalinguistic competence: The specific ways we use language to follow social rules.
Pragmatics: The choices that people make in conversation given the specific circumstances of the environment, including in relation to other people (i.e., how people decide *how* to say *what* to *whom* and *when*).
Presentation, Practice, Production (PPP): A method of language instruction where language forms are *presented*, *practiced* in a controlled manner, and then *produced* more freely.
Production: What a learner speaks or writes in the target language.
Productive knowledge: Language forms a learner produces during communication.

Proficiency: The degree to which a learner is able to use and understand a language.

Proficiency-based assessment: A type of assessment that is used to capture the extent to which a learner is communicatively competent in a variety of different situations or contexts.

Pushed output: When a learner is prompted or pushed to self-correct their speaking.

Realia: Authentic materials that were not created for educational purposes.

Recast: Reformulation or restatement of a learner's error with the correct form.

Receptive knowledge: Language forms that a learner might recognize and understand but is unlikely to produce.

Reliability: Refers to how consistent an assessment is regardless of the number of times an assessment or test is administered.

Repetition: Repeating what the learner said exactly, including the error, often with a rising intonation to let the learner know there's a reason for the repetition.

Reverse transfer: When knowledge of a second language begins to impact the first language, causing errors.

Second language settings: Settings where learners are taught or exposed to the majority language (e.g., a Japanese speaker taking English as a second language in classes in the UK).

Segmentals: Individual sounds of a language such as consonants and vowels.

Shallow orthography: A written system where sounds correspond to only one symbol/letter.

Sociopragmatic competence: The knowledge about what is or isn't appropriate in a certain social situation.

Speech acts: Language used for specific communicative actions (e.g., requests, apologies, refusals, suggestions, etc.).

Strategy-based instruction: The explicit instruction of different practices learners can independently use to support their language learning.

Suprasegmentals: Features "above" the level of sound such as rhythm, intonation, tone, and stress.

Synchronous computer-mediated communication(SCMC): Real-time communication mediated by technology/Internet (e.g., Zoom, Facetime, text chats, etc.).

Syntax: The order and structure of words and phrases.

Target language (TL): The language being taught or learned.

Target task: Tasks people do in their everyday lives; the skills learners need or wish to do in their L2.

Task-based assessment: A type of assessment which involves learners demonstrating their ability to successfully perform a real or simulated task. Part of a task-based approach to teaching (see **Task-Based Language Teaching (TBLT)**.

Task-Based Language Teaching (TBLT): An approach to language teaching organized around tasks, or what language learners need to be able to *do* with their language. See **focus on form** and **needs analysis**.

Task-Supported Language Teaching (TSLT): The use of tasks to supplement a pre-designed curriculum that is organized around discrete grammar forms/rules.

Translanguaging: An individual's use of their entire linguistics resources (including switching languages).

Validity: The meaningfulness and appropriateness of what an assessment measures and what interpretations it grants the teacher or test-taker.

Willingness to communicate: The threshold where learners feel comfortable producing the second language.

Working memory: A learner's capacity for storing, manipulating, and analyzing information in real time.

World language: Languages where learners' only exposure is through the input they receive in their language classroom (e.g., an English speaker taking German classes in the United States). See **foreign language setting**.

REFERENCES AND RESOURCES

Pre-Reading Self-Assessment

Bryfonski, L. (2019). Task-based teacher training: Implementation and evaluation in Central American bilingual schools. Georgetown University. Unpublished doctoral dissertation.

King, K. A., & Mackey, A. (2007). *The bilingual edge: Why, when, and how to teach your child a second language.* New York: Collins.

Ogilvie, G., & Dunn, W. (2010). Taking teacher education to task: Exploring the role of teacher education in promoting the utilization of task-based language teaching. *Language Teaching Research, 14*(2), 161–181.

Spada, N., & Lightbown, P. M. (2006). *How languages are learned.* Oxford University Press.

Chapter 1

de Saint Léger, D., & Storch, N. (2009). Learners' perceptions and attitudes: Implications for willingness to communicate in an L2 classroom. *System, 37*(2), 269–285.

García Mayo, M. D. P., & Alcón Soler, E. (2013). Negotiated input and output in interaction. In J. Herschensohn & M. Young-Scholten (Eds.), *The Cambridge handbook of second language acquisition* (pp. 209–229). Cambridge University Press.

McDonough, K. (2005). Identifying the impact of negative feedback and learners' responses on ESL question development. *Studies in Second Language Acquisition, 27*(1), 79–103.

McDonough, K., & Mackey, A. (2006). Responses to recasts: Repetitions, primed production, and linguistic development. *Language Learning, 56*(4), 693–720.

Oliver, R. (2000). Age differences in negotiation and feedback in classroom and pairwork. *Language Learning, 50*(1), 119–151.

Swain, M. (1993). The output hypothesis: Just speaking and writing aren't enough. *Canadian Modern Language Review, 50*(1), 158–164.

VanPatten, B. (2014). Creating comprehensible input and output. *The Language Educator, 7*(4), 24–26.

Chapter 2

Ellis, R., & Shintani, N. (2014). *Exploring language pedagogy through second language acquisition*. Routledge.

Fujii, A., Ziegler, N., & Mackey, A. (2016). Peer interaction and metacognitive instruction in the EFL classroom. In M. Sato & S. Ballinger (Eds.), *Peer interaction and second language learning: Pedagogical potential and research agenda* (pp. 63–89). John Benjamins.

Gass, S. M., & Mackey, A. (2006). Input, interaction and output in SLA. In J. Williams & B. VanPatten (Eds.), *Theories in second language acquisition: An introduction* (pp. 175–199). Lawrence Erlbaum.

Gass, S. M., & Varonis, E. M. (1994). Input, interaction, and second language production. *Studies in Second Language Acquisition, 16*(3), 283–302.

Koh, M. H., Barbour, M., & Hill, J. R. (2010). Strategies for instructors on how to improve online groupwork. *Journal of Educational Computing Research, 43*(2), 183–205.

Krashen, S. (1980). The input hypothesis. In J. Alatis (Ed.), *Current issues in bilingual education* (pp. 168–180). Georgetown University Press.

Krashen, S. (1982). *Principles and practice in second language acquisition*. Alemany Press.

Long, M. H. (1996). The role of the linguistic environment in second language acquisition. In W. C. Ritchie & T. K. Bhatia (Eds.), *Handbook of research on language acquisition: Second language acquisition* (Vol. II, pp. 413–468). Academic Press.

Long, M. H. (2007) Texts, tasks, and the advanced learner. In M. H. Long (Ed.), *Problems in SLA* (pp. 119–138). Lawrence Erlbaum.

Chapter 3

Bryfonski, L., & Ma, X. (2020). Effects of implicit versus explicit corrective feedback on Mandarin tone acquisition in a SCMC learning environment. *Studies in Second Language Acquisition, 42*(1), 61–88.

Li, S., & Vuono, A. (2019). Twenty-five years of research on oral and written corrective feedback in System, *System, 84*, 93–109.

Long, M. H. (2016). Recasts in SLA: The story so far. In M. Long (Ed.), *Problems in SLA* (pp. 75–116). Routledge.

Lyster, R., Saito, K., & Sato, M. (2013). Oral corrective feedback in second language classrooms. *Language Teaching, 46*(1), 1–40.

Mackey, A., Park, H. I., & Tagarelli, K. (2016). Error, feedback, and repair: Variations and learning outcomes. In G. Hall (Ed.), *The Routledge handbook of English language teaching* (pp. 499–512). Routledge.

Park, E. S., & Kim, O. Y. (2019). Learners' engagement with indirect written corrective feedback: Depth of processing and self-correction. In R. Leow (Ed.), *The Routledge handbook of second language research in classroom learning* (pp. 216–226). Routledge.

Chapter 4

Basterrechea, M., & Mayo, M. G. (2013). Language-related episodes during collaborative tasks. In K. McDonough & A. Mackey (Eds.). *Second language interaction in diverse educational contexts* (pp. 25–44). John Benjamins.

Choi, H., & Iwashita, N. (2016). Interactional behaviours of low-proficiency learners in small group work. In M. Sato & S. Ballinger (Eds.), *Peer interaction and second language learning: Pedagogical potential and research agenda*, (pp. 113–134). John Benjamins.

Fujii, A., Ziegler, N., & Mackey, A. (2016). Peer interaction and metacognitive instruction in the EFL classroom. In M. Sato & S. Ballinger (Eds.), *Peer interaction and second language learning: Pedagogical potential and research agenda* (pp. 63–90). John Benjamins.

Kim, Y., & McDonough, K. (2008). The effect of interlocutor proficiency on the collaborative dialogue between Korean as a second language learners. *Language Teaching Research*, *12*(2), 211–234.

Kim, Y., & McDonough, K. (2011). Using pretask modelling to encourage collaborative learning opportunities. *Language Teaching Research*, *15*(2), 183–199.

Philp, J., Adams, R., & Iwashita, N. (2013). *Peer interaction and second language learning*. Routledge.

Storch, N. (2002). Patterns of interaction in ESL pair work. *Language Learning*, *51*(1), 119–158.

Chapter 5

Graham, S., Woore, R., Porter, A., Courtney, L., & Savory, C. (2020). Navigating the challenges of L2 reading: Self-efficacy, self-regulatory reading strategies and learner profiles. *Modern Language Journal*, *104*(4), 693–714.

Gu, Y. (2019). Approaches to learning strategy instruction. In A. U. Chamot & V. Harris (Eds.), *Learning strategy instruction in the language classroom: Issues and implementation* (pp. 22–37). Multilingual Matters.

Khatib, S. A. A. (2010). Meta-cognitive self-regulated learning and motivational beliefs as predictors of college students' performance. *International Journal for Research in Education*, *27*, 57–72.

Kuo, Y.-C., Walker, A. E., Schroder, K. E. E., & Belland, B. R. (2014). Interaction, internet self-efficacy, and self-regulated learning as predictors of student satisfaction in online education courses. *The Internet and Higher Education*, *20*, 35–50.

Mezei, G. (2008). Motivation and self-regulated learning: A case study of a pre-intermediate and an upper-intermediate adult student. *Working Papers in Language Pedagogy*, *2*, 79–104.

Oxford, R. L. (2017). *Teaching and researching language learning strategies: Self-regulation in context* (2nd ed.). Routledge.

Puzziferro, M. (2008). Online technologies self-efficacy and self-regulated learning as predictors of final grade and satisfaction in college-level online courses. *American Journal of Distance Education*, *22*(2), 72–89.

Tsuda, A., & Nakata, Y. (2013). Exploring self-regulation in language learning: A study of Japanese high school EFL students. *Innovation in Language Learning and Teaching*, *7*(1), 72–88.

Chapter 6

Andringa, S., & Godfroid, A. (2020). Sampling bias and the problem of generalizability in applied linguistics. *Annual Review of Applied Linguistics*, *40*, 134–142.

Anya, U. (2011). Connecting with communities of learners and speakers: Integrative ideals, experiences, and motivations of successful black second language learners. *Foreign Language Annals, 44*(3), 441–466.

Anya, U. (2021). Critical race pedagogy for more effective and inclusive world language teaching. *Applied Linguistics, 42*(6), 1055–1069.

Blake, R. J., & Zyzik, E. C. (2003). Who's helping whom?: Learner/Heritage-speakers' networked discussions in Spanish. *Applied Linguistics, 24*(4), 519–544.

Bowles, M. A. (2011). Measuring implicit and explicit linguistic knowledge: What can heritage language learners contribute? *Studies in Second Language Acquisition, 33*(2), 247–271.

Carreira, M. (2020, September 22). *Instructed heritage language acquisition* [Podcast]. https://international.ucla.edu/nhlrc/article/238479.

Frieson, B. L. (2022). "It's like they don't see us at all": A Critical Race Theory critique of dual language bilingual education for black children. *Annual Review of Applied Linguistics, 42*, 47–54.

Flores, N., & Rosa, J. (2015). Undoing appropriateness: Raciolinguistic ideologies and language diversity in education. *Harvard Educational Review, 85*(2), 149–171.

Garcia, V., Pineault, C., & Bryfonski, L. (2022, March 19). An evaluation of a multidimensional identity measurement: The heritage language learner identity index. [Paper presentation]. American Association for Applied Linguistics Annual Conference, Pittsburgh, PA.

Henrich, J., Heine, S., & Norenzayan, A. (2010). Most people are not WEIRD. *Nature, 466*, 29.

Henshaw, F. G. (2015). Learning outcomes of L2-Heritage learner interaction: The proof is in the posttests. *Heritage Language Journal, 12*(3), 245–270.

Martin-Beltrán, M., & Montoya-Ávila, A. (2020). "I know there's something like that in Spanish": Heritage language learners' multifaceted interactions with linguistically diverse peers. *International Journal of Applied Linguistics, 30*(3), 530–552.

Park, E. S., Song, S., & Shin, Y. K. (2016). To what extent do learners benefit from indirect written corrective feedback? A study targeting learners of different proficiency and heritage language status. *Language Teaching Research, 20*(6), 678–699.

Ruggiero, D. M. (2015). "Más allá del fútbol": Teaching highland Afro-Ecuadorian culture and engaging race and racism through documentary film. *Hispania, 98*(3), 594–606.

Schoener, H., & McKenzie, K. (2016). Equity traps redux: Inequitable access to foreign language courses for African American high-school students. *Equity and Excellence in Education, 49*(3), 284–299.

Valdés, G. (2005). Bilingualism, heritage language learners, and SLA research: Opportunities lost or seized? *The Modern Language Journal, 89*(3), 410–426.

Valdés, G., & Geoffrion-Vinci, M. (2011). Heritage language students: The case of Spanish. In M. Díaz-Campos (Ed.), *The handbook of Hispanic sociolinguistics* (pp. 598–622). Wiley Blackwell.

Chapter 7

ACTFL. (2015). *NCSSFL-ACTFL Can-do statements*. Retrieved April 25, 2022 from https://www.actfl.org/educator-resources/ncssfl-actfl-can-do-statements.

Barkley, R. A. (2006). *Attention-deficit/hyperactivity disorder: A handbook for diagnosis and treatment* (3rd ed.). Guilford Press.

Cancer, A., Manzoli, S., & Antonietti, A. (2016). The alleged link between creativity and dyslexia: Identifying the specific process in which dyslexic students excel. *Cogent Psychology*, *3*(1), 1–13.

Cheatham, G. A., & Hart Barnett, J. E. (2017). Overcoming common misunderstandings about students with disabilities who are English language learners. *Intervention in School and Clinic*, *53*(1), 58–63.

Cioè-Peña, M. (2020). Raciolinguistics and the education of emergent bilinguals labeled as disabled. *The Urban Review*, 1–27.

Cockcroft, K., & Hartgill, M. (2004). Focusing on the abilities in learning disabilities: Dyslexia and creativity. *Education as Change*, *8*(1), 61–79.

Dawson, P., & Guare, R. (2009). *Smart but scattered: The revolutionary "executive skills" approach to helping kids reach their potential*. Guilford Press.

DuPaul, G. J., & Stoner, G. (2014). *ADHD in the schools: Assessment and intervention strategies* (3rd ed.). Guilford Press.

Greene, R. R., Beszterczey, S. K., Katzenstein, T., Park, K., & Goring, J. (2002). Are students with ADHD more stressful to teach? Patterns of teacher stress in an elementary school sample. *Journal of Emotional & Behavioural Disorders*, *10*(2), 79–89.

Hambly, C., & Fombonne, E. (2012). The impact of bilingual environments on language development in children with autism spectrum disorders. *Journalism of Autism and Developmental Disorders*, *42*(7), 1342–1352.

Kormos, J. & Smith, A. M. (2012) *Teaching languages to students with specific learning differences*. Multilingual Matters.

Kos, J. M., Richdale, A. L., & Hay, D. A. (2004). Children with attention deficit hyperactivity disorder and their teachers: A review of the literature. *International Journal of Disability, Development and Education*, *53*(2), 147–160.

Martínez-Álvarez, P. (2019). Dis/ability labels and emergent bilingual children: Current research and new possibilities to grow as bilingual and biliterate learners. *Race, Ethnicity, and Education*, *22*(2), 174–193.

Moats, L. C., & Dakin, K. E. (2008). *Basic facts about dyslexia and other reading problems*. The International Dyslexia Association.

O'Connor, R. E., Beach, K. D., Sanchez, V. M., Kim, J. J., Knight-Teague, K., Orozco, G., & Jones, B. T. (2019). Teaching academic vocabulary to sixth-grade students with disabilities. *Learning Disability Quarterly*, *42*(4), 231–243.

Ohan, J. L., Visser, T. A. W., Strain, M. C., & Allen, L. (2011). Teachers' and education students' perceptions of and reactions to children with and without the diagnostic label "ADHD." *Journal of School Psychology*, *49*, 81–105.

Peristeri, E., Baldimtsi, E., Vogelzang, M., Tsimpli, I. M., & Durrleman, S. (2021). The cognitive benefits of bilingualism in autism spectrum disorder: Is theory of mind boosted and by which underlying factors? *Autism Research*, 1–15.

Pfiffner, L. J., Barkley, R. A., & DuPaul, G. J. (2006). Treatment of ADHD in school settings. In R. A. Barkley (Ed.), *Attention-deficit hyperactivity disorder: A handbook for diagnosis and treatment* (pp. 547–589). Guilford Press.

Reetze, R., Zou, X., Sheng, L., & Katsos, N. (2015). Communicative development in bilingually exposed Chinese children with autism spectrum disorders. *Journal of Speech, Language, and Hearing Research*, *58*(3), 813–825.

Rogers, M., & Meek, F. (2015). Relationships matter: Motivating students with ADHD through the teacher-student relationship. *Perspectives on Language and Literacy*, *41*(1), 21–22.

Shaywitz, S. E., & Shaywitz, J. (2020). *Overcoming dyslexia* (2nd ed.). Hachette UK.

Chapter 8

Adolphs, C., Clark, L., Dornyei, Z., Glover T., Henry, A., Muir, C., & Valstar, M. (2018). Digital innovations in L2 motivation: Harnessing the power of ideal L2 self. *System, 78*, 173–185.

Alrabai, F. (2016). Factors underlying low achievement of Saudi EFL learners. *International Journal of English Linguistics, 6*(3), 21–37.

Deci, E. L. & Ryan, R. M. (1985). *Intrinsic motivation and self-determination in human behaviour*. Plenum

Dewaele, J. M., Witney, J., Satio, K., & Dewaele, L. (2018). Foreign language enjoyment and anxiety: The effect of teacher and learner variables. *Language Teaching Research, 22*(6), 676–697.

Dörnyei, Z. (2005). *The psychology of the language learner: Individual differences in second language acquisition*. Laurence Erlbaum.

Dörnyei, Z., & Csizér, K. (1998). Ten commandments for motivating language learners: Results of an empirical study. *Language Teaching Research, 2*(3), 203–229.

Dörnyei, Z., & Taguchi, T. (2009). *Questionnaires in second language research: Construction, administration, and processing*. Routledge.

Early, M., & Norton, B. (2012). Language learner stories and imagined identities. *Narrative Inquiry, 22*(1), 194–201.

Gardner, R. C. & Lambert, W. E. (1959) Motivational variables in second language acquisition. *Canadian Journal of Psychology 13*, 266–272.

Guilloteaux, M. J., & Dörnyei, Z. (2008). Motivating language learners: A classroom-oriented investigation of the effects of motivational strategies on student motivation. *TESOL Quarterly, 42*(1), 55–77.

Horowitz, E. K., Horowitz, M. B., & Cope, J. (1986). Foreign language classroom anxiety. *The Modern Language Journal, 70*(2), 125–132.

Liao, M. T., & Wong, C.T. (2010). Effects of dialogue journals on L2 students' writing fluency, reflections, anxiety, and motivation. *Reflections on English Language Teaching, 9*(2), 139–170.

MacIntyre, P. D., & Gardner, R. C. (1994). The subtle effects of language anxiety on cognitive processing in the second language. *Language learning, 44*(2), 283–305.

Mahmoodi, M. H., & Yousefi, M. (2021). Second language motivation research 2010-2019: A synthetic exploration. *The Language Learning Journal, 50*(3), 273–296.

Norton, B. (1997). Language, identity, and the ownership of English. *TESOL Quarterly, 31*(3), 409–429.

Norton, B. (2000). *Identity and language learning: Gender, ethnicity and educational change*. Pearson Education.

Norton, B. (2001). Non-participation, imagined communities, and the language classroom. In M. Breen (Ed.), *Learner contributions to language learning: New directions in research* (pp. 159–171). Pearson Education.

Norton, B. (2010). Language and identity. In N. Hornberger & S. McKay (Eds.), *Sociolinguistics and language education* (pp. 349–369). Multilingual Matters.

Norton, B., & Y. Gao (2008). Identity, investment, and Chinese learners of English. *Journal of Asian Pacific Communication, 18*(1), 109–120.

Norton, B., & C. McKinney (2011). Identity and second language acquisition. In D. Atkinson (Ed.), *Alternative approaches to second language acquisition* (pp. 73–94). Routledge.

Norton, B., & Pavlenko A. (Eds.). (2004). Gender and English language learners: Challenges and possibilities. In B. Norton & A. Pavlenko (Eds.), *Gender and English language learners* (pp. 1–12). Teachers of English to Speakers of Other Languages Inc.

Norton, B., & K. Toohey (2001). Changing perspectives on good language learners. *TESOL Quarterly, 35*(2), 307–322.

Norton, B., & K. Toohey (2002). Identity and language learning. In R. B. Kaplan (Ed.), *The Oxford handbook of applied linguistics* (pp. 115–123). Oxford University Press.

Norton, B., & K. Toohey (Eds.). (2004). *Critical pedagogies and language learning*. Cambridge University Press.

Norton, B., & Toohey, K. (2011). Identity, language learning, and social change. *Language Teaching, 44*(4), 412–446.

Papi, M. (2014). Language learner motivational types: A cluster analysis study. *Language Learning, 64*(3), 493–525.

Papi, M. (2021). The role of motivational and affective factors in L2 writing performance and written corrective feedback processing and use. In R. M. Manchón & C. Polio (Eds.), *The Routledge handbook of second language acquisition and writing* (pp. 152–165). Routledge.

Pfenninger, S. E., & Singleton, D. (2016). Affect trumps age: A person-in-context relational view of age and motivation in SLA. *Second Language Research, 32*(3), 311–345.

Rahimi, M., & Zhang, L. J. (2019). Writing task complexity, students' motivational beliefs, anxiety and their writing production in English as a second language. *Reading and Writing, 32*(3), 761–786.

Rassaei, E. (2015). Oral corrective feedback, foreign language anxiety and L2 development. *System, 49*, 98–109.

Shirvan, M. E., & Taherian, T. (2018). Anxiety dynamics in a virtual foreign language learning course. *Konin Language Studies, 4*, 411–436.

Stockwell, G. (2013). Technology and motivation in English-language teaching and learning. In E. Ushioda (Ed.), *International perspectives on motivation* (pp. 156–175). Palgrave Macmillan UK.

Teimouri, Y., Goetze, J., & Plonsky, L. (2018). Second language anxiety and achievement: A meta-analysis. *Studies in Second Language Acquisition, 41*, 363–387.

Ushioda, E. (2001) Language learning at university: Exploring the role of motivational thinking. In Z. Dornyei and R. Schmidt (Eds.), *Motivation and second language acquisition* (pp. 91–124). University of Hawaii Press.

Young, J. E. (1990). *Cognitive therapy for personality disorders: A schema-focused approach*. Professional Resource Press.

Zabihi, R., Mousavi, S. H., & Salehian, A. (2018). The differential role of domain-specific anxiety in learners' narrative and argumentative L2 written task performances. *Current Psychology, 39*(4), 1438–1444.

Chapter 9

Kormos, J. (2013). New conceptualizations of language aptitude in second language attainment. In G. Granena & M. Long (Eds.), *Sensitive periods, language aptitude, and ultimate L2 attainment* (pp. 131–154). John Benjamins.

Li, S. (2015). The associations between language aptitude and second language grammar acquisition: A meta-analytic review of five decades of research. *Applied Linguistics, 36*(3), 385–408.

Li, S. (2017). The effects of cognitive aptitudes on the process and product of L2 interaction: A synthetic review. In L. Gurzynski (Ed.), *Expanding individual difference research in the interaction approach: Investigating learners, instructors and researchers* (pp. 42–70). John Benjamins.

Sok, S., Shin, H. W., & Do, J. (2021). Exploring which test-taker characteristics predict young L2 learners' performance on listening and reading comprehension tests. *Language Testing, 38*(3), 1–23.

Wen, Z., & Skehan, P. (2021). Stages of acquisition and the P/E model of working memory: Complementary or contrasting approaches to foreign language aptitude? *Annual Review of Applied Linguistics, 41*, 6–24.

Yeldham, M., & Gao, Y. (2021). Examining whether learning outcomes are enhanced when L2 learners' cognitive styles match listening instruction methods. *System, 97*, 102435.

Chapter 10

Bulté, B., & Housen, A. (2012). Defining and operationalising L2 complexity. In A. Housen, F. Kuiken, & I. Vedder (Eds.), *Dimensions of L2 performance and proficiency: Investigating complexity, accuracy, and fluency in SLA* (pp. 21–46). John Benjamins.

Cysouw, M. (2013). Predicting language-leaning difficulty. In L. Borin & A. Saxena (Ed.), *Approaches to measuring linguistic differences* (pp. 57–82). De Gruyter Mouton.

Davis, C. (2005). *Shallow vs non-shallow orthographies and learning to read workshop. Report of the OECD-CERI Learning Sciences and Brain Research*. Cambridge University. www.oecd.org/dataoecd/54/39/35562310.pdf.

Everson, M. E. (2011). Best practices in teaching logographic and non-Roman writing systems to L2 learners. *Annual Review of Applied Linguistics, 31*, 249–274.

Flege, J. E. (1995). Second language speech learning: Theory, findings, and problems. In W. Strange (Ed.), *Speech perception and linguistic experience: Issues in cross-language research.* (pp. 233–277). York Press.

Housen, A., De Clercq, B., Kuiken, F., & Vedder, I. (2019). Multiple approaches to complexity in second language research. *Second Language Research, 35*(1), 3–21.

Kenner, C., Kress, G., Al-Khatib, H., Kam, R., & Tsai, K-C. (2014). Finding the keys to biliteracy: How young children interpret different writing systems. *Language Education, 18*(2), 124–144.

Klein, W., & Perdue, C. (1984). The learner's problem of arranging words. In B. MacWhinney & E. Bates (Eds.), *The cross-linguistic study of sentence processing.* (pp. 292–327). Cambridge University Press.

Osborne, C., Zhang, Q., & Zhang, G. X. (2020). Which is more effective in introducing Chinese characters? An investigative study of four methods used to teach CFL beginners. *The Language Learning Journal, 48*(4), 385–401.

Shen, H. H. (2005). An investigation of Chinese-character learning strategies among non-native speakers of Chinese. *System, 33*(1), 49–68.

Siok, W. T., Jin, Z., Fletcher, P., & Tan, L. H. (2003). Distinct brain regions associated with syllable and phoneme. *Human Brain Mapping, 18*(3), 201–207.

Chapter 11

Ellis, R. (2006). Current issues in the teaching of grammar: An SLA perspective. *TESOL Quarterly*, *40*(1), 83–107.

Ellis, R., Loewen, S., Elder, C., Erlam, R., Philp, J., & Reinders, H. (2009). *Implicit and explicit knowledge in second language learning, testing and teaching*. Multilingual Matters.

Li, S., Ellis, R., & Kim, J. (2018). The influence of pre-task grammar instruction on L2 learning: An experimental study. *Studies in English Education*, *23*(4), 831–857.

Liu, J. (2005). Chinese graduate teaching assistants teaching freshman composition to native English-speaking students. In E. Llurda (Ed.), *Non-native language teachers: Perceptions, challenges, and contributions to the profession* (pp. 155–177). Springer.

Long, M. H. (1998). Focus on form in task-based language teaching. *University of Hawaii Working Papers in ESL*, *16*(2), 35–49.

Nemtchinova, E. (2005). Host teachers' evaluations of nonnative-English-speaking teacher trainees: A perspective from the classroom. *TESOL Quarterly*, *39*(2), 235–261.

Norris, J., & Ortega, L. (2000). Effectiveness of L2 instruction: A research synthesis and quantitative meta-analysis. *Language Learning*, *50*(3), 417–528.

Spada, N., Jessop, L., Tomita, Y., Suzuki, W., & Valeo, A. (2014). Isolated and integrated form-focused instruction: Effects on different types of L2 knowledge. *Language Teaching Research*, *18*(4), 453–473.

Van Patten, B. (1990). Attending to form and content in the input: An experiment in consciousness. *Studies in Second Language Acquisition*, *12*(3), 287–301.

Chapter 12

Barriuso, T. A., & Hayes-Harb, R. (2018). High variability phonetic training as a bridge from research to practice. *The CATESOL Journal*, *30*(1), 177–194.

Bryfonski, L., & Ma, X. (2020). Effects of implicit versus explicit corrective feedback on Mandarin tone acquisition in a SCMC learning environment. *Studies in Second Language Acquisition*, *42*, 61–88.

Darcy, I. ; Ewert, D ; & Lidster, R. (2012). Bringing pronunciation instruction back into the classroom: An ESL teachers' pronunciation "toolbox." In. J. Levis & K. LeVelle (Eds.). *Proceedings of the 3rd Pronunciation in Second Language Learning and Teaching Conference, Sept. 2011*. (pp. 93–108). Iowa State University.

Eckstein, G. T. (2007). *A correlation of pronunciation learning strategies with spontaneous English pronunciation of adult ESL learners* (Publication No. 28109782) [Doctoral dissertation, Brigham Young University]. ProQuest Dissertations & Theses Global.

Flege, J. E. (1995). Second language speech learning: Theory, findings, and problems. In W. Strange (Ed.), *Speech perception and linguistic experience: Issues in cross-language research* (pp. 233–277). York Press.

Kuhl, P. (2004). Early language acquisition: Cracking the speech code. *Nature Reviews Neuroscience*, *5*(11), 831–843.

Lee, J., Jang, J., & Plonsky, L. (2014). The effectiveness of second language pronunciation instruction: A meta-analysis. *Applied Linguistics*, *36*(3), 345–366.

Levis, J. M. (2016). Research into practice: How research appears in pronunciation teaching materials. *Language Teaching*, *49*(3), 423–437.

Levis, J. M., Derwing, T. M., & Sonsaat-Hegelheimer, S. (Eds.). (2022). *Second language pronunciation: Bridging the gap between research and teaching*. John Wiley & Sons.

Mackey, A., Gass, S., & McDonough, K. (2000). How do learners perceive interactional feedback? *Studies in Second Language Acquisition*, *22*(4), 471–497.

Nazzi, T., & New, B. (2007). Beyond stop consonants: Consonantal specificity in early lexical acquisition. *Cognitive Development*, *22*(2), 271–279.

O'Brien, M. G. (2021). Easy and difficulty in L2 pronunciation teaching: A mini-review. *Frontiers in Communication*, *5*, 1–7.

Saito, K. (2013). Reexamining effects of form-focused instruction on L2 pronunciation development: The role of explicit phonetic information. *Studies in Second Language Acquisition*, *35*(1), 1–29.

Saito, K., & Lyster, R. (2012). Effects of form-focused instruction and corrective feedback on L2 pronunciation development of /ɹ/ by Japanese learners of English. *Language Learning*, *62*(2), 595–633.

Saito, K. & Plonsky, L. (2019). Effects of second language pronunciation teaching revisited: A proposed measurement framework and meta-analysis. *Language Learning*, *69*(3), 652–708.

Sardegna, V. G. (2009). *Improving English stress through pronunciation learning strategies* (Publication No. 3363085) [Doctoral dissertation, University of Illinois at Urbana-Champaign]. ProQuest Dissertations & Theses Global.

Sardegna, V. G., Lee, J., & Kusey, C. (2017). Self-efficacy, attitudes, and choice of strategies for English pronunciation learning. *Language Learning*, *68*(1), 83–114.

Chapter 13

Allen, H. W. (2018). Redefining writing in the foreign language curriculum: Toward a design approach. *Foreign Language Annals*, *51*(3), 513–531.

Bigelow, M., Delmas, R., Hansen, K., & Tarone, E. (2006). Literacy and the processing of oral recasts in SLA. *TESOL Quarterly*, *40*(4), 665–689.

Bigelow, M., & Tarone, E. (2004). The role of literacy level in second language acquisition: Doesn't who we study determine what we know? *TESOL Quarterly*, *38*(4), 689–700.

Bialystok, E. (2007). Acquisition of literacy in bilingual children: A framework for research. *Language Learning*, *57*(S1), 45–77.

Byrnes, H., Maxim, H. H., & Norris, J. M. (2010). Realizing advanced foreign language writing development in collegiate education: Curricular design, pedagogy, assessment. *The Modern Language Journal*, *94*, 1–235.

Flores, N. (2020). From academic language to language architecture: Challenging raciolinguistic ideologies in research and practice. *Theory into Practice*, *59*(1), 22–31.

Grabe, W., & Stoller, F. L. (2011). *Teaching and researching reading* (2nd ed.). Pearson Education.

Hammer, C. S., Hoff, E., Uchikoshi, Y., Gillanders, C., Castro, D., & Sandilos, L. E. (2014). The language and literacy development of young dual language learners: A critical review. *Early Childhood Research Quarterly*, *29*(4), 715–33.

Kern, R., & Schultz, J.M. (2005). Beyond orality: Investigating literacy and the literacy in second and foreign language instruction. *The Modern Language Journal*, *89*, 381–392.

Kim, Y. S., & Piper, B. (2019). Cross-language transfer of reading skills: An empirical investigation of bidirectionality and the influence of instructional environments. *Reading and Writing, 32*(4), 839–871.

Kuo, L. J., & Anderson, R. C. (2012). Effects of early bilingualism on learning phonological regularities in a new language. *Journal of Experimental Child Psychology, 111*(3), 455–467.

Leki, I. (2001). Material, educational, and ideological challenges of teaching EFL writing at the turn of the century. *International Journal of English Studies, 1*(2), 197–209.

National Institute of Child Health and Human Development (NICHD). (2000). Report of the National Reading Panel. Teaching children to read: An evidence-based assessment of the scientific research literature on reading and its implications for reading instruction (NIH Publication No. 00-4769). US Department of Health and Human Services.

Sun, Y.-C. (2010). Extensive writing in foreign-language classrooms: A blogging approach. *Innovations in Education and Teaching International, 47*(3), 327–339.

Troyan, F. J. (2014). Leveraging genre theory: A genre-based interactive model for the era of the Common Core state standards. *Foreign Language Annals, 47*(1), 5–24.

Yasuda, S. (2011). Genre-based tasks in foreign language writing: Developing writers' genre awareness, linguistic knowledge, and writing competence. *Journal of Second Language Writing, 20*, 111–113.

Chapter 14

Barcroft, J. (2008). Effects of synonym generation on incidental and intentional L2 vocabulary learning during reading. *TESOL Quarterly, 43*(1), 79–103.

Bisson, M., van Heuven, W. J. B., Conklin, K., & Tunney, R. J. (2014). The role of repeated exposure to multimodal input in incidental acquisition of foreign language vocabulary. *Language Learning, 64*(4), 855–877.

Brown, R., Waring. R., & Donkaewbua, S. (2008). Incidental vocabulary acquisition from reading, reading-while-listening, and listening to stories. *Reading in a Foreign Language, 20*(2), 136–163.

Cook, V. (2002). *Portraits of the L2 user*. Multilingual Matters.

Crossley, S., Salsbury, T., & Kyle, K. (2016). A usage-based investigation of L2 lexical acquisition: The role of input and output. *The Modern Language Journal, 100*(3), 702–715.

Gorsuch, G., & Taguchi, E. (2008). Repeated reading for developing reading fluency and reading comprehension: The case of EFL learners in Vietnam. *System, 36*(2), 253–278.

Hobson, V., & Schmitt, N. (2019). A review of current research on second language vocabulary learning. OASIS Summary of Schmitt (2008) in *Language Teaching Research*. https://oasis-database.org.

Hsueh-chao, M. H., & Nation, P. (2000). Unknown vocabulary density and reading comprehension. *Reading in a Foreign Language, 13*, 403–430.

Laufer, B., & Goldstein, Z. (2004). Testing vocabulary knowledge: Size, strength, and computer adaptiveness. *Language Learning, 54*(3), 399–436.

Legault, J., Zhao, J., Chi, Y. A., Chen, W., Klippel, A., & Li, P. (2019). Immersive virtual reality as an effective tool for second language vocabulary learning. *Languages, 4*(1), 13.

Lee, H., Warschauer, M., & Lee, J. H. (2019). The effects of corpus use on second language vocabulary learning: A multilevel meta-analysis. *Applied Linguistics, 40*(5), 721–753.

Malone, J. (2018). Incidental vocabulary learning in SLA: Effects of frequency, aural enhancement, and working memory. *Studies in Second Language Acquisition, 40*, 651–675.

Nation, I. S. P. (2006). How large a vocabulary is needed for reading and listening? *Canadian Modern Language Review, 63*, 59–82.

Pellicer-Sánchez, A. (2016). Incidental L2 vocabulary acquisition from and while reading. *Studies in Second Language Acquisition, 38*, 97–130.

Peters, E., Noreillie, A.-S., Heylen, K., Bulté, B., & Desmet, P. (2019). The impact of instruction and out-of-school exposure to FL input on learners' vocabulary knowledge in two languages. *Language Learning, 69*(3), 747–782.

Peters, E. (2018). The effect of out-of-class exposure to English language media on learners' vocabulary knowledge. *ITL International Journal of Applied Linguistics, 169*(1), 142–168.

Puimege, E., & Peters, E. (2019). Learners' English vocabulary knowledge prior to formal instruction: The role of learner-related and word-related variables. *Language Learning, 69*(4), 943–977.

Qiao, X., & Forster, K. I. (2017). Is the L2 lexicon different from the L1 lexicon? Evidence from novel word lexicalization. *Cognition, 158*, 147–152.

Schmitt, N. (2019). Understanding vocabulary acquisition, instruction, and assessment: A research agenda. *Language Teaching, 52*, 261–274.

Schmitt, N., & Schmitt, D. (1995). Vocabulary notebooks: Theoretical underpinnings and practical suggestions. *ELT journal, 49*(2), 133–143.

Suárez, M. M., & Gesa, F. (2019). Learning vocabulary with the support of sustained exposure to captioned video: Do proficiency and aptitude make a difference? *The Language Learning Journal, 47*(4), 497–517.

Sundqvist, P. (2019). Commercial-off-the-shelf games in the digital wild and L2 learner vocabulary. *Language Learning & Technology, 23*(1), 87–113.

Sylvén, L. K., & Sundqvist, P. (2012). Gaming as extramural English L2 learning and L2 proficiency among young learners. *ReCALL, 24*(3), 302–321.

Thompson, C.G., & von Gillern, S. (2020). Video-game based instruction for vocabulary acquisition with English language learners: A Bayesian meta-analysis. *Educational Research Review, 30*, 1–23.

Uchihara, T., Webb, S., & Yanagisawa, A. (2019). The effects of repetition on incidental vocabulary learning: A meta-analysis of correlational studies. *Language Learning, 69*(3), 559–599.

Waring, R., & Takaki, M. (2003). At what rate do learners learn and retain new vocabulary from reading a graded reader? *Reading in a Foreign Language, 15*(2), 130–163.

Webb, S., & Chang, A. C-S. (2015). How does prior word knowledge affect vocabulary learning process in an extensive reading program? *Studies in Second Language Acquisition, 37*(4), 651–675.

Zahar, R., Cobb, T., & Spada. N. (2001). Acquiring vocabulary through reading: Effects of frequency and contextual richness. *Canadian Modern Language Review, 57*(4), 541–572.

Zsiga, E. C. (2012). *The sounds of language: An introduction to phonetics and phonology.* John Wiley & Sons.

Chapter 15

Bardovi-Harlig, K. (2013). Developing L2 pragmatics. *Language Learning, 63*(Suppl. 1), 68–86.

Blyth, C. (2018). Immersive technology and language learning. *Foreign Language Annals, 51*, 225–232.

Culpeper, J., Mackey, A., & Taguchi, N. (2018). *Second language pragmatics: From theory to research*. Routledge.

Cunningham, J. D. (2019). L2 pragmatics learning in computer-mediated communication. In N. Taguchi (Ed.), *The Routledge handbook of SLA and pragmatics* (pp. 372–386). Routledge.

Holden, C., & Sykes, J. M. (2013). Complex L2 pragmatic feedback via place-based mobile games. In N. Taguchi & J. M. Sykes (Eds.), *Technology in interlanguage pragmatics research and teaching* (pp. 155–184). John Benjamins.

Ishihara, N., & Cohen, A.D. (2021). *Teaching and learning pragmatics: Where language and culture meet*. Routledge.

Kaplan-Rakowski, R., & Wojdynski, T. (2018). Students' attitudes toward high-immersion virtual reality assisted language learning. In P. Taalas, J. Jalkanen, L. Bradley, & S. Thouësny (Eds.), *Future-proof CALL: Language learning as exploration and encounters* (pp. 124–129). Research-publishing.net.

Kasper, G., & Rose, K.R. (2002). *Pragmatic development in a second language*. Blackwell.

Li, Q. (2019). L2 Chinese learners' pragmatic developmental patterns in data-driven instruction and computer-mediated communication (CMC): A case of Chinese sentence final particle ne. *Applied Pragmatics, 1*, 154–183.

Roever, C. (2021). *Teaching and testing second language pragmatics and interaction: A practical guide*. Routledge.

Taguchi, N. (2021). Learning and teaching pragmatics in the globalized world: Introduction to the special issue. *The Modern Language Journal, 105*(3), 615–622.

Tang, X. (2020). Task-based interactional sequences in different modalities: A comparison between computer-mediated written chat and face-to-face chat. *Applied Pragmatics, 2*, 174–198.

Sykes, J. M., & Dubreil, S. (2019). Pragmatics learning in digital games and virtual environments. In N. Taguchi (Ed.), *The Routledge handbook of SLA and pragmatics* (pp. 387–399). Routledge.

Watanabe, S. (1993). Cultural differences in framing: American and Japanese group discussions. In D. Tannen (Ed.), *Framing in discourse* (pp. 176–208). Oxford University Press.

Chapter 16

Butler, Y. G. (2011). The implementation of communicative and task-based language teaching in the Asia-Pacific Region. *Annual Review of Applied Linguistics, 31*, 36–57.

Gass, S. M., Behney, J., & Plonsky, L. (2020). *Second language acquisition: An introductory course* (5th ed.). Routledge.

Littlewood, W. (2014). Communication-oriented language teaching: Where are we now? Where do we go from here? *Language Teaching, 47*(3), 349–362.

Long, M. H. (2014). *Second language acquisition and task-based language teaching*. John Wiley & Sons.

Chapter 17

Ellis, R., Skehan, P., Li, S., Shintani, N., & Lambert, C. (2019). *Task-based language teaching: Theory and practice*. Cambridge University Press.

Erlam, R. (2016). "I'm still not sure what a task is": Teachers designing language tasks. *Language Teaching Research, 20*(3) 279–299.

Long, M. H. (2014). *Second language acquisition and task-based language teaching*. John Wiley & Sons.

Pica, T., Kanagy, R., & Falodun, J. (1993). Choosing and using communication tasks for second language instruction. In G. Crookes & S. Gass (Eds.), *Tasks and language learning: Integrating theory and practice* (p. 9–34). Multilingual Matters.

Robinson, P. (2011). Task complexity, cognitive resources, and syllabus design: A triadic framework for examining task influences on SLA. In P. Robinson (Ed.), *Cognition and second language instruction* (pp. 285–318). Cambridge University Press.

Van den Branden, K., M. Bygate, & J. Norris (2009). *Task-based language teaching: A reader*. John Benjamins.

Willis, D., & Willis, J. (2007). *Doing task-based teaching*. Oxford University Press.

Chapter 18

De Vos, J. F., Schriefers, H., Nivard, G., & Lemhofer K. (2018). A meta-analysis and meta-regression of incidental second language word learning from spoken input. *Language Learning, 68*(4), 906–941.

Gilmore, A. (2011). "I prefer not text": Developing Japanese learners' communicative competence with authentic materials. *Language Learning, 61*(3), 786–819.

Glisan, E., & Donato, R. (2017). *Enacting the work of language instruction: High-leverage teaching practices*. ACTFL.

Gorter, D. (2018). Linguistic landscapes and trends in the study of schoolscapes. *Linguistics and Education, 44*, 80–85.

Helmer, K. A. (2014). "It's not real, it's just a story to just learn Spanish": Understanding heritage language learner resistance in a southwest charter high school. *Heritage Language Journal, 11*(3), 186–206.

Long, M. (2020). Optimal input for language learning: Genuine, simplified, elaborated, or modified elaborated? *Language Teaching, 53*(2), 169–182.

Lorenzen, C. N. (2006). Heritage language learners' voices: The "Spanish for Spanish speakers," experience in a rural midwestern high school. In. D Schwarzer, M. Bloom & S. Shono (Eds.), *Research as a tool for empowerment: Theory informing practice* (pp. 191–220). Information Age Publishers.

Rose, M. (2012). Grammar in the real world: Enhancing grammar lessons with pragmatics. *Hispania, 94*(4), 670–680.

Schmidt, R. (2001). Attention. In P. Robinson (Ed.), *Cognition and second language instruction* (pp. 3–32). Cambridge University Press.

Simonsen, R. (2019). An analysis of the problematic discourse surrounding "authentic texts." *Hispania, 102*(2), 245–258.

Zyzik, E., & Polio, C. (2017). *Authentic materials myths: Applying second language research in classroom teaching*. University of Michigan Press.

Chapter 19

Blake, R. (2000). Computer mediated communication: A window on L2 Spanish interlanguage. *Language Learning & Technology*, 4(1), 111–125.

Eisenchlas, S. A., Schalley, A. C., & Moyes, G. (2016). Play to learn: Self-directed home language literacy acquisition through online games. *International Journal of Bilingual Education and Bilingualism*, 19(2), 136–152.

González-Lloret, M. (2020). Collaborative tasks for online language teaching. *Foreign Language Annals*, 53(2), 260–269.

González-Lloret, M., & Ortega, L. (2016). Towards technology-mediated TBLT. In M. Gonzalez-Lloret & L. Ortega (Eds.), *Technology-mediated TBLT: Researching technology and tasks* (pp. 1–21). John Benjamins.

González-Lloret, M. & Rock, K. (2022). Tasks in technology-mediated contexts. In N. Ziegler & M. González-Lloret (Eds.), *The Routledge handbook of second language acquisition and technology* (pp. 36–49). Routledge.

Groves, M., & Mundt, K. (2015). Friend or foe? Google translate in language for academic purposes. *English for Specific Purposes*, 37, 112–121.

Kern, R. (2006). Perspectives on technology in learning and teaching languages. *TESOL Quarterly*, 40(1), 183–210.

Koehn, P. (2010). *Statistical machine translation*. Cambridge University Press.

Michel, M., & Smith, B. (2017). Measuring lexical alignment during L2 chat interaction: An eye-tracking study. In S. Gass, P. Spinner, & J. Behney (Eds.), *Salience in second language acquisition* (pp. 244–268). Routledge.

Park, Y., Xu, Y., Collins, P., Farkas, G., & Warschauer, M. (2019). Scaffolding learning of learning structures with visual-syntactic text formatting. *British Journal of Educational Technology*, 50(4), 1896–1912.

Sauro, S. (2011). SCMC for SLA: A research synthesis. *CALICO Journal*, 28(2), 369–391.

Schmidt, R. (2001). Attention. In P. Robinson (Ed.), *Cognition and second language instruction* (pp. 3–32). Cambridge University Press.

Smith, B. (2003). Computer-mediated negotiated interaction: An expanded model. *The Modern Language Journal*, 87, 38–57.

Smith, B., & Gonzalez-Lloret, M. (2021). Technology-mediated task-based language teaching: A research agenda. *Language Teaching*, 54, 518–534.

Somers, H.L., & Lovel, J.H. (2006). Can AAC technology facilitate communication for patients with limited English? *ESRC Project Final Report*, University of Manchester. Available at https://personalpages.manchester.ac.uk/staff/harold.somers/ESRCfinal.pdf.

Sundqvist, P. (2019). Commercial-off-the-shelf games in the digital wild and L2 learner vocabulary. *Language Learning & Technology*, 23(1), 87–113.

Thomas, M., Reinders, H., & Warschauer, M. (Eds.). (2012). *Contemporary computer-assisted language learning*. Bloomsbury.

Wang, S., & Vásquez, C. (2014). The effect of target language use in social media on intermediate-level Chinese language learners' writing performance. *CALICO Journal*, 31(1), 78–102.

Winke, P., Gass, S., & Sydorenko, T. (2013). Factors influencing the use of captions by foreign language learners: An eye-tracking study. *The Modern Language Journal*, 97(1), 254–275.

Ziegler, N. (2016). Taking technology to task: Technology-mediated TBLT, performance, and production. *Annual Review of Applied Linguistics*, 36, 136–163.

Chapter 20

Berry, V., Sheehan, S., & Munro, S. (2019). What does language assessment literacy mean to teachers? *ELT Journal, 73*(2), 113–123.

Brown, H. D. & Abeywickrama, P. (2010). *Language assessment: Principles and classroom practice.* Pearson Longman.

Brown, N. A., Dewey, D. P., & Cox, T. L. (2014). Assessing the validity of can-do statements in retrospective (then-now) self-assessment. *Foreign Language Annals, 47*(2), 261–285.

Butler, Y. G., & Lee, J. (2010). The effects of self-assessment among young learners of English. *Language Teaching, 27*(1), 5–31.

Council of Europe. Council for Cultural Co-operation. Education Committee. Modern Languages Division. (2001). *Common European Framework of Reference for Languages: Learning, teaching, assessment.* Cambridge University Press.

Cox, T. L., Malone, M. E., & Winke, P. (2017). Future directions in assessment: Influences of standards and implications for language learning. *Foreign Language Annals, 51*, 104–115.

Hudson, T. (2005). Trends in assessment scales and criterion-referenced language assessment. *Annual Review of Applied Linguistics, 25*, 205–227.

Long, M. H. (2007). Texts, tasks, and the advanced learner. In M. H. Long (Ed.), *Problems in SLA* (pp. 119–138). Lawrence Erlbaum.

Nikolov, M. (2016). Trends, issues, and challenges in assessing young language learners. In M. Nikolov (Ed.), *Assessing young learners of English: Global and local perspectives* (pp. 1–18). Springer.

Norris, J. M. (2016). Current uses for task-based language assessment. *Annual Review of Applied Linguistics, 36*, 230–244.

Rudner, L. M., & Schafer, W. D. (2002). *What teachers need to know about assessment.* National Education Association.

Shohamy, E. (2001). Democratic assessment as an alternative. *Language Testing, 18*(4), 373–391.

Wiggins, G., & McTighe, J. (1998). *Understanding by design.* Association for Supervision and Curriculum Development.

Chapter 21

Agheshteh, H., & Mehrpur, S. (2021). Teacher autonomy and supervisor authority: Power dynamics in language teacher supervision in Iran. *Iranian Journal of Language Teaching Research, 9*(1), 87–06.

Ahmed, E., Nordin, Z. S., Shah, S. R., & Channa, M. A. (2018). Peer observation: A professional learning tool for English language teachers in an EFL institute. *World Journal of Education, 8*(2), 73–87.

Brannan, D. & Bleistein, T. (2012). Novice ESOL teachers' perceptions of social support networks. *TESOL Quarterly, 46*(3), 519–541.

Borg, S. (2003). Teacher cognition in language teaching: A review of research on what language teachers think, know, believe, and do. *Language Teaching, 36*(2), 81–109.

Burns, A. (2005). Action research: An evolving paradigm? *Language Teaching, 38*(2), 57–74.

References and Resources

Carvalho, V. L. L. (2020). Professional awareness among English language teacher educators: Individual and collaborative reflective practice. *Babel: Revista Eletrônica de Línguas e Literaturas Estrangeiras, 10*(1), 95–113.

Deyrich, M. C., & Stunnel, K. (2014). Language teacher education models: New issues and challenges. In J. D. M. Agudo (Ed.), *English as a foreign language teacher education: Current perspectives and challenges*, (pp. 83–105). Brill.

Farrell, T. S. (2018). Operationalizing reflective practice in second language teacher education. *Journal of Second Language Teacher Education, 1*(1), 1–20.

Freeman, D. (1982). Observing teachers: Three approaches to in-service training and development. *TESOL Quarterly, 16*(1), 21–28.

Freeman, D., & Johnson, K. E. (1998). Reconceptualizing the knowledge-base of language teacher education. *TESOL Quarterly, 32*(3), 397–417.

Graves, K. (2009). The curriculum of second language teacher education. In A. Burns, & J. C. Richards (Eds.), *The Cambridge guide to second language teacher education* (pp. 115–124). Cambridge University Press.

Johnson, A. P. (2012). *A short guide to action research* (4th ed.). Pearson Education.

Kubanyiova, M., & Crookes, G. (2016). Re-envisioning the roles, tasks, and contributions of language teachers in the multilingual era of language education research and practice. *The Modern Language Journal, 100*(S1), 117–132.

Mackey, A. (2017). Classroom-based research. In S. Loewen & M. Sato (Eds.), *The Routledge handbook of instructed second language acquisition* (pp. 541–561). Routledge.

Marsden, E., & Kasprowicz, R. (2017). Foreign language educators' exposure to research: Reported experiences, exposure via citations, and a proposal for action. *The Modern Language Journal, 101*(4), 613–642.

Miller, J. M. (2009). Teacher identity. In A. Burns & J. C. Richards (Eds.), *The Cambridge guide to second language teacher education* (pp. 172–181). Cambridge University Press.

Nassaji, H. (2012). The relationship between SLA research and language pedagogy: Teachers' perspectives. *Language Teaching Research, 16*(3), 337–365.

Negru, D. (2020). Lesson observation for professional development purposes. In *Calitate în educație-imperativ al societății contemporane* (Vol. II, pp. 293–298). Universitatea Pedagogică de Stat "Ion Creangă" din Chișinău.

.Nunan, D. (1989). *Understanding language classrooms: A guide for teacher-initiated action*. Prentice-Hall.

Nunan, D., & C. Lamb (1996). *The self-directed teacher: Managing the learning process*. Cambridge University Press.

Ortega, L. (2012). Language acquisition research for language teaching: Choosing between application and relevance. In B. Hinger, E. M. Unterrainer, & D. Newby (Eds.), *Sprachen lernen: Kompetenzen entwickeln? Performanzen (über)prüfen. [Language learning: Developing competency? (Re)assessing performances]* (pp. 24–38). Präsens Verlag.

Parathyras, V., & Zorbas, V. (2020). From observation of teaching practices to mentoring and teacher development in a multicultural setting: A case study. *Language Teaching Research Quarterly, 17*, 20–23.

Randolph, P. T. (2021). Professional growth through peer observation and idea implementation. *ORTESOL Journal, 38*, 41–44.

Richards, J., & Farrell, T. (2005). *Professional development for language teachers*. Cambridge University Press.

Tarone, E., & Allwright, D. (2005). Language teacher-learning and student language learning: Shaping the knowledge base. In D. J. Tedick (Ed.), *Language teacher education: International perspectives on research and practice* (pp. 5–23). Lawrence Erlbaum.

Tosriadi, T., Asib, A., Marmanto, S., & Azizah, U. A. (2018). In-service EFL teachers' reflection as a pathway to develop teacher professionalism. *International Online Journal of Education and Teaching, 5*(4), 921–932.

Webb, K. (2020). Peer observation for development: "If you don't have the right ingredients, you can't cook the dish." *ELTED Journal, 23*, 48–60.

INDEX

abjad script, 141
abugida system, 141
accent, 79, 168, 169, 172–173, 174, 178
accuracy, 51, 103, 123, 145, 153, 160, 163–164, 252, 255, 263, 286, 289, 299, 305, 312
achievement assessment, 299, 301
ACMC, 285–286
ACTFL, 88, 89, 103, 255, 263, 300, 301, 309
action plan, 46
action research, 8, 322–325, 326, 327, 329
ADHD, 95, 96, 97, 98, 234
advice letters, 70
anchor chart, 28
anxometers, 114
ASD. *See* autism spectrum disorder
Ask 3, then me, 11
assessments *for* learning, 298
assessments *of* learning, 298
asset-based perspective, 78
asynchronous computer-mediated contexts. *See* ACMC
attention
    attracted, 161
    directed, 161
attrition, 139
authentic materials, 267 *See* realia
authentic resources, 11, 84, 242, 254, 255, 267, 269, 270, 274, 276, 278, 280
automaticity, 7, 19
autonomous learners, 68, 69, 71, 132, 145
autonomy, 65, 70, 116, 118, 197, 321

backward design, 302
bidialectal children, 95

bilingual children, 95–96
bilingual labels, 30
bilingual programs, 24, 141
bilingual resources, 24
bilingualism, 28, 30, 96
Bill DeKeyser, 26
Bill VanPatten, 26

CALF, 305–306
CALL, 111, 284, 285, 287
CEFR, 255, 263, 300, 301, 309
choral answers, 16
chunks, 17, 101, 102, 104, 235
classroom observations, 321
CLIL. *See* content and language integrated learning
cognates, 66, 139, 188, 204, 208 *See also* vocabulary knowledge
cognitive creativity, 96, 130–131
cognitive resources, 36, 255
cognitive strategies, 64, 143, 149 *See also* learning strateiges
cold call, 12–13
Common European Framework of Reference. *See* CEFR
communication breakdowns, 18, 28, 38, 178
communication gaps, 18
communicative approaches, 236, 238, 239–240, 246
Compass Buddies, 56
complexity, 137–138, 143, 145, 163, 190, 305, 312
comprehensibility
    and literacy, 280
    and pronunciation, 168
comprehensible input, 25–26, 31–32, 132, 155
comprehension
    and literacy, 277

and pronunciation, 169–170, 171–174
computer-assisted language learning. *See* CALL
content and language-integrated learning, 235
content classes, 24
controlled response, 174
conversational style, 222, 227, 228
corrective feedback, 4–5, 23, 26, 36–37, 40, 44, 96, 159, 163, 164, 171, 175, 183, 237, 242, 244, 246, 284, 285, 286, 288 *See also* feedback
    clarification request, 36
    confirmation check, 36, 39
    metalinguistic feedback, 38
    recast, 35, 36, 38, 40, 58, 160, 171, 179
    repetition, 36
critical pedagogy, 319
crosslinguistic influence, 138

Deborah Tannen, 219
deep orthography, 142
deficit-based perspective, 78
developmental sequence, 158
    research, 250
diagnostic assessments, 194–195, 299, 301
dialect, 79, 95, 172, 222, 274
drill, 18, 159–160, 169, 172, 174, 179, 211, 239

elaborated input, 272, 273–274, 292
engagement, 7–8, 10, 12, 53, 67, 79, 84, 206, 207, 222, 273, 289, 324
enhanced input, 161
enriched input, 161

Index

example text, 45
executive functioning, 95, 97
explicit correction, 46
explicit instruction, 72, 94, 104, 127, 146, 156–157, 158–160, 162, 164, 186, 188, 189
explicit knowledge, 82, 143, 155, 158, 160–161, 162, 164
explicit learning, 154, 160, 236
explicit teaching, 64, 100, 224, 225

feedback. *See also* corrective feedback
  asynchronous feedback, 119
  box, 31
  direct written, 36, 37
  discussions, 40
  explicit, 36, 38–39, 127, 133, 171
  focused, 36, 39
  implicit, 38, 46, 100, 127, 160, 171
  indirect, 36, 44
  peer-to-peer feedback, 119
  preferences, 41
  unfocused, 36, 39
fluency, 19, 130, 163, 183, 196, 209, 212, 255, 286, 305, 306
focus on forms, 234
focus-on-form, 161, 163
foreign language settings, 23–24
formative assessments, 298, 309, 314 *See also* assessments for learning
form-focused instruction, 156–157, 160–161, 164
  integrated, 157
  isolated, 156–157, 163, 164

gallery walk, 58
gestures, 26, 28, 65, 102, 224, 235, 300
globalized languages, 80
grammar forms, 160, 162, 241, 298
grammar-based approaches, 234, 240, 246
grammar–translation approach, 234, 246
grapheme–phoneme correspondence, 141
grouping
  heterogenous, 50
  homogeneous, 51
  strategies, 54, 88
guided reflective practice, 66

heritage language learner, 83–84, 85, 86–87, 109, 112, 144, 273
high-variability phonetic training, 172

higher-proficiency learners, 36, 46, 143, 160, 203, 307

ideal self, 109
imagined L2 self, 79
immersion, 23, 144, 174
  contexts, 4
  programs, 69, 78, 140, 235
implicit correction, 46
implicit instruction, 155–156, 158–159, 160, 162
implicit knowledge, 82, 154, 161, 163, 164
implicit teaching, 224
incidental vocabulary learning, 202
indigenous languages, 24
individual differences, 26, 40, 113, 122, 124, 140, 144, 161, 175, 179, 181, 200, 203, 261, 263, 273, 292
  phonemic awareness, 94, 97
  phonological awareness, 94, 97, 100, 104
inductive reasoning, 95, 100
inference, 97, 187–188
input flood, 161, 225–226
intelligibility, 173
intentional vocabulary learning, 202
Interagency Language Roundtable scale, 263
interruptions, 226
intersectional identity research, 84

Jonathan Rosa, 80
journal, 69, 81, 113, 118, 190, 192, 214, 310

language environment, 24, 28, 69, 168, 274
language pledge, 17
language-related episodes, 49, 83–84
language routines. *See* automaticity
language teacher education, 324
language-bound listeners, 169, 173
learner autonomy, 11, 189, 196
learner interests, 10, 99
learner training. *See* strategy-based instruction
learner-centered texts, 268
lexicon, 200, 201
lexis, 137, 305–306, 312
linguistic landscape, 29, 274
listening strategies, 56, 69, 208, 277
literacy
  and phonemic awareness, 194, 196
  and phonological awareness, 184, 185, 194

LLAMA, 125, 127
logographic system, 141, 143
lower-proficiency learners, 30, 46, 50, 54, 160, 203

MALL. *See* Mobile-Assisted Language Learning
meaning-focused approaches, 235
  See naturalistic approaches
Merrill Swain, 4, 26
metacognitive strategies, 64, 145, 149, 186, 189
Mike Long, 26
minoritized communities, 95
minoritized learners, 80
mixed settings, 24
Mobile-Assisted Language Learning, 111
modality, 88, 111, 286, 310
modes of communication, 141, 291, 299, 301
  interpersonal mode, 291, 300
  interpretive mode, 291
  presentational mode, 141, 299, 300
modes of presentation
  presentational mode, 291
modified output, 6
monolingual children, 95–96, 185, 186
morphology, 154, 184, 195
motivation
  extrinsic, 108, 111
  instrumental, 108, 109, 111
  integrativeness, 108
  intrinsic, 108, 112, 113
multicultural studies, 319
multiple intersecting identities, 30, 79

natural approach, 141, 236
naturalistic approaches, 234, 235, 236, 237, 239–240
needs analysis, 250, 256–258, 262, 263
negotiation for meaning, 4, 23, 236, 239, 285
Nelson Flores, 80, 186
neurodiversity, 94, 100, 103, 309
  autism spectrum disorder, 95
  dyslexia, 95, 97, 98, 100
  grammatical sensitivity, 95
  hyper-focused attention, 96, 99
non-learner-centered texts, 268
noticing, 50–51, 83, 125, 129, 160, 170, 234, 272, 287
  a gap, 97, 100
  of corrections, 6
  of corrective feedback, 291
  of sociopragmatic rules and pragmalinguistic tools, 223

Index

OASIS. *See* Open Accessible Summaries in Language Studies
Open Accessible Summaries in Language Studies, 325
ought-to self, 79, 109

Paco Sentences, 27
parsing programs, 101
participation, 7, 58, 60, 80
peer interaction, 49–50, 54, 58, 60, 84, 90, 262
   direction-giver, 51
   strategy advisor, 70
performance-based assessment, 244, 301, 313
personality, 7, 50, 79, 113
phonological decoding, 94
phonological development, 168, 174–175
   and phonological awareness, 175, 179
phonological loop, 171
phonology, 83
placement tests, 244, 299, 301
positive transfer, 138, 149
Post-it reactions, 42
practicality, 303, 304, 314
pragmalinguistic competence, 220, 225
pragmatic appropriateness, 219
pragmatic competence, 218, 219–220, 223, 227, 229, 298
   See also pragmatic knowledge
pragmatic knowledge, 219, 221–222, 228
Presentation, Practice, Production, 250
prior knowledge, 64, 66, 184, 186, 187, 192, 193, 196, 255, 277
productive word knowledge, 201, 207
professional development, 147, 244, 312, 319–322, 324, 326, 328
proficiency-based assessment, 299
pushed output. *See* modified output

race, 78, 79–80, 84, 88, 180, 223, 319

read-aloud, 192
reading coaches, 94
reading strategies, 66, 183, 184, 191, 192, 203, 206
realia, 102, 267, 275, 279–280
receptive word knowledge, 201, 207
reflective teaching practices, 319, 326
register, 84
reliability, 304, 314
rephrasing, 66, 236
representation, 80–81, 85
resource analysis
   authentic input, 271
   bimodal input, 271
   simplified input, 271, 273
retention, 70, 143, 272, 321
reverse transfer, 139
Rod Ellis, 26

scaffolding, 13, 19, 64, 117, 192–193, 196, 229, 270, 310
SCMC, 285–286
script type, 141
second language settings, 24, 304
segmental, 170, 175
self-assessment, 306, 310
sentence starters, 14, 15, 19
shallow orthography, 142
signed languages, 4, 23, 27, 306
small-group work, 17, 51, 102, 118
sociopragmatic competence, 220, 224
sound–symbol correspondence, 184, 194, 196 *See* literacy
speaking strategies, 66 *See* learning strategies
specialized language use, 309
speech acts, 221, 223, 224, 227
spelling, 83, 84, 100, 133, 201
Stephen Krashen, 25–26
strategy-based instruction, 64
   strategy-specific instruction, 72
study abroad, 79, 109, 118, 237
summative assessments, 60, 298–299, 309, 314 *See* also assessments of learning
suprasegmental, 170, 171, 175
Susan Gass, 26

synchronous computer-mediated communication. *See* SCMC
syntax, 101, 138, 154, 305
system type, 141

Task Elements
   Familiarity, 252
   Planning time, 252
   Solutions, 252
Task-Based Language Teaching. *See* TBLT
TBLT, 237, 240, 250, 256–257
   pedagogic tasks, 251–252, 259, 261
   target tasks, 241, 251–252, 253, 258–260
   task-based assessment, 262
   task-based assessments, 298–299, 304
   task-based syllabus, 259–260
   task-supported language teaching, 256
teacher identity, 319
teacher knowledge, 320
teaching strategies, 8–9, 128, 157, 321
Think-Pair-Share, 14–15, 56
transfer, 138
translanguaging, 186

Uju Anya, 80

validity, 303–304, 314
visual support, 12–13
vocabulary knowledge, 17, 186, 195, 196, 203, 204, 207–208, 212, 215, 298
vocabulary mural, 210
vulnerable population, 85

WEIRD population, 78, 85
wait-time, 13, 14, 102
whole-class discussion, 9
willingness to communicate, 8–9
working memory, 38, 94, 97–98, 125–128, 171, 175, 204
writing strategies, 66, 188, 197
   social strategies, 145
   social/affective strategies, 64

Zoltán Dörnyei, 79